Handbook of Computer Games Technology

Volume II

Handbook of Computer Games Technology
Volume II

Edited by **Akira Hanako**

CLANRYE
INTERNATIONAL

New Jersey

Published by Clanrye International,
55 Van Reypen Street,
Jersey City, NJ 07306, USA
www.clanryeinternational.com

Handbook of Computer Games Technology: Volume II
Edited by Akira Hanako

International Standard Book Number: 978-1-63240-261-5 (Hardback)

Printed in the United States of America.

Contents

Preface

Computer games once were simple programs. But now, they have transformed into a complex programming technology. From simple flash games, this computer based technology has reached new heights, where one can play games by becoming the character itself. The action of performance in real world can now be converted into the gaming experience. Computer games are software development techniques which use artificial intelligence (AI), graphics of computer, multimedia programming, laws of physics, database designing, automata theory, database designing, input-output, and simulations. Games being developed these days can be categorised into Action, Action-adventure, Adventure, Role-playing, Simulation, Strategy, Vehicle Simulation etc.

The use of motion controllers, 3D tree models, Petri net models and adaptive-AR models are important technical models applied in advancing computer games technology.

This book provides a guideline for game development based learning. It also offers framework for adaptive game presenters with emotions and social comments. Some of the technical as well as conceptual aspects of game development and computer game technologies are discussed in this book.

I would like to express my sincere appreciation to the authors of this book for their excellent contributions and for their efforts involved in the publication process. I do believe that the contents in this book will be helpful to many researchers in this field around the world. Lastly, I would like to thank my family for being a constant source of support.

Editor

Analyzing the Effect of TCP and Server Population on Massively Multiplayer Games

Mirko Suznjevic,[1] **Jose Saldana,**[2] **Maja Matijasevic,**[1]
Julián Fernández-Navajas,[2] **and José Ruiz-Mas**[2]

[1] *Faculty of Electrical Engineering and Computing, University of Zagreb, Unska 3, 10000 Zagreb, Croatia*
[2] *Communication Technologies Group (GTC), Aragon Institute of Engineering Research (I3A), EINA, University of Zaragoza, 50018 Zaragoza Ada Byron Building, Spain*

Correspondence should be addressed to Mirko Suznjevic; mirko.suznjevic@fer.hr

Academic Editor: Alexander Pasko

Many Massively Multiplayer Online Role-Playing Games (MMORPGs) use TCP flows for communication between the server and the game clients. The utilization of TCP, which was not initially designed for (soft) real-time services, has many implications for the competing traffic flows. In this paper we present a series of studies which explore the competition between MMORPG and other traffic flows. For that aim, we first extend a source-based traffic model, based on player's activities during the day, to also incorporate the impact of the number of players sharing a server (server population) on network traffic. Based on real traffic traces, we statistically model the influence of the variation of the server's player population on the network traffic, depending on the action categories (i.e., types of in-game player behaviour). Using the developed traffic model we prove that while server population only modifies specific action categories, this effect is significant enough to be observed on the overall traffic. We find that TCP *Vegas* is a good option for competing flows in order not to throttle the MMORPG flows and that TCP SACK is more respectful with game flows than other TCP variants, namely, *Tahoe, Reno,* and *New Reno*. Other tests show that MMORPG flows do not significantly reduce their sending window size when competing against UDP flows. Additionally, we study the effect of RTT unfairness between MMORPG flows, showing that it is less important than in the case of network-limited TCP flows.

1. Introduction

Massively Multiplayer Online Role-Playing Games (MMORPGs) have become one of the most profitable genres in the gaming industry. The leading MMORPG in the market, namely, *World of Warcraft* (WoW) by *Activision Blizzard*, at its peak, had approximately 12 million players [1], and it reported around one billion US dollars of profit in 2010. MMORPG players demand interactive virtual worlds, so a good underlying network quality is needed. In other words, the traffic generated by virtual worlds of MMORPGs has very high quality of service demands in terms of delay and packet loss. While MMORPGs are real-time multiuser virtual worlds, many of them use TCP for communicating the actions of the player to the server and vice-versa.

The use of TCP as a transport protocol is not very widespread in the area of networked games. Besides flash based web games, TCP is not that common. Most of the games which feature full real time 3D virtual worlds use UDP, including First Person Shooters (FPS), racing, Real Time Strategy (RTS), and Multiplayer Online Battle Arena (MOBA). MMORPGs are one of the few game genres in which the use of TCP is employed (although UDP is used as well, depending on the game [2]). Most MMORPGs use the same client-server architecture with client holding all the application logic and 3D information, while the only thing exchanged with the server is the updates of specific entities in the virtual world. This enables very low requirements of these games on network bandwidth which are common in the whole genre [3]. WoW is, according to [4], still the most popular subscription based MMORPG in terms of number of players with around 8 million active subscribers (even after losing 4 million). Therefore, WoW still holds a very large portion of the market, and its traffic has more impact on the network than the traffic of next ten MMORPGs combined which makes it a logical choice for a study focused on effects of using TCP in an online game.

Using TCP has many implications, taking into account that TCP was initially designed for bulk transfers [5, 6], with the main objective of transmitting an existing amount of data with the maximum throughput, always maintaining fairness between flows. Since the throughput limit of bulk transfers mainly depends on network bandwidth, we can talk about *network-limited traffic*. However, an MMORPG sends information which does not previously exist but is continuously generated according to the player's actions. As a consequence, MMORPGs do not always exhaust their bandwidth share, as sometimes the application has nothing to send (*application-limited traffic*), and this makes some TCP mechanisms inefficient or even counterproductive. As an example, the authors of [6] reported that TCP back-off mechanism did not activate and also that fast retransmissions are very exceptional because of the high inter-packet times, leaving most recoveries to be made by timeout; furthermore, a correctly received TCP packet following a lost packet would be blocked from delivery to the application until the lost packet was eventually retransmitted successfully. In addition, some TCP mechanisms (e.g., delayed acknowledgment mechanism [2]) innately cause quality of service degradation.

While the impact of using TCP on MMORPGs performance has been studied [5], as well as the inspection of different TCP versions [6], limited work has been done on investigating how other TCP flows in a network would impact the MMORPG flows, as well as the analysis of RTT unfairness. MMORPG flows share a large portion of the network path with other flows, both in local networks of the end users (e.g., wireless LAN or DSL connection) as well as in the network operator core network. The rise of these games is modifying the traffic mix present in operator's networks, increasing the rate of small TCP packets which, due to the interactivity requirements of the games, cannot be considered as "best effort" flows. This fact makes it necessary to study the interaction of MMORPG application-limited TCP flows with "traditional" flows, such as TCP bulk transfers and UDP flows.

To perform realistic tests, accurate statistical models of the network traffic are commonly used. Such models are also useful for network capacity planning and optimization. However, the traffic of online games in general is very difficult to model [7] and strongly dependant on player behaviour at the application level [8]. What must be taken into account is that an MMORPG allows a wide range of activities, from picking flowers to fighting dragons with the help of some friends, and logically, the game interactivity and usage of network resources vary significantly depending on the deployed task.

To enable the characterization of the network traffic under different application conditions (i.e., picking flowers against fighting dragons), in previous work we have grouped activities within the game into different behaviour categories: *Questing, Trading, Player versus Player (PvP) combat, Dungeons, Raiding,* and *Uncategorized* [9]. We will follow this classification in the present work. As shown in Figure 1, which has been obtained from empirical traces, the traffic varies significantly depending on the player's activity. A source-based network traffic model based on defined behavioural categories was presented in [10]. This model comprises two main components: (1) a teletraffic model for each of the proposed categories and (2) player's behaviour (i.e., the probability of a player deploying an activity in a certain moment).

At the same time, one of the major problems for MMORPG's providers is scalability. To calculate the virtual world state when a large number of entities are in a small area of that world is a difficult task in real time [11]. Therefore, game operators often replicate the virtual world into multiple independent "shards" or servers and divide the player base across them. As a consequence, players cannot interact between shards. These techniques combined with Area of Interest (AOI) management (avatars out of the AOI of a player are considered not to interact with him) create significant load reductions. For different reasons, however, some of the shards become highly popular, whereas others are almost "deserted" (e.g., in WoW a highly popular server in Europe is *Outland*, while an almost deserted one is *Jaedenar*). The server population (i.e., the number of players on particular server or shard) has a significant effect on network traffic characteristics, mainly in the server-to-client direction. This is because the server has to send to the client application the updates of the state of all the entities in the AOI of the player, and this information increases in volume if the server is more crowded.

Having in mind the need for an accurate traffic model, we first deploy tests with the proposal of capturing the impact of the number of players in a shard onto the network traffic. In other words, the initial traffic model is extended to be able to modify Application Protocol Data Unit (APDU) sizes and Inter-APDU Arrival Times (IAT) according to the population of a particular server. This mainly affects the activities in which the number of players significantly varies, as *Trading* and *PvP combat*. This relationship between the server traffic and the number of players in the server has been measured for a concrete game, but this phenomenon is expected to happen in other similar games which use sharding.

Once the effect of server population has been statistically characterized, a full traffic model has been implemented in NS2 network simulator and used to deploy a number of tests with the aim to explore the interactions between MMORPG and other traffic flows. The competition between different flows when sharing a bottleneck is studied, including

(i) interaction of MMORPG and network-limited traffic using different TCP variants,

(ii) competition of MMORPG and UDP traffic,

(iii) influence of RTT on the behaviour of MMORPG flows (RTT unfairness),

(iv) global effect of the amount of players in a shard.

All in all, the contribution of this paper is threefold: first, the study of how MMORPG traffic characteristics change depending on the number of players which, to the best of our knowledge, is reported and measured for the first time. Second, once a realistic model is available, several

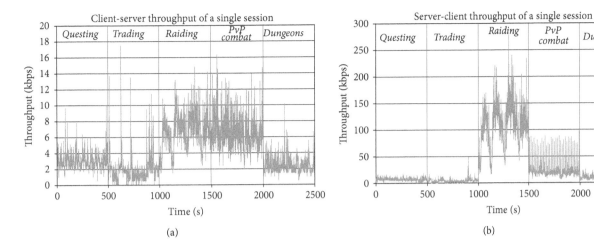

FIGURE 1: Bandwidth usage of the original game for different categories: (a) client-server and (b) server-client (the trace presented in the figure is a set of characteristic fragments obtained from separate captures).

tests exploring interactions between TCP MMORPG flows and other traditional applications have been deployed in order to illustrate the characteristics of competition between MMORPG flows with other network flows. Finally, the proposed model has been fully implemented in NS2. This NS2 script, which allows a wide range of tests, is offered to the research community. As previously stated, the model takes into account the variation of the player behaviour during the hours of the day, modifying the probability of the player's activity and the duration of each activity.

The structure of the paper is as follows: in Section 2, we review the previous work in MMORPG traffic classification, characterization, and interaction with other kinds of traffic. Section 3 addresses the question of obtaining the traffic model depending on the activity and population. Section 4 presents the MMORPG traffic competition tests deployed using the model, and the Conclusions section closes the paper.

2. Related Work

Network traffic of MMORPGs has been a target of a number of studies which are summarized in survey papers [3, 12]. Chen et al. and Wu et al. [2, 5] evaluate performance of TCP for online games in general and discuss whether TCP is in fact a suitable protocol for MMORPGs. They identify some network performance degradation problems derived from the traffic characteristics of this game genre: tiny packets, low packet rate, application-limited traffic generation, and bidirectional traffic. They remark that TCP is normally used by applications which deploy bulk transfers, so the bandwidth is limited by the network. In the case of MMORPGs, there are some moments in which the application has no data to send, and this may produce the effect of the TCP congestion window being reset unnecessarily. In other cases, the window may become arbitrarily large, producing bursts demanding a high amount of bandwidth from the network.

The authors of [6] investigate the performance of different TCP versions with respect to retransmission delay when

low-rate, real-time event streams are sent to clients. They tested the existing TCP variants, that is, *New Reno* (plain, with SACK, DSACK, FACK, and with DSACK and FACK), *Westwood*, BIC, and *Vegas* on Linux. They concluded that there are only small differences between TCP variants which are used for MMORPG flows, but also that multiplexing different flows into one TCP connection and a more aggressive timeout retransmission time promise a reduction of the delay perceived at the application level. In addition [13] explored the reservation on part of the path between a game server and a number of clients, discussing the implications of using it for network infrastructure. In our previous work [14] we presented a preliminary study of the coexistence of WoW and network-limited TCP using different variants. The present paper further explores this issue, including the effect of RTT, and it also extends the study to the coexistence with other flows.

In the area of network traffic modelling, WoW has been a use case in several studies, as it is the most popular subscription-based MMORPG. An initial traffic model for this game was presented by Svoboda et al. [15], together with the analysis of a traffic trace captured within a 3G mobile core network, which showed that WoW was one of the ten most popular TCP services in the monitored network. Other MMORPGs have also been modelled: *Lineage* [16] and *World of Legend* [17]. All the previously listed models are based on a methodology proposed in [18]; however, a different traffic model for WoW [19] is based on a transformational scheme developed for the highly erratic network traffic of online games.

While previous approaches focus on modelling the traffic of a game as a whole, another approach for addressing the highly variable network traffic of MMORPGs is based on classification of application level states. In [20] Park et al. applied such approach for MMORPG—WoW and a First Person Shooter (FPS)—*Quake 3*. The actions defined for WoW are *Hunting the NPCs, Battle with players, Moving,* and *No play.* Another classification has been proposed by Wang et al. [21], proposing *Hunting, Battlefield,* and *Downtown.*

The authors also inspect different scenarios of movement for the player (in the real world): subway, bus, and campus. In the following work, the same research group proposed traffic models for each category, which were implemented in NS2 [22].

There are several studies which focus on the number of players in MMORPGs [23–27]. The most in-depth analyses have been performed by means of cooperation between game providers with the research community by providing internal datasets. Such analyses have been performed for *EvE Online* [23] and *EverQuest II* [24].

Another approach to the investigation of the number of players is based on the use of application specific capabilities of clients, in order to obtain more information regarding the state of the virtual world. Through the development of scripts which run within the client, it is possible to obtain a range of information regarding currently active players in the virtual world. Notable studies using this approach are Pittman's [25, 26] and Lee's [27], both performed on WoW. Pittman investigated a number of players on *Aerie Peak,* a North American WoW server labelled as *full.* They noted that the average daily number of users peaks around 3,500 players [26]. The authors also concluded that the spatial distribution of players in the virtual world is not uniform, but there are hot spots in which players gather, while a large portion of the virtual world is empty. On the other side, Lee et al. presented a dataset comprising information regarding players on an Asian WoW server *Light's Hope,* captured for 1,107 days [27]. Lee's dataset only comprises the data about one of the two factions of the game and presents peaks below 500 players. Even if we double that value in an effort to estimate the number of both factions, it is still 3.5 times lower than the values reported by Pittman. Therefore, it is evident that different servers for the same game have significantly different player populations. The causes of this may vary, depending on social dynamics on each particular server, technical difficulties, server migrations, and so forth. The discrepancies in player population cause differences in both computational and network load.

In a previous work, we defined the following action categories: *Questing, Trading, Player versus Player (PvP) combat, Dungeons, and Raiding* [9], and we developed network traffic models for each of the categories, performed player behaviour measurements and modelling [28], and created a software architecture able to generate real traffic using the previously defined model [10].

Some traffic models of other game genres (i.e., FPS games) [29, 30] have considered the effect of the number of players sharing the virtual world. However, the number of concurrent players of these genres is limited to a few tens, whereas an MMORPG shard can host thousands of players, adding a high degree of complexity which requires different techniques like, for example, the definition of the Area of Interest. The specific contribution of the current paper, regarding traffic modelling, is the study of the modification of the MMORPG's patterns for specific action categories which are affected by differences in server population. The most affected category is *Trading,* due to the previously identified phenomena of players grouping in one or more "hubs," which are usually

capital cities [25]. In addition, *PvP combat* traffic shows a strong dependence on the number of players, since this category is designed for a number of players ranging between 4 and 100. To the best of our knowledge, none of the existing traffic models for MMORPGs takes into account the server population (i.e., the number of players on the server).

3. Population and Player-Dependant Traffic Model

As previously shown, the population of different servers in MMORPGs varies significantly. The causes of this phenomenon can be various, but they can mostly be attributed to sociological and game related influences. For example, in WoW, the English speaking server *Outland* in Europe (at the time of writing this paper) is one of the most popular servers and "it is well known" among the player population that this is the server where there are a lot of players focused on *PvP combat.* In addition, some servers are designed for different languages (e.g., German, French, etc.) and this fact can also impact their population. Game mechanics such as division of server by types, instability of certain server hardware, and migrations between shards, also have an impact on overall server population.

We consider that modelling traffic at application level is a more accurate approach than doing it at packet level, adopting the approach in [15]. In addition, this makes the model independent of the underlying network technology. Thus, we characterize APDU size and IAT, instead of working with packets. In addition, we avoid the simplification of considering that the player always generates traffic with the same statistical distribution: as seen in Figure 1, traffic strongly varies depending on player's activities. As a consequence, the advanced traffic model uses two steps: we first model the player's behaviour, and then we devise the parameters which rule the traffic generation. A previous model, including the behavioural parameters as well as the teletraffic statistic distributions for each of the action categories, can be found in [10]. As we have already said, we want to construct an improved model which modifies its statistics according to the population of the server.

3.1. Identification of Action Categories in Which Traffic Depends on Population. We now describe the tests we have deployed in order to identify the activities in which the traffic significantly varies with the number of players in the server. The client generates a traffic flow transmitting the player's actions to the server. At the same time, the server calculates the next state of the virtual world and transmits it to the client. Thus, the server has to communicate to the client the movements and characteristics of the rest of the avatars in its area of Interest. So logically, the population of the server influences server to client traffic, whereas the information sent by the client is not population dependant.

First, the traffic of *Trading* category has shown its strong dependency on the server population. The reason is that *Trading* is mostly performed in capital cities in WoW, which have been proven to be "hot spots" for player gathering [26], so interaction between players is frequent. Also, points in the virtual world in which the players can perform offline trading through auctioning items (i.e., *Auction Houses*) are located in the big cities. On the other hand, *Questing* is performed in very large areas, so even in highly populated servers there are never more than a few players in the vicinity. The results in [31] also indicate that stay time of players in quest areas is dependent on the level for which the questing area has been designed, further lowering the density of the players in those areas.

Regarding the rest of activities, they are based on "instancing." Instances are areas of the virtual world which are replicated for each group of players who enter them, and the number of players is fixed during the activity. As a consequence, they do not depend on the server population but on the number of players in the instance. *Raiding* and *Dungeons* are the categories which are defined with a fixed number of players, so we do not model these action categories as dependant on number of players, and we use the models described in [10].

On the other hand, we have modelled *PvP combat* to be aware of the number of players, as each *PvP* area is designed for a different number of players (from four to eighty). It should be noted that the population of the particular server does not have an effect on *PvP combat*; only the population of the specific area in which the player has been assigned has an influence. All in all, we will model the statistics of *Trading* and *PvP combat* as population dependant. In the next subsections we describe in detail the developed statistical models.

3.2. Measurement Methodology. The method for measuring the number of players performing a particular activity is similar to the one proposed in [25]: the use of the "/who" call of the WoW command line user interface. This call is used to obtain the list of online players in a certain zone, of specific level, class, or name. As a parameter, we use a name of the zone in which the avatar was located in order to obtain the number of players in the surrounding area.

In order to characterize these activities, we performed measurements of the number of players in two WoW servers with different population: *Bladefist*, a low populated realm, and *Outland*, a server labelled as "full." Measurements were performed between 20:00 and 21:00 hours. This time frame is considered as "prime" time (i.e., when the number of players on the shard is among the highest). The results showed that there are up to six times more players on *Outland*. This difference in the number of players results in significantly different traffic characteristics of server-to-client traffic.

First, we have captured network traces with different numbers of active players in the vicinity. With that aim, we have placed a virtual character in *Stormwind*, a capital city of the *Alliance* faction, and performed trading activities (e.g., browsing auction house, visiting bank, checking mail, etc.); we captured network traffic for 30 minutes and also measured the number of avatars in the area. As a result, we obtained seven traffic traces with different numbers of active players around, from 30 to over 600. We also obtained a trace of a player in a completely deserted area, with no other players around, in order to obtain the characteristics of traffic when only "keep alive" data is sent.

PvP combat in WoW is a quite complex activity, but it always involves two teams who fight to ensure victory through either killing all the members of the opposing team (arenas) or gathering a certain number of points or objectives depending on the map (battlegrounds). The number of players is fixed to brackets which can be 4, 6, and 10 for arenas and 20, 30, and 80 for battlegrounds. For the purposes of player-dependant *PvP combat* modelling, we used 20 traces of arena matches and battlegrounds [28].

3.3. Population-Dependant Teletraffic Model of Trading. It has been previously noted that Weibull distribution shows the best fit for both APDU size and IAT of the general WoW traffic [10, 15]. While we previously modelled *Trading* category with Lognormal distribution [10], we obtained better results with Weibull distribution when performing fitting for a specific number of players. We determined the parameters of the Weibull distribution for each of the captured traces and defined a relationship between those parameters and the number of players. Using nonlinear regression, we estimated the parameters of APDU size dependence of number of players in this way:

$$\alpha = 55.067 * N^{0.357},$$
$$\gamma = 1.02 + 0.000406 * N, \tag{1}$$

where α and γ are the *scale* and *shape* factors of the Weibull distribution and N is the number of active players in the AOI.

Trading IAT is described with the following formulae:

$$\alpha = 118,508 + 298,763 * e^{(-0,0119498*N)},$$
$$\gamma = 1.149 * N^{0.068}. \tag{2}$$

As shown in Figure 2 (where M stands for "Measured" and G stands for "simulation Generated"), the fit is quite good, especially for the APDU (Figure 2(a)), while for IAT the trend is captured (Figure 2(b)), but with more significant discrepancies. For the sake of clarity, we only plot the two measurement cases which we consider borderline (30 and 602 players) and one common case (121 player). The rest of the measurements have between 100 and 500 players average and behave similarly to the depicted curves.

3.4. Statistical Model of PvP Combat. We show the characteristics of both APDU and IAT for every *PvP* activity in Figure 3, as well as the respective statistical models (common for IAT, and based on the number of players for APDU). According to the results shown in Figure 3(b), we have not modelled IAT for *PvP* combat as depending on the number of players, since the IAT distribution has shown to be fairly constant for every *PvP* activity, regardless of the number of players. This is due to the fact that *PvP* is a very dynamic action category with constant movement and use of various abilities, which results in very frequent updates from the server, regardless of the number of players [28].

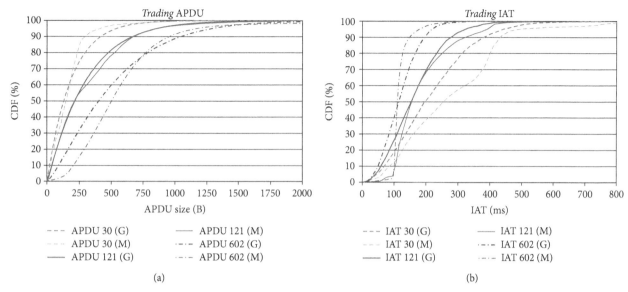

FIGURE 2: CDFs of (a) APDU and (b) IAT for different numbers of players for measured (M) and simulation generated (G) traces of *Trading*.

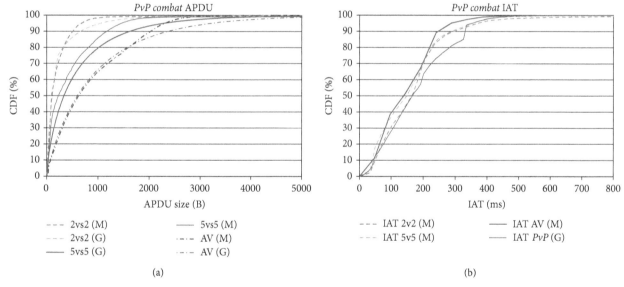

FIGURE 3: CDFs of (a) APDU (b) IAT, for different numbers of players for measured (M) and simulation generated (G) traces of *PvP combat*.

We model APDU size as dependant on the number of players (i.e., the arena bracket or specific battleground). For arenas the modelling procedure is simpler, as they are small areas in which players are constantly in the AOI of the others. Through comparison of arena traces of different brackets, we extracted how much additional data is transferred per additional player, obtaining a mean APDU increase of 38 bytes per player. Thus, we fit the APDU size to a Weibull distribution dependant on the number of players. The formula is as follows:

$$\text{Mean}(N) = \text{Mean}(4) \cdot 38 \cdot (N - 4),$$

$$\alpha = \frac{\text{Mean}(N)}{1.178}, \qquad (3)$$

$$\gamma = 0.76,$$

where Mean(i) is the mean of the distribution describing i players and Mean(4) = 258.33 (estimated from the measurements).

For battlegrounds the case is more complex, as they are larger in terms of virtual space, and not all players are always in the AOI of all other players. That is why we first estimate the average number of players in the AOI, depending on the battleground. The estimation is based on the measurement traces of each particular battleground and the values obtained from measurements of arenas in which we know exactly how many players are in the AOI. The estimated values of the average number of users are listed in Table 1.

The formula for battlegrounds has also been slightly modified in comparison with arenas, as in arenas there is constant fight until someone "dies," whereas in battlegrounds there are also time periods in which players wait to be "reborn" after

TABLE 1: Estimated Average Number of Players per Battleground.

Battleground	Average number of players
Alterac Valley	21.32
Arathi Basin	10.90
Warsong Gulch	10.11
Eye of the Storm	13.14
Strand of the Ancients	15.03

they have been killed, time periods in which the player is travelling from one end of the battleground to another, and so forth. These differences reflect on the characteristics of the Weibull distribution. The final battleground formula for server APDU sizes is

$$\text{Mean}\,(N) = \text{Mean}\,(4) \cdot 38 \cdot (N - 4),$$

$$\alpha = \frac{\text{Mean}\,(N)}{1.073}, \tag{4}$$

$$\gamma = 0.87,$$

where the parameter N is representing an estimated average number of players in the AOI for the battleground and Mean(4) = 258.33. In Figure 3 the results of the model are plotted versus the measured data for cases of *2v2* and *5v5* arenas and for *Alterac Valley* (AV) battleground. As it can be observed, the models tend to slightly overestimate the empirical distribution, but the general trend is captured well.

As *PvP combat* has been fractionated into arenas and battlegrounds and some parameters of the model are dependent on the battleground type, we have to fully adapt the behavioural model. We make two assumptions here: first, we consider the duration of the *PvP* activity as independent of whether it is a battleground or an arena; second, we assume a battleground/arena ratio of 50% : 50%, since there is no reliable empirical data from which the values for this parameter could be extracted.

Our model makes the decision of a player entering a specific bracket of arena or battleground, based on data gathered by WoW add-on census (the dataset and the add-on are further described on http://www.warcraftrealms.com/). The parameters of popularity of each particular arena bracket or battleground are displayed in Tables 2 and 3, respectively. The popularity parameter describes how often players join specific battleground map or specific arena bracket.

3.5. Implementation of the Advanced Model. Once we have obtained the statistics of the traffic for each activity, the model has been fully implemented in NS2. It includes the probability of a player deploying each activity, which varies with the hour of the day. This script, allowing a wide range of tests, is offered to the research community. As an example of the use of the model, Figure 4 shows the daily behavioural variation obtained when simulating 3,000 players during a whole day. It can be seen that it does capture the main trends in player behaviour such as the high rise of *Raiding* in the evening [10]. The slight discrepancies with respect to previous results

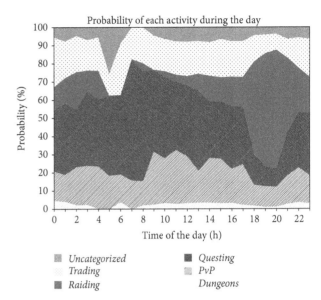

FIGURE 4: Daily pattern of players' activities.

TABLE 2: Popularity of arena brackets.

Arena	Popularity
2v2	45.05%
3v3	45.16%
5v5	9.79%

TABLE 3: Popularity of specific battlegrounds.

Battleground	Popularity
Arathi Basin	24.56%
Warsong Gulch	32.50%
Eye of the Storm	7.96%
Strand of the Ancients	2.08%
Alterac Valley	32.89%

[10] are mainly caused by the fact that we do not model the fluctuation of the players during the day.

All in all, as an example of the results of the developed model, Figure 5(a) shows the client-server traces generated by the NS2 script, for each activity. To illustrate the bandwidth difference depending on the number of players and activity, Figure 5(b) shows the effect of the server population for server-client traffic of *Trading* and the same effect depending on the different scenarios for *PvP combat*. As it can be seen, the script captures the differences in traffic characteristics for particular player behaviour (note that Figure 5(b) is not comparable with Figure 1(b), since it only shows the activities that modify their behaviour with the number of players).

4. Tests and Results

In this section we present the results of different experiments using the complete NS2 traffic model described previously, with the aim of illustrating the behaviour of these flows when they share the network with other traffic. Thus, we

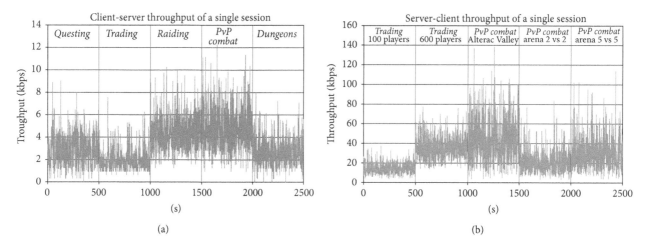

FIGURE 5: Throughput generated by the model for (a) client to server for each category and (b) server to client for *Trading* and *PvP combat* with different options.

will mainly focus on the competition between application-limited TCP game traffic and other flows, and how this competition modifies the communication parameters. The considered competing flows are FTP, which use TCP so as to get as much throughput as possible (network-limited), and UDP Constant Bit Rate (CBR), which generates the same throughput despite the status of the network.

The obtained results will be presented in terms of the most interesting parameter for each kind of traffic.

(i) For the MMORPG TCP traffic we will mainly focus on Round Trip Time (RTT), taking into account that latency is the most important parameter, because the interactivity of the game mainly depends on it. In order to estimate the RTT in NS2, we will use the parameters that govern TCP dynamics (e.g., retransmissions), namely, "smoothed RTT" and "RTT *variation*," which are calculated and updated frequently, according to the network conditions. They are subsequently used to obtain the value of Retransmission TimeOut (RTO) [32]. If this timeout expires, the packet is retransmitted.

(ii) For the FTP background traffic, we will present the achieved throughput, since these flows try to get as much as possible of the bandwidth share. The size of the sending window of TCP will also be presented if required.

(iii) For the CBR traffic, the results can be presented in terms of bandwidth or packet loss rate which are directly related to this case, since the traffic is sent in an open loop.

In order to create a scenario where the different flows share a bottleneck, we have configured a dumbbell topology (Figure 6): two pairs of client-server connections (*A* and *B*) correspond to game nodes and the other pair is used for generating background traffic.

Regarding the parameters of the simulations, when activity exchange is not explicitly required by the test, we will use

by default *Questing* traffic, one of the most popular activities, which also presents a relatively stable traffic profile. The advantage of using a single activity in those tests is that we avoid the influence of player behaviour, which may obscure the observations. In the last subsection we include activity exchange so as to better observe the characteristics of the realistic traffic generated through the model. Each *Questing* flow generates about 2.2 kbps in the client-server connection and roughly 18 kbps in the server-client one. By default, the bandwidth in the bottleneck is 10 Mbps in both directions. Queue sizes are 100 packets. The Round Trip Time (RTT) delay of the bottleneck (RTT0) is 40 ms. By default, the rest of RTTx delays are set to 0. Each simulation lasts 200 seconds, and a "tick" of 1 second is used to calculate the average RTT or throughput during each interval. The tick is 0.1 seconds for the TCP window size.

4.1. Competition of MMORPG and FTP Flows: The Effect of TCP Variants. In this subsection we will study the competition of application-limited (MMORPG) and network-limited TCP flows (we will use FTP as a typical application). To this aim, 100 MMORPG sessions are established between *client A* and *server A,* and 10 FTP upload and 10 FTP download sessions are set between *background* 1and 2, with a packet size of 1,500 bytes.

In order to correctly imitate the behaviour of WoW, which uses a single session, piggybacking the ACKs in packets in the opposite direction [15], the *Full-TCP* NS2 TCP implementation (using *Reno*) has been used for game sessions. For the FTP sessions, five TCP variants are tested: *Tahoe, Reno, New Reno, SACK,* and *Vegas,* using the standard NS2 implementations for these protocols. Each TCP session is started using a different random delay, in order to avoid the effect of the synchronization of TCP window sizes [30]. Thus, the first seconds of the presented graphs may present a transient behaviour different from the stationary.

The effect of the different TCP variants used for the background flows can be observed in Figure 7 (on behalf of clarity, only *New Reno, SACK,* and *Vegas* are shown), where

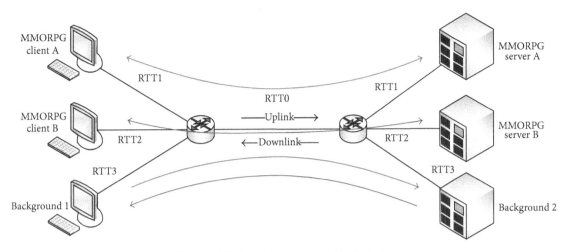

FIGURE 6: Network topology used in the tests.

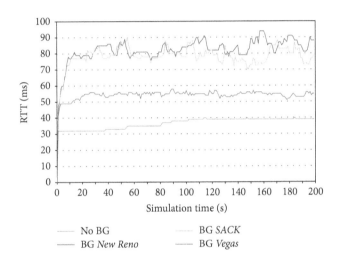

FIGURE 7: Competition of MMORPG versus FTP traffic for different TCP variants: smoothed RTT of a game flow.

TABLE 4: Average RTT between all the game flows when different TCP variants are used for the background traffic.

BG TCP variant	avg smoothed RTT	avg RTT variation
No BG	38.76 ms	3.05 ms
Tahoe	82.61 ms	7.24 ms
Reno	81.23 ms	7.36 ms
New Reno	84.54 ms	6.76 ms
SACK	77.64 ms	6.85 ms
Vegas	54.74 ms	3.65 ms

the smoothed RTT is presented. Table 4 presents the average RTT on each case, between all the game flows. This RTT increase is caused by queuing delay at the bottleneck. These results are complemented with those in Figures 8, 9, and 10, which present the aggregate throughput obtained by the FTP flows and the TCP window size for *New Reno*, *SACK*, and *Vegas*. Finally, Table 5 summarizes the FTP throughput results for all the tested TCP variants.

TABLE 5: Average throughput obtained by the FTP background flows using different TCP variants.

BG TCP variant	Avg throughput uplink	Avg throughput downlink
Tahoe	871.15 kbps	736.08 kbps
Reno	866.58 kbps	746.53 kbps
New Reno	874.58 kbps	749.85 kbps
SACK	849.84 kbps	717.88 kbps
Vegas	814.76 kbps	672.24 kbps

It can first be observed that when no background traffic is present, the estimated latency is roughly 40 ms. The behaviour of *New Reno* and *SACK* is very similar, but it can be seen that game traffic obtains better results when *SACK* is used for the background traffic: 7 ms are reduced from the RTT, at the cost of a slighter share of the bandwidth of the link for the FTP flows (an average of 849 kbps instead of 874 kbps per flow, i.e., a 3% throughput reduction). The reason for this can be that *SACK* reduces the retransmissions, since its ACK mechanism is able to acknowledge packet ranges, so the behaviour results are a bit less aggressive. The results for *Tahoe* and *Reno* are very similar to those of *New Reno*.

TCP *Vegas* behaves in a very different way, as shown in Figure 10: the window size does not grow aggressively, but it remains constant. Because of this *timid* behaviour [33], when TCP *Vegas* notices the RTT increase, it maintains its sending rate, even in the absence of packet loss. In the uplink, *Vegas* only gets 814 kbps (which means a reduction of 9% with respect to *New Reno*), and in the downlink the reduction is roughly 10%. However, as a counterpart, this is translated into a significant reduction of the RTT of the MMORPG flows: only 14 ms are added to the 40 ms of default RTT, whereas in *New Reno* this figure is 44 ms.

It should be noted that in all these cases the game is still playable, taking into account that the literature has reported that MMORPG players can tolerate up to some hundreds of milliseconds of RTT [34].

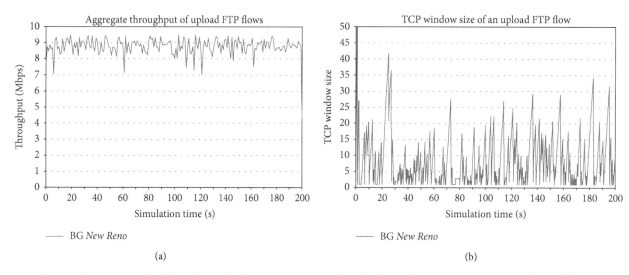

FIGURE 8: Competition between MMORPG and FTP background traffic using TCP *New Reno*: (a) aggregate throughput of the 10 FTP flows and (b) evolution of the TCP window of one of the flows.

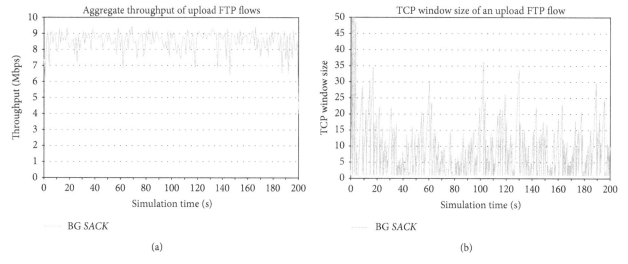

FIGURE 9: Competition of MMORPG and FTP background traffic using TCP *SACK*: (a) aggregate throughput of the 10 FTP flows and (b) evolution of the TCP window of one of the flows.

As a result, we can conclude that the most popular TCP variants (i.e., *New Reno* and *SACK*) can be respectful with competing MMORPG traffic, although they add some latency due to their behaviour trying to get the maximum bandwidth share. On the other hand TCP *Vegas* could be considered as a good option for competing flows in order not to throttle the MMORPG flows and by that to better preserve the quality of game experience for the MMORPG players.

4.2. Competition of MMORPG and UDP Background Traffic. It is normally assumed [35] that, when TCP and UDP flows compete for a shared link, UDP gets all the required bandwidth while TCP uses the remainder of the bandwidth, because of TCP flow control mechanism. However, in the case of MMORPGs, in which the traffic is not limited by the network but is application limited, a different behaviour can be observed.

We have set this scenario: 100 MMORPG *Questing* sessions (roughly 2 Mbps in the server-client direction) are run from *client A* to *server A*. At the same time, three UDP flows are sent between *backgrounds* 1 and 2. The total amount of UDP traffic is the aggregation of these three flows: small packets (40 bytes, 50% of the packets), medium packets (576 bytes, 10% of the packets), and large packets (1,500 bytes, 40% of the packets) [36].

In Figure 11, 7 Mbps of UDP traffic share the link with 100 MMORPG sessions. Since there is enough bandwidth, each flow obtains the required amount. The first row of Table 6 summarizes the results: first, it can be seen that the RTT of the MMORPG connections is not affected, since the obtained value is similar to the result obtained when no background traffic was present (Table 4). In addition, it can be seen that the packet loss rate of the CBR traffic is residual. When 8 Mbps of UDP CBR traffic are sent (Figure 12), the average

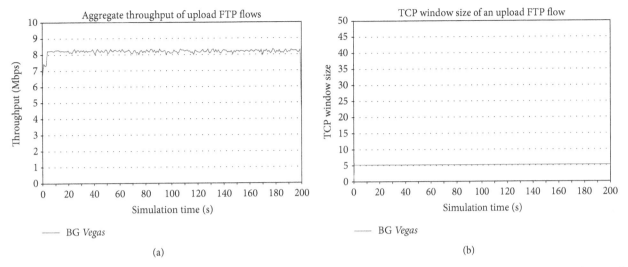

FIGURE 10: Competition of MMORPG and FTP background traffic using TCP *Vegas*: (a) aggregate throughput of the 10 FTP flows and (b) evolution of the TCP window of one of the flows.

TABLE 6: Summary of the tests: average RTT of all the MMORPG flows; packet loss rate in the downlink.

CBR throughput (downlink)	Average RTT MMORPG	Average packet loss rate CBR
7 Mbps	39.35 ms	0.05%
8 Mbps	48.16 ms	0.34%
8.5 Mbps	38.58 ms	4.61%
9 Mbps	76.78 ms	11.67%

RTT rises up to 48 ms. At the same time, the packet loss rate of the UDP flows is slightly increased.

However, when UDP traffic is 8.5 Mbps (Figure 13) and the total offered traffic is above the bandwidth limit, the tendency is that MMORPG traffic maintains its bandwidth use of roughly 2 Mbps, whereas UDP traffic only obtains the remaining throughput.

This is also observed in Figure 14, where the offered UDP traffic is 9 Mbps. The bandwidth obtained by the UDP flows is roughly the same as in the previous case, whereas MMORPG maintains its bandwidth, with a slight increase of 3.22%, caused by duplicate game packets. All in all, it can be seen that MMORPG traffic flows roughly obtain the same throughput, despite the amount of competing UDP traffic.

All in all, this behaviour is the opposite of that normally expected in the TCP-UDP competition [33], where TCP only obtains the traffic not used by UDP. The reason for this is that the bandwidth demand of the MMORPG flows is not governed by the congestion window, since they do not have an amount of traffic ready to be transferred but keep on generating new information while the game evolves. In order to illustrate this, Figure 15(a) shows the TCP window of an MMORPG session, in the case where no background traffic is present (negligible queuing delay), and (Figure 15(b)) in the case of having 8.5 Mbps of UDP background traffic.

Although the size of the TCP window is reduced when background traffic is present, the flows keep on sending their traffic, since they do not need a high value of the TCP window in order to send it. This fits with the two opposed effects reported in [6]: on one hand, the thinness of each stream makes that few packets are sent by RTT, making the window hardly grow. On the other hand, the flows do not correctly react to congestion, so they may keep on sending the same amount of traffic.

4.3. RTT Unfairness Tests. The aim of this subsection is the study of RTT unfairness between different MMORPG TCP flows. As reported in the literature [34], when two TCP flows with different RTTs compete for the same bottleneck link, the one with a smaller RTT has an advantage with respect to the other. The cause of this is that the most popular TCP versions *(New Reno, SACK)* increase their sending windows according to the received ACKs, so different delays will make them increase their rates differently.

However, in the case of MMORPG flows, we cannot expect a modification in the throughput, since the traffic is application limited instead of network limited. As we have already said, the main figure of merit for MMORPGs is RTT. Hence, an increase of the network RTT should be translated into a direct increase of the smoothed RTT seen by TCP. So the aim of this subsection is to check if there is any additional impairment caused by RTT unfairness, leaving apart the RTT increase itself.

In order to answer this question, we have set the parameters of the scenario this way: 100 MMORPG flows are established between *client A* and *server A*, and at the same time, 100 MMORPG flows are active between *client B* and *server B*. Background traffic consists of 10 FTP upload and 10 FTP download sessions using TCP *SACK*, between *background 1* and *background 2* nodes. The value of RTT1 (Figure 6) is set to different values, higher than 0, so the flows having a higher RTT, and thus the flows between *client A*

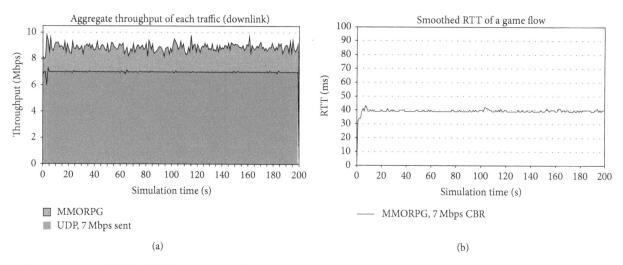

(a)

(b)

FIGURE 11: Coexistence of 100 MMORPG flows and 7 Mbps of UDP CBR traffic: (a) received throughput in the downlink by each traffic and (b) smoothed RTT of one of the game flows.

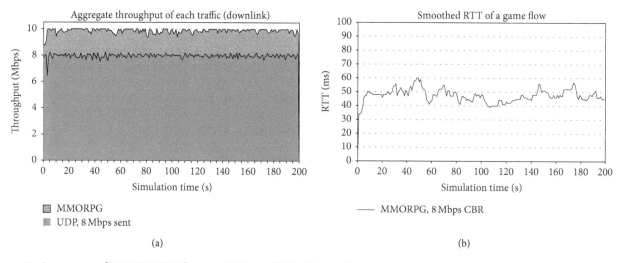

(a)

(b)

FIGURE 12: Coexistence of 100 MMORPG flows and 8 Mbps of UDP CBR traffic: (a) received throughput in the downlink by each traffic and (b) smoothed RTT of one of the game flows.

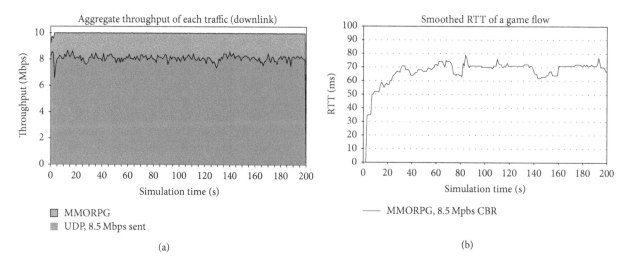

(a)

(b)

FIGURE 13: Coexistence of 100 MMORPG flows and 8.5 Mbps of UDP CBR traffic: (a) received throughput in the downlink by each traffic and (b) smoothed RTT of one of the game flows.

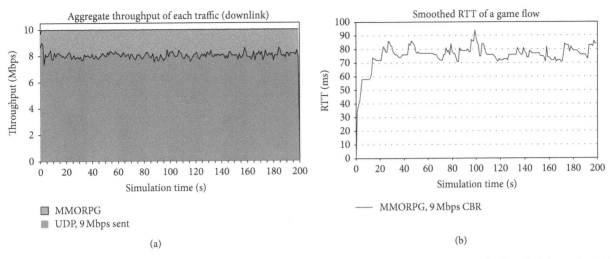

(a)

(b)

FIGURE 14: Coexistence of 100 MMORPG flows and 9 Mbps of UDP CBR traffic: (a) received throughput in the downlink by each traffic and (b) smoothed RTT of one of the game flows.

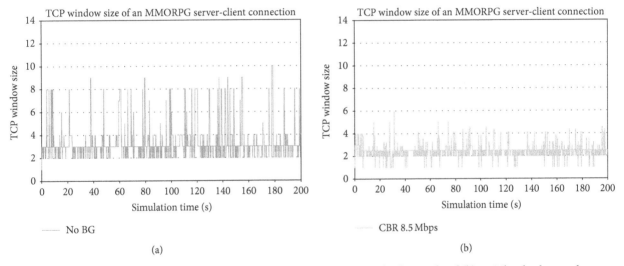

(a)

(b)

FIGURE 15: TCP window size, and server-client MMORPG traffic: (a) no background and (b) 8.5 Mbps background.

and *server A* are at a disadvantage. The RTT of the bottleneck (RTT0) is always 40 ms.

Figure 16 presents the results obtained when 100 game flows from *client A* to *server A,* experiencing different amounts of RTT (from 50 to 90), share the bottleneck with 100 game flows from *client B* to *server B,* always with an RTT of 40 ms. Regarding the value of smoothed RTT, two things can be appreciated in Figure 16(a): first, the difference between the columns is roughly the difference in terms of network RTT: for example, when 100 flows with an RTT of 60 ms share the bottleneck with 100 flows with an RTT of 40 ms, the difference in terms of smoothed RTT is 21.85 ms (i.e., roughly 20 ms). This happens (with very small variations) for all the values. Second: the RTT value for the *client B* to *server B* connections always remains the same.

Regarding the results of RTT *variation* (Figure 16(b)), it can be appreciated that the variation of the RTT is significantly higher for the flows experiencing a higher RTT, which will be translated in high jitter values.

The results of the throughput are not shown here, since the throughput variations between *A-A* and *B-B* flows are negligible (up to 3%), as it could be expected. We can conclude saying that smoothed RTT is not affected by this unfairness, but only RTT *variation* is worse for the flows with a higher RTT.

4.4. The Effect of Server Population on the Aggregate Traffic. We have previously mentioned the importance of the number of players present on a server, since this can have an effect on the global traffic. This subsection uses the proposed model to confirm that the traffic can significantly vary according to the server population, and also depending on the hour of the day. The developed model takes into account both variables.

In the tests of this subsection we have established 100 MMORPG traffic flows between *client A* and *server A,* competing with 10 FTP upload flows, 10 FTP download flows (using TCP *SACK*), and UDP background traffic of 6 Mbps

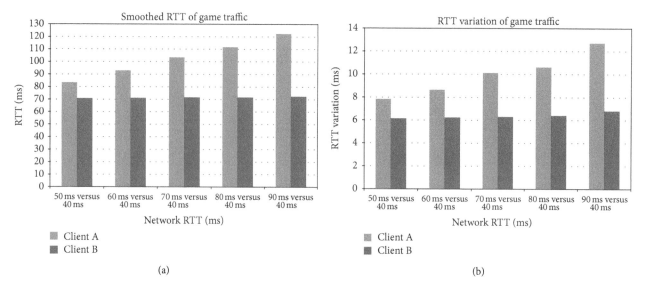

FIGURE 16: Latency of MMORPG flows from *client A* and *client B* (a) Smoothed RTT and (b) RTT *variation*.

in both uplink and downlink. We have considered that the players are using low-populated servers (30 players) in one case, and high-populated ones (600 players) in the other. Taking into account that the two activities in which traffic significantly varies with the server population are *PvP combat* and *Trading*, we have selected three different hours of the day (see Figure 4):

(i) 8:00 as an example of low *PvP combat* and high *Trading*;

(ii) 11:00 where both activities have a high probability of being performed;

(iii) 20:00 where both activities have low probability.

In this case, the aggregate traffic (100 MMORPG flows) is composed of flows corresponding to the six action categories, according to their probabilities, which also depend on the hour of the day. In this way, we investigate if the variation of the APDU and IAT of *Trading* and *PvP combat* has a global effect, which can be observed on the aggregate server-to-client traffic.

The results are shown in Figure 17, where 200 simulation seconds are run for each case. The left figure displays the case of players in low populated servers, while the right displays the case of highly populated servers. During the initial seconds, there is a transient status in which FTP connections need some time in order to increase their sending windows. As a first observation, we see that the throughput of these 100 MMORPG sessions strongly varies with the hour of the day: at 8:00 it can vary from 2 to 2.4 Mbps, depending on the global population of the servers where the players are. However, at 20.00 it varies from 3.5 to 4.1 Mbps. It should be remarked that these variations are not caused by a different number of flows, but only by the global population of the servers to which these players are connected.

At the same time, it can be observed that, at 11.00 (Figures 17(c) and 17(d)), the difference between the traffic

TABLE 7: Average smoothed RTT of all the MMORPG flows.

Hour of the day	Smoothed RTT 30 players	Smoothed RTT 600 players
8:00	91.39 ms	87.69 ms
11:00	90.46 ms	89.23 ms
20:00	93.61 ms	96.32 ms

is significant: 2.18 Mbps with 30 players and 2.96 Mbps with 600 players (35%). At 20:00 (Figures 17(e) and 17(f)), the difference is only from 3.5 to 4.1 (17%). At 8.00 (Figures 17(a) and 17(b)) the traffic ranges from 2 to 2.44 Mbps (22%).

Finally, in order to explore if the variation of the bandwidth with the hour of the day has any influence on the RTT (measured as smoothed RTT), Table 7 shows its average value for the 100 MMORPG flows. It can be seen that the variations are really small (between 1% and 4%), and this fits with another phenomenon that can be observed in Figure 17; that is, we see that in all the cases the UDP flows get reduced their 6 Mbps of bandwidth share, whereas MMORPG flows maintain their throughput. FTP flows are only able to get the bandwidth that the two other kinds of flows leave free. This is in concordance with the results shown in Sections 4.1 and 4.2, and with the effect reported in [6]; that is, the flows do not react to congestion due to their thinness, and they keep on sending the same amount of traffic.

The high variability of MMORPG traffic depending on the hour of the day and on the population of a server makes it difficult to calculate the number of servers required for provisioning an online game. In addition, many other factors have an influence; for example, the release of a new game or of new content of an existing one can cause a traffic rush. Although game developers may experience difficulties when predicting the success of a game, they may be interested in using statistical models in order to predict the demand variations according to the hour of the day.

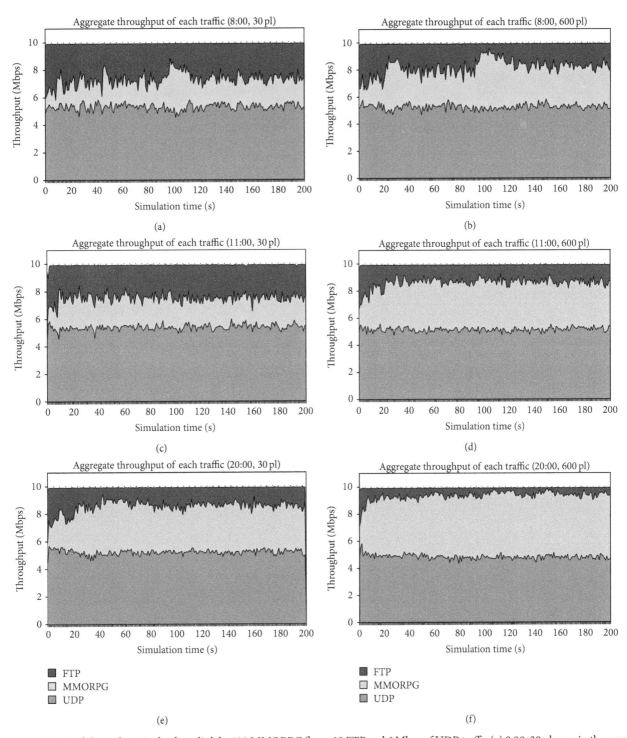

FIGURE 17: Received throughput in the downlink by 100 MMORPG flows, 10 FTP and 6 Mbps of UDP traffic (a) 8:00, 30 players in the servers; (b) 8:00, 600 players in the servers; (c) 11:00, 30 players; (d) 11:00, 600 players; (e) 20:00, 30 players; (f) 20:00, 600 players.

4.5. Discussion of the Results. This subsection summarizes and discusses the results presented in this section. In the first tests, we measured the competition of MMORPG and FTP flows using different variants of TCP. We first observed that the MMORPG flows are able to work properly even with network-limited TCP connections in the background. The most important parameter for players, namely, RTT can be kept low for all the TCP variants. TCP *SACK* shows a more

respectful behaviour with game flows: it increases less the game RTT, at the cost of achieving a slightly lower amount of bandwidth share than *Tahoe, Reno,* and *New Reno.* This tradeoff is more accentuated with TCP *Vegas,* which reduces even more its throughput but as a counterpart adds less delay (up to 30 ms) to the RTT of the game flows.

The second subsection has studied the mutual influence of MMORPG TCP flows and UDP CBR ones. In contrast with what normally happens with TCP flows, which only get the bandwidth share not used by UDP ones, the tests have shown that TCP game flows are able to maintain their throughput despite the amount of UDP traffic. The reason is that the bandwidth demand of the game flows is not governed by the congestion window, since they do not have an amount of predefined data to transfer, but they keep on generating new information according to the player actions and the game evolution.

The third battery of tests has explored the RTT unfairness, normally observed when several TCP flows with different RTTs share a bottleneck. This difference is not as important as for network-limited TCP flows. In this case, the bandwidth obtained does not vary with the RTT, taking into account that the traffic is mostly signalling. In addition, the RTT experienced by the game (measured in terms of TCP smoothed RTT) varies according to the real network RTT. Only the RTT *variation* shows worse results for the flows with a higher RTT, which will be translated into a higher jitter in the game traffic.

Finally, we have used the developed model of the game traffic so as to obtain results illustrating the effect of the number of players in a server (server population). Different hours of the day have been selected, drawing some conclusions that mainly affect server-to-client traffic: the bandwidth may vary up to 35% depending on the population of the server, and this difference may also vary according to the hour of the day. The cause of this phenomenon is that, in some moments, the activities preferred by the players are more server-population dependant. In addition, it has again be observed that game flows are able to maintain their throughput and a reasonable RTT, even in the presence of high amounts of combined FTP and UDP traffic flows.

5. Conclusion

This paper has studied the interactions between application-limited TCP traffic, typical of MMORPGs, and other flows. In order to do this, an advanced traffic model of a popular MMORPG game has been first developed. By using measurements deployed in real servers of the game, we have analyzed how the APDU and IAT of some activities vary with the number of players on the server, and this effect has been included in the statistics that rule the traffic generation in the model. In addition, the model is able to simulate user behaviour, generating traffic according to different activities, which have different probabilities depending on the hour of the day.

The traffic model has also been implemented in a network simulator, and a set of tests of the coexistence between traffic flows have been deployed: the coexistence of the game traffic with FTP using different TCP variants; the competition with UDP flows; the effect of different values of RTT between game flows; and the global effect of the server population on the aggregate traffic. It has been shown that TCP *SACK* is more respectful with game flows than *Tahoe, Reno*, and *New Reno;* that is, it achieves a slightly lower throughput but adds less delay to MMORPG flows. Furthermore, the behaviour of TCP *Vegas* is even better, not throttling the MMORPG flows and causing no growth on their RTT, since it does not increase aggressively its window size. Interestingly, we found

that MMORPG flows are resilient to UDP traffic: since they do not need significant sizes of the TCP window, they are able to maintain their bandwidth share while maintaining their RTT in reasonable limits. The RTT unfairness for application-limited TCP traffic has also been studied, showing that only the RTT variation is affected. Finally, we have confirmed that the player population on the server has significant impact on the overall traffic (up to 30%). Although game developers may experience difficulties when predicting the success of a new game, the use of statistical models able to predict the demand variations according to the hour of the day is seen as very convenient. As future work, we plan to improve the model so as to include players' arrivals and departures. In addition, the influence of different buffer sizes and policies on the coexistence of MMORPG traffic with other flows will be studied.

Conflict of Interests

The authors declare that there is no conflict of interests regarding the publication of this paper.

Acknowledgments

This work has been partially financed by the Project "Content Delivery and Mobility of Users and Services in New Generation Networks," by the Ministry of Science, Education, and Sports of the Republic of Croatia; the European Community Seventh Framework Programme under Grant Agreement no. 285939 (ACROSS); CPUFLIPI Project (MICINN TIN2010-17298); Project TAMA, Government of Aragon; Project Catedra Telefonica, University Zaragoza; European Social Fund in collaboration with the Government of Aragon. The authors would like to thank John Miller for his advice regarding some details of the game traffic. they also want to thank Tanja Kauric for her help in obtaining the traffic traces of the game.

References

[1] Activision Blizzard, "World of Warcraft subscriber base reaches 12 million worldwide," October 2010, http://us.blizzard.com/en-us/company/press/pressreleases.html?id=2847881.

[2] K.-T. Chen, C.-Y. Huang, P. Huang, and C.-L. Lei, "An empirical evaluation of TCP performance in online games," in *Proceedings of the ACM SIGCHI International Conference on Advances in Computer Entertainment Technology (ACE '06)*, Hollywood, Calif, USA, June 2006.

[3] M. Suznjevic and M. Matijasevic, "Player behavior and traffic characterization for MMORPGs: a survey," *Multimedia Systems*, vol. 19, no. 3, pp. 199–220, 2012.

[4] I. V. Geel, "MMOData: Keeping track of the MMORPG scene," August 2013, http://mmodata.net/.

[5] C.-C. Wu, K.-T. Chen, C.-M. Chen, P. Huang, and C.-L. Lei, "On the challenge and design of transport protocols for MMORPGs," *Multimedia Tools and Applications*, vol. 45, no. 1–3, pp. 7–32, 2009.

[6] C. Griwodz and P. Halvorsen, "The fun of using TCP for an MMORPG," in *Proceedings of the 16th Annual International Workshop on Network and Operating Systems Support for Digital Audio and Video (NOSSDAV '06)*, pp. 1–7, New York, NY, USA, May 2006.

[7] K. Shin, J. Kim, K. Sohn, C. J. Park, and S. Choi, "Transformation approach to model online gaming traffic," *ETRI Journal*, vol. 33, no. 2, pp. 219–229, 2011.

[8] K.-T. Chen, P. Huang, and C.-L. Lei, "Game traffic analysis: an MMORPG perspective," *Computer Networks*, vol. 51, no. 3, pp. 19–24, 2007.

[9] M. Suznjevic, O. Dobrijevic, and M. Matijasevic, "MMORPG Player actions: Network performance, session patterns and latency requirements analysis," *Multimedia Tools and Applications*, vol. 45, no. 1–3, pp. 191–214, 2009.

[10] M. Suznjevic, I. Stupar, and M. Matijasevic, "A model and software architecture for MMORPG traffic generation based on player behavior," *Multimedia Systems*, vol. 19, no. 3, pp. 93–101, 2012.

[11] B. De Vleeschauwer, B. van den Bossche, T. Verdickt, F. de Turck, B. Dhoedt, and P. Demeester, "Dynamic microcell assignment for massively multiplayer online gaming," in *Proceedings of the 4th ACM SIGCOMM Workshop on Network and System Support for Games (NetGames '05)*, pp. 1–7, Hawthorne, NY, USA, 2005.

[12] X. Che and B. Ip, "Packet-level traffic analysis of online games from the genre characteristics perspective," *Journal of Network and Computer Applications*, vol. 35, no. 1, pp. 240–252, 2012.

[13] C. Majewski, C. Griwodz, and P. Halvorsen, "Translating latency requirements into resource requirements for game traffic," in *Proceedings of the International Network Conference (INC '06)*, pp. 113–120, Plymouth, UK, 2006.

[14] J. Saldana, M. Suznjevic, L. Sequeira, J. Fernandez-Navajas, M. Matijasevic, and J. Ruiz-Mas, "The effect of TCP variants on the coexistence of MMORPG and best-effort traffic," in *Proceedings of IEEE ICCCN 8th International Workshop on Networking Issues in Multimedia Entertainment (NIME '12)*, pp. 1–5, Munich, Germany, 2012.

[15] P. Svoboda, W. Karner, and M. Rupp, "Traffic analysis and modeling for world of warcraft," in *Proceedings of the IEEE International Conference on Communications (ICC '07)*, pp. 1612–1617, Glasgow, UK, June 2007.

[16] J. Kim, E. Hong, and J. Choi, "Measurement and analysis of a massively multiplayer online role playing game traffic," in *Proceedings of Advanced Network Conference*, pp. 1–8, 2003.

[17] Y. Wu, H. Huang, and D. Zhang, "Traffic modeling for Massive Multiplayer On-line Role Playing Game (MMORPG) in GPRS access network," in *Proceedings of the International Conference on Communications, Circuits and Systems (ICCCAS '06)*, pp. 1811–1815, Guilin, China, June 2006.

[18] V. Paxson, "Empirically derived analytic models of wide-area TCP connections," *IEEE/ACM Transactions on Networking*, vol. 2, no. 4, pp. 316–336, 1994.

[19] K. Shin, J. Kim, K. Sohn, C. J. Park, and S. Choi, "Transformation approach to model online gaming traffic," *ETRI Journal*, vol. 33, no. 2, pp. 219–229, 2011.

[20] H. Park, T. Kim, and S. Kim, "Network traffic analysis and modeling for games," in *Internet and Network Economics*, vol. 3828 of *Lecture Notes in Computer Science*, pp. 1056–1065, Springer, 2005.

[21] X. Wang, H. Kim, A. V. Vasilakos et al., "Measurement and analysis of world of warcraft in mobile WiMAX networks," in *Proceedings of the 8th Annual Workshop on Network and Systems Support for Games (NetGames '09)*, Paris, France, November 2009.

[22] X. Wang, T. Kwon, Y. Choi, M. Chen, and Y. Zhang, "Characterizing the gaming traffic of World of Warcraft: from game scenarios to network access technologies," *IEEE Network*, vol. 26, no. 1, pp. 27–34, 2012.

[23] W.-C. Feng, D. Brandt, and D. Saha, "A long-term study of a popular MMORPG," in *Proceedings of the 6th ACM SIGCOMM Workshop on Network and System Support for Games (NetGames '07)*, pp. 19–24, Melbourne, Australia, September 2007.

[24] J. Kawale, A. Pal, and J. Srivastava, "Churn prediction in MMORPGs: a social influence based approach," in *Proceedings of the International Conference on Computational Science and Engineering*, pp. 423–428, Vanoucer, Canada, August 2009.

[25] D. Pittman and C. G.Dickey, "A measurement study of virtual populations in massively multiplayer online games," in *Proceedings of the 6th ACM SIGCOMM Workshop on Network and System Support for Games (NetGames '07)*, pp. 25–30, Melbourne, Australia, September 2007.

[26] D. Pittman and C. G. Dickey, "Characterizing virtual populations in massively multiplayer online role-playing games," in *Advances in Multimedia Modeling*, vol. 5916 of *Lecture Notes in Computer Science*, pp. 87–97, Springer, 2010.

[27] Y.-T. Lee, K.-T. Chen, Y.-M. Cheng, and C.-L. Lei, "World of warcraft avatar history dataset," in *Proceedings of the 2nd Annual ACM Multimedia Systems Conference (MMSys '11)*, pp. 123–128, San Jose, Calif, USA, February 2011.

[28] M. Suznjevic, I. Stupar, and M. Matijasevic, "MMORPG player behavior model based on player action categories," in *Proceedings of the 10th Annual Workshop on Network and Systems Support for Games (NetGames '11)*, Ottawa, Canada, October 2011.

[29] P. A. Branch, A. L. Cricenti, and G. J. Armitage, "An ARMA(1,1) prediction model of first person shooter game traffic," in *Proceedings of the IEEE 10th Workshop on Multimedia Signal Processing (MMSP '08)*, pp. 736–741, Cairns, Australia, October 2008.

[30] T. Lang, P. Branch, and G. Armitage, "A synthetic traffic model for quake3," in *Proceedings of the ACM SIGCHI International Conference on Advances in Computer Entertainment Technology (ACE '04)*, pp. 233–238, Singapore, June 2005.

[31] X. Zhuang, A. Bharambe, J. Pang, and S. Seshan, "Player dynamics in massively multiplayer online games," Tech. Rep. CMU-CS-07-158, School of Computer Science Carnegie Mellon University, Pittsburgh, Pa, USA, 2007.

[32] T. Issariyakul and E. Hossain, *Introduction to Network Simulator NS2*, Springer, 2011.

[33] G. Marfia, C. E. Palazzi, G. Pau, M. Gerla, and M. Roccetti, "TCP Libra: derivation, analysis, and comparison with other RTT-fair TCPs," *Computer Networks*, vol. 54, no. 14, pp. 2327–2344, 2010.

[34] M. Ries, P. Svoboda, and M. Rupp, "Empirical study of subjective quality for massive multiplayer games," in *Proceedings of the 15th International Conference on Systems, Signals and Image Processing (IWSSIP '08)*, pp. 181–184, Bratislava, Slovakia, June 2008.

[35] H. Sawashima and Y. H. H. Sunahara, "Characteristics of UDP packet loss: effect of TCP traffic," in *Proceeeding of the 7th Annual Conference of the Internet Society (INET '97)*, p. 6, Kuala Lumpur, Malaysia, 1997.

[36] Cooperative Association for Internet Data Analysis (CAIDA), "NASA Ames Internet Exchange Packet Length Distributions," March 2008, http://www.caida.org/research/traffic-analysis/AIX/plen_hist/.

2

Desirable Elements for a Particle System Interface

Daniel Schroeder and Howard J. Hamilton

Department of Computer Science, University of Regina, Regina, SK, Canada S4S 0A2

Correspondence should be addressed to Howard J. Hamilton; howard.hamilton@uregina.ca

Academic Editor: Ali Arya

Particle systems have many applications, with the most popular being to produce special effects in video games and films. To permit particle systems to be created quickly and easily, Particle System Interfaces (PSIs) have been developed. A PSI is a piece of software designed to perform common tasks related to particle systems for clients, while providing them with a set of parameters whose values can be adjusted to create different particle systems. Most PSIs are inflexible, and when clients require functionality that is not supported by the PSI they are using, they are forced to either find another PSI that meets their requirements or, more commonly, create their own particle system or PSI from scratch. This paper presents three original contributions. First, it identifies 18 features that a PSI should provide in order to be capable of creating diverse effects. If these features are implemented in a PSI, clients will be more likely to be able to accomplish all desired effects related to particle systems with one PSI. Secondly, it introduces a novel use of events to determine, at run time, which particle system code to execute in each frame. Thirdly, it describes a software architecture called the Dynamic Particle System Framework (DPSF). Simulation results show that DPSF possesses all 18 desirable features.

1. Introduction

A *particle system* is a structure used to control the behavior of many elements called particles, where a *particle* is an object with some properties such as position, velocity, and size. Particle systems are typically implemented in software, and each particle is visualized on screen as a colored pixel, a texture (i.e., an image), or a polygon. Particle systems are widely used in video games and films to generate special effects and model fuzzy objects that do not have well-defined shapes, such as fire, smoke, flowing liquids, dust, clouds, fog, snow, rain, hair, fur, sparks, explosions, and abstract visual effects such as magic spells and glowing trails. These effects help immerse viewers in virtual environments by adding detail to them, as well as by making them more attractive. In addition to creating special effects, particle systems have many practical and research applications, such as visualizing and controlling implicit surfaces [1–6] and mesh deformation [5, 7].

When creating a particle system, a number of issues confront the client, where the *client* is the person creating the particle system, such as a designer or programmer. These issues include deciding how the particles should be drawn, how the particles should be managed in memory for efficient performance, which properties the particle system and its particles should have, and how algorithms should be coded for common particle system operations, such as updating the position of a particle according to its velocity.

To avoid dealing with these issues, every time a new particle system is required, Particle System Interfaces have been developed to assist clients with creating particle systems. A *Particle System Interface* (PSI) is a piece of software designed to perform common tasks related to particle systems for clients, while providing them with a set of parameters whose values can be adjusted to create different particle systems. PSIs allow clients to quickly create particle systems, which in turn produce new effects. By using a PSI, clients can also avoid having to design and implement the particle systems themselves. Instead, clients simply use the interface of the PSI to create particle systems and run simulations, which avoids issues such as how particles should be drawn and how they should be managed in memory. Additional terminology related to PSIs is described in Section 2.

A PSI is typically either interactive software with a Graphical User Interface (GUI), a set of related code that can be added to a client program, or a software library with an

Application Program Interface (API). Although many PSIs exist that can be used to create great visual effects, most PSIs are only useful for creating specific types of effects and are not easily extended. For example, the Particles [8] and Particle 3D [9] PSIs are capable of producing impressive fire and explosion effects, but they are not designed to handle collisions between particles and the virtual environment. Therefore, they are not suited to producing effects such as water cascading down over multiple surfaces or smoke from a fire accumulating near the ceiling in an enclosed area. If clients require some functionality that is not supported by a PSI, such as particle-environment interactions, they must either find another PSI that meets their requirements or create their own particle system or PSI. Unless the effect that the client is trying to create is simple or common, he or she will most likely have to create a particle system or PSI from scratch.

The goal of our research was to design, implement, and evaluate a software framework that is flexible enough to support creating particle systems for diverse applications while making the process of creating particle systems fast and easy for clients. This paper makes three original contributions to research. The first original contribution, as described in Section 3, is the identification of 18 features that are appropriate for a PSI capable of creating a wide variety of effects. A PSI with all these features should be applicable to the great majority of applications that require particle systems. Clients will likely be able to use such a PSI to meet their requirements while leveraging the functionality already present in the PSI, which can potentially save a significant amount of effort. Existing PSIs are evaluated with respect to these 18 desirable features in Section 4.

The second original contribution, as described in Section 5, is the idea of using events to determine when code for updating particles and particle systems should be executed. The event approach has three advantages over the traditional approaches of either using Boolean values to determine whether or not specific code should be executed or setting a parameter to a specific value, so that it does not affect the output. First, using events can increase performance since they avoid unnecessarily executing code. Secondly, using events can increase modularity by making it easier for clients to add or remove code. Thirdly, because events can be added or removed at run time, particle and particle system behavior can easily be changed at run time.

The third original contribution, as described in Section 6, is the Dynamic Particle System Framework (DPSF) software, which provides the 18 features mentioned above. DPSF was developed to help clients create PSIs. Rather than starting from scratch, clients can build upon DPSF to create PSIs, allowing them to avoid implementing common particle system tasks, such as managing particles in memory, while still being able to program desired functionality into the PSI. The experimental results and the Demo software, as described in Section 7, show that DPSF can be used for applications that other PSIs cannot. The results of experiments conducted with the Demo software, reported elsewhere [10], also show that DPSF runs fast enough to be used for interactive applications, such as video games. By integrating features from other existing PSIs into a single framework, DPSF enables the creation of visual effects that are qualitatively different from those possible with other PSIs. These features make using DPSF suitable for a wide variety of applications that require a particle system.

2. Terminology

This section defines terminology relevant to particles, particle systems, and PSIs. *Particle properties* are properties possessed by every particle in a particle system. Such properties are used to control a particle's behavior. Some typical particle properties are position, velocity, color, size, and *lifetime* (how long the particle should remain active). Particles that have an elapsed time less than their lifetime are referred to as *active particles*; all other particles are referred to as *inactive particles*. *Particle update functions* are functions that update the values of a particle's properties, such as by updating a particle's position according to its velocity. *Particle system properties* are properties of the particle system itself and are typically used to control the particle system as a whole. Examples of particle system properties include the maximum number of particles that can exist in the particle system, the rate at which particles are added to the particle system, and the magnitude of an external force that affects the trajectories of all particles in the particle system. *Particle system update functions* are functions that update the particle system's properties, such as by changing the rate at which particles are added. Particle and particle system properties are collectively referred to as *Particle System Interface properties (PSI properties)*, and particle and particle system update functions are collectively referred to as *Particle System Interface update functions (PSI update functions)*.

A *Particle System Interface parameter (PSI parameter)* is a parameter provided by a PSI whose value can be adjusted by clients to affect the behavior or visualization of the particle system and its particles. When a PSI parameter value is changed, it changes the value of one or more PSI properties, or changes the way that the PSI properties are updated internally by the particle system, causing a new particle system to be produced. PSI parameter values are typically specified by clients through code, a script, or a visual tool. Examples of common PSI parameters include the lifetime, initial position, and initial velocity of particles added to the particle system and the texture used to draw the particles. By allowing clients to set different values for the PSI parameters, many different particle systems can be created from a single PSI.

Figure 1 shows the relationship between a PSI, a particle system, and a visual effect. An example of a PSI is shown at the top of Figure 1. It provides functions to add, update, and draw particles; the particle properties called elapsed time, lifetime, position, and velocity which every particle will have; a particle system property called texture, which is used to draw the particles; and PSI parameters to set the lifetime, initial position, initial velocity, and texture of the particles. Below the PSIs in Figure 1 are examples of two particle systems created from the PSI. Each of the Fire and Smoke particle systems was created by specifying values for the PSI parameters. When particle system simulations run, they create effects, where an

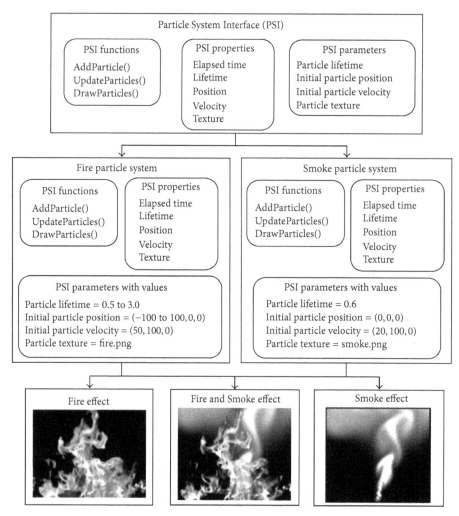

FIGURE 1: One Particle System Interface, creating two particle systems and creating three effects.

effect is the overall perception of the individual particles of the particle system. When an effect is visualized, such as by being shown on screen, it is referred to as a *visual effect*. Three visual effects created from the Fire and Smoke particle systems are shown at the bottom of Figure 1.

3. Desirable PSI Features

While many published works describe applications of particle systems, few describe the components that a PSI should possess in order to be suitable for many applications. Reeves [11] and van der Burg [12] identified the following desirable PSI properties: lifetime, velocity, and color for the particles, having a particle system texture, and external force. Identifying the desirable features of a PSI facilitates evaluation of PSIs. Arguably, a PSI is more likely to meet clients' requirements if it has a greater number of these desirable features.

A PSI flexible enough to support creating a wide range of diverse effects should offer the following features, which are discussed in more detail below.

(F1) Provide a method to add and update particles.

(F2) Provide some built-in PSI properties.

(F3) Provide PSI parameters to specify values for built-in PSI properties.

(F4) Provide a method to draw the particles.

(F5) Provide a method for inspecting the active particles in the particle system.

(F6) Allow clients to create PSI properties.

(F7) Allow clients to specify how the new PSI properties are updated each frame, and how they affect other PSI properties.

(F8) Allow clients to create PSI parameters.

(F9) Allow updates to be made when a particle condition is met.

(F10) Allow updates to be made when a particle system condition is met.

(F11) Allow particles to be affected by objects and forces in the virtual environment.

(F12) Allow particles to be affected by other particles in the same particle system.

(F13) Allow PSI parameters to be updated at run time by software events.

(F14) Allow PSI parameters to be updated at run time by user input, enabling real-time interaction with the particle system.

(F15) Allow PSI parameters to update the properties of active particles.

(F16) Allow PSI parameters to affect a subset of the active particles.

(F17) Provide support for animated particles.

(F18) Provide support to use multiple particle images in a particle system.

Adding new particles to the particle system and updating existing particles (F1) are essential particle system tasks. Ways to perform these tasks are apparently always included in a PSI. Also, every PSI apparently provides some built-in particle and particle system properties (F2), but the number and types of PSI properties that they provide may differ. Having more PSI properties typically allows clients to define more detailed particle behaviors and create a wider range of effects.

A PSI property is only useful for creating diverse effects if the client is able to change its value. A PSI property's value can be changed by clients through the use of a PSI parameter (F3). For example, a particle system might emit particles at a rate corresponding to a ParticlesPerSecond particle system property. If the value of this property cannot be changed by clients, then they will not be able to use it to create a new effect. However, if clients are able to change the value of the ParticlesPerSecond property using a PSI parameter, then they will be able to create several different effects by adjusting that value. If a PSI provides more PSI parameters, clients will have more options available to them, which allows them to create more diverse effects.

Many particle system applications require visualizing the effect on screen, so providing a function to draw the particles (F4) can be very useful for allowing clients to visualize their effects with minimal effort. To allow clients to display their effects in a variety of ways, the PSI should also provide a function or property that allows clients to iterate through all of the active particles in the particle system and inspect their property values (F5). For example, if clients want to visualize their effect in a custom manner, such as by forming a mesh where particles correspond to vertices in the mesh and these vertices are connected by lines, they will likely be able to accomplish this by iterating over the particles but not by using the PSI's built-in drawing function. Providing feature F5 also has the benefit of allowing clients to collect information about the particles during the simulation, such as by tracking the positions of the particles over time or recording other information about them.

While there is a general set of PSI properties that are required to create many common effects, it is impossible to provide every property that a client may potentially require. Thus, it can be beneficial to allow clients to create their own PSI properties (F6). For example, if clients want their particles to each have an Orientation property, and it is not provided

by the PSI, they could add it as a new particle property. This property would allow each particle to be oriented differently. Unless the values of the properties that clients create are intended to be constant and do not affect other properties, clients will also require the ability to define how the new PSI properties are updated and the effects, if any, that they have on the other PSI properties (F7). For example, clients may decide that they want the Orientation property of a particle to change based on a rotational velocity. In this case, they need to create a RotationalVelocity particle property and define how it affects the Orientation property (e.g., Orientation += RotationalVelocity ∗ ElapsedTime). Similarly, if clients want the velocities of particles to be affected by acceleration or friction, they need to define these new properties and specify how they affect the Velocity particle property. In addition to creating new PSI properties and defining how they are updated, clients will likely require the ability to specify values for these properties. This means that clients should also be able to create PSI parameters (F8) in order to specify values for the new PSI properties.

While particle systems are generally stochastic in nature, they are often intended to follow some general pattern of behavior. More complex patterns of behavior can be created by allowing updates to be triggered when specific particle conditions are met (F9). For example, clients may want each particle to randomly change its direction when half of its lifetime has elapsed or to change colors when it reaches a certain speed. Alternatively, they may want a counter to be incremented every time a particle collides with a specific object. Similarly, allowing updates to be triggered when specific particle system conditions are met (F10) can also allow more complex effects to be created. For example, clients might want the color of new particles to change after 1000 particles have been emitted from the particle system or to apply a gravitational force to all particles after the particle system has existed for 10 seconds. Being able to trigger updates according to internal particle and particle system conditions as well as specifying the updates that should be performed can allow clients to conveniently define deterministic aspects of particle system behavior and thus create more complex effects.

Providing a particle system with information about the surrounding virtual environment can allow particles to react to objects or forces in this environment (F11), which can enhance realism. For example, if a particle system in a video game is emitting sparks, it may be desirable to have the sparks bounce off the walls and floor in the virtual environment of the game instead of passing through them. A virtual environment is *dynamic* if it contains objects with properties that are updated at run time. Having particles that react to dynamic virtual environments can further increase the realism of an effect. Similarly, clients may want particles to be affected by other particles in the particle system (F12), such as by having particles collide instead of passing through one another. Because these operations can be computationally expensive to perform, a client is unlikely to use them frequently, but they should be available.

In addition to particle systems reacting to the environment, it can be beneficial to have them reacting to software events. Therefore, PSI parameters should be responsive to

TABLE 1: A list of PSIs, a PSI created using DPSF, and the features from Section 3 that they support.

Label	Particle System Interface	F1	F2	F3	F4	F5	F6	F7	F8	F9	F10	F11	F12	F13	F14	F15	F16	F17	F18
PSI0	Particle Chamber	X	X	X	X									X	X				
PSI1	Microsoft XNA Unleashed	X	X	X	X														
PSI2	Building a Particle Engine	X	X	X			X	X	X					X	X				
PSI3	Particle Systems API	X	X	X	X	X						X	X	X	X	X	X		
PSI4	Particles	X	X	X	X									X	X				
PSI5	Particle 3D	X	X	X	X									X	X				
PSI6	Balls	X	X	X	X							X		X	X				
PSI7	Declarative API	X	X	X	X		X	X	X	X		X		X	X	X			
PSI8	Autodesk 3ds Max	X	X	X	X	X	X	X	X	X	X	X	X	X			X	X	X
PSI9	Autodesk Maya	X	X	X	X	X	X	X	X	X	X	X	X	X			X	X	X
DPSF	PSI created using DPSF	X	X	X	X	X	X	X	X	X	X	X	X	X	X	X	X	X	X

software events at run time (F13), where a *software event* is triggered by something in the software that is external to the virtual environment. For example, clients may want the particle system to emit particles of a different color when the user accomplishes some goal, such as collecting 100 coins or achieving a mission objective. Also desirable is the ability to update PSI parameters at run time according to user input (F14). This feature allows for real-time interaction between users and the particle system and has many potential applications. For example, it could be used to allow users to control a fire-hose particle system, where they spray water at fires to put them out. Real-time interaction with particle systems at the particle level can also be achieved by allowing PSI parameters to affect the properties of active particles (F15), rather than only affecting the properties of particles added to the particle system after the PSI parameter value has been updated. Being able to change the properties of active particles at run time allows particle behavior to be updated at run time. For example, a particle system may initially emit particles that are attracted to some object. Clients may want the particles to change behavior and be repelled from the object when specific user input is received. By allowing the properties of active particles to be updated, this type of behavior can be achieved.

In addition to updating active particle properties, clients may want to change the behavior of only some of the active particles in the particle system. For example, when specific user input is received, clients may want to change the color of only 100 random particles or only the particles that meet some criteria, such as having a velocity greater than 100 or being within a certain distance of another object. For these cases, PSI parameters should be able to update a subset of the active particles (F16).

In order to create certain effects, clients may require the individual particles to be animated (F17). For example, clients may want to create a particle system representing hundreds of butterflies, where each butterfly is flapping its wings. Similarly, clients may want a particle system to display its particles using several different images (F18). For example, clients may want to simulate a tornado picking up many different objects, such as rocks, sticks, and clumps of dirt. In order for these different objects to be visualized properly, the particle system would need to support displaying its particles with multiple images.

The 18 features listed above are neither exhaustive nor independent. They are not exhaustive because someone might devise a new feature of general interest, but they correspond to all features of interest we observed in existing PSIs. They are not independent because several of them are interrelated. For example, F14 depends on F13, because the user input referred to in F14 is a specific type of software event, as referred to in F13. Nonetheless, we believe that it is worth distinguishing them, so we can better evaluate existing PSIs. For example, some systems react to some types of events (F13), but they do not react to input events (F14).

4. Evaluation of Current PSIs

Particle systems have become popular in recent years and many PSIs have been developed to make creating particle systems easier. Table 1 shows ten representative existing PSIs and the features from Section 3 that each supports. For simplicity, we refer to the PSIs as PSI0 to PSI9: PSI0-Particle Chamber [13], PSI1-Microsoft XNA Unleashed [14], PSI2-Building a Particle Engine [15], PSI3-Particle Systems API [16, 17], PSI4-Particles [8], PSI5-Particle 3D [9], PSI6-Balls [18], PSI8-Autodesk 3ds Max [19], and PSI9-Autodesk Maya [20]. For completeness, our DPSF software is also included in the table.

A PSI provides clients with a set of parameters (PSI parameters) whose values may be altered to produce different particle systems and, hence, different effects. Some PSIs, such as PSI0, allow clients to simply select the effect they want from a list of effects (e.g., fire, smoke, snow, etc.) and then the PSI sets all of the PSI parameters accordingly, allowing an effect to be created quickly and easily. If the PSI has the exact effect the client wants, this feature is ideal. Other PSIs allow clients to pick an effect and then accept default PSI parameter values or manually specify new ones. For example, a client might specify the permissible range for a particle's initial velocity and lifetime. Some PSIs, such as PSI0, provide a GUI that clients can use to adjust PSI parameter values and visualize the particle systems in real time as the PSI parameter values are changed. Some PSIs, such as PSI8 and PSI9, allow PSI parameter values to be specified from a script, allowing new particle systems to be created by editing a simple text file. Several PSIs, such as PSI1, PSI4, and PSI5, are available as a set of related codes that can be added to a client program. In more detail, PSI1 provides Update and Draw functions and a Settings class to configure particle properties, and PSI4 and PSI5 both provide a base ParticleSystem class with Update and Draw functions that client classes can inherit. Finally, PS4 is available as a software library with a well-defined API. Recently, Krajcevski and Reppy have specified a declarative API for particle systems (PSI7) [21]. With their approach, a particle system is described in a declarative fashion by an emitter, which specifies how new particles are generated, an action, which specifies how particles are updated, and a renderer, which specifies how particles are drawn. A particle system can be targeted for either CPU or GPU execution.

Although space concerns prohibit a discussion of all features for all PSIs, a few observations are appropriate. As can be seen in Table 1, all ten existing PSIs support features F1, F2, and F3. Adding and updating particles (F1) and providing some built-in PSI properties (F2) and PSI parameters (F3) are essential PSI features. The PSIs differ in the PSI properties they contain and the PSI parameters that they provide to the client. The PSI parameters provided by most of the PSIs include setting the particles' lifetime, initial position, initial velocity, size, and an external force to affect the trajectory of all of the particles, as well as setting the texture used to draw the particles, the maximum number of particles that the particle system can contain, and the rate at which particles should be emitted. All PSIs except PSI2 provide a method to draw particles (F4). Only PSI3, PSI8, and PSI9 provide a method for inspecting the active particles in the particle system (F5).

The PSI parameters mentioned above are adequate for creating some simple visual effects, but these parameters alone are not capable of producing sophisticated effects, such as having the particles follow a path, react to environmental forces, or behave according to physically accurate rules, such as those used in fluid flow simulations. The main problem is that the PSIs are limited in the number of PSI parameters they provide to clients, and the PSI parameters they do provide typically do not allow clients to specify these sorts of behaviors.

By allowing clients to create PSI properties (F6), to specify how the new PSI properties are updated each frame and how they affect other PSI properties (F7), and to create PSI parameters (F8), PSI2, PSI7, PSI8, and PSI9 provide this type of flexibility. Two features that are not provided by most existing PSIs are allowing updates to be triggered when specific particle conditions are met (F9) and when specific particle system conditions are met (F10). Of the systems examined, only PSI8 and PSI9 provided both those features, although PSI7 provides F9.

Of the PSIs inspected, all but PSI1 support updating PSI parameters at run time according to software events (F13). PSI1 allows PSI parameters to be specified during initialization, but it does not allow them to be changed after the PSI

has been initialized. The only three PSIs that do not support user interaction with the particle system at run time (F14) are PSI1, PSI8, and PSI9. This limitation is inherent in the design of PSI8 and PSI9 because they are both offline renderers. In other words, they do not perform the simulations in real time. Instead they precompute the simulation and record it as an animation (i.e., video). Clients can incorporate the animations in applications. However, as mentioned, since the users of the application are then simply watching videos, they are not able to interact with the particle systems. Although PSI8 and PSI9 provide more features than the other PSIs inspected, their applications are limited to recorded animation.

The only PSIs inspected that support animated particles (F17) and using multiple images for a particle system's particles (F18) are PSI8 and PSI9. These features are especially useful for films and video game cut scenes, where emphasis is put on the visualization of the particles. By allowing particles to be animated or using multiple images for the particles, more realistic and convincing visual effects can be created. However, because PSI8 and PSI9 are offline renderers, they cannot be used to generate particle systems for the interactive parts of video games.

No single previous PSI supports all 18 features, as shown in Table 1. When clients want to create an effect, they may need to investigate and test multiple PSIs, with no guarantee that the PSIs will support the effects that they require. This can be a time consuming process since clients will not only need to find the PSIs but also learn how to use each of them. To avoid this process, it is preferable to have a PSI that is capable of creating many diverse effects; since once clients learn to use the PSI, they will be able to create any effects they require.

5. Event-Based Updating

As mentioned in Section 2, when using a PSI, clients can define particle and particle system update functions to update the particle and particle system properties, respectively. Once these functions have been defined, clients can choose (1) which functions should be used to update the particles and particle system, (2) when the functions should be called, and (3) the order of their execution. The *event-based approach to particle and particle system updating* accomplishes this purpose through the use of events, where an *event* is a delegate (i.e., function pointer) with some extra data, such as the order of execution. Two classes of events are of interest. A *particle event* points to a particle update function and is used to update particle properties. A *particle system event* points to a particle system update function and is used to update the particle system properties. To cause an update function to be executed, an event pointing to that update function is added to the particle system. Events can be added and removed when initializing a particle system, as well as at run time. Because events can be added and removed at run time, real-time interaction with the particles can be achieved.

When an event *fires*, it executes the particle or particle system update function to which it points, updating the particles or particles system, respectively. When and how often an event fires depends on the type of event being used. Four types of events are distinguished.

(1) *Every Time Events:* these events fire every time the particle system is updated and are applied to every active particle in the particle system. Every Time Events are used for updates that should be performed for every frame, such as updating a particle's position according to a velocity or interpolating a particle's color between two color values.

(2) *One-Time Events*: these events fire the next time the particle system is updated and are then removed. Thus, each event only fires once. Like Every Time Events, One-Time Events are applied to every active particle in the particle system. One-Time Events are useful for interactively controlling particles at run time. For example, clients could add a One-Time Event to the particle system each time a specific button is pressed, allowing an effect such as changing the color or size of all particles to occur each time the button is pressed.

(3) *Timed Events*: these events fire at a specific moment in a particle's lifetime and are only applied to that particle. For example, if a particle is set to live for 4 seconds and clients want it to change colors half way through its lifetime, a Timed Event could be specified to fire after 2 seconds (absolute time) or 0.5 of the lifetime (relative time) to change the color of the particle. Timed Events are useful for deterministically controlling a property of a group of particles, such as changing the velocities of all particles at specific times to have them move in a planned pattern.

As mentioned above, Every Time Events and One-Time Events are applied to every active particle in the particle system. If clients only want specific particles to be updated, they can code a condition into the particle update function. For example, if clients want some smoke particles to be moved around when an object passes by them, they can code the particle update function to take into account the particle's distance from the object when updating the particle's velocity. This allows particles close to the object to be greatly affected by it and particles far from it to not be affected by it. By allowing clients to write the particle update functions, triggered by events, the event-based approach allows update functions to affect only some of the active particles (F16).

When a Timed Event fires, it executes the particle update function on only the particles that have reached a specified age. Timed Events typically only fire once, but if clients explicitly change the age or lifetime of a particle, then these events could fire several times. For example, a Timed Event could be set to fire when the particle reaches half of its lifetime. If some update resets the lifetime of a particle to 0.25 when it reaches 0.75 of its lifetime, the event would fire a second time.

Using events allows clients to choose which update functions should be used to update the particle system and its particles. By selecting which PSI update functions to use and by being able to modify the selection at run time, many diverse effects can be created with a single general-purpose PSI. Specific particle systems can be created from such a PSI by specifying the events and update functions that the particle system should use. For example, a PSI might provide three different particle update functions for updating the transparency of a particle as it ages. The first function might linearly interpolate the transparency to have the particle fade evenly during its lifetime. The second function might leave the particle opaque for the first half of its life then fade it out during the last half, and the third function might do the same except restrict the fade out to the last 20% of the lifetime. Clients could then choose which fade out method to use by adding an Every Time Particle Event that points to the appropriate particle update function.

Similar functionality could be offered by traditional PSIs by allowing clients to set a fade out variable with a value from an enumeration listing the possible fade out methods and then using a series of if/else statements to select one. However, using this approach would require that the value of the fade out variable be checked once for every update for every particle in the particle system in order to determine which fade out method to use. If the particle system is being updated 60 times per second and the particle system contains 5000 particles, this method would require 300,000 extra operations every second in the best case scenario, which would be when the fade out variable's value matched the first if statement's conditions. It is expected that this method would decrease performance, especially if the PSI offered similar variables for controlling how the particle's position, velocity, acceleration, color, size, orientation, and so forth were updated, and each of these variables had many possible values. By using events, this potential performance loss is avoided, since the functions to perform the necessary operations are called directly without requiring any additional operations to check variable values. Also, using the method just described, if clients wanted to add additional methods to fade out particles, they would need to add a new value to the fade out enumeration, add an if statement to the logic controlling which fade out method is used, and write the actual operations to perform the new fade out method. By using events, clients only need to define a single new function and specify that it should be called by adding to the particle system a new event that points to the function.

Events can be used to further increase speed over traditional PSIs. Because clients can choose which particle update functions they want to use, they can avoid wasting CPU cycles updating particle properties that are not being utilized. For example, if the particles contain an acceleration property, but the clients do not want to use acceleration to update the velocity of the particles, they simply need not to add an event to update the particle velocity according to the acceleration. In a traditional PSI, clients would set the acceleration of each particle to zero, and during each update the new velocity of every particle would be calculated. Since the acceleration is zero, these operations would be pointless. With an event-based approach, these calculations are avoided altogether by simply not specifying events to update the velocity.

Using events along with PSI update functions provides support for several of the features listed in Section 3. Because events can be added and removed at run time, real-time interaction with the particles is possible (F14). By giving clients the ability to create PSI update functions, which have access to the particle and particle system properties, updates can be triggered by specific particle conditions (F9) and by specific particle system conditions (F10). Similarly, this ability also allows clients to update PSI properties according to the forces in the virtual environment (F11) and other particles in the particle system (F12), as well as to specify which, if any, of the active particles should be updated (F16).

6. DPSF

The Dynamic Particle System Framework (DPSF) is a framework written in C# and XNA that provides the 18 features mentioned in Section 3. It consists of two base classes (the base particle class and the base particle system class) and two default classes (a default particle class and a default particle system class). To use DPSF, clients incorporate it into their code, add variables to represent PSI properties, and add functions for initializing and updating. The base particle and particle system classes included in DPSF provide features F1 to F4. Clients can have the list of active particles returned to the external software by using the Active Particles property (F5), allowing them to explicitly draw the particles themselves or to perform other operations such as analyzing the particles and collecting data. Since these base classes can easily be extended, clients can define new PSI properties (F6), new PSI update functions (F7), and new PSI parameters (F8). The *base particle class* contains only the essential particle properties, which are specifically the particle's lifetime, elapsed time, and visibility. Clients can create particle classes that inherit from this base particle class, allowing them to specify any additional particle properties that they may require, such as position, velocity, acceleration, size, color, or mass. The *base particle system class* contains functions to perform common particle system functions, such as adding, updating, and removing particles in the simulation. As with particle classes, clients can then create particle system classes that inherit from the base particle system class, allowing them to add new PSI properties, PSI update functions (to update the new PSI properties), and PSI parameters (to specify values for the PSI properties). Also, clients must specify a *particle initialization function*, which is a function used to specify the initial values of particle's properties when it is added to the simulation. Once clients have created their particle and particle system classes, they have effectively created a PSI; DPSF can then run the simulation using the particle and particle system classes specified by the clients.

This extensibility gives clients freedom to create many types of effects with DPSF. For example, if clients want to create an effect where hot particles ascend and cool particles descend, they could first create a particle class with position and temperature particle properties, by copying the base particle class and inserting two instance variables, one for position and one for temperature. Then they would create a particle system class that includes the following: (1) a particle system property for ambient temperature; (2) a particle update function that updates the particle's temperature to slowly approach the ambient temperature; (3) a particle update function to update the particle's vertical position according to its temperature; (4) a particle initialization function to specify a particle's initial position and temperature; and (5) PSI parameters to specify the ambient temperature and the minimum and maximum values for a particle's initial temperature. They would then run the simulation simply by specifying values for the PSI parameters and calling the Update() and Draw() functions provided by the base particle system class. By extending DPSF, clients do not have to decide how to manage particles in memory or draw them to the screen and can instead focus on the remaining components required to create the desired effect.

DPSF provides default particle and particle system classes. They are useful because many effects require similar sets of PSI properties, PSI update functions, and PSI parameters. The default classes include the components required for particle position, velocity, acceleration, rotation, friction, color, size, and so forth. By using default classes, clients can create common effects quickly, as with existing PSIs. They can also easily extend them to create uncommon effects, such as those required in research applications.

Because DPSF allows clients to create PSI properties (F6), write PSI update functions (F7), and create PSI parameters (F8), they are able to quickly integrate their code into a PSI, allowing custom behaviors to be created. This feature removes many of the restrictions that other PSIs place on clients. Clients can be more productive, because they can incorporate their behaviors and constraints into an existing PSI instead of having to create one from scratch. Because DPSF allows clients to inject their own code into a DPSF PSI, the PSIs described in Section 4 could be implemented using DPSF. Also, because DPSF supports creating a wide variety of effects, clients will likely be able to use DPSF to create all of the particle systems that their applications require, instead of having to use multiple PSIs. Thus, clients will not need to learn to use multiple PSIs and integrate them into a single project.

7. Results

To evaluate the capabilities of DPSF, software called *Demo* was implemented that uses DPSF to create 35 different effects. Table 2 lists 8 of the effects and the features from F1 to F18 that a PSI must possess in order to create them. The table shows that DPSF supports creating PSIs with all 18 of the features listed in Section 3. As shown previously in Table 1, none of the existing PSIs analyzed in Section 4 provides all 18 features.

For example, Demo demonstrates that PSIs can interact with the virtual environment (F11). In Demo's *Fountain* effect, balls are emitted in an upward direction and are affected by gravity, which pulls them downward. When the balls hit the floor, they bounce off it. This bouncing is shown in Figure 2(a), which displays the particle trajectories over a span of three seconds.

Demo's *Smoke* effect demonstrates interaction with objects in the virtual environment, where smoke particles are attracted to an orb that moves past them from left to right, as shown in Figures 2(b) and 2(c).

TABLE 2: Effects created in Demo, the features they demonstrate, and the number of lines of code used to create them.

Feature	Brief feature description	Fire and Smoke	Fountain	Smoke	Square Pattern	Figure-eight	Image	Sprite force	Animated butterflies
F1	Add and update particles	X	X	X	X	X	X	X	X
F2	Built-in PSI properties	X	X	X	X	X	X	X	X
F3	Built-in PSI Parameters	X	X	X	X	X	X	X	X
F4	Method to draw particles	X	X	X	X	X	X	X	X
F5	Method to return active particles						X	X	X
F6	Create new PSI properties	X	X	X			X	X	X
F7	Create new update functions	X	X	X	X	X	X	X	X
F8	Create new PSI Parameters	X		X			X	X	X
F9	Trigger updates on particle conditions	X			X		X		
F10	Trigger updates on PS conditions						X		
F11	Particles affected by environment		X	X					X
F12	Particles affected by other particles							X	
F13	Update PSI parameters from events	X	X	X	X	X	X	X	
F14	Update PSI parameters from user input	X	X	X	X	X	X	X	
F15	Update properties of active particles		X	X	X		X	X	
F16	Update a subset of active particles			X			X	X	
F17	Animated particles								X
F18	Multiple particle images						X		
Lines of code	N/A	187	76	107	89	61	322	413	275

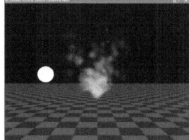

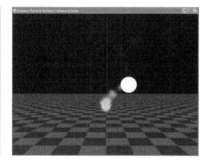

(a) Fountain effect interacting with the floor (shown over a span of three seconds)

(b) Smoke effect before orb attracts particles

(c) Smoke effect while orb attracts particles

FIGURE 2: Two effects showing interaction with the virtual environment.

Deterministic particle systems can also be created using DPSF. For example, Demo's *Square Pattern* effect shows a simple deterministic effect where each particle follows a square path. This effect is created by using three timed events (F9), which change a particle's velocity direction at 25%, 50%, and 75% of the particle's lifetime. Figure 3 shows the particle trajectories over a span of five seconds.

The *Figure-Eight* effect shown in Figure 4 also displays deterministic behavior, where the particles follow the path of a figure-eight. This effect was achieved by writing a function with code to make a particle travel in two circles and then adding it as a Timed Event (F7). The three screen shots in Figure 4 show the particles as they travel in a figure-eight pattern.

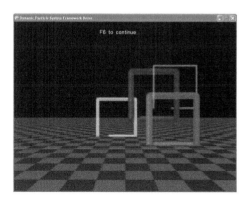

FIGURE 3: Particles traveling in square patterns.

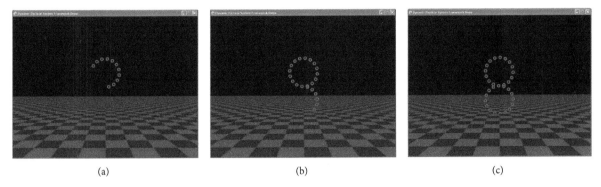

(a)   (b)   (c)

FIGURE 4: Particles traveling in a figure-eight pattern.

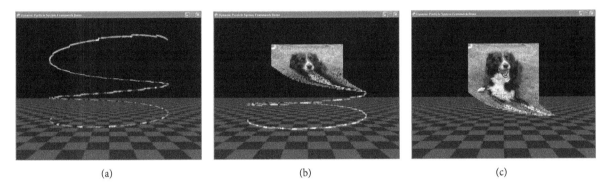

(a)   (b)   (c)

FIGURE 5: Particles traveling in a spiral before coming to rest at their final positions, which forms an image.

The *Image* effect provided by DPSF Demo also shows that complex deterministic effects can be created. In this effect, particles travel in a spiral before coming to rest at their final positions, as shown in Figure 5. The combination of all particles in their final positions forms a single image (F18).

Almost all of the effects created in Demo allow for interaction between the user and the particle system (F14). Most effects allow the user to move and change the orientation of the emitter at run time, affecting where particles are emitted and the direction they travel. Many effects offer other types of user interactions as well. For example, with the Fountain effect, shown in Figure 2(a), users can turn collisions between the balls and the floor on and off. Figures 2(c) and 6(a) show particles being attracted to a user-controlled particle, and Figure 6(b) shows particles being repelled from a user-controlled particle. These effects also demonstrate interactions between particles (F12) as well as control at the individual particle level (F16), because the particle that the user controls is one of the particles in the particle system.

The *Animated Butterflies* effect, shown in Figure 7, demonstrates animated particles (F17) by creating animated butterfly particles that flap their wings. The animation class allows the animations for the individual butterflies to be played at different speeds simultaneously and to have these speeds updated at run time. By increasing the animation speed as particles travel upward, the butterflies appear to flap their wings faster when ascending and slower when descending, producing a more convincing effect.

By looking at the number of lines of source code used to create the effects in Demo, which were counted using Code Line Counter Pro [22] and are listed in Table 2, one can see that few lines of code are required on the clients' part to create a PSI. In contrast, many more lines of code would be needed to create a PSI from scratch or to modify an existing one to meet the clients' requirements. The small size of the source code provides evidence that many effects can be created quickly and easily by using the given templates and default classes.

8. Conclusion

The goal of this research was to design, implement, and evaluate a software framework that is flexible enough to support creating particle systems for diverse applications while making the process of creating particle systems fast and easy for clients. The DPSF software was developed to accomplish this goal. To simplify learning how to use DPSF and to make creating PSIs faster and easier, templates are provided that clients can use when creating PSIs. In addition, DPSF provides default classes that include particle properties and update functions that are required by many common effects. The default classes make it faster and easier for clients to

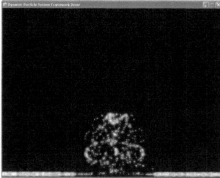
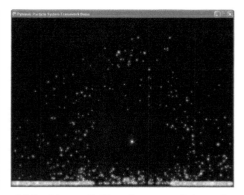

(a) Particles attracted to a client-controlled particle   (b) Particles repelled by a client-controlled particle

FIGURE 6: Particles being attracted to and repelled away from a client-controlled particle.

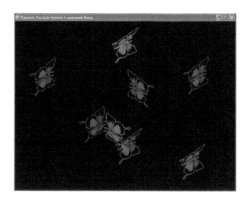

FIGURE 7: Animated butterfly particles.

create common particle system effects. DPSF is available for download at http://www.xnaparticles.com/Download.php.

The Demo software demonstrates that DPSF provides the 18 features listed in Section 3 and shows that DPSF can be used to create many diverse effects. Since DPSF supports these features, it can be used for traditional particle system applications as well as new ones. Because DPSF allows clients to create their own rules and constraints, it is a good candidate to be used in research applications. Also, performance tests reported elsewhere [10] show that the speed of DPSF is comparable to existing PSIs, except GPU-based systems give significantly faster performance for 10,000 or more particles.

Up to the time of writing, DPSF has been used in Holophone 3D [23] (a holographic phone app for Windows-Phone), an XNA-based game engine called PloobsEngine [24] and 18 independent video game development projects [25], including AvaGlide [26], Cannon number 12 [27], Defy Gravity [28], Orbitron: Revolution [29], and Perkuna's Dragon [30]. DPSF could be improved in several ways. More features could be added to the default classes, such as automatic collision detection and reaction between particles and the virtual environment, nearest neighbor detection, and a bounding box containing the particle system. As well, a Graphical User Interface (GUI) could be provided to allow clients who lack programming knowledge to create particle systems using DPSF.

Conflict of Interests

The authors declare that there is no conflict of interests regarding the publication of this paper.

Acknowledgment

This work was supported by the Natural Sciences and Engineering Research Council of Canada via a Discovery Grant to H. J. Hamilton.

References

[1] E. Galin, R. Allègre, and S. Akkouche, "A fast particle system framework for interactive implicit modeling," in *Proceedings of the IEEE International Conference on Shape Modeling and Applications (SMI '06)*, p. 32, June 2006.

[2] J. C. Hart, E. Bachta, W. Jarosz, and T. Fleury, "Using particles to sample and control more complex implicit surfaces," in *Proceedings of the ACM International Conference on Computer Graphics and Interactive Techniques (SIGGRAPH '05)*, p. 269, ACM, Los Angeles, Calif, USA, 2005.

[3] M. Meyer, B. Nelson, R. M. Kirby, and R. Whitaker, "Particle systems for efficient and accurate high-order finite element visualization," *IEEE Transactions on Visualization and Computer Graphics*, vol. 13, no. 5, pp. 1015–1026, 2007.

[4] W. Y. Su and J. C. Hart, "A programmable particle system framework for shape modeling," in *Proceedings of the International Conference on Shape Modeling and Applications (SMI '05)*, pp. 114–123, IEEE Computer Society, Cambridge, Mass, USA, June 2005.

[5] R. Szeliski and D. Tonnesen, "Surface modeling with oriented particle systems," in *Proceedings of the 19th Annual Conference on Computer Graphics and Interactive Techniques (SIGGRAPH '92)*, pp. 185–194, ACM, Chicago, Ill, USA, 1992.

[6] A. P. Witkin and P. S. Heckbert, "Using particles to sample and control implicit surfaces," in *Proceedings of the 21st Annual Conference on Computer Graphics and Interactive Techniques (SIGGRAPH '94)*, pp. 269–277, ACM, Orlando, Fla, USA, 1994.

[7] P. Volino and N. Magnenat-Thalmann, "Simple linear bending stiffness in particle systems," in *Proceedings of the ACM SIGGRAPH/Eurographics Symposium on Computer Animation*

(SCA '06), pp. 101–105, Eurographics Association, Aire-la-Ville, Switzerland, 2006.

[8] Microsoft, Particles, April 2007, http://creators.xna.com/en-us/sample/particle.

[9] Microsoft, Particle 3d, May 2007, http://creators.xna.com/en-us/sample/particle3d.

[10] D. Schroeder, *Dynamic particle system framework: a framework for building custom particle system interfaces [M.S. thesis]*, Department of Computer Science, University of Regina, 2009.

[11] W. T. Reeves, "Particle systems—a technique for modeling a class of fuzzy objects," *ACM Transactions on Graphics*, vol. 2, no. 2, pp. 91–108, 1983.

[12] J. van der Burg, "Building an advanced particle system," *Game Developer*, vol. 3, pp. 44–50, 2000.

[13] R. Benson, Particle chamber, June 2000, http://archive.gamedev.net/archive/reference/listce83.html?categoryid=225.

[14] C. Carter, *Microsoft XNA Unleashed: Graphics and Game Programming for Xbox 360 and Windows*, Sams, 2007.

[15] Michael Fotsch, Building a Direct3D Particle Engine, December 2000, http://realmike.org/blog/articles/building-a-direct3d-particle-engine/.

[16] D. K. McAllister, "The design of an API for particle systems," Tech. Rep., Department of Computer Science, University of North Carolina at Chapel Hill, Chapel Hill, NC, USA, 2000.

[17] D. K. McAllister, Particle Systems API, December 2008, http://archive.gamedev.net/archive/reference/listce83.html?categoryid=225.

[18] bjackdl, Balls, March 2008, http://en.pudn.com/downloads102/sourcecode/windows/csharp/detail416495_en.html.

[19] Autodesk, Autodesk 3ds Max, September 2013, http://usa.autodesk.com/3ds-max/.

[20] Autodesk, Autodesk Maya, September 2013, http://usa.autodesk.com/maya/.

[21] P. Krajcevski and J. Reppy, "A declarative API for particle systems," in *Practical Aspects of Declarative Languages*, vol. 6539 of *Lecture Notes in Computer Science*, pp. 130–144, Springer, Berlin, Germany, 2011.

[22] BistoneSoft, Code Line Counter Pro—C# Version 3.8, May 2009, http://www.softplatz.net/Downloads/Development/Compilers-Interpreters/Code-Line-Counter-Pro-C-Version.html.

[23] Holophone3D, Experience 3D holograms on Windows Phone, September 2013, http://dpsf.freeforums.org/holophone3d-experience-3d-holograms-on-windows-phone-t110.html.

[24] tpastor, PloobsEngine, September 2013, http://dpsf.freeforums.org/ploobsengine-t94.html.

[25] DPSF Forums, Projects that use DPSF, September 2013, http://dpsf.freeforums.org/.

[26] Haiku Interactive, AvaGlide, September 2013, http://haikuinteractive.com/.

[27] SquigglyFrog Studios/Microsoft Games Studios, Cannon #12, September 2013, http://cannon12.squigglyfrog.com/.

[28] Fish Factory Games, Defy Gravity, September 2013, http://dpsf.freeforums.org/defy-gravity-t81.html.

[29] Firebase Industries, Orbitron: Revolution, September 2013, http://dpsf.freeforums.org/orbitron-revolution-t106.html.

[30] Middle Lands Studios, Perkuna's Dragon, September 2013, http://www.wp7connect.com/tag/middle-lands-studios/.

3

A New Methodology of Design and Development of Serious Games

André F. S. Barbosa,[1] Pedro N. M. Pereira,[1] João A. F. F. Dias,[1] and Frutuoso G. M. Silva[1,2]

[1] *University of Beira Interior, Rua Marques de Avila e Bolama, 6201-001 Covilhã, Portugal*
[2] *Instituto de Telecomunicações (IST), Torre Norte, Piso 10, Avenida Rovisco Pais 1, 1049-001 Lisboa, Portugal*

Correspondence should be addressed to Frutuoso G. M. Silva; fsilva@di.ubi.pt

Academic Editor: Daniel Thalmann

The development of a serious game requires perfect knowledge of the learning domain to obtain the desired results. But it is also true that this may not be enough to develop a successful serious game. First of all, the player has to feel that he is playing a game where the learning is only a consequence of the playing actions. Otherwise, the game is viewed as boring and not as a fun activity and engaging. For example, the player can catch some items in the scenario and then separate them according to its type (i.e., recycle them). Thus, the main action for player is catching the items in the scenario where the recycle action is a second action, which is viewed as a consequence of the first action. Sometimes, the game design relies on a detailed approach based on the ideas of the developers because some educational content are difficult to integrate in the games, while maintaining the fun factor in the first place. In this paper we propose a new methodology of design and development of serious games that facilitates the integration of educational contents in the games. Furthermore, we present a serious game, called "Clean World", created using this new methodology.

1. Introduction

In recent years there was a growing interest in serious games (i.e., games for purposes beyond entertainment) because they facilitate the learning process, by engaging the user and increasing his motivation. Eck argues that "games are effective not because of what they are, but because of what they embody and what learners are doing as they play a game" [1]. These kinds of games have been used in a wide range of sectors such as military, healthcare, education, and corporate, among others. However, only a few methodologies were proposed to guide the design of serious game [2]. This is due to the fact that the development of a serious game is a process that involves a high degree of creativity.

The development of serious games, besides the game designers and developers, requires a tight collaboration with domain experts. Notwithstanding the gathering of information via traditional mechanisms (e.g., meetings and interviews with experts) for serious game design can be a difficult task. In serious games the critical point is the relationship between the game and the educational content.

But according to Zyda [3] the pedagogy must be subordinate to story. Often the game design relies on a detailed approach based on the ideas of the designers and developers because some knowledge is difficult to integrate in the games, while maintaining the fun factor in the first place [4].

2. Serious Games on Education

Currently, there are several research projects and literature about serious games in very diverse areas but we will restrain our focus on education alone.

The use of serious games for educational purposes can have a very positive effect, since they provide an effective way to engage students in learning activities and have the ability to stimulate cognitive processes like acknowledging displayed information, deductive and inductive reasoning, and also problem-solving [5].

Zielke et al. [6] described a serious game that lets players increase their cultural expertise in simulated Afghan rural and urban environments. It is a serious game for immersive cultural training by creating a living world. A similar serious game is also described by Losh [7]. This game aims to accelerate a learner's acquisition of spoken Arabic to assist in the rapid deployment of soldiers into tactical situations. Both games aim to prepare the soldiers for real war scenarios. The military industry was one of the first that used serious games for learning.

The United Nations organization has also launched some serious games to support their own initiatives, for example, to learn about the crisis in Darfur, related to HIV and AIDS prevention, and to stop disasters.

The serious game "Fast Car: Travelling Safely around the World" [8] launched by the United Nations Educational, Scientific, and Cultural Organization (UNESCO) aims to provide young people over the age of 16 with accurate and reliable information about HIV prevention, while educating, entertaining, and promoting healthy behavior. While racing on circuits on five different continents and virtually visiting some of UNESCO's World Heritage sites, players will receive information on existing prevention practices, treatment, and care for HIV and AIDS.

"Darfur is Dying" [9] serious game provides a window into the experience of the 2.5 million refugees in the Darfur region of Sudan. Players must keep their refugee camp functioning and avoid the attacks by militias. It allows the players to learn more about the humanitarian crisis in Darfur.

Muratet et al. [10] presented a serious game dedicated to learn computer programming. The basis for their serious game is a real-time strategy game, since it is the genre most played by the target audience. The players can command game entities with their own behaviors and have contests with other players in the multiplayer mode.

Barbosa and Silva [11] described a serious game to teach young students the basic functioning of the human circulatory system. It is a real-time strategy game where the player has to control a group of entities, such as red blood cells, white blood cells, and platelets, to avoid the bacteria. For that, the player has to understand the function of each entity to progress in the game.

Cowley et al. [12] presented a serious game to teach energy efficient knowledge and behavior to users of public buildings around Europe. It is one part of the project Save Energy that, by the use of information and communication technologies and real-time information from sensors and actuators, aims to transform the behavior of users of public buildings regarding energy efficiency.

The United States Environment Protection Agency (EPA) has a web page dedicated to recycling, called Recycle City, to visit and to explore how the city's residents recycle, reduce, and reuse waste [13]. It has also a serious game, the Dumptown game, where the player can create his own Recycle City. When starting the game the player sees Dumptown at its worst; it is littered and polluted, and nothing is being recycled or reused. But the player can start programs that encourage Dumptown's citizens and businesses to recycle and reduce waste. Each time the player tries out a new program, he can see immediately how the Dumptown landscape changes and how much waste he is preventing from going into the landfill.

More recently, Martins et al. [14] presented a serious game in Oncobiology that will allow the player to support clinical decisions with biological data, with the aim of promoting hypothesis-driven clinical research. They decided to develop a serious game as a point and click adventure, because they think it would best fit the theme and experience that they wanted for the player. They opted for a hospital themed game, where the player assumes the role of a medical doctor in residency training, who is put in charge of a clinical case and has to make step-wise decisions based on clinical and biological information.

Allegra et al. [15] describe a serious game that aims to introduce and foster an entrepreneurial mindset among young people. The focus of this game is on the management of a touristic company, in a complex market in which players compete with other companies/players.

Most of the serious games referred to above run on web browsers, which is not a platform dedicated to games. On the contrary, the consoles are platforms dedicated to games. Thus, a serious game designed for a console should be more effective than one designed for browser because players usually associate the games to consoles, which provide a more immersive experience due to their peripherals. A clear example of that is the exergames: games that promote the physical exercise [16], which are a success in consoles (e.g., fitness games).

Nevertheless, there are also some interesting approaches used in serious games and virtual environments for learning, where the knowledge is associated with task-based learning theory. For example, Bellotti et al. [17] proposed a new architecture for a class of serious games, the sand box serious games. The model of these games consists in a virtual world where knowledge is distributed in contextualized tasks spread by the world. In this context, they proposed decoupling contents from their delivery strategy, that is, by creating a task repository. The contents can be embodied in instances of simple task models, such as mini-games, quizzes, visiting a limited virtual world zone, interactions with 3D objects, or conversations with virtual humans. Their approach was later applied in the TiE project, which is designed to promote the knowledge of the European cultural heritage to a wider audience, where a visual authoring tool of tasks was introduced [18].

The same concept of task-based learning (e.g., mini-games, quizzes, and puzzles) was tested for interactivity and serious gaming for educational TV [19]. In this case, the authors have explored how to combine the media-driven nature of TV programs with the active user's participation which is typical of interactive games.

Recently, Bellotti et al. [20] presented a serious game model for cultural heritage that is based on previous works [17, 18] and tested with TiE game. They defined a model for games that are set in realistic virtual worlds enriched with embedded educational tasks, where the tasks are implemented as mini-games. They proposed a top-down methodology for content preparation, starting from a city-level analysis down to the single points of interest and associated tasks, which are instances of simple predefined mini-game/quiz typologies.

Smith and Sanchez [21] presented a strategy for developing mini-games that can be embedded in game-based training. They described how mini-games can be used for conceptual or procedural knowledge and they also present descriptions of several case studies that use mini-games as part of the learning strategy. They concluded that mini-games have become sophisticated enough to be included in serious games.

Procci et al. [22] described a serious game to teach deploying military personnel about available mental health resources and coping skills, as well as to determine whether the inclusion of mini-games improved learning outcomes. They concluded that including mini-games to provide practice in a game-based training environment such as a serious game improves learning outcomes.

In this paper we propose a new methodology of design and development serious games, which is aligned with the idea of embedded educational tasks in parallel to the main game, for example, through the use of mini-games because they have the potential to reinforce a single or small group of learning objectives by providing engaging and motivating learning experiences. Next section describes in detail the proposed methodology.

3. Methodology of Design and Development of Serious Games

As referred before, in a serious game the fun factor must be maintained in the first place. Therefore, to provide a rich and engaging environment that presents educational goals the best practices of pedagogical psychology are needed. But the best pedagogic practices are those that are interpreted as fun [23].

Real learning does happen in games, and this learning process shares many characteristics with the pedagogy of problem-based learning. Players must solve problems to progress through the game and they can only solve a given problem by accumulating the necessary experience and tools in lower levels of the game.

The pedagogy used is akin to problem-based learning where the structure and narrative of the game provide the purpose of learning and an immediate motivation for pursuing the knowledge required. Furthermore, it must include meaningful problems to solve with the purpose of learning the contents.

The learning must occur within multiple mechanisms, such as mini-games, puzzles, and quizzes, played in parallel to the main game environment but also by the gameplay and solving quests in the game. The educational component must be mainly based on the interaction with these learning mechanisms, where the concepts to be learned are embedded. However, the player must have missions to complete in the main game in order to obtain the requirements and tools to progress in game through the access to these mechanisms. For example, collect several items to be used in a mini-game or in a puzzle for a specific learning outcome. Thus, the player has the opportunity to learn some contents provided by a specific learning mechanism, keeping the main game more fun and engaging.

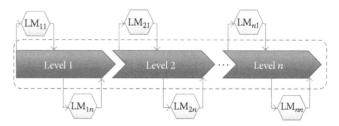

FIGURE 1: Diagram of our methodology; a game with several levels and the learning mechanisms associated to each layer.

This methodology must be applied also into each game layer, which means that the learning contents can be distributed by all layers. Therefore, the player must have several quests to complete per layer and also several learning mechanisms to overcome, in order to learn the concepts associated to each layer of the game. Figure 1 shows the diagram of our methodology, where a game is divided by levels and each level can be composed by several learning mechanisms (i.e., LM_{ij} in Figure 1). For each layer of the game, the player has missions to overcome as a way to access the learning mechanisms and thus progress in the game.

In short, our methodology proposes two main components for the design and development of a serious game, a main game with quests and a set of learning mechanisms. These learning mechanisms are related with the main game but they are independent and played in parallel with main game. Thus, it is easier to include learning contents in the game by defining independent learning mechanisms.

Note that this kind of learning mechanisms can be diverse, for example, quizzes, puzzles, or mini-games. But the knowledge is embodied mainly in those mechanisms that appear during the game, which means that the main game can be more oriented for fun factor engaging the player more.

4. "Clean World" Game

To test the methodology presented was developed a serious game, called "Clean World." "Clean World" is a 3D game created to raise awareness to environmental problems that we face today and tries to show what we can do to protect nature and keep our planet clean from pollution. For this, it intends to teach important concepts about recycling and renewable energies by combining classical platform and role-play game elements with mini-games and puzzles as learning mechanisms. Thus, the first step in designing of "Clean World," after deciding the theme, was the creation of a story to support the game.

4.1. The Story of the Game. The game takes place on the Anglas islands, in the year 2022. Due to the greed of big corporations, planet Earth is now completely polluted. People cannot walk on the streets without breathing masks due to the polluted air, and the big cities became giant industrial complexes where industries try to explore to the maximum the last resources of the planet.

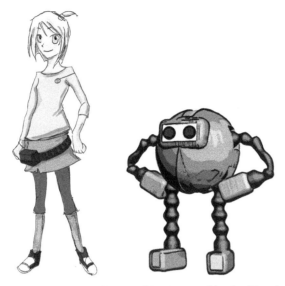

FIGURE 2: Concepts of Kate and Boris created by the 2D artist.

In one of the Anglas islands, the remote island of Cypricene, Kate, a 16-year-old girl, struggles against a disease that now affects almost the entire human population. Kate is alone on the island and she is too weak to get out. So, she uses technology to find help and builds a small robot with unique abilities, called Boris, which she sends in search of help. Boris is the character that the player controls in the game to search for help for Kate, a nonplayable character (see Figure 2). Note that the use of a robot is related with the theme of the game because the robot needs energy to move. Thus, the player needs to control the energy level of the robot to progress in the game.

After the beginning of the adventure Boris leaves in search of the medical center of the island, in order to help Kate (i.e., it is the first mission of the player in the game). There he meets Dr. Jacob, a brilliant scientist and doctor. The doctor explains to Boris that Kate is sick because she was infected with the Stigma, a new disease that has been affecting the human population almost for a decade. Dr. Jacob explains that the Stigma has no known cure; however, he has been studying the disease for a long time and he believes that the illness is connected to the pollution in the world. He describes to Boris his theory: if we reduce the pollution in the world probably the disease will disappear.

With the medicine on its hand, Boris goes back home to give it to Kate. Feeling a lot better, Kate is willing to test Dr. Jacob's theory with Boris's help. Thus, together they start to clean the island from pollution, starting by recycling the garbage (i.e., it is the second mission of the player in the game).

Later on, Boris meets Tom A. Toe, the engineer responsible for the wastewater treatment plant of the island. Then, with the help of this engineer, Boris starts to convert the plant and the machines to use clean energy sources, like the sun and the wind (i.e., it is the other mission of the player). Figure 3 shows the concepts of Dr. Jacob and Tom A. Toe created by the 2D artist.

FIGURE 3: Concepts of Dr. Jacob and Tom A. Toe created by the 2D artist.

4.2. *Main Game.* "Clean World" game was developed to be played with the Xbox controller making it more attractive for players, because consoles games are normally more addictive.

To implement the story, the "Clean World" game was divided in three levels. The first level's theme is recycling of garbage where Boris has to collect items spread through the island. Besides, Boris has to maintain his energy during this task, which means that he needs to recharge his batteries from time to time. For this purpose he needs to return to Kate's home because at this stage he cannot recharge by himself. If he loses all of his energy the player loses one life and starts the level again.

After completing most of the quests in this level, Boris gains a solar panel as a new ability. This solar panel allows to Boris recharging his batteries alone, that is, without returning to Kate's house, which is an advantage to progress faster in the game.

Figure 4 shows an overview of the first level of the game, where we can see some fog to simulate the environmental pollution. As we can see later, in the third level, the environment

FIGURE 4: Screenshot of the first level, where the environment is polluted.

FIGURE 5: Screenshot of the second level, the cave.

is less dark because to reach the third level the player has to complete some tasks to clean the environment.

During each level of the game there are several learning mechanisms that the player has to complete in order to advance and finish the level. These learning mechanisms will be presented in more detail in next section.

The second level has a new scenario that corresponds to a cave (see Figure 5). In this level, the player has to collect several items that can contaminate the soil (e.g., toxic garbage). Like in the previous level there are several learning mechanisms related to environmental issues that the player has to complete and that provide valuable information on how we can help to improve the planet's health.

In the third level the player will find a cleaner environment with less fog. This shows to the player that his tasks have had a positive impact on the environment and in Kate's health. The goal of this level is to teach some contents about renewable energies (e.g., using the sun and wind). In this case, the player has to complete tasks such as activating solar panels, building wind towers, repairing water mills, and providing clean and renewable energies to a wastewater treatment plant. Additionally, the player can now use the power of the sun to recharge his batteries using the solar panel available (see Figure 6).

During the entire game the player is assisted by two nonplayable characters (NPCs), Dr. Jacob and Tom A. Toe, who give instructions and quests to Boris. Figure 7 shows both characters that assist Boris during the game. For example, in Figure 7(b), in bottom right corner, we can see a dialog with Tom, the engineer that assists Boris in the third level.

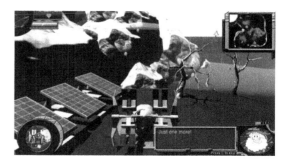

FIGURE 6: Screenshot of the third level, where the environment is less polluted.

(a)

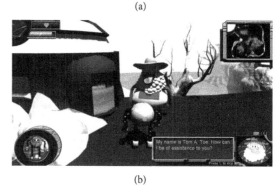

(b)

FIGURE 7: Nonplayable characters: (a) Dr. Jacob in level 1; (b) Tom A. Toe in level 3.

Boris has several skills that can be acquired and used during the game. For example, he can simply walk or use his skills to transform into a sphere to roll or even recharge his batteries using a solar panel. His skills are displayed on the bottom left corner of the interface. As we can see, Figures 4, 5, and 6 show these three different skills, walk, roll, and recharge, respectively. On the top left corner of the screen, Boris health and energy bars are displayed. A map of the level is displayed on the top right corner of the screen where the position of Boris and other important information are located (e.g., the location of Kate's house).

Figure 8 shows the workflow of the first level of the game, where we can see the quests and the learning mechanisms of this level. As we can see, the learning mechanisms in this case are the two mini-games referred to in Figure 8.

In Figure 8 we can also see that after completing quest 9, the player obtains a new ability; that is, Boris gains a solar panel that enables him to recharge his batteries by himself.

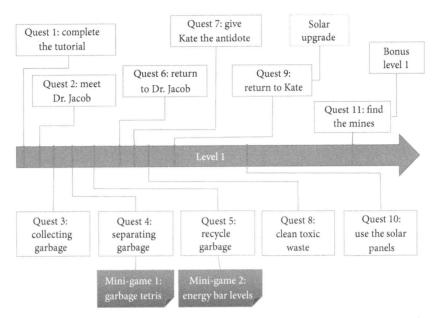

FIGURE 8: Workflow of the first level of the game, where we can see the several quests and the two learning mechanisms that run in parallel to main game (i.e., two mini-games).

The same strategy is used in the second and third levels of the game. Thus, the player has several quests to complete in the main game and has several learning mechanisms to overcome, in order to learn the concepts associated to the game thematic.

4.3. Learning Mechanisms. To include educational contents in the game without disfiguring it (i.e., keeping the fun factor in first), several learning mechanisms were spread along the game, in particular some mini-games and puzzles associated to the thematic of recycle and renewable energies. These mini-games and puzzles allow teaching some educational content about the environment and how to protect it, such as garbage separation. Furthermore, in all the game the tasks related to garbage collection and separation are associated with the colors of the Xbox buttons, taking into account the type of the garbage, that is, green button to glass, blue button to paper, yellow button to metal, and red button to plastic (see Figure 9).

Some learning mechanisms are based on several successful games that already proved to engage the players. For example, the mini-game associated to the separation of garbage uses mechanics similar to the Tetris game. But the mini-game of energy bar levels associated with the recycling machines uses mechanics similar to Guitar Hero game. These learning mechanisms introduce new gameplay mechanics and diverse experiences in parallel to the main game. This way, the game teaches important concepts about the protection of the environment, through fun, engaging the player with diverse experiences.

In the mini-game based on the Tetris game (see Figure 9(b)) the player has to separate the garbage according to its type using the joystick of Xbox controller.

During the evaluation process with different users we observed that these learning mechanisms were the most exciting part of the game for the players. For example, the mini-game associated with the energy bar levels of the recycling machines was considered very exciting by the players. Although it was a very simple game, its mechanics were very challenging for the players (see Figure 9(c)). In this mini-game the player needs to maintain the energy bars level below the line. For that, the player needs to press the correspondent buttons of the Xbox controller, but only one at a time is allowed.

Figure 10(a) shows a mini-game based on the Guitar Hero game, where the player has to collect the maximum number of items that appear in front of him. Players can move to the right and to the left and have to press the corresponding button to catch the items (i.e., press the button with the same color of the illuminated item).

Finally, Figure 10(b) shows a mini-game that is a puzzle of pipes, where the player has to reorient several parts of pipes to create a path from one side to the other, to create a functional path for energy to pass through. Boris can use the resulting energy to recharge or to give clean energy to other machines.

5. Conclusions and Future Work

People differ in their behavior, play styles, and learning methods. But some forms of learning are more fun than others; thus, serious games can provide mutual goals of entertainment and education.

The "Clean World" game aims to teach important concepts about recycling and renewable energies to players. But the players see it more as a game and less as a serious game, which means that educational contents were very well included in the game. The methodology proposed here was to include educational contents mainly out of the main game, that is, as independent learning mechanisms proved to be very efficient. This methodology demonstrated a more

(a)

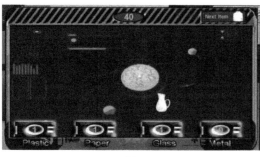

(b)

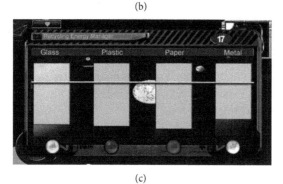

(c)

FIGURE 9: Xbox controller and two examples of learning mechanisms from level 1: (a) Xbox command; (b) associated to the separation of garbage; (c) energy bar levels associated to the recycling machines.

(a)

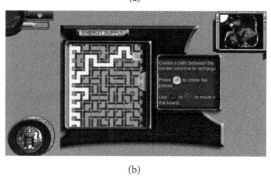

(b)

FIGURE 10: Other learning mechanisms: (a) mini-game associated to garbage collection; (b) mini-game associated to the recharge of batteries.

effective way to create serious games that engage the players, when its learning contents are included mainly in learning mechanisms, as, for example, mini-games and puzzles, since it enables keeping the main game a simple game without disfiguring it with learning contents.

Besides, we could observe that the target people of the game (i.e., young people) liked to play the game and consider it addictive due to the challenge provided by mini-games and puzzles, which means that these learning mechanisms are really effective. But note that this game was designed for the Xbox controller, which is also a controller dedicated to games that are more interesting for players.

Playing "Clean World" helps young people to develop a positive attitude to help the planet Earth. Doing this will increase the chances of the young people to grow and become responsible adults, recycling, and using the renewable energies.

In the future we hope to include new characters in the game, for example, enemies that compete with the player in some tasks, making the game even more interesting and challenging (i.e., include nonplayer characters). Furthermore, we hope to test the game in some secondary schools to evaluate its effectiveness with more detail, namely, based on a protocol of evaluation of the knowledge before and after playing the game.

Conflict of Interests

The authors declare that there is no conflict of interests regarding the publication of this paper.

References

[1] R. V. Eck, "Digital game-based learning: it's not just the digital natives who are restless," *EDUCAUSE Review*, vol. 41, no. 2, pp. 16–30, 2006.

[2] A. C. Vidani and L. Chittaro, "Using a task modeling formalism in the design of serious games for emergency medical procedures," in *Proceedings of the Conference in Games and Virtual Worlds for Serious Applications (VS-GAMES '09)*, pp. 95–102, IEEE Computer Society, March 2009.

[3] M. Zyda, "From visual simulation to virtual reality to games," *Computer*, vol. 38, no. 9, pp. 25–32, 2005.

[4] C. Aldrich, *The Complete Guide to Simulations and Serious Games: How the Most Valuable Content Will Be Created in the Age Beyond GutenBerg to Google*, Pfeiffer, 2009.

[5] D. R. Michael and S. L. Chen, *Serious Games: Games That Educate, Train, and Inform*, Cengage Learning PTR, 2005.

[6] M. A. Zielke, M. J. Evans, F. Dufour et al., "Serious games for immersive cultural training: creating a living world," *IEEE Computer Graphics and Applications*, vol. 29, no. 2, pp. 49–60, 2009.

[7] E. Losh, "In country with tactical iraqi: trust, identity, and language learning in a military video game digital experience," in *Proceedings of the Digital Arts and Culture Conference*, pp. 69–78, 2005.

[8] Unesco, "Fast car: Travelling safely around the world," unesco, http://www.unesco.org/new/en/communication-and-information/crosscutting-priorities/hiv-and-aids/fast-car-travelling-safely-around-the-world/.

[9] Dying. Darfur is dying, unric, http://www.darfurisdying.com/.

[10] M. Muratet, P. Torguet, J.-P. Jessel, and F. Viallet, "Towards a serious game to help students learn computer programming," *International Journal of Computer Games Technology*, vol. 2009, Article ID 470590, 12 pages, 2009.

[11] A. F. S. Barbosa and F. G. M. Silva, "Serious games—design and development of oxyblood," in *Proceedings of the 8th International Conference on Advances in Computer Entertainment Technology (ACE '11)*, pp. 15:1–15:8, 2011.

[12] B. Cowley, J. L. Moutinho, C. Bateman, and A. Oliveira, "Learning principles and interaction design for "Green My Place": a massively multiplayer serious game," *Entertainment Computing*, vol. 2, no. 2, pp. 103–113, 2011.

[13] Recycle City, "United states environment protection agency (epa)," http://www.epa.gov/recyclecity/.

[14] A. Martins, F. Freitas, P. Gonçalves et al., "Design choices in the development of an oncobiology serious game for medical education," in *Proceedings of the 5th International Conference on Education and New Learning Technologies*, pp. 1031–1039, IATED, 2013.

[15] M. Allegra, V. dal Grande, M. Gentile, D. la Guardia, and S. Ottaviano, "A serious game to promote and facilitate entrepreneurship education for young students," in *Proceedings of the International Conference on Education and Educational Technologies*, Recent Advances in Education and Educational Technologies, pp. 256–263, 2013.

[16] J. Sinclair, P. Hingston, M. Masek, and K. Nosaka, "Using a virtual body to aid in exergaming system development," *IEEE Computer Graphics and Applications*, vol. 29, no. 2, pp. 39–48, 2009.

[17] F. Bellotti, R. Berta, A. De Gloria, and L. Primavera, "Adaptive experience engine for serious games," *IEEE Transactions on Computational Intelligence and AI in Games*, vol. 1, no. 4, pp. 264–280, 2009.

[18] F. Bellotti, R. Berta, A. De Gloria, and L. Primavera, "Supporting authors in the development of task-based learning in serious virtual worlds," *British Journal of Educational Technology*, vol. 41, no. 1, pp. 86–107, 2010.

[19] F. Bellotti, R. Berta, A. De Gloria, and A. Ozolina, "Investigating the added value of interactivity and serious gaming for educational TV," *Computers and Education*, vol. 57, no. 1, pp. 1137–1148, 2011.

[20] F. Bellotti, R. Berta, A. De Gloria, A. D'ursi, and V. Fiore, "A serious game model for cultural heritage," *Journal of Computing and Cultural Heritage*, vol. 5, no. 4, article 17, 2012.

[21] P. A. Smith and A. Sanchez, "Mini-games with major impacts," in *Serious Game Design and Development: Technologies for Training and Learning*, J. Cannon-Bowers and C. Bowers, Eds., pp. 1–12, 2010.

[22] K. Procci, C. Bowers, C. Wong, and A. Andrews, "Minigames for mental health: improving warfighters' coping skills and awareness of mental health resources," *Games for Health Journal*, vol. 2, no. 4, pp. 240–246, 2013.

[23] K. Royle, "Game based learning: a different perspective," *Innovate Online*, vol. 4, no. 4, pp. 39–48, 2008.

4

Concert Viewing Headphones

Kazuya Atsuta,[1] Masatoshi Hamanaka,[2] and SeungHee Lee[3]

[1] *Graduate School of Systems and Information Engineering, University of Tsukuba, 1-1-1 Tennodai, Tsukuba, Ibaraki 305-8573, Japan*
[2] *Faculty of Engineering, Information and Systems, University of Tsukuba, 1-1-1 Tennodai, Tsukuba, Ibaraki 305-8573, Japan*
[3] *Faculty of Human Sciences, University of Tsukuba, 1-1-1 Tennodai, Tsukuba, Ibaraki 305-8573, Japan*

Correspondence should be addressed to Kazuya Atsuta, kazuya@music.iit.tsukuba.ac.jp

Academic Editor: Suiping Zhou

An audiovisual interface equipped with a projector, an inclina-tion sensor, and a distance sensor for zoom control has been developed that enables a user to selectively view and listen to specific performers in a video-taped group performance. Dubbed *Concert Viewing Headphones*, it has both image and sound processing functions. The image processing extracts the portion of the image indicated by the user and projects it free of distortion on the front and side walls. The sound processing creates imaginary microphones for those performers without one so that the user can hear the sound from any performer. Testing using images and sounds captured using a fisheye-lens camera and 37 lavalier microphones showed that sound locali-zation was fastest when an inverse square function was used for the sound mixing and that the zoom function was useful for locating the desired sound performance.

1. Introduction

In this paper, we describe an audiovisual interface dubbed *Concert Viewing Headphones* that enables someone viewing a video-taped musical concert to select particular performers or areas to view and listen to.

We define two requirements for the interface. First, the user can control it by simply performing the natural actions related to listening. Such actions are those of people in the audience at a concert hall; for example, they turn their heads in the direction of the viewing and/or listening target. Thus, with this interface, a user can better enjoy videos of concerts by selecting particular areas and/or performers on the stage by turning his or her head in their direction and cupping a hand to an ear. Second, the constructed device incorporating this interface is small enough for home use. Since projectors have been getting smaller and smaller, we were able to develop a headphone device equipped with a compact projector, an inclination sensor, and a distance sensor. This device detects the user's head direction, detects the distance between the user's cupped hand and ear, and outputs the corresponding image and sound. Moreover, it

is small enough to be used in the home and many other environments.

Figure 1 shows the system flow of this interface. First, the user's head direction is detected by the inclination sensor. Next, the portion of the wide-angle image covering the whole stage corresponding to the head direction is extracted, and this portion is projected on the screen. At the same time, the recorded sounds are mixed so as to emphasize the sounds of the performers within the extracted portion (i.e., the projected image). If the user cups a hand to an ear to hear better, the projected image is enlarged to a degree corresponding to the distance between the user's hand and the distance sensor attached to the one of the headphones, enabling the user to better focus on a particular performer.

This interface has three features in particular.

(1) Use of Imaginary Microphones. Ideally, we would capture the sound for each performer through a microphone attached to the performer's music stand because the sounds are mixed so as to emphasize those within the selected ambit. However, this is difficult in terms of time and cost if there are many performers, as in an orchestra. There is

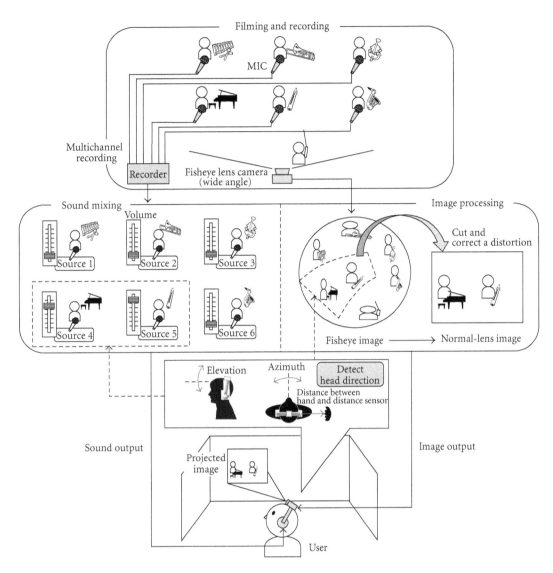

FIGURE 1: System flow of audiovisual interface.

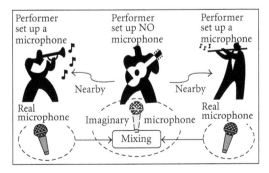

FIGURE 2: Creation of imaginary microphones.

thus a problem with mixing sounds if performers without a microphone are in the selected ambit. We solve it by creating imaginary microphones for those performers without a real microphone, making it possible to mix sounds as if each

performer had a real microphone. The creation of these imaginary microphones is illustrated in Figure 2. The sounds for two performers with real microphones who were near a performer without one are mixed, and this mixed sound is used as the sound recorded by an imaginary microphone for that performer. The sounds are mixed in proportion to the distances between the performer without a real microphone and the two performers with real microphones.

(2) Use of Image Captured with Fisheye Lens. A wide-angle image covering the whole stage is captured using a camera with a circular fisheye lens. The user selects the target ambit from this image, enabling the user to selectively appreciate a particular portion of the image. The lens captures a 180° image that is characterized by low distortion at the center and large distortion around the edges. The distortion in the extracted area is corrected when the image corresponding to the gaze orientation is extracted. A nondistorted image is then projected. This is described in detail in Section 3.1.1.

FIGURE 3: Concert Viewing Headphones.

(3) Projection of Image on Front Wall and Two Side Walls.
The image is projected on the front wall and two side walls
relative to the user. If the 180° image covering the whole stage
was projected on only the front wall, it could be difficult to
clearly see the performers at the ends of the stage. For this
reason, *Concert Viewing Headphones* is premised on being
used indoors and on the images being projected on not only
the front wall but also the two side walls. Thus, the user
can view the whole stage evenly because the performers at
the ends of the stage appear on the corresponding side wall
when the user's head turns in the direction of a side wall.
However, when an image is projected on a side wall, it is
projected at a tilt, so it is distorted and forms a trapezoid
(*keystone distortion*). This distortion is compensated for by
distorting the image counter to the *keystone distortion* before
it is projected. This is described in detail in Section 3.1.2.

The *Concert Viewing Headphones* device developed in this
study is shown in Figure 3. A projector and an inclination
sensor are mounted on top of the headphones (i.e., above the
user's head). This enables the image to be projected in the
direction of the user's gaze.

We tested *Concert Viewing Headphones* by using a video
of a musical concert recorded with a fisheye-lens camera and
37 microphones. Ten participants used our device to view the
concert. They enjoyed listening to the music and watching
the performance and were able to zero in on the sounds of
particular performers.

2. Related Research

This is the first report of a device based on a pair of
headphones with a projector that enable images and sound
source to be viewed and listened to selectively. There has been
some related research.

2.1. Immersive Displays. *Immersive displays* project images
onto screens or on monitors that surround a user. We discuss
two major systems below.

The first one is *TWISTER*, which presents stereoscopic
images to a user [1, 2]. The user stands in a cylindrical
booth, which displays live full-color 360-degree panoramic
and stereoscopic images. There are many units arranged in a
cylindrical pattern around the user. Each one of these units
consists of two LED arrays (one array for the right eye,
the other for the left) and a douser. When these units are
spinning at high speed, a binocular parallax is caused by the
douser, giving the images a stereoscopic effect.

The other one is *Ensphered Vision*, which projects images
onto a full-surround spherical screen that surrounds the user,
enabling him or her to experience virtual reality [3]. A single
projector and a spherical convex mirror are used in order
to display a seamless image. The spherical convex mirror
diverges the light from the projector in the spherical screen.
A planar mirror then bends this light so that the user can
see the image from the center. These optical configurations
enable the user to view a seamless wide-angle image.

These systems are not suitable for home use because they
must be large enough to cover either one's whole body or
one's head.

2.2. Multiview or Wide-Angle Image Systems. One can selectively appreciate the images on a DVD containing multiview images and contents captured with wide-angle images
by switching among the images arbitrarily [4, 5]. In conventional DVDs containing live images, one cannot selectively
switch among images because the images were captured with
cameras having a narrow field of view. In contrast, with a
DVD containing multiview images, one can select images
for particular points on the stage. In contents using wide-
angle images, one can arbitrarily select the portion of an
image to be viewed from a panoramic image captured with
omnidirectional cameras or with a camera equipped with a
fisheye lens. Such systems are controlled by manipulating a
remote control, or a mouse. Therefore, one cannot appreciate
the image and sound by simply performing the natural
actions related to listening. Moreover, in the course of using
a mouse to select a portion of an image to be viewed from
a panoramic image, one sometimes loses his or her place in
the image. In contrast, if a user wearing the *Concert Viewing
Headphones* device turns his or her head, the projected image
is switched corresponding to this movement. Thus, the user
can recognize in which direction he or she is looking at in the
image.

2.3. Sound Scope Headphones. We previously developed an
interface called "*Sound Scope Headphones*" that enables a user
to appreciate sounds by selecting particular sound sources
[6]. In conventional DVDs containing live images, one
cannot select particular sound sources because the sounds
are already mixed and cannot be remixed. In contrast, *Sound
Scope Headphones* mixes the sounds on the basis of the
user's head direction. The interface does not handle images.
Furthermore, the interface does not use real sounds recorded
at a concert but rather the music in the *RWC Music Database*
[7]. In this study, we use real sounds recorded at a concert.

2.4. Head-Mounted Display. A system using a *head-mounted
display* changes the images on the basis of the user's head
direction [8]. The user wears a device, such as a pair of
goggles or a helmet, and experiences virtual reality produced
by images displayed on a monitor close to the user's eyes.
However, only one person can use it at a time, and the user's
eyes tend to become tired.

In a computer game using a *head-mounted display* (e.g.,
SONY HMZ-T1 [9]), a player experiences only the virtual

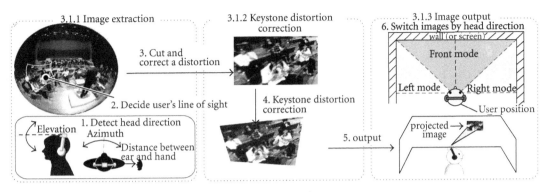

FIGURE 4: Image processing system.

world. In contrast, a computer game using an interface based on *Concert Viewing Headphones* can combine the real world with the virtual world by projecting the virtual images onto real-world objects. We discuss such a game more fully in Section 6.

2.5. Motion Captures. If the motions of a user turning his or her head and cupping a hand to an ear are captured with Microsoft's Kinect for the Xbox 360 [10], it is possible to produce images and sound corresponding to the motions. In this method, the image is projected on a monitor. However, it is unnatural visually to project 180° images that capture a whole stage on a flat surface, and, as mentioned in Section 1, it could be difficult to clearly see the performers at the ends of the stage. However, if the projection surface is extended by using monitors, it is difficult in terms of cost. In contrast, *Concert Viewing Headphones* projects a 180° image not only on the front wall but also on the two side walls relative to the user. That is, the performers at the ends of the image appear on the corresponding side walls. Thus, the user can view the whole stage evenly.

3. Description

Concert Viewing Headphones, equipped with a projector, an inclination sensor, and a distance sensor, comprises two systems: image processing and audio processing. It first detects the angle of elevation and direction of the user's head. It then extracts the portion of the image corresponding to the elevation and direction and projects it onto the front wall or a side wall. At the same time, it mixes the sounds recorded by the microphones for that portion of the image and outputs those sounds.

3.1. Image Processing System. The image processing system comprises image extraction, keystone distortion correction, and image output, as illustrated in Figure 4.

3.1.1. Image Extraction. The first step in image extraction is to detect the user's head direction by using the elevation and azimuth of the user's head measured with a three-axis attitude sensor. Next, the gaze orientation, that is, the direction of the user's eyes, is determined on the basis of

FIGURE 5: Coordinates on a stage.

the detected head direction. Specifically, the sensors detect the user's head direction (elevation φ, azimuth θ), and the coordinates on the stage corresponding to the head direction are calculated. Thus, the image processing system determines which portion of the stage the user is looking at. As Figure 5 shows, the coordinates on the stage are calculated on the basis that the center of the fisheye image is $\varphi = 0°$, $\theta = 0°$ and of the ends of an image are $-90°$ and/or $90°$.

Furthermore, if the user cups a hand to an ear to hear better, the image is enlarged so as to enable looking at a particular area of the stage more closely. The degree of enlargement is proportional to the distance between the user's hand and the distance sensor. The corresponding portion of the image is then extracted.

In this study, we used only one camera in order to reduce cost and to enable a more convenient installation position. Therefore, we captured a whole stage with a circular fisheye-lens camera that can capture a wide-angle image at around 180°. We will now describe the principle for capturing with a fisheye lens and the method for distortion correction.

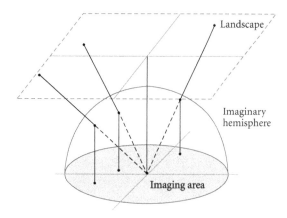

FIGURE 6: Principle for capturing with a circular fisheye-lens camera.

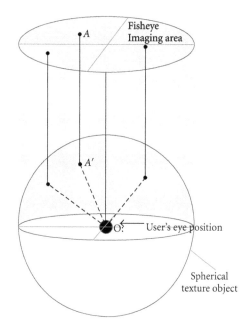

FIGURE 7: Texture mapping for distortion correction.

FIGURE 8: Distorted image and corrected image.

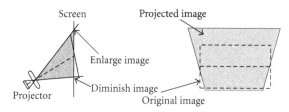

FIGURE 9: Image projected at a tilt on side wall.

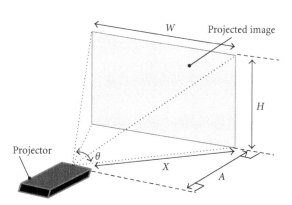

FIGURE 10: Configuration of projected image.

As Figure 6 shows, in a camera using the circular fisheye lens, the landscape is reflected in an imaginary hemisphere and projected onto the imaging area at right angles. Thus, a fisheye image is produced and output with low distortion at the center and large distortion around the edges.

The distortion is corrected for by centering the extracted image onto a point detected by the three-axis attitude sensor. Specifically, we correct the distortion by reversing the process based on the principle for capturing with a fisheye lens. In this study, we used OpenGL [11] for the process in this distortion correction. As Figure 7 shows, the fisheye image is projected onto the upper hemisphere of a spherical texture object in OpenGL. We define the center of this object as the user's eye position. Thus, when the user views the spherical surface from the center of the object, a nondistorted image is presented to the user. Figure 8 shows a distorted image and a corrected (non-distorted) image.

3.1.2. Keystone Distortion Correction. The image projected on a side wall is at a tilt, so it is either magnified or demagnified and forms a trapezoid, as illustrated in Figure 9. This *keystone distortion* must be corrected. The image is thus processed in accordance with the elevation and direction of the user's head so that it is not distorted when it is projected. This processing distorts the image counter to the keystone distortion. The correction is calculated by using the measurements from the direction and inclination sensors. The magnification or reduction percentage is determined by comparing the projection distance with the image projected on the front wall.

We use A as the minimum distance between the projector and screen, H as the height of the projected image, W as the width of the projected image, θ as the angle of view, and X as the distance between the projector and the edge of the projected image. Figure 10 shows the relationships among these elements.

In addition, when we tilt the projector, θ_1 is the angle between the center of the front wall and the major axis of the

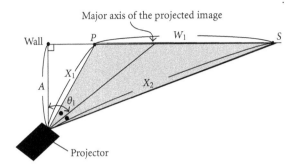

FIGURE 11: Configuration of image projected at a tilt.

projected image. X_1 and X_2 are the right and left edges of the projected image. Figure 11 shows the relationships among these elements.

The angle between the major axis of the projected image and the left end of the projected image, P, is $\theta/2$. Therefore,

$$X_1 = \frac{A}{\cos(\theta_1 - \theta/2)}. \tag{1}$$

The left side in the image is a maximum of X_1/X times enlarged compared to when it is projected in front of the wall.

Similarly,

$$X_2 = \frac{A}{\cos(\theta_1 + \theta/2)}. \tag{2}$$

The right side in the image is a maximum of X_2/X times enlarged compared to when it is projected in front of the wall. Therefore, the output image is corrected so that the left side in the image is a maximum of X_1/X times reduced, and the right side in the image is a maximum of X_2/X times reduced.

3.1.3. Image Output.

Since it is visually unnatural to project 180° images on a flat surface, *Concert Viewing Headphones* is premised, as mentioned above, on being used indoors and on the images being projected on not only the front wall but also the two side walls. When an image is projected on a side wall, correction processing switches its shape appropriately for sidewall projection.

3.2. Audio Processing System.

The audio processing system comprises *imaginary microphone creation, distance calculation,* and *mixing.* The system flow is shown in Figure 12.

3.2.1. Imaginary Microphone Creation.

As mentioned in Section 1, ideally, there would be a sound source for every performer, but this is difficult in practice. Moreover, it would result in an enormous amount of audio data. Therefore, we record sound sources with microphones corresponding to each of the instrumental parts of the music. That is, a microphone is attached to the music stand of one performer for each group of performers playing the same instrument. For those performers without a microphone, an imaginary microphone is created for each one by mixing the sounds

recorded with nearby real microphones on the basis of the distance between the performer and the position of the real microphones. It is possible that the sound of an imaginary microphone might include instrumental sounds that are distant from the imaginary microphone because, in general, microphones pick up sounds from all directions. However, sound pressure is decreased in inverse proportion to the square of the distance between a microphone and the position of a sound source. Moreover, in typical concerts, because the size of the stage is large enough, the performers are spaced out on the stage with enough distance between each instrumental part of the music. Therefore, in this study, most of the sounds picked up by microphones are from nearby the microphones and made up of one instrumental part. For this reason, we used a method that creates imaginary microphones on the basis of the distance between the performer and the position of the real microphones. We will discuss methods for creating a more realistic sound for those performers without a real microphone. These methods are discussed more fully in Section 6.

The sounds from all microphones are used to control the mixing rate for each performer's sound.

3.2.2. Distance Calculation.

The mixing rate for each performer's sound is calculated on the basis of the distance between the performer and the center of the image extracted by the image processing system. The distance is calculated from the current projected image and the position of each performer in the coordinate system of the image captured with a circular fisheye lens.

3.2.3. Mixing.

Whether there are any performers in the projected image is determined from the distance calculation information. The sound volume for those performers not in the projected image is set to zero. That is, their sound is muted. For performers who are in the projected image, their sound is emphasized so that they approach the center of the projected image. Prepared functions are used to determine the mixing rates needed to adjust the sound volumes so as to increase the volumes with a decrease in the calculated distance. Each performer's sound is multiplied by the corresponding mixing rate, the sounds are added together, and they are output. We prepared five mixing rate functions, as shown in Figure 13.

We normalized the height of the projected image from 0 to 1. When the distance from the center of the image is 0, the volume amplification rate of each function is normalized so that it has a value of 1. When the distance from the center of the image is 0.5, the volume amplification rate of each function is normalized so that it has a value of 0.1.

In Figure 13, line 1 is constant with the distance, and the volume is the same for all microphones. Line 2 is a negative gradient. If this function is applied, each performer's projected volume has an inverse relationship to the performer's distance from the center of the image. Line 3 is a normal distribution. If his function is applied, the user can hear the performers located at the center of the image and around the center. The volume for the performers at the edge of the

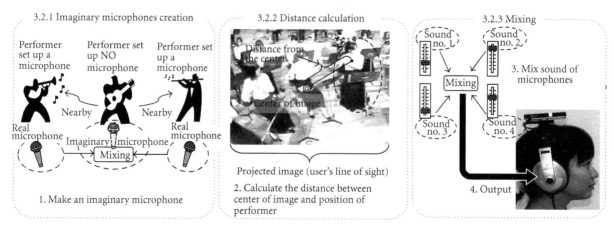

FIGURE 12: Audio processing system.

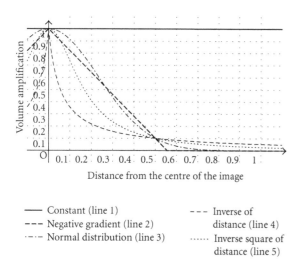

FIGURE 13: Mixing rate functions.

image is almost zero. Line 4 is the inverse of the distance from the center of the image. If this function is applied, each performer's projected volume has an inverse relationship to the performer's distance from the center of the projected image. Line 5 is the inverse square of the distance from the center of the projected image. If this function is applied, each performer's projected volume has an inverse relationship to the performer's distance from the center of the image. In Section 4, we describe our evaluation of these functions.

If a user controls the projected image so as to be able to view the whole stage, it is possible that the user does not want to emphasize a particular performer's sound but listen to all performers' sounds. For this reason, the user can select from two sound mixing modes. The first one is "constant mode," in which the volume is the same for the sounds of all performers who are in the projected image (line 1 in Figure 13). The other one is "emphasis mode," in which, as mentioned above, the sounds of the performers who are in the projected image are emphasized so that the performers approach the center of the projected image (e.g., line 5 in Figure 13).

Concert Viewing Headphones changes the image and sound mixing in accordance with the orientation of the user's head. When the user operates the zoom function by cupping an ear, performers at edge of the image are out of the enlarged image or are away from the center of the enlarged image. As a result, the sounds of the performers at the center of the projected image are emphasized.

3.3. Implementation. We used an attitude heading reference system (3DM-GX3-25, MicroStrain) as both a direction sensor and an inclination sensor. It outputs the Euler angles, rotation matrix, delta angle, delta velocity, acceleration angular rate, and magnetic field to a USB device small enough to be mounted on a pair of headphones.

We use a proximity sensor (Asakusa Giken Co., Ltd.) as the distance sensor. It detects the distance in the 0–6 cm range by infrared reflectance, making it well suited for measuring the distance between the hand and ear. It is mounted on the right headphone. We initially used an ultrasonic sensor, but it was unable to provide accurate measurements at close range.

Data is transmitted from the proximity sensor by using the *Arduino* which is an open-source electronics prototyping platform. Because the proximity sensor outputs data using serial communication, connecting it to a PC is problematic. We used a USB-serial conversion substrate (FT232RX) to enable the proximity sensor-to-USB connection.

A *mini USB projector* was mounted on the headphones. Because the 3DM-GX3 system is susceptible to magnetic force, we selected a projector with less magnetic force.

4. Evaluation

We evaluated our *Concert Viewing Headphones* by first creating an image and sound source. We video-taped and recorded a University of Tsukuba Symphonic Band concert at Nova Hall (a concert hall in Tsukuba city, Japan). The microphones and camera were configured as shown in Figure 14. The microphones were placed on the music stands. Because there were 37 instrumental parts in the performance, we used 37 lavalier microphones to record the

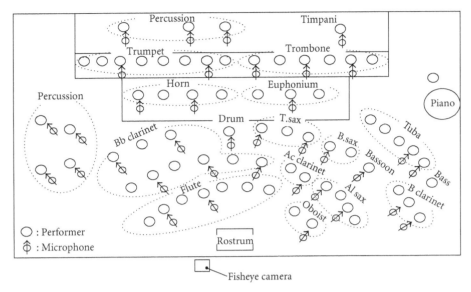

FIGURE 14: Microphone and camera positions.

TABLE 1: Average time to locate 440 Hz sine wave.

Function	Time without zoom system [s]	Time with zoom system [s]
Constant	112.5	56.2
Negative gradient	29.2	24.0
Normal distribution	32.6	17.8
Inverse of distance	30.9	20.8
Inverse square of distance	23.8	16.9

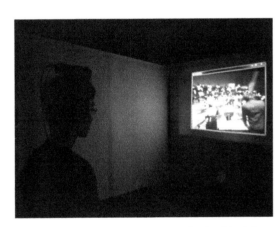

FIGURE 15: Participant using *Concert Viewing Headphones*.

sounds. An image of the entire stage with all performers visible was captured with a 2.5 m high fisheye-lens camera. We experimented with the mixing functions described in Section 3.2.3 to identify the natural correspondence between changes in the image and the sound mixing.

4.1. Evaluation of Functions for Mixing.

We located a point at which one could hear a 440 Hz sine wave at random positions in the image. The ten evaluation participants attempted to locate this point with only their ears so as to identify the natural correspondence between head movement and changes in the sound mixing. We recorded the time it took to do this. Each time a participant located the point, the sine wave shifted to another point at random. This was repeated five times for each function. We defined the function with which the participants could find the sine wave the fastest as the best one. The average times for each function are shown in Table 1. The time was the shortest for the "inverse square of distance" function with the zoom function.

All ten participants were adults in their 20's. In addition, three of them had been playing musical instruments on a daily basis, another three had been playing musical instruments for a period of time, and the other four had hardly played an instrument. We determined that there was not any difference that depended on the participants' musical experience in the result of each function. Figure 15 shows a participant using *Concert Viewing Headphones*.

4.2. Evaluation of Sound and Image.

We demonstrated that the targeted ambit naturally corresponded to the changes in the sound mixing by using an eye-mark recorder. Specifically, the participants repeated the action of looking at a particular performer arbitrarily and transferring their gaze to another performer. In the meantime, we examined the relation between their viewpoint and the mixing rate of each performer's sound. As a result, we determined that the sound volume of a performer who the participant was looking at was highest in the mixing. When the participant was transferring his or her gaze, the mixing was switched in real time so that the sound volume of a performer who was closest to the participant's viewpoint was highest. However, when the participant turned his or her head quickly, we determined that the shifting of the image sometimes lagged behind that of the sound. If we reduced the file size of the image and/or sound, this lag would be improved, but

TABLE 2: Average score of each function.

Function	Average score rated by ten participants			Average
	Q1: Is the relation between the shifting of the image and that of the sound natural?	Q2: is the instrumental sound emphasized so that it approaches the center of the projected image?	Q3: when you turn your head quickly, is the relation between the shifting of the image and that of the sound natural	
Constant	2.6	2.7	3.1	2.8
Negative gradient	3.9	4.1	3.9	3.9
Normal distribution	3.4	3.6	3.6	3.5
Inverse of distance	3.6	3.3	3.1	3.3
Inverse square of distance	3.7	3.7	4.0	3.8

we think that the image and sound quality should not be degraded in the audiovisual interface. Therefore, we will improve the program of this interface so that the shifting of the image and sound is more natural.

4.3. Questionnaire. A questionnaire containing four questions was completed by the participants after the testing. Questions nos. 1 to 3 were rated on a 5-point scale with the following possible responses: completely disagree (1), somewhat disagree (2), uncertain (3), somewhat agree (4), and completely agree (5). Table 2 shows the average score of each function rated by the ten participants for each question. The score was highest for the "negative gradient" and "inverse square of distance" functions. For question no. 4, we asked "What is your feeling about the characteristic or difference among each of the five functions?" In the "inverse square of distance function," most participants had positive opinions, for example, "I could hear the difference among the sounds very clearly," and "I could notice many different instrumental sounds." Therefore, we could determine the effectiveness of using the inverse square of distance function.

5. Conclusion

Our *Concert Viewing Headphones*, equipped with a projector, an inclination sensor, and a distance sensor for zoom control, enables a user to selectively view and listen to specific performers in a video-taped group performance. It has both image and sound processing functions. The image processing extracts the portion of the image selected by the user and projects it free of distortion on the front and side walls. The sound processing creates imaginary microphones for those performers without one so that the user can hear the sound from any performer. Testing using images and sounds captured using a fisheye-lens camera and 37 lavalier microphones showed that sound localization was fastest when an inverse square function was used for the sound mixing. Moreover, the zoom function enabled the participants to indicate the desired sound performance.

6. Future Work

We will discuss the creation of the imaginary microphones in the audio processing system and design a method so as to be able to create a more realistic sound. For example, we will record the instrumental sounds within a more narrow area on the stage by using directional microphones and adjusting the position of the microphones. Besides this, we will estimate the acoustic transfer function in the position of the performers without a real microphone.

Furthermore, we will apply this interface to virtual reality games. As mentioned above, *Concert Viewing Headphones* can combine the real world with the virtual world because it can project virtual images onto real-world objects. For example, we plan to devise a game that uses an interface based on *Concert Viewing Headphones*. In a darkish room, there are real objects (e.g., clocks, shelves, boxes, etc.) located around a player wearing the interface. The player finds a particular imaginary musical instrument from among the imaginary instruments hidden in the objects similar to putting a spotlight on something. Specifically, each one of these objects corresponds to an instrumental sound and the image of a performer playing the instrument on the projected image. If the player's viewpoint is close to an object, an instrumental sound corresponding to the object is emphasized, and a performer playing the instrument is projected on the object. That is, the player can find the imaginary instruments from the change of sounds and the projected images by turning his or her head.

In order to improve on *Concert Viewing Headphones*, we plan to conduct further experiments on the image functions to determine whether the zooming and image changes are natural. Furthermore, we will conduct experiments with the participants of all ages.

Acknowledgments

The author would like to express our deepest gratitude to Sawako Miyashita who provided helpful comments and suggestions. They would also like to thank Atsushi Usami whose meticulous comments were an enormous help to them.

References

[1] Y. Kunita, N. Ogawa, A. Sakuma, M. Inami, T. Maeda, and S. Tachi, "Immersive autostereoscopic display for mutual telexistence: TWISTER I (Telexistence Wide-angle Immersive STEReoscope Model I)," in *Proceedings of the IEEE Virtual Reality Annual International Symposium*, pp. 31–36, Yokohama, Japan, 2001.

[2] S. Tachi, "TWISTER: immersive ominidirectional autostereoscopic 3D booth for mutual telexistence," in *Proceedings of the Asiagraph in Tokyo*, pp. 1–6, Tokyo, Japan, 2007.

[3] H. Iwata, "Full-surround image display technologies," *International Journal of Computer Vision*, vol. 58, no. 3, pp. 227–235, 2004.

[4] Google Maps with Street View, http://maps.google.com/intl/en/help/maps/streetview/.

[5] Immersive Media, http://www.immersivemedia.com/demos/index.php.

[6] M. Hamanaka and S. Lee, "Sound scope headphones: controlling an audio mixer through natu-ral movement," in *Proceedings of the International Computer Music Conference*, pp. 155–158, New Orleans, La, USA, 2006.

[7] M. Goto, H. Hashiguchi, T. Nishimura, and R. Oka, "RWC music database: music genre database and musical instrument sound database," in *Proceedings of the 4th International Conference on Music Information Retrieval (ISMIR '03)*, pp. 229–230, October 2003.

[8] Y. Onoe, K. Yamazawa, H. Takemura, and N. Yokoya, "Telepresence by real-time view-dependent image generation from omnidirectional video streams," *Computer Vision and Image Understanding*, vol. 71, no. 2, pp. 154–165, 1998.

[9] Sony Introduces the Worlds First Personal 3D Viewer, http://news.sel.sony.com/en/press_room/consumer/television/release/60813.html.

[10] Xbox 360 + Kinect, http://www.xbox.com/en-US/Kinect.

[11] OpenGL: The Industry's Foundation for High Perfor-mance Graphics, http://www.opengl.org/.

5

Epitomize Your Photos

Peter Vajda,[1] Ivan Ivanov,[1] Jong-Seok Lee,[2] and Touradj Ebrahimi[1]

[1] *Multimedia Signal Processing Group (MMSPG), École Polytechnique Fédérale de Lausanne (EPFL), 1015 Lausanne, Switzerland*
[2] *School of Integrated Technology, Yonsei University, Incheon 406-840, Republic of Korea*

Correspondence should be addressed to Peter Vajda, peter.vajda@epfl.ch

Academic Editor: Mark Green

With the rapid growth of digital photography, sharing of photos with friends and family has become very popular. When people share their photos, they usually organize them into albums according to events or places. To tell the story of some important events in one's life, it is desirable to have an efficient summarization tool which can help people to receive a quick overview of an album containing large number of photos. In this paper, we present and analyze an approach for photo album summarization through a novel social game "Epitome" as a Facebook application. This social game can collect research data, and, at the same time, it provides a collage or a cover photo of the user's photo album, while the user enjoys playing the game. The proof of concept of the proposed method is demonstrated through a set of experiments on several photo albums. As a benchmark comparison to this game, we perform automatic visual analysis considering several state-of-the-art features. We also evaluate the usability of the game by making use of a questionnaire on several subjects who played the "Epitome" game. Furthermore, we address privacy issues concerning shared photos in Facebook applications.

1. Introduction

Rapid growth of digital photography in recent years has increased the size of personal photo collections. People use their digital cameras or mobile phones equipped with cameras to take photos. Besides storing them on computer hard drives, they often share their digital photos with friends, family, and colleagues through social networks. Facebook (http://www.facebook.com/), Flickr (http://www.flickr.com/), and Picasa (http://picasa.google.com/) are examples of such photo sharing web sites. Some people also print their photos on post cards, calendars, or photo books, often to give them as presents or to create physical souvenirs.

Photos are often organized into albums (collections) based on places, events or dates, and people. Consumers tend to take several photos from one scene, hoping that one of them will be outstanding, and this leads to large number of similar photos. Therefore, it can be very time-consuming to go through all photos in one of these albums. Summarization is an effective way to provide a quick overview of a set of photos. In this paper, album summarization is defined as selecting a set of photos from a larger collection which best represents the visual information of the entire collection.

Selected photos can be used to create a collage of a given album or a cover for an album or to be included in a photo book. However, as already mentioned, manual photo album summarization can be very time-consuming.

Which photos are the most suitable to summarize a photo album? Creation of a photo summary is a very subjective task. There are different criteria upon which a human user would rate digital photos. The color, composition, content, lighting, and sharpness of a photo, all contribute to viewer's response to that photo (http://comminfo.rutgers.edu/conferences/mmchallenge/2010/02/10/hp-challenge-2010/). These characteristics are used extensively by professionals on web sites, magazine covers, and printed advertisements to draw attention, communicate a message, and leave a lasting emotional impression. There is a gap between what people think the summary should look like and what we get with an automatic summarization. For example, funny photos are usually chosen within summarized photos, and they are not easy to detect using computer vision techniques. Therefore, including photos containing humans, such as one's family or friends, in the process of album summarization is needed.

Besides spending a lot of time sharing and consuming content in online social networks, people also use online applications, especially social games. Players pour huge amounts of time and efforts into games. For example, a recent survey [1] revealed that most players (95%) play social games several times a week, with 64% playing daily. The average game session lasts more than half an hour (i.e., how long 61% play), while 10% may play more than three hours at a time. Work by Von Ahn and Dabbish [2] showed the tremendous power that networks of people possess to solve problems while playing social games. Therefore, the time and effort in playing a game can be utilized to address some issues in image processing community, that is, users entertain themselves while playing an enjoyable game, with the added side effect that they are doing useful work in the process, for example, summarizing one's photo album. This is one of our motivations to develop a novel approach for photo album summarization through gaming.

In this paper, we present and evaluate an approach for photo album summarization through a novel social game "Epitome," which was previously introduced in [3]. It has been implemented as a Facebook application and as an application for mobile phones on the Android OS platform. The main idea of this approach is to show a reduced set of photos from a Facebook album, ask users to play the game, and then integrate results of several users in order to produce a summarization for the whole album. There are two games involved in this approach: "Select the Best!" and "Split it!." In the first game, a user has to select the better of two photos randomly selected from one Facebook album. The goal of the second game is to mimic separation of one album into different events or scenes, by selecting a pair of photos that are more different. The results achieved in the two games are compared with those of other users, and every user receives a score based on his/her performance. A sequence of photos which gets the largest number of users' votes represents a summarization sequence of the album. The proof of concept of the proposed method is demonstrated through a set of experiments on several photo albums. We compare results obtained by this game with an automatic image selection, by making use of visual and temporal features. Furthermore, the usability of the game is evaluated by making use of a questionnaire (a user study) on several subjects who played the "Epitome" game. We also address privacy issues concerning shared photos in Facebook applications.

The paper is organized as follows. We introduce related work in Section 2. The proposed social game application is presented in Section 3. Evaluation methodologies and results are discussed in Section 4. Finally, Section 5 concludes the paper with a summary and some perspectives for future study.

2. Related Work

The proposed game is related to different research fields including visual analysis, automatic photo album summarization, and gaming. Therefore, the goal of this section is to review the most relevant work in these fields.

2.1. Automatic Photo Album Summarization. State-of-the-art techniques for automatic photo album summarization are based on time-separated events, spatial information using GPS coordinates, and content-based image similarities. Harada et al. [4] developed an interface for automatic personal photo structuring, considering the time difference between two consecutive photos in order to determine different events. Naaman et al. [5] developed a system which automatically organizes digital photographs considering their geographic location or event-based description extracted from user tags. For photo collection clustering, combination of spatial, temporal, and content-based similarity is then used. This clustering can be used for photo navigation for different categories, such as elevation, season, time of the day, location, weather status, temperature, and time zone. Once photos are clustered, different page layouts are shown. Atkins [6] proposed a photo collection page layout generation method, considering hierarchical partition of the page, which provides explicit control over the aspect ratios and relative areas of photos. This approach attempts to maximize page coverage without having overlapping photos. Geigel and Loui [7] emphasized the aesthetic side of a page layout for image collections. They used a genetic algorithm to optimize aspects such as balance and symmetry for a good placement of images in the personalized album pages. In general, however, automatic summarization has its limitations. There is usually a gap between what people think the summary should look like and what automatic summarization produces. A promising solution to narrow the gap is to incorporate human knowledge and preference into the summarization process.

Regarding content-based image similarity, various visual features have been used in automatic photo album summarization. Bag of Words (BoW) model is based on the histogram of local features [8]. Zhang et al. [9] presented a comparative study on the performance of different local features on texture and object recognition tasks based on global histogram of features. BoW method gives a robust, simple, and efficient solution for measuring image similarity without considering the spatial information in images. The BoW mostly uses local feature descriptors, and the Scale Invariant Feature Transform (SIFT) [10] is based on an approximation of the human visual perception. A faster version of the SIFT descriptor with comparable accuracy, called Speeded Up Robust Features (SURF), is proposed in [11]. Another popular feature is the Histogram of Oriented Gradient (HOG) [12]. It is a grid-based histogram on gradient information of the image. This feature was first proposed for human detection, while the recent literature also considers it for general image retrieval. In this paper we use the feature called "tiny", which is a simple 32×32 color image, resized from the original image [13]. It was motivated by psychophysical results showing the remarkable tolerance of the human visual system to degradations in image resolution.

2.2. Crowdsourcing through Games. Ames and Naaman [14] showed that providing incentives to users in form of entertainment or rewards, for example, games, can motivate them to tag photos in online and mobile environments.

Gaming also provides a new way of motivating people by making the subjective data acquisition interesting and enjoyable. The most famous examples of these kind of games are the ESP game and the Peekaboom, developed for collecting information about image content. In the *ESP game* [2], two players, who are not allowed to communicate with each other, are asked to enter a textual label which describes a shown image. The task of each user is to enter the same word as his/her partner in the shortest possible time. In the *Peekaboom* game [15], one player is given a word related to the shown image, and the aim is to communicate that word to the other player by revealing portions of the image, while the second player sees an empty black space in the beginning. This idea served as a basis for several other games [16], such as video tagging, music description and tagging, tag description, object segmentation, visual preference, and image similarities. Foldit [17] is a game that presents simplified three-dimensional protein chains to players and provides a score according to the predicted quality of the folding done by the player. All actions by the player are performed in a three-dimensional virtual world. It requires training to solve complex open protein puzzles which in turn requires a lot of commitment by the players.

Following the presented state-of-the-art techniques, a game-based approach for photo album summarization called "Epitome" was developed first in [3], which provides a collage or a cover photo of the user's photo album, while, at the same time, the user enjoys playing a game. It can also collect research data. In this way, both users and research community can benefit. In this paper, we present an improved version of the game and evaluate it. We compare results obtained by this game with an automatic image selection, by making use of visual and temporal features. Furthermore, the usability of the game is evaluated by making use of a questionnaire (a user study) on several subjects who played the "Epitome" game. We also address privacy issues concerning shared photos in Facebook applications.

3. Algorithms

In this section two algorithms for photo album summarization are described. First, the proposed "Epitome" game is described which takes advantage of many casual gamers to solve the complex problem of album summarization. Then, an automatic visual algorithm is presented as a comparison benchmark to the task.

3.1. Social Game "Epitome". A social game, "Epitome," provides an intuitive and enjoyable user interface as a Facebook application, as shown in Figure 1. The main purpose of the game is to create photo collages for Facebook photo albums considering the feedback of the owners' Facebook friends.

The scenario of the game is as follows. A Facebook user, denoted as a player in this paper, installs the game in his/her Facebook applications page and allows access to his/her photo gallery, as shown in Figure 9(a). Then, the player can select between two games. In the first game, called "Select the Best!," two random photos are shown to the player from one of his/her friends' photo albums chosen randomly and he/she

has to choose a better photo, which the player likes more. If the player chooses the photo which is the most frequently selected, then the player's score increases. The second game is called "Split it!." In this game, two pairs of consecutive photos are shown, where the player should select a photo pair which is more different. The results of the two games by many players are combined to produce the summarization of a photo album. In this way, the summarization is conducted based on the feedback of the album owner's friends. The game has appealing look using different visual and audio effects, as shown in Figure 1.

In order to perform summarization using players' inputs, the application calculates three different values: *Importance*, *Segmentation*, and *UserScore*.

Importance value is determined in the "Select the Best!" game for each photo album separately. Two randomly chosen photos are shown to the user and he/she selects the better one in his/her opinion. A feature vector $Selected_n^{best}$, $n \in [1, \ldots, N]$, is calculated for each player, n among N players, as follows:

$$Selected_n^{best}[i] = \delta_{i,s},$$
$$Appeared_n^{best}[i] = \delta_{i,j} + \delta_{i,s},$$
$$\delta_{i,j} = \begin{cases} 1, & \text{if } i = j, \\ 0, & \text{if } i \neq j, \end{cases} \tag{1}$$

where $i, j, s \in [1, \ldots, M]$, M is the size of a particular Facebook album, j, s are indices of the two photos shown to the player, and s is index of the selected photo. The vector $Appeared_n^{best}$ of dimension M stores the frequency of all photos that appear in the game. At the end, we perform normalization on vector $Selected_n^{best}$ by element-wise division in order to obtain *Importance*:

$$Importance[i] = \frac{\sum_n Selected_n^{best}[i]}{\sum_n Appeared_n^{best}[i]}, \tag{2}$$

which is an M-dimensional vector showing the distribution of the most representative photos within one Facebook album.

Segmentation vector is calculated in the "Split it!" game for each photo album separately in an analogous way to that for *Importance*. Two pairs of consecutive photos are chosen randomly from the album and the player selects the more different pair of photos. A feature vector $Selected_n^{segm}$, $n \in [1, \ldots, N]$, is calculated for each player, n among N players, as follows:

$$Selected_n^{segm}[i] = \delta_{i,s},$$
$$Appeared_n^{segm}[i] = \delta_{i,j} + \delta_{i,s}, \tag{3}$$

where $i, j, s \in [1, \ldots, M - 1]$, M is the size of a particular Facebook album, $j, j + 1$ and $s, s + 1$ are indices of the the photo pairs, shown to the player, and $s, s + 1$ are indices of selected photo pair. The vector $Appeared_n^{segm}$ of dimension M stores the frequency of all photos that appear in the game. At

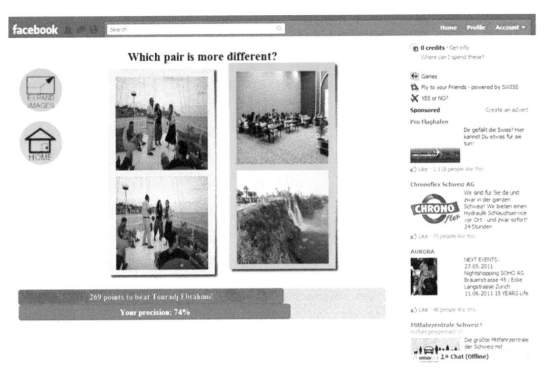

FIGURE 1: Screenshot from the Epitome game.

the end, we perform normalization on vector $Selected_n^{segm}$ by element-wise division in order to obtain $Segmentation$:

$$Segmentation[i] = \frac{\sum_n Selected_n^{segm}[i]}{\sum_n Appeared_n^{segm}[i]}, \qquad (4)$$

which is an M-dimensional vector showing the frequency with which each photo in one Facebook album is selected as a starting photo in a new segment.

Finally, vectors $Importance$ and $Segmentation$ are used to automatically select L most representative photos within one Facebook photo album, as shown in Figure 2. In this game L was arbitrarily set to five. First, $L - 1$ maximum values from the vector $Segmentation$ of the album are determined in order to segment the album into L most probable segments. For each of these segments, a photo with the highest score in the vector $Importance$ is chosen. These L photos represent a collage of the album, which is shown to the owner of the album if he/she reaches a certain level of $UserScore$.

$UserScore$ value is defined to motivate players to play this game frequently. For example, in the "Select the Best!" game, the player increases his/her own $UserScore$ if he/she selects the photo which has the higher or equal $Importance$ value among two photos. The same approach is used in the "Split it!" game, where the player increases his/her $UserScore$ if he/she selects the separation place where $Segmentation$ value is the highest among two separation places. Initially $UserScore$ is set to zero. $UserScore$ values for all players are sorted to show ranking of players in the "Epitome" game.

3.2. Automatic Photo Album Summarization. Automatic photo album summarization is performed considering different visual and temporal features. After extracting these

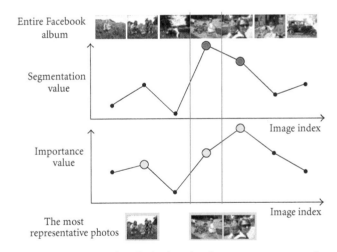

FIGURE 2: An example of selecting the three most representative photos within one Facebook album through the "Epitome" game.

features, the album is segmented into five parts by calculating the four highest Euclidean distances of the consecutive photos features. For each image in a particular segment, we calculate the sum of the Euclidean distances between that feature of the photo and the rest of the image features in the segment. The image with the lowest sum is then selected as the most representative photo in that segment.

Different features can be used for segmentation and to select the most representative photo in the segments. We considered the following features: Bag of Words (BoW) method based on Speeded Up Robust Features (SURF), Histogram of Oriented Gradient (HOG), HSV (Hue, Saturation,

Value) color histogram, "tiny" features, and time stamp, as described below.

Bag of Words model in computer vision was derived from BoW model in natural language processing (NLP) [8]. A similar method in computer vision documents represents images or objects, and visual clusters of local features are considered as a word. In our case, SURF features were used as local features [11]. BoW is a vector which represents the histogram of visual features. Therefore, this method does not consider spatial information or order of visual features. 1000 feature clusters were calculated by a hierarchical k-means algorithm. Each image is represented by 1000 normalized values.

Histogram of Oriented Gradients [18] calculates the histogram of gradients in the region around one keypoint. It is evaluated on a dense grid of uniformly spaced cells and uses overlapping local contrast normalization for improved accuracy. Using gradient information for feature description is very robust to different illumination conditions. The dimensions of the HOG features are around 1000.

Color histogram descriptor is extracted from photos in the HSV domain. Color descriptors often fail in image retrieval in different lighting conditions; however, in our case photos from one Facebook album are compared and assumed to have similar lighting conditions. The dimensions of the HSV color features are around 1000.

Tiny feature is used as baseline representing scaled 32×32 grayscale tiny images.

Time stamp is extracted from EXIF for further analysis. It corresponds to the time order by which photos were uploaded to Facebook.

4. Evaluation and Results

Evaluation of the "Epitome" game can be performed in two ways: performance and usability of the game.

4.1. Performance Evaluation. The performance of summarizing albums with the "Epitome" game is evaluated with respect to the ground truth given by humans.

The dataset of photos used for performance evaluation is the official dataset from "HP Challenge 2010: High Impact Visual Communication" at the "Multimedia Grand Challenge 2010" [19]. Some example photos are shown in Figure 3. It consists of six albums, each with 20 photos. These albums cover photos that are usually taken during a vacation, describing a variety of topics: photos depicting different landmarks and famous sightseeing places, photos with parents and kids, and photos of cars, flowers, and sea animals. Figure 7 provides example photos within one of the albums.

We first constructed a ground truth by asking different people to subjectively perform summarization and then tested our algorithm against the ground truth data. We recruited 63 participants, among whom 61% were males and 39% were females, aged 18–65 (average age was 31), with different backgrounds and cultural differences. In the collection of the ground truth data, participants were shown 20 photos belonging to the same album. The task of the

participants was to select the five most representative photos of the whole album, while looking at all photos of that album.

For simplicity of the explanation on how the designed photo selection tool (social game) was evaluated, let us consider only one album with $M = 20$ photos. First, ground truth data is collected. Every user n among N users is asked to select the five most representative photos. After his/her participation in collecting the ground truth data, the corresponding feature vector $Selected_n$, $n \in [1, \ldots, N]$, is formed as follows:

$$Selected_n[i] = \sum_{k \in [1, \ldots, 5]} \delta_{i,s_k}, \qquad (5)$$

where $i, s_k \in [1, \ldots, M]$ and for all $k, l \in [1, \ldots, 5] : s_k \neq s_l$. s_k for $k \in [1, \ldots, 5]$ are the five indexes of the photos which were chosen as the representative ones. The selected indexes are distinctive. Feature vectors of the users n and m, $n, m \in [1, \ldots, N]$, are then compared to each other, and the score of their matching $S_{n,m}$ is calculated as

$$S_{n,m} = Selected_n \cdot Selected_m^T. \qquad (6)$$

In other words, the higher the number of identical photos that are chosen by two users, the better the score of the match between them. Note that the maximum score of the match is 5. Finally, to each user n, $n \in [1, \ldots, N]$, a value $Performance_n$ is assigned as

$$Performance_n = \sum_{i=1}^{N} S_{n,i}. \qquad (7)$$

The maximum value in the vector $Performance$ shows the best performing participant who has the highest number of selected photos which are matched with all other users. The maximum possible value of the performance is $5 \times N$, which in our case becomes 315. These results are considered as the ground truth data and compared with the results obtained from the games and from the automatic album summarization algorithms, in order to prove the concept of the approach. All computations are repeated in a same way for all albums.

Then, the participants are asked to play our game with the selected dataset. The vectors $Importance$ and $Segmentation$ of dimension M are determined for each album, which are described in Section 3.1. These values are used to automatically select the $L = 5$ most representative photos within each album in the dataset. These L photos are then represented as a choice of the proposed method. Then, the complete procedure of measuring similarity between the choice of the proposed method and all other users is repeated and the final scores are computed according to (6) and (7).

Furthermore, the performance of this game is compared to the performance of an automatic image selection which considers different visual and time features described in Section 3.2. We calculated the performance of 20 different feature pairs, considering five features for segmentation and four features for choosing the representative images, as shown in Figure 4. The result shows that the best

FIGURE 3: Some example photos for each of six albums. Photos in each row belong to the same album. The albums cover a large variety of objects and scenes usually taken during a vacation.

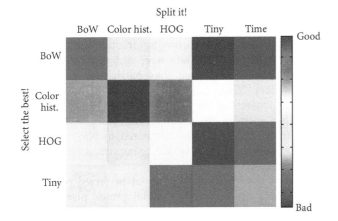

FIGURE 4: Comparison between different visual and time features. The best performance is achieved with "color histogram" feature for both "Split it!" and "Select the best!" tasks. Dark red color indicates the best (*Performance* ≈ 100) and dark blue color indicates the worst performing algorithm (*Performance* ≈ 70). For example, using "time" feature for segmenting an album and "BoW" feature for selecting the most representative images gives poor results on evaluation.

performance (around 100) is achieved by the pair of "color histogram" features for album segmentation and best photo selection in the segment. In the following the performance of automatic visual analysis, represented by color histogram, is compared with the "Epitome" game.

Figure 5 shows the distribution of the participants' performance, including the choice of the proposed method and the automatic visual analysis. All performances are sorted in a descending order. As one can see, the performance of the proposed method is better than the automatic visual analysis since it is closer to the best performance of users for ground truth generation. On average, this approach achieves 80% of the performance of the best user for each album, which proves the concept of the game. It also outperforms the automatic visual analysis, which can achieve performance of 64%. For albums three and five, this value is even higher, that is, about 95%. The most representative photos for one of the albums selected by the proposed method are shown in Figure 7. Figure 6 shows the comparison of performance in summarizing photo albums performed by the "Epitome" game, automatic photo selection using color histogram, and users who participated in creating the ground truth data.

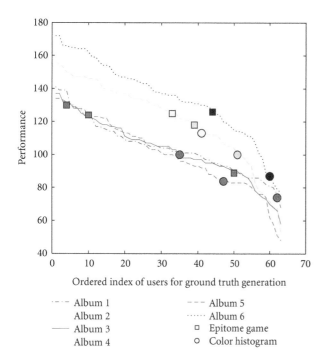

FIGURE 5: The distribution of the participants' performance. The results of the "Epitome" game are shown with square markers and the results of automatic visual analysis with circle marker. Different colors of the markers correspond to different albums.

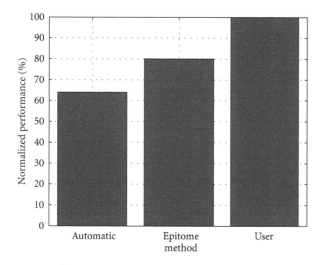

FIGURE 6: The comparison of normalized performance in summarizing photo albums performed by the "Epitome" game, automatic photo selection using color histogram, and users who participated in creating the ground truth data.

4.2. Usability Evaluation. The usability of the "Epitome" game is evaluated through a user study. We asked participants (users) to play the game with different Facebook photo albums and to provide us with their feedback on the game in the form of a questionnaire.

We recruited 40 participants, aged 23–46 (average age was 28), with different cultural backgrounds. First, all participants were introduced to the "Epitome" game by showing

them basic rules on how to play the game. Then, all participants spent sufficient time to play the game. After a participant played with the "Epitome" game with different Facebook photo albums, a questionnaire was used to obtain the feedback from the participant. The questionnaire consists of three groups of questions:

(i) general questions about motivation to play the game and enjoyment;

(ii) questions to assess different platforms for playing the game (mobile, Facebook, or simple web page), for example, satisfaction with visual presentation for each of them;

(iii) questions about privacy issues regarding showing one's photos to his/her friends, friends of friends, and everybody or nobody.

In this study, we used discrete rating scales with adjective description of each level. Depending on the question, participants had to choose one of the answers or to rank answers according to their preferences. For each of the questions we calculated mean of the participants responses.

In this paper, we do not describe the whole questionnaire and results, but we rather discuss some of the interesting outcomes from our study. All questions are listed in the appendix. The questionnaire with choices is publicly available (http://mmspg.epfl.ch/files/content/sites/mmspl/files/shared/questionnaire_epitome.pdf).

4.2.1. Motivation to Play the Game. Questions (1)–(6), (9)–(14), and (21) listed in the appendix belong to questions about motivation to play the game. Results showed that 70% of the players are very satisfied with the game. We further asked players of the "Epitome" game what *motivated* them most to play the game. Results are shown in Figure 8. Players enjoyed the most to watch their Facebook friends' photos, which was even more preferred than the original goal of the game, that is, getting their own albums summarized. We observed another interesting value of the game that people like the idea of watching (browsing) friends' photos through the "Epitome" game. Players were not motivated to play "Epitome" by the fact that they participate in collecting research data. This shows that fun and enjoyment are important aspects of the game that should be considered. In another question about motivation, players prefer more to see their friends' photos compared to photos of some unknown people. This promotes the importance of the social part of the game.

One of the questions was about preferred patterns of playing the game. Like other casual games, players would like to play our game several times a month, and around five minutes every time.

4.2.2. Platform. An important question we discuss here is about *different platforms* for playing the "Epitome" game (questions (7) and (8) listed in the appendix), such as a simple web page, a mobile phone, and a Facebook application. Average ranks for these platforms are 2.3, 2.2, and 1.5, respectively, which shows that players prefer Facebook

FIGURE 7: Photos from album 3. The most representative photos selected by the proposed method are marked with green bounding box, while the red bounding box denotes photos selected by making use of color histogram.

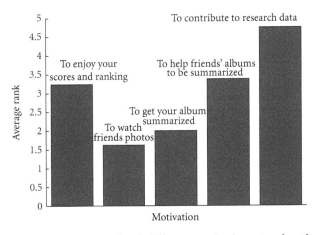

FIGURE 8: Average rank of different motivations to play the "Epitome" game. Lower average ranks are better.

the most. Surprisingly, players have similar preferences for mobile phone application and simple web page. One of the reasons for this could be that the mobile phone had limited bandwidth in wireless connection and the game was faltering while loading some images from Facebook.

4.2.3. Privacy Issues. We also addressed *Facebook permission issues.* To play the third party applications, like the "Epitome," users should accept an agreement with an application on accessing users' data stored in Facebook. But, we note that users' privacy settings in Facebook are different from what the third party application actually access. If the user allows the third party applications to access his/her photos, they get right to distribute and modify (resize, rotate, change in color perception, etc.) photos of the user. Before using this application for the first time, Facebook shows to the player a permission page informing him/her what kind of data will

be retrieved from his/her Facebook account if he/she allows access to the application, as shown in Figure 9(a). People are usually not concerned about this issue and easily allow access to data by the application. In order to address the privacy issue regarding this process of allowing access to the data, we created new visually intuitive permission pages, as shown in Figure 9(b)–9(d).

In our experiments, users were asked whether they allow access to their data using the default Facebook permission page either on the mobile phone or in Facebook, and were separately asked if they would allow access to any of the three new permission pages. We measured how many players allow the "Epitome" game to access photos they have uploaded, photos they have been tagged in, and photos their friends have uploaded. Results are depicted in Figure 10. Clearly, the players understand the risk better by viewing our illustrative permission pages than the default Facebook permission page, and more than 90% of the players did not allow the application to retrieve their photos that can be further modified or distributed within "Epitome." This shows that the default Facebook permission page is neither sufficiently intuitive nor informative.

The users do not have sufficient control over details about permission in Facebook applications. From the questions related to permission settings of shared photos (questions (15)–(20) listed in the appendix), we conclude that players would not like to give more permissions to the application compared to the permission they already set for their photos in Facebook. For example, 86% of the users would like to share their private photos through this application only with their friends.

4.3. Statistics of the Game. The "Epitome" game was published on Facebook in June 2011, and during two months, 49 users played it 5870 times on a dataset of 21780 photos. Distribution of players' score is shown in Figure 11. A few

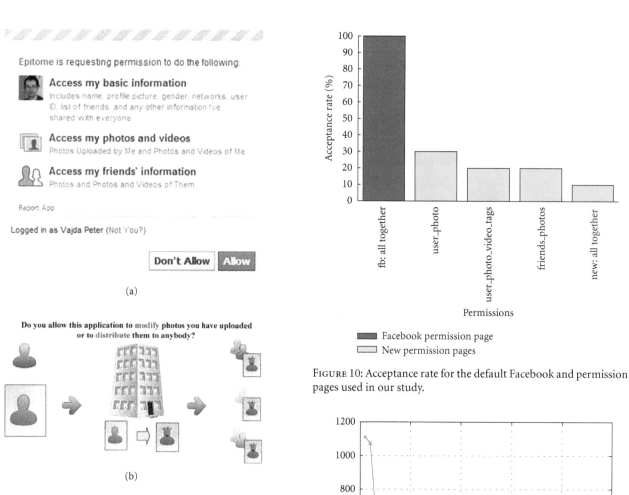

Epitome is requesting permission to do the following:

Access my basic information
Includes name, profile picture, gender, networks, user ID, list of friends, and any other information I've shared with everyone

Access my photos and videos
Photos Uploaded by Me and Photos and Videos of Me

Access my friends' information
Photos and Photos and Videos of Them

Report App

Logged in as Vajda Peter (Not You?)

Don't Allow   Allow

(a)

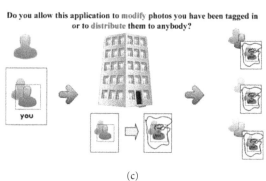

Do you allow this application to modify photos you have uploaded or to distribute them to anybody?

(b)

Do you allow this application to modify photos you have been tagged in or to distribute them to anybody?

you

(c)

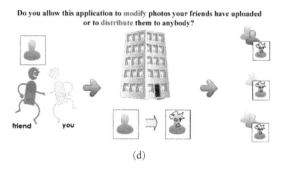

Do you allow this application to modify photos your friends have uploaded or to distribute them to anybody?

friend   you

(d)

FIGURE 9: Different permission pages used in our study: (a) default Facebook permission page, (b) *user_photos* permission page, (c) *user_photo_video_tags* permission page, and (d) *friends_photos* permission page.

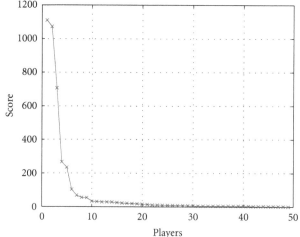

Acceptance rate (%)

Permissions

■ Facebook permission page
□ New permission pages

FIGURE 10: Acceptance rate for the default Facebook and permission pages used in our study.

FIGURE 11: The distribution of players' score in the "Epitome" game. Scores are sorted in descending order.

players played the game frequently and thus had higher scores than the others. Many new users started recently playing this game and therefore they still have low scores. Figure 12 shows the distribution of the photos' score, that is, the number of votes per appearance of each photo. Again, since the "Epitome" game was recently published online, there are much more photos available, especially from new users, than those photos users played with in the game, and therefore many photos are not shown yet to users. This is the reason for many extreme values (score of zero and one) in Figure 12. Figure 13 shows the number of pictures changed in collages over time. It can be concluded from this figure that it converges.

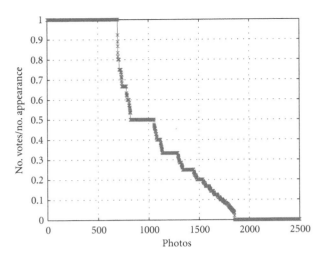

FIGURE 12: The distribution of photos' scores in the "Epitome" game, that is, the number of votes per appearance of each photo. Scores are sorted in descending order. The rest of the photos did not yet appeared or nobody voted for them.

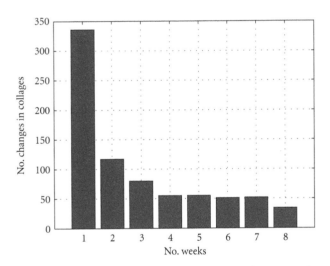

FIGURE 13: The number of photos changed in collages over time since the "Epitome" game was launched.

4.4. Advantages and Disadvantages. In summary, the "Epitome" game has the following advantages.

(1) Performance of the game-based album summarization is better than using only computer vision approaches, which was shown in [20].

(2) People like to watch their friends' photos through this game, which also encourages social interaction between them.

(3) The game itself is interesting and people can have fun through the game.

However, a disadvantage is the processing time for generating fine album summarization, as shown in [20].

5. Conclusion

In this paper, we described and analyzed a social game, "Epitome," for photo album summarization on Facebook. The game is a social application to enjoy photos of one's Facebook friends, while contributing to summarization of their photo albums and collecting research data. The proof of concept of the game was demonstrated and validated through a set of experiments on several photo albums. The results of the experiments showed that the summarization game achieves 80% of the best performance of different participants and significantly outperforms automatic visual summarization methods (64%). The usability of this game was validated by making use of a questionnaire. The results of our user study showed that the main motivation for a player of the game is to watch his/her friends' photos and obtain his/her album summarization. Finally, a default Facebook permission page was analyzed and considered as not sufficiently intuitive nor informative.

As a future study, we will make the game more attractive for users and also consider to include in this approach more sophisticated visual analysis. We also plan to improve the game by reducing the bandwidth which is necessary to load all images.

Appendix

The usability of the "Epitome" game is evaluated by making use of a questionnaire (a user study) on several subjects who played the game. The questionnaire consists of three groups of questions: (1) general questions about motivation to play the game and enjoyment, (2) questions to assess different platforms for playing the game, and (3) questions about privacy issues regarding showing one's photos to his/her friends, friends of friends, and everybody or nobody. Questions are listed in the following.

(1) Are you satisfied with the Epitome game? If not completely satisfied, what is the main reason for that?

(2) Please rank the motivations to play the Epitome game according to your preferences in order to make it more enjoyable?

(3) Please rank the improvements of the Epitome game according to your preferences in order to make it more enjoyable?

(4) How often would you play the Epitome game?

(5) How long would you play the Epitome game at once?

(6) Would you prefer to play only one integrated game?

(7) Please rank three platforms for playing the Epitome game according to your preferences?

(8) How do you like the Mobile interface? How do you like the Facebook interface?

(9) Would you enjoy the Epitome game more if you play with less than nine images? If yes, how many images should be displayed?

(10) How much do you prefer to watch your friends' photos compared to the photos of unknown people?

(11) Is it good to show your rank and compare it with your friends' ranks for the enjoyment of Epitome?

(12) Is it good to have your summarization sequence as a result of the Epitome game?

(13) How many images in album summarization sequence of photos would you prefer?

(14) There are two statements: 1st statement—to have perfectly summarized Facebook album, but waiting for it long time period; 2nd statement—to have preliminarily summarized Facebook album after a short time. Which of these statements is more important for you?

(15) To whom would you allow Epitome to show your private photos which are not shared even with your friends in order to receive a good summarization of your Facebook albums?

(16) To whom would you allow Epitome to show your private photos which are shared just with your friends in order to receive a good summarization of your Facebook albums?

(17) To whom would you allow Epitome to show your private photos which were shared with friends of friends in order to receive a good summarization of your Facebook albums?

(18) To whom would you allow Epitome to show photos in which you were tagged in order to receive a good summarization of your Facebook albums?

(19) To whom would you allow Epitome to show photos of your friends in order to receive a good summarization of your Facebook albums?

(20) Do you want to play with photos of your friends even if they do not play Epitome?

(21) Any suggestions to improve the game?

Acknowledgments

This work was supported by the Swiss National Foundation for Scientific Research in the framework of NCCR Interactive Multimodal Information Management (IM2) and the Swiss National Science Foundation Grant "Multimedia Security" (no. 200020-113709), partially supported by the European Network of Excellence PetaMedia (FP7/2007-2011).

References

[1] "Social games: news and survey findings," http://content.usatoday.com/communities/gamehunters/post/2010/02/social-games-news-and-survey-findings/1.

[2] L. Von Ahn and L. Dabbish, "Labeling images with a computer game," in *the Conference on Human Factors in Computing Systems (CHI '04)*, pp. 319–326, April 2004.

[3] I. Ivanov, P. Vajda, J. S. Lee, and T. Ebrahimi, "Epitome—a social game for photo album summarization," in *the 1st ACM Workshop on Connected Multimedia (CMM '10)*, pp. 33–38, October 2010.

[4] S. Harada, M. Naaman, Y. J. Song, Q. Wang, and A. Paepcke, "Lost in memories: interacting with photo collections on PDAs," in *Proceedings of the 4th ACM/IEEE Joint Conference on Digital Libraries (JCDL '04)*, pp. 325–333, June 2004.

[5] M. Naaman, Y. J. Song, A. Paepcke, and H. Garcia-Molina, "Automatic organization for digital photographs with geographic coordinates," in *Proceedings of the 4th ACM/IEEE Joint Conference on Digital Libraries (JCDL '04)*, pp. 53–62, June 2004.

[6] C. B. Atkins, "Adaptive photo collection page layout," in *the International Conference on Image Processing (ICIP '04)*, pp. 2897–2900, October 2004.

[7] J. Geigel and A. Loui, "Using genetic algorithms for album page layouts," *IEEE Multimedia*, vol. 10, no. 4, pp. 16–27, 2003.

[8] F. F. Li and P. Perona, "A bayesian hierarchical model for learning natural scene categories," in *IEEE Computer Society Conference on Computer Vision and Pattern Recognition (CVPR '05)*, pp. 524–531, June 2005.

[9] J. Zhang, M. Marszałek, S. Lazebnik, and C. Schmid, "Local features and kernels for classification of texture and object categories: a comprehensive study," *International Journal of Computer Vision*, vol. 73, no. 2, pp. 213–238, 2007.

[10] D. G. Lowe, "Distinctive image features from scale-invariant keypoints," *International Journal of Computer Vision*, vol. 60, no. 2, pp. 91–110, 2004.

[11] H. Bay, T. Tuytelaars, and L. Van Gool, "Surf: Speededup robust features," in *Proceedings of the 9th European Conference on Computer Vision*, pp. 404–417, 2006.

[12] P. Felzenszwalb, D. McAllester, and D. Ramanan, "A discriminatively trained, multiscale, deformable part model," in *the 26th IEEE Conference on Computer Vision and Pattern Recognition (CVPR '08)*, June 2008.

[13] A. Torralba, R. Fergus, and W. T. Freeman, "80 million tiny images: a large data set for nonparametric object and scene recognition," *IEEE Transactions on Pattern Analysis and Machine Intelligence*, vol. 30, no. 11, pp. 1958–1970, 2008.

[14] M. Ames and M. Naaman, "Why we tag: motivations for annotation in mobile and online media," in *the 25th SIGCHI Conference on Human Factors in Computing Systems (CHI '07)*, pp. 971–980, May 2007.

[15] L. Von Ahn, R. Liu, and M. Blum, "Peekaboom: a game for locating objects in linages," in *the Conference on Human Factors in Computing Systems (CHI '06)*, pp. 55–64, April 2006.

[16] E. Law and L. von Ahn, "Input-agreement: a new mechanism for collecting data using human computation games," in *the Conference on Human Factors in Computing Systems (CHI '09)*, pp. 1197–1206, 2009.

[17] F. Khatib, F. Dimaio, S. Cooper et al., "Crystal structure of a monomeric retroviral protease solved by protein folding game players," *Nature Structural and Molecular Biology*, vol. 18, no. 10, pp. 1175–1177, 2010.

[18] N. Dalal and B. Triggs, "Histograms of oriented gradients for human detection," in *IEEE Computer Society Conference on Computer Vision and Pattern Recognition (CVPR '05)*, pp. 886–893, June 2005.

[19] "HP Challenge 2010 Dataset: High Impact Visual Communication," http://comminfo.rutgers.edu/conferences/mmchallenge/2010/02/10/hp-challenge-2010.

[20] P. Vajda, I. Ivanov, L. Goldmann, and T. Ebrahimi, "Social game epitome versus automatic visual analysis," in *Proceedings of IEEE International Conference on Multimedia and Expo*, July 2011.

6

Enhancing a Commercial Game Engine to Support Research on Route Realism for Synthetic Human Characters

Gregg T. Hanold[1] and Mikel D. Petty[2]

[1] *Oracle National Security Group, Reston, VA 20190, USA*
[2] *Center for Modeling, Simulation, and Analysis, University of Alabama in Huntsville, Huntsville, AL 35899, USA*

Correspondence should be addressed to Mikel D. Petty, pettym@uah.edu

Academic Editor: Kok Wai Wong

Generating routes for entities in virtual environments, such as simulated vehicles or synthetic human characters, is a long-standing problem, and route planning algorithms have been developed and studied for some time. Existing route planning algorithms, including the widely used A* algorithm, are generally intended to achieve optimality in some metric, such as minimum length or minimum time. Comparatively little attention has been given to route realism, defined as the similarity of the algorithm-generated route to the route followed by real humans in the same terrain with the same constraints and goals. Commercial game engines have seen increasing use as a context for research. To study route realism in a game engine, two developments were needed: a quantitative metric for measuring route realism and a game engine able to capture route data needed to compute the realism metric. Enhancements for recording route data for both synthetic characters and human players were implemented within the Unreal Tournament 2004 game engine. A methodology for assessing the realism of routes and other behaviors using a quantitative metric was developed. The enhanced Unreal Tournament 2004 game engine and the realism assessment methodology were tested by capturing data required to calculate a metric of route realism.

1. Introduction

Entities in virtual environments, such as simulated vehicles or synthetic humans, move from place to place in the virtual environment. Algorithms to automatically generate those routes have been developed and studied for some time. The A* graph search algorithm, because of its simplicity and effectiveness, has been applied in a range of simulation environments, including Close Combat Tactical Trainer, Combat XXI, and OneSAF Objective System, and games such as Warcraft and Civilization; some of these applications use variants of the basic A* algorithm [4]. Most route planning algorithms, including A*, are designed to produce or approximate *optimum* routes, where optimality is measured in terms of some application-specific metric; examples include minimum distance for individual humans moving in urban terrain [5], minimum distance for vehicles moving in a road network [6], minimum exposure to threats for combatants moving in a battle area [7], or maximum sensor coverage for

search platforms surveying a target area [8]. In contrast, very little attention has been given to producing *realistic* routes, where realism is defined as the similarity of the generated route to a route that would be followed by a real human in the same terrain with the same constraints (e.g., starting and ending locations and movement capabilities) and goals (e.g., minimizing exposure to threats). The route realism research performed to date has been largely focused on very short routes (e.g., within a single room [9]) or highly specific circumstances (e.g., avenues of approach for large vehicle formations [10]).

Commercial game engines have been quite successful at their primary purpose, which is to provide a framework within which to develop engaging and entertaining virtual environments. As their architectures have matured in terms of software design and become more open to external modification, game engines have seen increasing use as a context for research in human behavior modeling (e.g., [5]). Generating realistic behavior in a game engine-generated virtual

FIGURE 1: Satellite view of the real world McKenna MOUT facility [1].

environment requires, among other things, that the virtual environment replicate those aspects of the real world that affect the behavior to be generated. The game industry has approached this goal with the massively multiplayer online role-playing games such as World of Warcraft and first-person shooter games such as Quake III Arena, Half-Life, and Americas Army. However, validation of the realism of behavior generated for algorithm-controlled characters (hereinafter known as "Bots") in a game engine is still a developing discipline [11]. To date, such validation has largely been limited to face validation by subject matter experts (e.g., see [5, 10]; for more information on face validation, see [12]), due to both limitations in the facilities provided by the game engines to capture validation data and gaps in the quantitative methods available to validate human behavior.

To study route realism for synthetic human characters in the context of a commercial game engine, two developments were needed: a quantitative metric for measuring the realism of a route, and a game engine appropriately enhanced to capture the data about routes executed in the game engine needed to compute that metric [13]. This paper describes those developments. Enhancements for extracting and recording route data (time, location, heading, velocity) for both Bots and human players as they follow routes within the Unreal Tournament game engine are described in Sections 2 and 3. The bot and human data recording through the API during scenario execution required dynamic storage external to the game engine. That data was used as input to a quantitative realism metric for analysis of the routes' realism. A new seven-step methodology for the creation and use of an objective quantitative or statistical metric based on the data captured from a virtual environment and the application of that methodology to develop a metric of route realism is described in Section 4. The methodology was tested and refined through live data collection. The enhancements are specific to the particular game engine used, but suggest what may be required in another game engine. The methodology is applicable to any game engine.

2. Simulation Environment

As previously reported [13, 14], the selection of the simulation or virtual environment to implement the realism metric considered several factors. First, the environment itself must present a realistic representation of the real world with respect to the behavior in question. Second, the API must

allow for the collection, measurement, and storage of game and environmental data during run time without impacting game engine performance. Third, the API must support integration with the game engine physics and artificial intelligence engines. Finally, the virtual environment (map or level) must have an interface to allow route data (or other behavior data) collected from humans executing defined scenarios in the physical environment to be input for statistical comparison.

2.1. Game Engines. Three commercial game engines were considered: Quake III Arena, Half-Life 2, and Unreal Tournament 2004. While Quake III Arena and Half-Life 2 met the criteria, Unreal Tournament 2004 (UT2004) ships with synthetic agents or Bots and provides through the custom scripting language, UnrealScript, both an interface to these bots and an interface through which game developers can modify the host game without access to the complex game engine source code. UnrealScript provides a rich object-oriented interface to the UT2004 game engine or modifications to it such as Ravenshield and Infiltration. Other UT2004-based games, such as America's Army and Vegas, lock or limit the ability to make modifications through UnrealScript. With its object-oriented interface and the availability of an Integrated Development Environment (IDE), UT2004 was selected as the base game engine. Since the initial research and selection of UT2004, Epic Games has released Unreal Tournament 3, which offers significant improvements to game and level design. However, at the time of this writing, the port of the API and IDE was not complete.

2.2. Virtual Environment. An important step in the creation of a virtual environment suitable for the measurement of the realism of behaviors is the creation of the virtual world. The virtual environment should model a real-world location to potentially allow the comparison of algorithm-generated behaviors with those of humans executing similar behaviors in the real world. The UT2004 virtual world developed was modeled after Fort Benning's McKenna Military Operations in Urban Terrain (MOUT) training facility; the real-world McKenna facility is shown in Figure 1, and its UT2004 virtual recreation is shown in Figure 2.

The game engine must provide an algorithm to generate bot behavior of the type to be assessed for realism. For this research, the behavior was route planning and execution; route planning for the bot used the A* algorithm and route execution used the game engine's standard route following process. In UT2004, A* requires only one custom object, to mark the destination. Native to the UT2004 is the UnrealScript language through which custom map objects can be added. The BotDestinationPathNode was added to the available map objects to provide a destination for the A* route calculation; the script to do so is in (Algorithm 1.) The A* algorithm required nodes to be added to the virtual terrain and their edges to be computed. The "Build AI Paths" function in the UnrealEd creates an internal search graph of nodes (pathnodes) and edges (reachspecs), as shown in Figure 3.

FIGURE 2: "Satellite" view of the virtual McKenna MOUT facility [2].

```
// BotDestinationPathNode. Goal Node
class BotDestinationPathNode extends PathNode
    placeable;
```

ALGORITHM 1: Unrealscript pathnode listing.

2.3. Application Programming Interface (API). The first key element to the development of a virtual environment suitable for measuring realism was the existence of an API to both the game engine hosted on a server and the human player and bot clients. As previously noted, UT2004 was one of the first game engines to ship with algorithm-controlled characters, that is, with bots. UT provides a custom scripting language, UnrealScript, through which game developers can modify the host game. In addition to an interface with the UT2004 game Engine, UnrealScript also supports integration with the map editor, UnrealEd, and several integrated development environments. Through the API, we developed an architecture that implements the instrumentation interface required to monitor and record bot and human player execution data from which the realism metric can be calculated.

2.4. Integrated Development Environment. A second key element of virtual environment suitable for measuring realism was the Integrated Development Environment (IDE). Several IDEs can be used with the UT2004 Game Engine. These include Visual Studio (.NET framework with C# and C++), Netbeans (Java), and Eclipse (IDE). For this work, we used the Netbeans IDE. Netbeans was configured with the Pogmut2 plug-in to UT2004 [3] for bot development and data recording, jdbc drivers for database connectivity, and JChart for near-real-time charting. The architecture required to implement the UT2004 simulation environment includes the following software packages: (1) UT2004 and (2) Netbeans (JChart and Pogamut 2 plug-in) and (3) Gamebots 2004 (GB2004) UnrealScript Library and (4) Database with Spatial Libraries.

FIGURE 3: Close up view of UT2004 pathnodes and reachspecs in the virtual McKenna.

3. Architecture and Implementation

Implementing an architecture that supports realistic behavior representation revealed several challenges. The first was to develop an interface that would allow player route data to be collected and recorded without triggering the UT2004 cheat protection code. The second was to develop a mechanism through which route data for humans executing the defined scenarios in the real world could have route data imported into the UT2004 virtual environment for statistical comparison to route data from routes executed in the virtual environment. To solve these challenges, GB2004 and the Pogamut Libraries were modified. By using GB2004 and Pogamut, all data collection was independent of UT2004, thereby avoiding the anticheat triggers.

3.1. Component Overview. The components required to implement an environment suitable for the development of a metric that would measure the realism of bot actions consist of the server node which hosts the UT2004 game engine server, the client node hosting the Unreal client, the IDE node hosting the bot and experiments, and the database node hosting a database with the spatial libraries for data storage and route planning.

GB2004 is an UnrealScript package jointly developed by University of Southern California and Carnegie Mellon University as an interface between the server and the clients that provide an interface to the UT2004 engine. The interface with UT2004 can access sensory information, such as the location and rotation of a player or bot in the game world, messages generated through game play, and UT2004 action commands that control bot behavior.

The interface with the client provides a synchronous and asynchronous messaging interface that allows bot action commands to be issued from client to server and data and game information to be requested and received by the client. Marshall implemented this capability through a higher-level interface, called JavaBot API [15], which handled the specific GB2004 protocol, network socket interface, and client-server messaging. That work demonstrated an environment that supports the development of bot logic using the UT2004 engine.

Expanding on the JavaBot API and extending the GB2004 UnrealScript, Gemrot developed the Pogamut plug-in to the Netbeans IDE. The base Pogamut Architecture, shown in

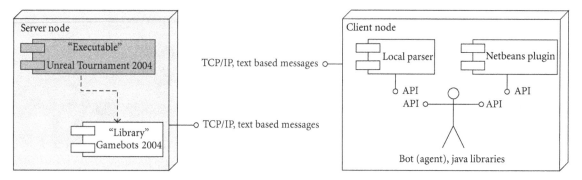

FIGURE 4: Pogamut architecture overview [3].

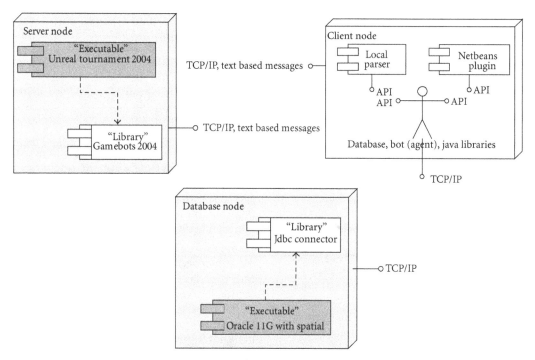

FIGURE 5: Pogamut database component overview.

Figure 4, integrates the UT2004 Server through the GB2004 API with the Client and Netbeans IDE.

The Pogamut architecture consists of four components: (1) GB2004 and (2) Parser and (3) Client and (4) IDE. To support the realism metric, the basic Pogamut architecture was extended with a database component as shown in Figure 5. This added component provided storage and access to recorded data for both bot and human behaviors for use in calculating the realism metric. The database allows for the additional asynchronous and synchronous processing of game information required to control bot actions and offload processing from the UT2004 game engine and Client. In addition to the database, the Pogamut Experiment Class in the IDE was modified to connect with the database and provide for human player monitoring on the UT2004 server.

3.2. GameBots 2004. GB2004 is programmed in UnrealScript and makes the UT2004 environment available to the Client/IDE which runs the bot through libraries and the

TCP/IP-based API. It defines a text protocol that the client must implement to successfully run a bot in the UT2004 environment. This protocol consists of commands (sent from Client to GB2004) and messages (sent from GB2004 to Client). Commands are used to control bot actions. Messages serve to acknowledge the command and transmit information about events (asynchronous messages) or about state of the game (synchronous messages).

Communication between GB2004 and Client/IDE is based on TCP/IP. The bot is run through the Netbeans IDE and its Pogamut plug-in. This off-loads the bot's use of system resources to the IDE; thereby ensuring game engine performance is not confounded by bot execution.

Leveraging the concepts introduced in work on behavior believability in video games [16], GB2004 was modified to extract from the UT2004 game engine the same run time behavior data as are extracted for bots. Java classes were also added to extend the Pogamut agent class API libraries to allow a human player to communicate with GB2004 and

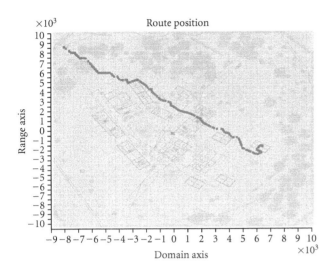

FIGURE 6: Bot A* route in virtual McKenna.

record the human player behavior data. Access to human player behavior data in the simulation environment is a critical prerequisite to the validation of the realism of bot actions.

3.3. Parser and Mediator. The Pogamut Parser translates text messages to Java objects and implements compression for transmission between GB2004 and the Client/IDE. The Pogamut parser class generates two threads for each bot. The first thread implements the communication from GB2004 to the bot (messages for the bot) and the second one implements the communication from the bot to the GB2004 (commands to the bot in UT2004). The Pogamut Mediator class creates the listener between the parser and client for detecting and delivering messages from parser to client and vice versa. The mediator recognizes the GB2004 protocol allowing communication with the UT2004 and GB2004.

To provide for player monitoring and human action simulation, the Pogamut Parser class was modified to generate two additional threads. The first thread implements the equivalent communication from the modified GB2004 to the human player objects within UT2004 (messages for the human player) and the second implements the communication from the UT2004 human player objects to the GB2004 (commands to the human player Objects in UT2004). This modification does not interact with the players themselves, only the human player Objects within the UT2004 game engine through the GB2004 human player modifications. To ensure the integrity of the human player actions within the game, these threads only serve to collect and provide to the IDE human player data.

A minor modification to the Pogamut Mediator class in the Java API used in the IDE was required for communication with the human player. A supporting modification was made to the GB2004 messaging interface.

3.4. Bot Client/IDE. The Bot Client/IDE consists of the Pogamut libraries and APIs which are used in the development of

the bot. The libraries and APIs manage the communication between the bot's logic and the UT2004 server through the Parser and Mediator as described above. The Bot Client/IDE also uses the information received from the Parser through the Mediator to build a world model for each bot executing in the game and updates the model with information received from the bot. The parameters that describe this world model are stored in a database whose access process executes in its own thread to avoid impacting the bot logic thread during execution. The database also provides for asynchronous data analysis to update the game model near real time. This allows the bot logic access to a game model that more closely mimics what is available to the human player so as to more closely mimic human player actions.

The Bot Client/IDE provides these services to bots' behavior control logic:

(i) communication with Parser via Mediator,

(ii) map representation,

(iii) bot memory,

(iv) inventory,

(v) access for logic,

(vi) database access.

3.5. Experiment Client. The development of a realism metric required a new client capable of interfacing with both bot and human player data in UT2004 as well as the world model. Using the modifications made to the Pogamut libraries and GB2004, we developed the Experiment Client. The Experiment Client runs in a Netbeans IDE to provide an IDE for development of metric experiments to record route data. We used the bots' execution of the A* algorithm for route planning and execution as the test case.

As with the Bot Client/IDE, the Experiment Client consists of the modified Pogamut libraries and APIs described above. In addition to the modifications made to support human player behavior data recording, the Pogamut Experiment Class was extended to support a threaded database and JChart interface. The database provides storage for data analysis and bot action input. This enhancement allows real-time animation of bot or human player routes during scenario execution, as illustrated in Figure 6. An example of off-line data analysis for realism measurement is shown in Figure 7.

Unlike the Bot Client/IDE, the Experiment Client does not execute any bot or game logic. This allows all bot and game logic to be executed on distributed clients, which prevents the data recording from impacting bot game performance. The Experiment Client generates bot and human player Agents running in threads during execution.

These agents inherit all the bot and human player attributes with the exception of bot logic and human player commands. The attribute inheritance exposes the bot and human player behavior data without violating the game engine's anticheat code or exposing the data to the bot or human player during execution. The Experiment Client also uses the information received from the Parser through the

Normalized change in direction (0–180)

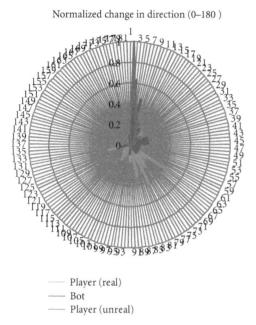

—— Player (real)
—— Bot
—— Player (unreal)

Figure 7: Radar chart of normalized heading change metric.

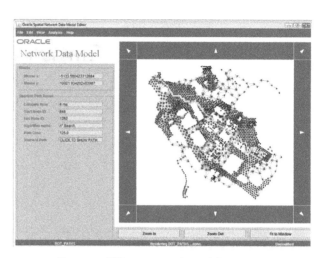

Figure 8: UT2004 network model A* route.

Mediator for each bot and human player, and the world model generated by the Bot Client or in the absence of a bot, by the Experiment Client. The Experiment Client interface to the database also provides for asynchronous data analysis to update the game model near real time in the absence of a bot. The interface also allows implementation of metrics in the database for real-time and off-line analysis and display.

The Experiment Client provides the following services:

(i) communication with the Parser through the Mediator,

(ii) map representation,

(iii) access to bot and human player memory,

(iv) game inventory (weapons for both human player and bots),

(v) access for experiment and metric logic,

(vi) database access.

3.6. Database with Spatial Libraries. The database node forms the final component of the simulation environment. For this simulation environment, we used an Oracle 11 g database with its spatial option. The Oracle 11 g database provides two important functions. First, it provides for the behavior data storage and subsequent quantitative analysis of the realism metrics collected through a database thread implemented in the Pogamut bot (agent) interface with GB2004 and UT2004 server. Second, a dynamic world model is maintained within the database to provide near real time access by the bot's logic to more closely mimic human actions based on the changing game world environment. In addition, we used the spatial module to develop a network model of the UT2004 world model collected during Bot Client or Experiment Client initiation. The network model allows for

real-time modification to the edges for the UT2004 generated search graph during game play and subsequent updates to the A* routes for the bots (Figure 8).

4. Measuring Realism

The previous section defined the game engine modifications required to support the collection of environmental (map or level) world model and player and bot behavior data within the virtual environment. This section describes the development of the virtual environment necessary to support bot and player behavior data collection and a methodology for using those data to calculate the realism metric.

4.1. Physical and Virtual Environments. In addition to the UnrealScript GB2004 and Java API modifications that permit access to the physics and artificial intelligence components of the game engine, Bot Client, and Experiment Client described above, the UT2004 editor provided the interface to the virtual world through which both the bot and human player actions could be programmed and added to the environment. In addition, the virtual space had to physically exist and have the capacity to record human actions and behavior. The McKenna facility was found to meet these requirements. McKenna is fully instrumented for recording training scenarios and has been modeled in the UT2004 MODS America's Army and Ravenshield. While not trivial, the McKenna Ravenshield model was ported to UT2004 and the GB2004 UnrealScript components required for player and bot monitoring added. The accuracy and realism of the bots' and players' actions could then be measured for a quantitative analysis of their realism. Finally, the modeling of a physical location in the virtual world will allow future with truth (recorded human execution of defined scenarios and actions) for validation of realism metrics.

There are several characteristics and properties that the physical and virtual environment must possess for realism to be accurately measured and quantitatively compared.

```
/**
 * New Pogamut Class for Storing Player Parameters during game play
 * Class to Create MonitoredPlayerBody for storing GB2004 Messages
 * @author fabien tence initial code
 * @author gregg hanold extended for player and A-star
 */
public class MonitoredPlayerBody extends AgentBody {
    public MonitoredPlayerBody(Logger logger, String playerUnrealID) {
        helloMessage = MessageType.HELLO_MONITORING;
        knownObjects = new KnownObjects();
        platformLog = logger;
        for (MessageType type: MessageType.values()) {
            this.typeMessageListeners.put(type,
                new ArrayList<RcvMsgListener>()); }
        initializer = new MonitoringInitializer(playerUnrealID); }}
```

ALGORITHM 2: MonitoredPlayerBody class listing.

(i) The virtual world must provide the same type of activity using the same methods as the physical world.

(ii) The virtual world must contain the same number and types of objects (actors) as the physical world.

(iii) The virtual world must convey the same level of detail that would be encountered in the physical world and change in a manner that is believable, realistic, and faithfully mimics the physical world.

The virtual world must mimic the experience and milieu of the physical world and present the user with an experience that is unpredictable and nonscripted in addition to being believable and realistic [17].

4.2. Data Recording and Measurement. A significant challenge in producing quantitative measures was developing an interface to the UT2004 server that could record the same data from both the bot and human players executing a scenario in the virtual world and humans in the real world. To accomplish this, GB2004 UnrealScript and the Pogamut Core Java Libraries were modified to provide for advanced player messaging and a new database thread integrated with Experiment Client. The listings for the Player Monitoring classes are shown in (Algorithms 2 and 3). In addition, an input mechanism to display and compare in the virtual world route data recorded in the physical world was developed.

Bot and human player monitoring functions occur in separate executables. Bot monitoring is executed as part of the bot spawning. To initiate player monitoring, a Pogamut Experiment must be executed. The Main listing for executing player monitoring is shown in (Algorithm 4). The message listener was added to an extension of the AgentBody class to interface with GB2004. Both bot and player monitoring implement a database thread through a Java dbConn class that constructs a jdbc connector with select, insert, update, and delete methods for an Oracle 11 g database. The dbConn class was constructed during the bot and player monitoring initialization and is populated with the map representation, bot and player memory, and object inventory. It is updated with each doLogic() logic cycle. The doLogic() override for the player monitoring logic cycle is given in (Algorithm 5).

The simulation architecture called for an Experiment Client to execute the monitoring and recording functions of both bot and human players. This client runs on its own dedicated computer which offloads the processing from the bot and UT2004 clients. Distribution of this processing makes possible the simultaneous collection of both bot and human player behavior data without impacting the UT2004 game engine, player, or Bot Client performance. The Experiment Client makes possible near real time recording and analysis of both bot and human player route data.

4.3. Methodology. The proposed general methodology for measuring the realism of algorithm-generated bot behavior, such as route planning and following, has seven steps.

(1) *Create scenarios.* Create a scenario (or set of scenarios) that includes the behavior for which a realism measurement is desired and that can be executed by both bots and human players in the virtual environment.

(2) *Identify data.* Determine the virtual environment data variables that describe the behavior as it is executed at run time.

(3) *Execute with humans in virtual environment.* Execute the scenario in the virtual environment with human players, recording the behavior data during execution.

(4) *Execute with bot in virtual environment.* Execute the scenario in the virtual environment with a bot, recording the behavior data during execution.

(5) *Execute with humans in real world.* If possible, execute the scenario in the real world with humans, recording the behavior data during execution.

(6) *Measure realism.* Calculate the realism metric values for the behaviors of the bots and human players in the

```
/**
 * New Pogamut Class for Monitoring Player Parameters during game play
 * Class to Create MonitoredPlayer Instance and tie to GB2004 Messages
 * @author fabien tence initial code
 * @author gregg Hanold extended for player and A-star
 */
public class MonitoredPlayer extends Agent {
    private String unrealID;
    public MonitoredPlayer(String unrealID) {
        this.unrealID = unrealID; //needed in initBody can't call super
        Agent.instancesAlive + = 1;
        // init of compounds
        initLogging();
        initBody(); // preceeds memory, memory needs to register listener in body
        initMemory();
        initGameMap(); // must be called as the last item !
        // uses reference to the memory, body ( For A* search must know
        //where the agent is)
        this.body.addTypedRcvMsgListener(this,
            MessageType.MAP_FINISHED); }
    @Override
    protected GameBotConnection initGBConnection(URI gameBots)
        throws UnknownHostException {
        return new MonitoringConnection(gameBots.getHost(),
        gameBots.getPort() == −1 ? 3003: gameBots.getPort()); }
    @Override
    protected void initBody() {
        this.body = new MonitoredPlayerBody(platformLog, unrealID);
        this.body.addRcvMsgListener(this); //GB20004 Messaging
        this.body.exceptionOccured.addListener(
            new FlagListener<Boolean>() {
                public void flagChanged(Boolean changedValue,
                    int listenerParam) {
                if (changedValue) {
                    platformLog.severe("Exception occured, stopping agent.");
                    exceptionOccured = true; }}} );
    }}
```

ALGORITHM 3: MonitoedPlayer class listing.

virtual environment, and if available, for the humans in the real world.

(7) *Assess realism.* Compare the values of the realism metrics. Using a suitable statistical hypothesis test, determine if the realism metric values for the human players in the virtual environment and the humans in the real world are distinguishable from those of the bot in the virtual environment. The closer the bot's realism metric values are to the human's values, the more realistic the algorithm-generated behavior is.

4.4. Testing. To test the enhanced UT2004 simulation environment, it was used to collect route data from a group of volunteer human players who were persons attending the 2010 Huntsville Simulation Conference [18]. The data collection process exercised both the enhanced simulation environment and five of the seven steps of the methodology; the two unexercised steps remain for future work, as detailed

in Section 5. The testing process is described within the framework of the methodology's steps.

(1) *Create scenarios.* Because possible differences in routes resulting from differing amounts of terrain information available were of interest, three scenarios, denoted A (no terrain knowledge), B (partial terrain knowledge), and C (complete terrain knowledge), were developed. All three scenarios required route planning and following, the realism of which was the subject of the test.

(2) *Identify data.* The data variables needed to measure the realism of routes were determined to be location, heading, and velocity. Sources for these data were found in the game engine.

(3) *Execute with humans in the virtual environment.* The volunteer human players were told that their objective was to navigate within the virtual environment as they would in the physical world. Because the objective of this test was measuring route realism and not actual game play, each human players was given an introduction and demonstration of the

```
public class Main extends Experiment {
    Vector<MyMonitoring> monitoredPlayers;
    private boolean isMonitoring;
    public Main(ExperimentDescriptor descriptor, UTServer server) {
        super(descriptor, server); }
    @Override
    protected void stageOneInit() throws Exception {
        monitorPlayingPlayers(); }
    @Override
    protected void stageOneInit() throws Exception {
        getLogger().info("Experiment started.");
        if (isMonitoring) {
            createControlPanel(); //Small panel to stop the experiment
            //Wait for all monitored player to stop playing (or an error occurs
            //in the monitoring)
            Iterator<MyMonitoring> iter = monitoredPlayers.iterator();
            while (iter.hasNext()) {
                iter.next().getSemaEndMonitor().acquire(); }}
        setResultAndTerminate(new ExperimentResult()); }
    private void monitorPlayingPlayers() throws PogamutException {
        Set<Player> players = getServer().getInfo().getPlayers();
        if (players != null && !players.isEmpty()) {
            Iterator<Player> iter = players.iterator();
            monitoredPlayers = new Vector<MyMonitoring>();
            while (iter.hasNext()) {
                Player player = iter.next();
                MyMonitoring theMonitoredPlayer =
                        new MyMonitoring(player.UnrealID);
                getServer().monitorPlayer(theMonitoredPlayer);
                monitoredPlayers.add(theMonitoredPlayer);
                isMonitoring = true; }}}
    @Override
    protected void stageThreeFinish() {
        getLogger().info("Experiment finished.");
        if (isMonitoring) {
            Iterator<MyMonitoring> iter = monitoredPlayers.iterator();
            while (iter.hasNext()) {
                MyMonitoring plr = iter.next();
                plr.disconnect(); }}}
    private void createControlPanel() {
        final JFrame frame = new JFrame();
        JButton stopButton = new JButton("Stop");
        stopButton.addActionListener(new ActionListener() {
            public void actionPerformed(ActionEvent arg0) {
                Iterator<MyMonitoring> iter = monitoredPlayers.iterator();
                while (iter.hasNext()) {
                    MyMonitoring plr = iter.next();
                    plr.saveData();
                    plr.getSemaEndMonitor().release();}
                frame.dispose(); }});
        frame.add(stopButton);
        frame.setPreferredSize(new Dimension(200, 75));
        frame.setVisible(true);
        frame.pack(); }
    public static void main(String[] args) {}}
```

Algorithm 4: Player monitoring Main class listing.

```
// Player doLogic() parameter recording segment
//Overrides Experiment doLogic in Pogamut Library to add db recording
   @Override //doLogic() to capture player movement and position
   protected void doLogic() throws PogamutException {
      long time = System.currentTimeMillis(); //Time of current execution
      if (time − lastSaveTime > 60000) {
      dbConn.Insert ("tbl_PParams",time, vel, dir, loc); //Update Player Table
         lastSaveTime=time; } //Set data recording interval
      totalTS++;
      Triple vel = getMemory().getAgentVelocity(); //Player velocity
      Triple dir = getMemory().getAgentRotation(); //Player movement direction
      Triple loc = getMemory().getAgentLocation(); //Player postion
      if (vel.x != 0 || vel.y != 0) { //the player is moving
         wasImmo = false;
      } else { //the player is not moving
         if (wasImmo) {
            consecImmoTS++; }
         wasImmo = true;
         immoTS++; }
      . . .
   }
//BOT doLogic() parameter recording segment
   protected void doLogic() throws PogamutException {
      long time = System.currentTimeMillis(); //Time of current execution
      if (time − lastSaveTime > 60000) {
      dbConn.Insert ("tbl_BParams", time, vel, dir, loc); //Update BOT Table
         lastSaveTime=time; } //Set data recording interval
      totalTS++;
      Triple vel = memory.getAgentVelocity(); //BOT velocity
      Triple dir = memory.getAgentRotation(); //BOT movement direction
      Triple loc = memory.getAgentLocation(); //BOT position
      if (vel.x != 0 || vel.y != 0) { //the BOT is moving
         wasImmo = false;
      } else { //the BOT is not moving
         if (wasImmo) {
            consecImmoTS++; }
         wasImmo = true;
         immoTS++; }
      . . .
         action_run_roamAround(); //BOT Path following Navigation command
   }
```

ALGORITHM 5: Player monitoring dologic () listing.

UT2004 navigation controls available: stop, walk, run, jump, crouch, and turn. All other UT2004 game-related controls were turned off. The human players were provided a period of time to familiarize themselves with the game controls and to ask the experimenter any questions related to the scenario. The familiarization period and the disabling of nonmovement controls were intended to eliminate the effects of player familiarity with the game engine on the recorded route data.

All of the human players from whom data was collected were unfamiliar with the specific terrain area before the experiment. The players were randomly assigned to one of the three scenarios and were given terrain information consistent with the scenario.

For scenario A (no terrain knowledge), the human players were given the following briefing: "You are to locate and enter a building with a chain link fence surrounding it. The fence will have a single gate. The building is green with a black roof, a single door, and windows on all sides. Once in the building you are to enter the room with two windows, one above the other. The lower window will have its view obstructed by a jersey barrier. You will be given a few minutes to familiarize yourself with the UT2004 Client controls, while the database is initialized for collection." No map was provided to the human player.

For scenario B (partial terrain knowledge), the human players were given the same briefing as in Scenario A. The map in Figure 6 was provided to them, showing the starting and destination points, but no routes.

For scenario C (complete terrain knowledge), the human players were given the same briefing as in Scenario A. As with

TABLE 1: Sample route data recording.

Time stamp	X-Coordinate	Y-Coordinate	Z-Coordinate	Velocity-X	Velocity-Y	Velocity-Z
1288187592014	−8144.53	8358.18	−605.41	100.79	−68.13	0.00
1288187592264	−8047.99	8292.91	−603.25	364.52	−246.42	0.00
1288187592514	−7957.77	8231.93	−601.60	364.53	−246.41	0.00
1288187592796	−7852.70	8160.07	−600.03	357.64	−256.31	0.00
1288187592999	−7758.46	8078.95	−597.98	324.40	−297.26	0.00
1288187593249	−7670.81	7989.45	−595.45	288.14	−332.54	0.00
1288187593499	−7610.44	7912.54	−592.89	269.10	−348.13	0.00
1288187593749	−7536.66	7814.22	−589.56	258.49	−356.07	0.00

scenario B, the map in Figure 6 was provided, showing the starting and destination points, but no routes. During the scenario execution, a display of the Figure 6 map was updated near-real-time with the player's current position.

The mechanism for recording the route data within the game engine has been described. Table 1 shows a small sample of the recorded route data for a typical route. Figure 9 illustrates typical routes for each of the three scenarios; in the figure they are identified as "None" (scenario A), "Partial" (scenario B), and "Complete" (scenario C).

(4) *Execute with bot in the virtual environment.* A bot generated and followed a route using the A* algorithm. Figure 9 also shows the bot route.

(5) *Execute with humans in the real world.* This step of the methodology remains for future work; see Section 5. Because the terrain used for the test models the real-world McKenna facility, which is regularly used for training, data may be available at some point in the future.

(6) *Measure realism.* As of this writing, the route realism metrics are currently under development. Several candidate metrics are under development, including (1) the ratio of route length to straight line distance from the starting point to the ending point, and (2) the normalized heading change for each route. Calculating the former is straightforward; calculating the latter proceeds as follows.

(i) Filter out all route segments in which the bot or human player was not moving.

(ii) Convert the individual route headings for each of the route segments, both bot and human player, to normalized values as $H_n = H - H_{sl}$, where H_{sl} is the straight line heading from start to destination; all negative values are converted to positive by adding 360.

(iii) Calculated the heading change for each route segment as $H_c(x) = |H_n(x-1) - H_n(x)|$, converting to a 0 to 180 degree scale to include both left and right heading changes under the assumption that a heading change of 1 to 179 degree was a right heading change and 181 to 359 degrees was a left heading change.

(iv) Compute the mean, standard error of the mean, and standard deviation of the heading changes for each of the record routes, both bot and human players.

The results of these calculations are summarized in Table 2 and Figure 10.

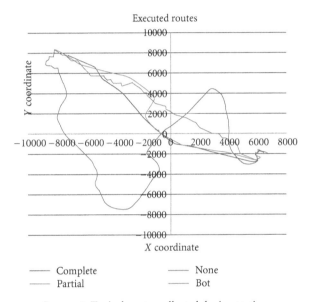

FIGURE 9: Typical routes collected during testing.

(7) *Assess realism.* This step of the methodology remains for future work; see Section 5.

5. Results and Future Work

The primary objective of this paper was to describe the enhancements made to a commercial game engine in order to collect data that might be used to measure and assess the realism of algorithm-generated behaviors, such as route planning. This section summarizes the results and future work.

5.1. Results. An implementation of an instrumented commercial game engine in which route realism can be quantitatively measured and a methodology for collecting route data needed for those measurements was presented. Analysis of data collected for bots and human players executing routes within the virtual environment will provide quantitative data required to develop route realism metrics, which will in turn be used to validate or assess the realism of algorithm-generated routes. UT2004 with the Pogamut Java Libraries and Netbeans IDE and GB2004 provided a suitable platform for the acquisition of the needed route data.

TABLE 2: Sample bot and human realism metric calculations.

Type	Variable	N	N*	Mean	SE_Mean	StDev
A-BOT	BOTHdg(D)	255	1	13.17	1.02	16.24
B-NK	P5Hdg(D)	484	1	6.06	0.84	18.52
B-NK	P6Hdg(D)	387	1	2.83	0.25	4.87
B-NK	P13Hdg(D)	397	1	1.07	0.21	4.23
B-NK	P16Hdg(D)	412	1	5.93	0.79	16.03
B-NK	P17Hdg(D)	603	1	4.26	0.39	9.51
B-NK	P18Hdg(D)	564	1	4.29	0.37	8.68
C-Part	P7Hdg(D)	235	1	5.99	1.32	20.26
C-Part	P8Hdg(D)	451	1	1.60	0.34	7.25
C-Part	P10Hdg(D)	400	1	1.85	0.28	5.61
C-Part	P14Hdg(D)	515	1	1.96	0.28	6.24
C-Part	P15Hdg(D)	489	1	1.94	0.44	9.73
D-Comp	P3Hdg(D)	118	1	4.57	0.87	9.45
D-Comp	P4Hdg(D)	190	1	2.53	0.59	8.09
SL	SLhdg(D)	218	1	0.41	0.18	2.66

Where type is defined by: A-BOT: BOT, B-NK: Human Player No Knowledge, C-Part: Human Player Partial Knowledge, D-Comp: Human Player Complete Knowledge. Variable represents the test run for BOT-BOT Heading, Pxx-Player xx Heading. SL-Straight Line Heading. N: Number of sample points. N*: Number of missing sample points. Mean: Mean of the Variable Heading in Degrees. SE: Mean-Standard Error of the Mean. StDev: Standard Deviation.

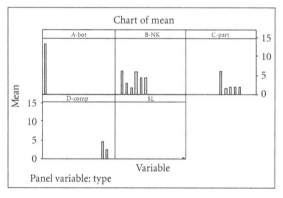
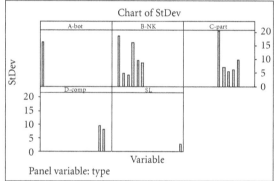

FIGURE 10: Plot of mean and standard deviation of normalized heading change metric.

The enhancements to UT2004 are specific to that game engine, but they suggest what may be required in another game engine to collect similar data. The overall methodology is applicable to any game engine with a suitable API.

5.2. Future Work. The next phase of this research will focus on the development of a quantitative realism metric based on route data that can be applied to any given route to measure its realism. Validation of the realism metric will be performed via comparisons of realism metric values for routes followed by algorithms and humans executing the same scenarios in the virtual environment. Statistical hypothesis tests will be used to demonstrate that the realism metrics reliably distinguish between algorithm-generated and human-generated routes.

Based on lessons learned from the data collection testing, an improved set of scenarios will be used in the next phase of the research. Four human player scenarios will be used.

(1) *No terrain knowledge.* The player is given no information before route planning and execution.

(2) *Incomplete terrain knowledge.* The player is shown a map of the terrain with starting and destination points marked before planning and execution.

(3) *Incomplete terrain knowledge with preplanned route.* The player is shown a hardcopy map of the terrain with starting and destination points marked before route planning and execution. He/she is given the opportunity to plan a route on the map before starting route execution; the player retains the map during route execution.

(4) *Complete knowledge of the terrain with preplanned route.* The player is shown a hardcopy map of the terrain with starting and destination points marked before route planning and execution. He/she is given the opportunity to plan a route on the map before starting route execution; the player retains the map during route execution. During route execution, the player is shown his/her current position plotted in near real time on an animated terrain map.

TABLE 3: Experimental design for human player data collection.

Players	Map	Start	Destination	Category	Player	Map	Start	Destination	Category
1	1	1	1	1	64	2	1	1	1
2	1	1	2	1	63	2	1	2	1
3	1	1	3	1	62	2	1	3	1
4	1	1	3	1	61	2	1	3	1
5	1	1	1	1	60	2	1	1	1
6	1	1	2	1	59	2	1	2	1
7	1	1	3	1	58	2	1	3	1
8	1	1	4	1	57	2	1	4	1
9	1	1	1	1	56	2	1	1	1
10	1	1	2	1	55	2	1	2	1
11	1	1	3	1	54	2	1	3	1
12	1	1	4	1	53	2	1	4	1
13	1	1	1	1	52	2	1	1	1
14	1	1	2	1	51	2	1	2	1
15	1	1	3	1	50	2	1	3	1
16	1	1	4	1	49	2	1	4	1
17	1	2	1	2	48	2	2	1	2
18	1	2	2	2	47	2	2	2	2
19	1	2	3	2	46	2	2	3	2
20	1	2	3	2	45	2	2	3	2
21	1	2	1	2	44	2	2	1	2
22	1	2	2	2	43	2	2	2	2
23	1	2	3	2	42	2	2	3	2
24	1	2	4	2	41	2	2	4	2
25	1	2	1	2	40	2	2	1	2
26	1	2	2	2	39	2	2	2	2
27	1	2	3	2	38	2	2	3	2
28	1	2	4	2	37	2	2	4	2
29	1	2	1	2	36	2	2	1	2
30	1	2	2	2	35	2	2	2	2
31	1	2	3	2	34	2	2	3	2
32	1	2	4	2	33	2	2	4	2
33	1	3	1	3	32	2	3	1	3
34	1	3	2	3	31	2	3	2	3
35	1	3	3	3	30	2	3	3	3
36	1	3	3	3	29	2	3	3	3
37	1	3	1	3	28	2	3	1	3
38	1	3	2	3	27	2	3	2	3
39	1	3	3	3	26	2	3	3	3
40	1	3	4	3	25	2	3	4	3
41	1	3	1	3	24	2	3	1	3
42	1	3	2	3	23	2	3	2	3
43	1	3	3	3	22	2	3	3	3
44	1	3	4	3	21	2	3	4	3
45	1	3	1	3	20	2	3	1	3
46	1	3	2	3	19	2	3	2	3
47	1	3	3	3	18	2	3	3	3
48	1	3	4	3	17	2	3	4	3
49	1	4	1	4	16	2	4	1	4
50	1	4	2	4	15	2	4	2	4

Table 3: Continued.

Players	Map	Start	Destination	Category	Player	Map	Start	Destination	Category
51	1	4	3	4	14	2	4	3	4
52	1	4	3	4	13	2	4	3	4
53	1	4	1	4	12	2	4	1	4
54	1	4	2	4	11	2	4	2	4
55	1	4	3	4	10	2	4	3	4
56	1	4	4	4	9	2	4	4	4
57	1	4	1	4	8	2	4	1	4
58	1	4	2	4	7	2	4	2	4
59	1	4	3	4	6	2	4	3	4
60	1	4	4	4	5	2	4	4	4
61	1	4	1	4	4	2	4	1	4
62	1	4	2	4	3	2	4	2	4
63	1	4	3	4	2	2	4	3	4
64	1	4	4	4	1	2	4	4	4

Two maps will be used, each with four starting and ending points, giving 16 possible combinations per map. Each human player will execute one scenario on each of the two maps. Table 3 summarizes the resulting experimental design. The minimum number of human required is 64.

If the necessary data are available, the routes followed in the virtual environment will also be compared with routes followed by humans moving in the real world. To allow for this possibility, the virtual environment used for data collection was a recreation of a real location, the Fort Benning McKenna MOUT facility. The routes of real soldiers in the McKenna facility would be compared to algorithm-generated and human-generated routes in the virtual environment.

Since the development of the UT2004 simulation environment, Epic Games has released the UT3 Engine and UnReal Developers Kit. The UT2004 environment should be ported to UT3 to take advantage of the additional engine access and behavior control available through this update. Finally, further development of the Pogamut Experiment classes to include parameter identification and statistical analysis should be explored.

Appendix

Selected Source Code

Selected source code excerpts for key parts of the implementation are provided. For more details, see Algorithms 1, 2, 3, 4, and 5.

Disclosure

This research received no specific grant from any funding agency in the public, commercial, or not-for-profit sectors.

References

[1] P. Fua, "McKenna MOUT Site, Fort Benning, Georgia," 2009, http://www.ai.sri.com/~fua/rcvw/Benning.html.

[2] D. R. Scribner and P. H. Wiley, "The development of a virtual McKenna Military Operations in Urban Terrain (MOUT) site for command, control, communication, computing, intelligence, surveillance, and reconnaissance (C4ISR) studies," Tech. Rep. ARL-TR-4139, June 2007.

[3] M. Dorfler, "Pogamut 2 IDE for Agents in UT2004," 2009, https://artemis.ms.mff.cuni.cz/pogamut/tiki-index.php?page=Architecture/.

[4] E. Beeker, "Potential error in the reuse of Nilsson's a algorithm for path-finding in military simulations," *Journal of Defense Modeling and Simulation*, vol. 1, no. 2, pp. 91–97, 2004.

[5] Z. Shen and S. Zhou, "Behavior representation and simulation for military operations on urbanized terrain," *Simulation*, vol. 82, no. 9, pp. 593–607, 2006.

[6] J. E. Bell and P. R. McMullen, "Ant colony optimization techniques for the vehicle routing problem," *Advanced Engineering Informatics*, vol. 18, no. 1, pp. 41–48, 2004.

[7] D. A. Reece, M. Kraus, and P. Dumanoir, "Tactical movement planning for individual combatants," in *Proceedings of the 9th Conference on Behavior Representation in Modeling and Simulation*, pp. 301–308, Orlando, Fla, USA, May 2000.

[8] D. R. Van Brackle, M. D. Petty, C. D. Gouge, and R. D. Hull, "Terrain reasoning for reconnaissance planning in polygonal terrain," in *Proceedings of the 3rd Conference on Computer Generated Forces and Behavioral Representation*, pp. 285–306, Orlando, Fla, USA, March 1993.

[9] D. Brogan and N. Johnson, "Realistic human walking paths," in *Proceedings of the Computer Animation and Social Agents*, pp. 94–101, May 2003, New Brunswick, NJ, USA.

[10] R. G. Burgess and C. J. Darken, "Realistic human path planning using fluid simulation," in *Proceedings of the 13th Conference on Behavior Representation in Modeling and Simulation*, pp. 3–12, Arlington, Va, USA, May 2004.

[11] D. E. Diller, W. Ferguson, A. M. Leung, B. Benyo, and D. Foley, "Behavior modeling in commercial games," in *Proceedings of the 13th Conference on Behavior Representation in Modeling and Simulation*, pp. 257–268, Arlington, Va, USA, May 2004.

[12] M. D. Petty, "Verification, validation, and accreditation," in *Modeling and Simulation Fundamentals: Theoretical Underpinnings and Practical Domains*, J. A. Sokolowski and C. M. Banks, Eds., pp. 325–372, John Wiley & Sons, Hoboken, NJ, USA, 2010.

[13] G. Hanold and D. Hanold, "Route generation for a synthetic character (BOT) using a partial or incomplete knowledge route generation algorithm in UT2004," in *MODSIM World*, Virginia Beach, Va, USA, October 2009.

[14] G. Hanold and D. Hanold, "A method for quantitative measurement of the realism of synthetic character (BOT) actions within the UT2004 virtual environment," in *MODSIM World*, Virginia Beach, Va, USA, October 2009.

[15] A. N. Marshall, J. Vaglia, J. M. Sims, and R. Rozich, "Unreal Tournament Java Bot," 2006, http://sourceforge.net/projects/utbot.

[16] F. Tence and C. Buche, "Automatable evaluation method oriented toward behaviour believability for video games," in *Proceedings of the 9th International Conference on Intelligent Games and Simulation*, Valencia, Spain, November 2008.

[17] M. R. Stytz and S. B. Banks, "Considerations for human behavior modeling interoperability within simulation environments," in *Proceedings of the Fall Simulation Interoperability Workshop*, Orlando, Fla, USA, September 2006.

[18] G. T. Hanold and M. D. Petty, "Developing a modeling and simulation environment and methodology for the measurement and validation of route realism," in *Proceedings of the Huntsville Simulation Conference*, Huntsville, Ala, USA, October 2010.

7

Immersion in Computer Games: The Role of Spatial Presence and Flow

David Weibel and Bartholomäus Wissmath

Department of Psychology, University of Bern, Muesmattstrasse 45, 3000 Bern 9, Switzerland

Correspondence should be addressed to David Weibel, david.weibel@psy.unibe.ch

Academic Editor: Daniel Thalmann

A main reason to play computer games is the pleasure of being immersed in a mediated world. *Spatial presence* and *flow* are considered key concepts to explain such immersive experiences. However, little attention has been paid to the connection between the two concepts. Thus, we empirically examined the relationship between presence and flow in the context of a computer role-playing game ($N = 70$), a racing game ($N = 120$), and a jump and run game ($N = 72$). In all three studies, factor analysis revealed that presence and flow are distinct constructs, which do hardly share common variance. We conclude that presence refers to the sensation of being there in the mediated world, whereas flow rather refers to the sensation of being involved in the gaming action. Further analyses showed that flow and presence depend on motivation and immersive tendency. In addition, flow and presence enhanced performance as well as enjoyment.

1. Introduction

In a broad survey, Yee [1] assessed motivations and experiences of 30,000 game users. He found that many users play computer games because they like to be immersed in a fantasy world. Immersion into mediated environments in general and computer games in particular has previously been explained through (spatial) *presence* (e.g., [2, 3]) and *flow* (e.g., [4–6]). Flow and presence share conceptual similarities such as an immersive component and intense feelings of involvement (cf. [7, 8]), but there are clear differences (cf. [6, 9]) whereas flow can be defined as immersion or involvement in an activity (i.e., the gaming action), presence rather refers to a sense of spatial immersion in a mediated environment. In the last decades, a plethora of studies have been conducted to investigate presence and flow in various media contexts. Surprisingly, however, there is not one single comprehensive empirical study that investigates the relationship between the two concepts. Within the study in hand, we therefore aim to empirically analyse the relationship between flow and (spatial) presence. In order to validate differences and similarities, we accomplished three large-scale experiments using three different computer games.

Since presence as well as flow can be described as immersive experiences, Draper et al. [7] suggest that presence is a particular type of flow experience that occurs during teleoperations. This is in line with Bystrom et al. [10] who assume that presence—just like flow—occurs due to a feedback loop between task characteristics and attention allocation. Alike, Hoffman and Novak [8] propose that attention and involvement are essential components of the sensation of presence as well as the experience of flow. Despite these conceptual similarities, both concepts are used independently to describe and explain immersive experiences in the context of media use.

Furthermore, we are interested whether and to what extent certain personal characteristics play a crucial role in both, presence and flow. Previous studies suggest that the users' *motivation* and *immersive tendency*—as proposed by Witmer and Singer [11]—predict immersive experiences. The influence of immersive tendency on presence has been shown by Weibel et al. [12], the influence of motivation on flow was found by Engeser et al. [13]. However, it is not yet clear whether these two variables also exert a strong influence in the context of computer games. Additionally, the relationships between motivation and presence as well as between immersive tendency and flow have not yet been examined.

To provide even deeper insights into the role of presence and flow in the context of computer games, we intend to shed light on the question whether presence and flow influence *enjoyment* and *performance*. Existing literature speculates that these two variables depend on both, flow and presence (e.g., [2–4, 14]). To date, however, there still is a lack of compelling empirical evidence. To our knowledge, there is no empirical study investigating the influence of flow and presence on enjoyment and performance in the context of computer games. Also, the relation between presence and performance is so far mere speculation and has not yet been investigated. We feel that investigating all variables together may help understanding the bigger picture of the processes involved in computer gaming and to identify possible mediating effects.

As aforementioned, we conducted three studies using different computer game settings. Study 1 was accomplished in the context of a computer role-playing game. In order to replicate the findings, we conducted a second study using a racing game running on Sony Playstation 3. In order to further enhance external validity and to investigate whether the relation between presence and flow depends on the vividness of the virtual environment, we conducted a third study within the jump and run game Sonic the Hedgehog. This game lacks of vividness and portrays the elements of the virtual world rather cartoon-like and less realistically. Thus, it seems less ideal to induce presence compared to the racing game and the role-playing game.

2. Theoretical Considerations

2.1. Spatial Presence. In the recent decades, technological development formed the basis for a completely new experience. The sensation of being spatially present at remote places displayed by technical interfaces. *Presence*, also referred to as telepresence or spatial presence, describes a state of consciousness that gives the impression of being physically present in a mediated world. According to Steuer [15], (tele)presence is the extent to which an individual feels present in the mediated environment, rather than in the immediate physical environment. Mediated contents become real and one's self-awareness is immersing into another world [7]. Slater and Wilbur [16] define this experience as a "state of consciousness, the (psychological) sense of being in the virtual environment" (page 604). According to Lombard and Ditton [2], presence is a perceptual illusion of nonmediation. A more recent approach was proposed by Wirth et al. [3]. Their two-level process model of spatial presence suggests attention allocation and the establishment of a mental model of the mediated environment to be prerequisite conditions for the sensation of presence. Once these preconditions are met, the individual-mediated environment will define the primary subjective frame of reference.

Due to enhanced vividness and new ways of interaction, virtual reality (VR) technology including computer games are assumed to elicit stronger presence experiences than more traditional media offerings such as TV [17]. In accordance, Tamborini [18] points out the capability of computer games to induce feelings of immersion and involvement, which are both essential components of presence [11].

2.2. Flow. The holistic experience of flow was first proposed by Csikszentmihalyi in 1975 [19]. Csikszentmihalyi describes flow as a mental state of operation in which a person is fully immersed in what he/she is doing. This gratifying mental state is characterized by a feeling of energized focus, full involvement, and success in the process of the activity. The concept suggests that the psychological experiences of various leisure activities such as rock climbing, dancing, or chess playing have several common dimensions. The characteristics of such intrinsically rewarding flow experiences are intense involvement, clarity of goals and feedback, concentrating and focusing, lack of self-consciousness, distorted sense of time, balance between the challenge and the skills required to meet it, and finally the feeling of full control over the activity [14].

An issue of recent research is the investigation of flow experience in the context of computer use (e.g., [4, 5, 20–23]). An adaptation of Csikszentmihalyi's concept of flow with regard to the specific experiences of human-computer interactions was assessed by Rheinberg et al. [24, 25]. In a factor analytical approach, they found that the construct contains the two dimensions: (1) smooth and automatic running and (2) absorption. The first factor refers to the feeling of utmost concentration and focusing, control over the activity, clarity of the operations, and smooth and automatic cogitations. The second factor refers to the feeling of full involvement, distorted sense of time, optimal challenge, and absent mindedness.

Preliminary research on flow and computer games suggests that the psychological experience of gaming is consistent with the dimensions of flow experiences as outlined by Csikszentmihalyi and Rheinberg and Engeser. Thus, the concept of flow "form(s) the basis of the psychological presence of gamers within the game and provides a useful framework" (paragraph 3, Psychological Presence section, [20]). The importance of flow in the context of media consumption was also pointed out by Sherry [4], who argues that media enjoyment is after all the result of flow experiences. According to Sherry, flow experiences especially occur while playing computer and video games: "video games possess ideal characteristics to create and maintain flow experiences in that the flow experience of video games is brought on when the skills of the player match the difficulty of the game" (page 328). In line with these assumptions, Voiskounsky et al. [5] as well as Rheinberg and Vollmeyer [22] experimentally demonstrated that players of Multi-User Dungeons experience high levels of flow. Voiskounsky et al. as well as Klimmt [26] propose flow to be one the main sources of the attractiveness of computer games.

2.3. Presence and Flow as Process Variables in Media Use. Presence and flow describe some sort of immersive experiences and both are process variables referring to the actual media use. According to Draper et al. [7], presence can be defined as a special type of flow experience that occurs during teleoperations. Bystrom et al. [10] assume a feedback loop between task characteristics, attention allocation, and presence. They consider this loop to be similar to the flow concept. In 1996, Hoffman and Novak [27] hypothesized that within computer-mediated environments, presence leads to more attention and more flow. Novak et al. [28] supported this assumption. In a compelling online environment, they found that presence and flow correspond. A positive correlation between presence and flow was also found by Weibel et al. [6] in the context of a computer game. The similarities of flow and presence are also pointed out by Fontaine [9] who states that the flow experience produces peaks of involvement that seem to be similar to the "vividness" of presence.

Yet, not only similarities but also differences between the two concepts are discussed (e.g., [6, 9]). As aforementioned, presence has often been described as immersion into a virtual environment; in contrast, flow rather refers to an experience of being involved in an action (cf. [6]). The concept of flow focuses more on the task characteristics, while the concept of presence is more focused on technological characteristics of a medium. Flow could thus be described as immersion into an activity (i.e., the gaming action), whereas presence rather refers to a sense of spatial immersion in a mediated world. Fontaine describes this distinction as follows: "flow involves a narrow focus on a limited range of task characteristics, whereas presence involves a broader awareness of the task ecology" (p. 485). Furthermore, Fontaine states that flow is associated with feelings of *control*, whereas presence is rather associated with novel ecologies that lack of predictability. According to Fontaine, it is these differences that make flow a state of consciousness most suitable for performance in familiar ecologies and presence rather in unfamiliar ones.

As mentioned above, theoretical articles suggest differences as well as similarities between presence and flow. To date, there is a lack of empirical evidence concerning the connection between the two concepts. Therefore, our first objective is to answer the question whether and how the presence and flow are related to each other in the context of computer games.

2.4. The Influence of Motivation and Immersive Tendency on Flow and Presence.
Lombard and Ditton [2] assume that certain traits facilitate the occurrence of presence experiences. Accordingly, Witmer and Singer [11] propose a disposition of individuals—immersive tendency—which influences whether someone experiences presence. According to Witmer and Singer, someone who scores high on immersive tendency has the capability to become involved in situations, shows a tendency to maintain focus on current activities, and generally likes playing video games. Furthermore, they propose that this trait relates to involvement in tasks. Thus, immersive tendency might not only influence presence, but also flow.

A further personal factor discussed in the literature is the user's motivation. According to Lombard and Ditton [2] and Wirth et al. [3], motivation is a prerequisite to experience presence. To date, convincing empirical evidence that proves these considerations is missing. Csikszenthimalyi believes

flow and motivational factors to be connected. Accordingly, Engeser et al. [13] showed that students with higher motivation reported stronger flow experiences during statistic lectures. Weibel et al. [29] replicated these findings within an e-learning environment. Thus, the motivation of an individual seems—at least to a certain amount—to determine the level of presence and flow.

Taken together, we assume that personal traits in terms of immersive tendency and motivation at least partly determine the degree of presence and flow.

2.5. The Influence of Flow and Presence on Enjoyment and Performance.
There seems to be a connection between presence and enjoyment (e.g., [6, 30]). Wirth et al. [3] assume that "spatial presence can intensify existing media effects such as enjoyment" (page 495). Accordingly, Teng [31] proposes that immersion in games is pleasurable and does satisfying the user's need. Since flow is a gratifying experience, flow and enjoyment should also be related. Sherry [4] as well as Weber et al. [32] suggest that media enjoyment after all results from flow experiences. Correspondingly, Ghani and Deshpande [21] could experimentally demonstrate the positive connection between flow and enjoyment.

Performance is yet another factor that is assumed to be influenced by presence and flow. Witmer and Singer [11] as well as Lombard and Ditton [2] assume a positive correlation between presence and task performance. In an experimental setting, Sheridan [33] showed that participants scoring high on presence indeed performed better. Csikszentmihalyi [14] states that the balance between challenges and required skills is a central aspect of flow experiences. He assumes that flow rather occurs if this balance is reached on a superior performance level. Thus, flow should lead to higher performance. Engeser et al. [13] could prove this assumption in the context of a statistic lecture, Weibel et al. [29] within an e-learning environment. In both studies, students scoring higher on flow during the lectures performed better in the subsequent test. Thus, we expect that presence and flow positively influence enjoyment and performance.

2.6. Summary of the Expected Relationships.
To sum up, existing literature suggests that the actual media use in terms of presence and flow is determined by the personal characteristics immersive tendency and motivation. In turn, presence and flow are assumed to enhance enjoyment as well as performance. Our second aim—besides testing the relation between presence and flow—is to empirically investigate this relationship in three studies within three different computer games. The expected relations are shown in Figure 1.

3. Study 1

3.1. Method

3.1.1. Participants. A total of 70 students of a large public university in Switzerland participated. All of them were undergraduate students enrolled in psychology. Thirty-seven females and 33 males took part in the experiment. The average age was 23.9 years (SD = 5.42). All participants received

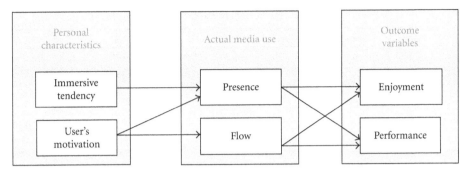

FIGURE 1: Expected relationship between personal characteristics, flow and presence, and outcome variables.

a credit in their introductory courses for participating. All participants were treated according to the declaration of Helsinki [34].

3.1.2. Design and Statistical Methods. Before starting the experiment, we assessed the participants' motivation and their immersive tendency. The participants' spatial presence, flow, and enjoyment were captured expost. Furthermore, we measured the gaming performance.

We examined the dimensionality of presence and flow by means of factor analysis. To investigate the relationship between personal characteristics, actual media use, and outcome variables, a path analysis was conducted.

3.1.3. Stimulus Material. The computer role-playing game *Neverwinter Nights* produced by BioWare [35] was used. It is setting is a medieval fantasy world, a player is traveling through. There, an adventurous mission has to be completed. We divided the game into two parts. In the first part, the participants had to travel through the virtual world with the mission to find as many so-called rubies as possible. These rubies were said to provide power. The duration of this part of the game was exactly 15 minutes. After the expiration of the time the avatars were automatically transported into an arena where they had to compete against an opponent over five rounds. For reasons of standardization, the combat itself was programmed in a way that all players lost the final combat in the fifth round.

The game was played on a desktop system. Thereby, we used a 46″ LCD large-screen television.

3.1.4. Measurements. All data besides performance were captured by means of self-report. The subjects rated all items on five-point Likert scales.

Immersive Tendency. The immersive tendency was assessed before the experiment started. We used the immersive tendency questionnaire by Witmer and Singer [11]. The questionnaire consists of 29 items (example item: "how frequently do you find yourself closely identifying with the characters in a story line?"). According to Witmer and Singer the reliability of the scale is between 0.75 and 0.81.

(Pre)Motivation. The motivation was measured with one single item. The participants were asked the following question

before playing the computer game: "How motivated are you to play the game?" (1 = not at all; 5 = very much).

Presence. We used the presence scale by Kim and Biocca [36]. Kim and Biocca define the term presence in line with Lombard and Ditton as a sense of (spatially) being there in a mediated environment. The questionnaire was originally designed to measure presence in the context of televised media contents and was also used to assess presence in the context of computer games. The scale had been used in previous studies and turned out to be valid and reliable (e.g., [6, 28, 37]). The scale consists of eight items (example item: "the computer game came to me and created a new world for me, and the world suddenly disappeared when the game ended"). The authors do not mention the scale's reliability. In our study, the scale was reliable (Cronbach's *alpha* = .75).

Flow. Flow was assessed using the flow short scale by Rheinberg et al. [25] (example item: "I was totally absorbed in what I am doing"). This scale was previously used in the context of computer games (e.g., [6, 22]) and turned out to be a valid and reliable. According to the authors, the consistency of the scale (Cronbach's *alpha*) is around 0.90.

Enjoyment. In line with various other studies [6, 38, 39], we measured enjoyment with one single item: "Did you enjoy the game?" (1 = not at all; 5 = very much).

Performance. The participants had to travel through the virtual world in the first part of the game. Their mission was to find as many rubies as possible. The performance measure was the amount of rubies found.

3.2. Results

3.2.1. Reliabilities. Sufficient reliabilities were revealed for presence (Cronbach's *alpha* = .75), immersive tendency (Cronbach's *alpha* = .74), and the flow scale (Cronbach's *alpha* = .84).

3.2.2. Descriptives. Table 1 shows the intercorrelations between the measured variables including means and standard deviations. Individuals rated all items on five-point Likert scales. A value of 1 indicates the lowest, and 5 the highest

TABLE 1: Bivariate correlations between the measured variables.

Variables	Mean	Standard deviation	1	2	3	4	5	6
(1) Presence	2.88	0.52	—	.42**	.48**	.40**	.53**	.13
(2) Flow	3.10	0.62		—	.43**	.52**	.50**	.29*
(3) Immersive tendency	2.94	0.45			—	.19	.19	.11
(4) Motivation	3.24	0.55				—	.32**	.22
(5) Enjoyment	2.79	0.72					—	.15
(6) Performance	7.84	2.87						—

Note: $^*P < .05$, $^{**}P < .01$.

TABLE 2: Presence and flow: principal axis factoring*.

Factor		1	2
A prior classification	Item		
	When the game ended, I felt like I came back to the "real world" after a journey.	.003	**.819**
	The computer game came to me and created a new world for me, and the world suddenly disappeared when the game ended.	−.003	**.733**
	During the game, I felt I was in the virtual environment.	.132	**.751**
Presence	During the game, my body was in the room, but my mind was inside the world created by the computer.	.281	.372
	During the game, the computer-generated world was more real or present for me compared to the "real world."	.373	**.629**
	During the game, I NEVER forgot that I was in the middle of an experiment. (inverse coded)	−.007	.329
	The computer-generated world seemed to me only "something I saw" rather than "somewhere I visited." (inverse coded)	.030	.367
	During the game, my mind was in the room, not in the world created by the computer. (inverse coded)	.090	.329
	I knew what I had to do each step of the way.	.301	.190
	The right thoughts/movements occurred of their own accord.	**.766**	.000
	I felt that I had everything under control.	**.574**	.210
	I had no difficulty concentrating.	**.465**	−.104
Flow	My mind was completely clear.	**.644**	−.034
	My thoughts/activities were running fluidly and smoothly.	**.647**	.248
	I was totally absorbed in what I was doing.	**.743**	.215
	I felt just the right amount of challenge.	**.609**	.089
	I was completely lost in thought.	**.599**	.022
	I did not notice the time passing.	**.603**	.364
% of variance explained		**22.0**	**16.7**

* Rotation method: Varimax with Kaiser Normalisation.
Note: values less than 0.4 are suppressed.

possible value. The mean performance reflects the average amount of collected rubies. These findings show that overall presence, flow, and enjoyment ratings were medium.

3.2.3. Dimensionality of Flow and Presence: Factor Analysis. Presence correlates positively with flow, $r(70) = .42, P < .01$, but how are these concepts related to each other? To examine the dimensionality of presence and flow, we additionally conducted a factor analysis. Our focus lied on identifying the underlying variables, concepts, and items. Therefore, a principal axis factor analysis was conducted. First, we tested if the output variables belong together. The measure of sampling adequacy (MSA) criterion is acceptable (MSA = .78)

(cf. [40]). The scree test suggests a two-factor-solution. The two-factor solution suggested by the scree-test explains 38.7 percent of variance. The varimax rotation extracts a first factor, which explains 22 percent of variance. It consists of eight out of ten flow-items, which load higher than .4 on the particular factor. The second factor which explains 16.7 percent of the variance mainly consists of four out of eight items of the presence scale. No items of different constructs load high on the same factor. Table 2 shows these findings.

In order to further test construct validity, we additionally computed a confirmatory factor analysis. Thereby, we tested the solution as suggested by the exploratory factor analysis. The findings show that the data fitted the model well

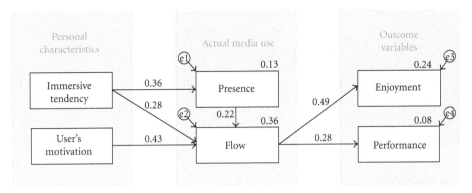

FIGURE 2: Relationship between personal characteristics, actual media use, and outcome variable: resulting model for study 1.

(χ^2 = 53.10; df = 47; P = .25; GFI = .89; CFI = .98; RMSEA = .04). Furthermore all path coefficients turned out to be significant. Thus, the results of confirmatory factor analysis confirm the two-factor structure.

3.2.4. Relationship between Personal Characteristics, Actual Media Use, and Outcome Variables: Path Analysis. To test the relationship between personal characteristics (immersive tendency and motivation), actual media use (presence and flow), and outcome variables (enjoyment and performance), a path analysis was conducted. Thereby, we tested the model proposed in the introduction section. Figure 2 shows the resulting model. Nonsignificant paths were removed from this model. The indices suggest a good fit (χ^2 = 11.04; df = 9; P = .27; GFI = .95; CFI = .97; RMSEA = .05).

All paths are significant on the 0.01 level except the path between presence and flow which is significant on the 0.05 level. The two exogenous variables immersive tendency and motivation are uncorrelated, $r(70)$ = .19, P > .05. As expected, the results reveal that the actual media experience depends on personal characteristics. The process variables presence and flow—which both refer to the actual use—in turn influence both, enjoyment and performance.

The exogenous variable immersive tendency influences the endogenous variable presence and thereby explains 13 percent of variance. Immersive tendency also affects flow directly as well as indirectly over presence. Thus, presence partly mediates the relationship between immersive tendency and flow. Motivation only influences flow, but not presence. Together, motivation, immersive tendency, and presence explain over one third of variance in the endogenous variable flow (36%). Flow in turn influences enjoyment as well as performance, whereby 24 percent (enjoyment), respectively 8 percent (performance) of variance is explained. In contrast, presence does not directly influence enjoyment and performance, but indirectly via flow. Additional analyses using the Baron and Kenny steps [41] show that flow fully mediates the relationship between presence and enjoyment as well as the relationship between presence and performance.

3.2.5. Summary of the Results of Study 1. Flow and presence positively correlate. Still, the results suggest that flow and presence are distinct constructs. The factor analysis revealed

a two-factorial solution with one factor representing flow and the other representing presence. Path analysis showed that presence and flow are influenced by immersive tendency. Motivation, in contrast, only influenced flow experiences. Furthermore, flow influenced enjoyment as well as performance, whereby the latter influence was not very strong. Presence, on the other hand, only influenced the two outcome variable indirectly over flow. Thus flow was identified as an important mediator.

4. Study 2

To replicate the findings of study 1 and to enhance external validity, we conducted a second study in the context of a different computer game.

4.1. Method

4.1.1. Participants. 120 participants took part in the second study (80 women and 40 men). All of them were students of a large public university in Switzerland. The average age was 22.50 years (SD = 3.51). The sample consists of undergraduate students enrolled in psychology, who obtained a credit for participating. All participants were treated according to the declaration of Helsinki [34].

4.1.2. Design and Statistical Methods. The same variables as in study 1 were assessed (motivation, immersive tendency, spatial presence, flow, enjoyment, and performance) and the same analyses were conducted.

4.1.3. Stimulus Material

The Game Formula 1. Championship Edition [42] for Playstation 3 was used, whereby the circuit "Autodroma Nazionale Monza" was chosen. Participants drove the car using a steering-wheel and a foot pedal. To exercise the handling, there was a two minutes training phase. Then, the testing phase began. Participants were instructed to drive as fast as possible without crashing. The duration of the testing phase was ten minutes.

The game was played on a desktop system by using a 46″ LCD large-screen television.

TABLE 3: Bivariate correlations between the measured variables.

Variables	Mean	Standard deviation	1	2	3	4	5	6
(1) Presence	3.04	1.11	—	.34**	.33**	.06	.16	.01
(2) Flow	3.51	0.89		—	.20*	.46**	.46**	.26*
(3) Immersive tendency	3.25	0.58			—	.31**	−.04	.08
(4) Motivation	4.20	0.96				—	.21*	.17
(5) Enjoyment	3.78	1.34					—	.21*
(6) Performance	5.05	0.77						—

Note: *$P < .05$, **$P < .01$.

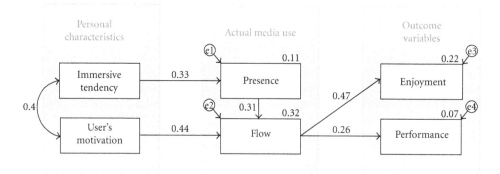

FIGURE 3: Relationship between personal characteristics, actual media use, and outcome variable: resulting model for study 2.

4.1.4. Measurements. To measure immersive tendency, motivation, flow, and enjoyment, the same instruments as in study 1 were used.

Since the presence scale we used in study 1 was originally designed to measure presence in the context of television, we chose to use another scale in study 2, namely, the *I group Presence Questionnaire* [43]. According to the authors, this scale builds upon other existing presence questionnaires and is more commonly used than Kim and Biocca's scale (e.g., in the following studies: [44, 45]). We used the spatial presence subscale, which consists of five items on a five-point scale (example item: "somehow I felt that the virtual world surrounded me."). Since another computer game was used, the *performance* was also measured differently.

The number of rounds completed during the 10-minute testing phase served as performance measure.

4.2. Results

4.2.1. Reliabilities. Reliabilities for the presence scale (Cronbach's *alpha* = .74) and the immersive tendency questionnaire (Cronbach's *alpha* = .77) were acceptable. The flow scale turned out to be reliable as well (Cronbach's *alpha* = .83).

4.2.2. Descriptives. Table 3 shows the means and standard deviations of the variables, we captured, as well as their intercorrelations. The mean performance reflects the average number of rounds that were completed in the racing game. The findings show that presence, flow, and enjoyment ratings were above the midpoint of the scales and thus slightly higher than in study 1.

4.2.3. Dimensionality of Flow and Presence: Factor Analysis. The MSA criterion is acceptable (MSA = .77) and the scree test suggests a two-factor solution. The varimax rotation extracts a first factor which explains about one-fourth of the variance. It consists of six flow items. The second factor explains 18 percent of the variance and mainly consists of four out of five presence items. Like in study 1, no items of different constructs load high on the same factor. Table 4 shows these results.

The result of a confirmatory factor analysis shows that the data fits the model well (χ^2 = 14.81; df = 20; P = .79; GFI = .97; CFI = 1.00; RMSEA = .00), whereby all path coefficients were significant. Hence, the results of confirmatory factor analysis confirm the two-factorial structure of the data.

4.2.4. Relationship between Personal Characteristics, Actual Media Use, and Outcome Variables: Path Analysis. The relationship between personal characteristics (immersive tendency and motivation), actual media use (presence and flow), and outcome variables (enjoyment and performance) was again tested with a path analysis. Figure 3 shows the resulting model. The fit of the model turned out to be good (χ^2 = 6.83; df = 9; P = .66; GFI = .98; CFI = 1.00; RMSEA = .00).

All paths are significant on the 0.01 level. All nonsignificant paths were removed from the model as well. In contrast to the first study, the two exogenous variables immersive tendency and motivation are correlated. Like in study 1, the findings show that personal characteristics can predict the actual media use in terms of presence and flow. Actual media use in terms of presence and flow in turn affects enjoyment as well as performance.

TABLE 4: Presence and Flow: principal axis factoring*.

Factor		1	2
A priori classification	Item		
	Somehow I felt that the virtual world surrounded me.	.052	**.605**
	I felt like I was just perceiving pictures (inverse coded).	.139	.286
Presence	**I did not feel present in the virtual space** (inverse coded).	.007	**.408**
	I had a sense of acting in the virtual space, rather than operating something from outside.	.045	**.814**
	I felt present in the virtual space.	.063	**.904**
	I knew what I had to do each step of the way.	**.542**	.020
	The right thoughts/movements occurred of their own accord.	**.724**	.084
	I felt that I had everything under control.	**.734**	.064
	I had no difficulty concentrating.	**.567**	.098
	My mind was completely clear.	**.723**	.086
Flow	**My thoughts/activities were running fluidly and smoothly.**	**.885**	.146
	I was totally absorbed in what I was doing.	.362	.111
	I felt just the right amount of challenge.	.287	−.001
	I was completely lost in thought.	.335	.015
	I did not notice the time passing.	.298	.123
% of variance explained		**24.7**	**18.0**

* Rotation method: varimax with Kaiser normalisation.
Note: values less than 0.4 are suppressed.

The exogenous variable immersive tendency influences the endogenous variable presence, whereby 11 percent of variance is explained. In contrast to study 1, immersive tendency does not influence flow directly. Only an indirect influence via presence occurs. Thus, presence totally mediates the relationship between immersive tendency and flow. This mediation was tested by using the steps by Baron and Kenny [41]. Motivation only influences flow, but not presence. Immersive tendency, motivation, and presence together explain about one-third of variance in the endogenous variable flow. Flow in turn influences enjoyment as well as performance and thereby explains 22 percent (enjoyment) and 7 percent (performance) of variance. Like in the first study, presence does not directly influence enjoyment and performance, but indirectly via flow. Again, the Baron and Kenny steps show that flow fully mediates the relationship between presence and enjoyment and between presence and performance.

4.2.5. Summary of the Results of Study 2. Generally, the results were quite similar to those of study 1. Flow and presence are positively related, but the results of the factor analysis again suggest that flow and presence are distinct constructs and do hardly share common variance. The findings of the path analysis suggest that presence is influenced by immersive tendency, whereas flow is influenced by motivation. Flow in turn low influenced enjoyment as well as performance, whereby more variance was explained in the variable enjoyment. Presence influenced enjoyment and flow indirectly. Alike study 1, these relations were mediated by flow.

5. Study 3

In the games we used for study 1 and study 2, the elements of the virtual environments were rather vivid and realistic

and thus ideal to induce spatial presence. We therefore aimed to further replicate the findings of study 1 and 2 in the context of a computer game that portrays the elements of the environment less realistically.

5.1. Method

5.1.1. Participants. 78 participants took part in the third study (37 women and 41 men). All of them were students of a large public university in Switzerland. The average age was 23.82 years (SD = 8.12). All participants were treated according to the declaration of Helsinki [34].

5.1.2. Design and Statistical Methods. The same variables as in studies 1 and 2 were assessed (motivation, immersive tendency, spatial presence, flow, enjoyment, and performance) and the same analyses were conducted.

5.1.3. Stimulus Material. The game *Ultimate Flash Sonic* was used (FlashGames.de, n.d.). It is a flash version of the Sonic the Hedgehog Game [46]. Ultimate Flash Sonic is a jump and run game. Compared to the games used for study 1 and 2, the design and the graphics are rather poor as well as cartoon-like. Participants had to control their avatar by using the keyboard. First, there was a two-minute training phase. Then, the participants were instructed to complete the first level as fast as possible.

The game was played on a desktop system. Like in the previous studies, we used a 46″ LCD large-screen television.

5.1.4. Measurements. To measure immersive tendency, motivation, flow, and enjoyment, the same instruments as in studies 1 and 2 were used.

TABLE 5: Bivariate correlations between the measured variables.

Variables	Mean	Standard deviation	1	2	3	4	5	6
(1) Presence	1.93	0.87	—	.26*	.42**	.19	.25*	−.07
(2) Flow	3.23	0.89		—	.38**	.47**	.29*	−.35**
(3) Immersive tendency	3.18	0.73			—	.03	.13	−.08
(4) Motivation	3.42	1.20				—	.06	−.42**
(5) Enjoyment	3.34	1.58					—	−.01
(6) Performance	111.49	64.96						—

Note: *$P < .05$, **$P < .01$

To further enhance external validity, we again chose to use another scale to assess spatial presence, namely, the *MEC Spatial Presence* Questionnaire [47]. The questionnaire was tested with different types of media stimuli and was found reliable and valid [48]. As we were particularly interested in the spatial dimension of presence, we restricted ourselves to the subscale *Spatial Presence: Self Location*. This subscale consists of 8 items, which have to be judged on a five-point Likert scale (1 = I do not agree at all; 5 = I fully agree).

Since another computer game was used, the *performance* was also measured differently. The time to complete the first level of the game comprised the performance measure.

5.2. Results

5.2.1. Reliabilities. Reliabilities for the presence scale (Cronbach's *alpha* = .93), the flow scale (Cronbach's *alpha* = .75), and the immersive tendency questionnaire (Cronbach's *alpha* = .84) were acceptable.

5.2.2. Descriptives. Table 5 shows the means and standard deviations of the variables, we captured, as well as their intercorrelations. The mean performance reflects the average amount of time needed to complete the first level (in seconds). The findings show that flow and enjoyment ratings were above the midpoint of the scales and thus comparable to the values of studies 1 and 2. The presence ratings were lower compared to the other studies. This may be due to the poor graphics of the game used for study 3.

5.2.3. Dimensionality of Flow and Presence: Factor Analysis. An acceptable MSA criterion resulted (MSA = .79). The scree test suggests a three-factor solution. The varimax rotation extracts a first factor which explains 28.8% percent of the variance. It consists of all eight presence items. The second and the third factor consist of all flow items and together explain slightly more than the presence items (32 percent of the variance). The second factor mainly consists of six flow items. In accordance with the classification of Rheinberg et al. [25], these items cover the flow aspect *smooth and automatic running* and reflect the sensation of focusing and control over the activity as well as smooth and automatic cogitations. The third factor consists of the remaining four flow items. In line with Rheinberg's classification, these items cover the flow aspect *absorption*, which includes full involvement, distorted sense of time, optimal challenge, as well as absent-mindedness. Like in studies 1 and 2, no items of different

constructs load high on the same factor. Table 6 shows these results.

To confirm the factorial structure, we additionally conducted a confirmatory factor analysis. The results show an acceptable model fit (χ^2 = 110.79; df = 109; P = .43; GFI = .87; CFI = 1.00; RMSEA = .02) and all path coefficients turned out to be significant. Thus, the three-factorial structure of the data could be confirmed.

5.2.4. Relationship between Personal Characteristics, Actual Media Use, and Outcome Variables: Path Analysis. The relationship between personal characteristics (immersive tendency and motivation), actual media use (presence and flow), and outcome variables (enjoyment and performance) was tested with path analysis. The results of the factor analysis suggest flow to be a two-factorial construct. Therefore, and in contrast to studies 1 and 2, the two flow subdimensions *absorption* and *smooth and automatic running* were both included. Figure 4 shows the resulting model. The fit of the model turned out to be acceptable (χ^2 = 16.64; df = 12; P = .16; GFI = .94; CFI = 93; RMSEA = .07).

All nonsignificant paths were removed from the model. Like in the previous studies, personal characteristics influence presence and flow. Presence and flow in turn affect the outcome variables enjoyment and performance.

Immersive tendency influences presence, whereby 17 percent of variance is explained. Immersive tendency also indirectly affects the flow subdimension absorption. Thus, presence mediates the relationship between immersive tendency and absorption. This mediation was tested using the procedure described by Baron and Kenny [41]. Motivation neither influences presence nor absorption. However, the user's motivation affects the second flow subdimension *smooth and automatic running*, explaining 19 percent of variance. Smooth and automatic running in turn influences performance. Performance is also influenced by absorption. Thereby, 12 percent of variance is explained. No mediation was found between presence and performance. Thus, in contrast to studies 1 and 2, presence has neither a direct nor an indirect influence on the participants' performance. Enjoyment is only affected by absorption. Similar to studies 1 and 2, we also observed an indirect effect of presence on enjoyment. The steps proposed by Baron and Kenny [41] show that absorption fully mediates between presence and enjoyment. In total, 7 percent of variance of the enjoyment ratings is explained.

TABLE 6: Presence and flow: principal axis factoring*.

A priori classification	Item	1	2	3
Factor				
	I had the feeling that I was in the middle of the action rather than merely observing.	.536	−.007	.422
	I felt like I was a part of the environment of the game.	.788	−.018	.153
	I felt like I was actually there in the environment of the game.	.933	−.065	.068
	I felt like the objects in the game surrounded me.	.783	.100	.188
Presence	It was as though my true location had shifted into the environment of the game.	.719	.046	.251
	It seemed as though myself was present in the environment of the game.	.888	−.095	.135
	I felt as though I was physically present in the environment of the game.	.816	−.080	.048
	It seemed as though I actually took part in the action in the game.	.728	.058	.210
	I knew what I had to do each step of the way.	.068	.771	−.113
	The right thoughts/movements occurred of their own accord.	.004	.669	−.075
	I felt that I had everything under control.	.077	.813	−.202
	I had no difficulty concentrating.	−.105	.399	.244
	My mind was completely clear.	.001	.616	.169
Flow	My thoughts/activities were running fluidly and smoothly.	−.095	.925	.051
	I was totally absorbed in what I was doing.	.020	.155	.898
	I felt just the right amount of challenge.	.268	−.028	.691
	I was completely lost in thought.	.341	−.034	.625
	I did not notice the time passing.	.279	−.097	.626
% of variance explained		28.8	17.6	14.4

* Rotation method: varimax with Kaiser normalisation.
Note: values less than 0.4 are suppressed.

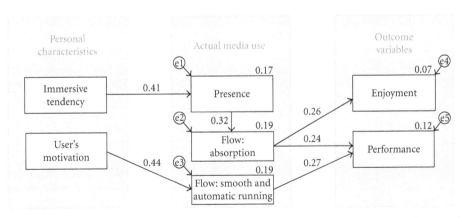

FIGURE 4: Relationship between personal characteristics, actual media use, and outcome variable: resulting model for study 3.

5.2.5. Summary of the Results of Study 3. The correlation between flow and presence is also significant in study 3, but the findings again suggest that flow and presence differ from each other. The factor analysis revealed a three-factorial solution with one factor representing presence and the second and third factor representing flow. Thus, in contrast to studies 1 and 2, flow turned out to be a two-factorial construct with one factor representing the aspect *absorption* and the other representing the aspect *smooth and automatic running* (cf. [25]). Hence, both flow dimensions were included in the path analysis. The results revealed that presence is dependent on immersive tendency. Motivation influenced smooth and automatic running, but not absorption. Furthermore, both flow dimensions influenced performance. In contrast to studies 1 and 2, presence had neither a direct nor an indirect effect on performance. Enjoyment was only directly affected by absorption, but there was also an indirect effect of presence on enjoyment. Thus, flow was again identified as a mediator. However, the influenced on enjoyment was rather small compared to studies 1 and 2.

6. Discussion

The aim of the present study was to analyse the relationship between flow and (spatial) presence. Furthermore, we investigated whether these two variables depend on the users' motivation and immersive tendency and whether presence and flow influence enjoyment and performance. We first analysed these questions within the computer role-playing game Neverwinter Nights and then replicated the findings in the context of the racing game Formula 1 for Playstation 3. To examine whether the relation between presence and flow depends on the vividness of the virtual environment, we conducted a third study within the jump and run game Sonic the Hedgehog. In contrast to the other games we used, Sonic the Hedgehog lacks of vividness and portrays the elements of the virtual world less realistically, but rather cartoon-like. Thus, it seems less ideal to induce sensations of presence. All studies revealed quite similar results even though different games and different presence scales were used and the handling of the games was different (keyboard versus steering wheel).

Presence and flow are positively correlated in all studies. However, the three principal axis factor analyses provide evidence that presence and flow are two distinct constructs, which do hardly share common variance. The results of all three studies show that there is not even one single item of different constructs that loads high on the same factor. In the first two studies, two-factor solutions were suggested by the screen tests. These solutions go in line with the prior classification. One factor represents presence, the other factor represents flow. In the third study, a three-factorial solution resulted. One factor represents presence, whereas flow is represented by two factors. In line with the conceptualisation of Rheinberg et al. [25], one factor is referring to *absorption*—the sensation of involvement, absent mindedness, and distorted sense of time—the other is referring to *smooth and automatic running*, the experience of utmost focus and control over the activity. The findings of the three studies suggest that even though the two constructs correlate and are thus related, presence and flow represent different aspects of immersive experiences. It is by all means plausible that spatial presence refers to the feeling of being involved or present in a virtual reality. A user experiencing presence is highly immersed in the virtual world portrayed by the computer game. Thus, the concept seems to cover spatial aspects. In contrast, we assume that flow rather describes a mental state in which a person is fully immersed in a task. Thus, flow seems to be related to the gaming action. This in line with Weibel et al. [6] Fontaine [9] who considers that flow involves a narrow focus on task characteristics, whereas presence involves a broader awareness of the task ecology. Taken together, the experience of flow seems to refer to the sensation of being highly involved in the gaming action, but not to the sensation of being spatially immersed in the world portrayed by the game. Therefore, we conclude that immersive experiences can be divided into (1) spatial immersion—the sensation of being there (presence)—and (2) immersion in the task—the sensation of being involved in the gaming action (flow). As the flow factor explained more variance than the presence

factor within all three computer games, we suggest that flow is more important for immersive experiences in computer games.

Our second objective was the investigation of the relationship between motivation and immersive tendency, actual media use in terms of presence and flow, and the outcome variables enjoyment and performance. The results of the three studies support the predicted relations. Presence and flow are positively affected by motivation and immersive tendency and in turn influence enjoyment and performance.

Witmer and Singer [11] suggest that immersive tendency is a disposition which can predict the amount of immersion a person is able to experience. The findings of all three studies support this assumption. We can therefore conclude that mediated environments designed to absorb and immerse their users are most effective for users scoring high on immersive tendency. Furthermore, our study shows that motivational factors play a crucial role and enhance flow experiences. Users rather immerse in the gaming action if they are motivated before interacting with a medium. As a consequence, designers of e-learning environments should try to evoke the users' motivation. To sum up, the results are in line with Wirth et al. [3], who state that user characteristics may support the processes that lead to immersive experiences.

The results furthermore show that flow experiences positively affect enjoyment and performance. Presence, in contrast, does only indirectly influence enjoyment (in all studies) and performance (in studies 1 and 2) via flow, which was identified a mediator. This again suggests that presence is an ancestor of flow. In line with Weibel et al. [6], the two sensations seem not to occur simultaneous, but rather sequential. It might be that the sensation of being there in the computer game facilitates smooth and automatic running of the gaming task because the primary frame of reference is in the world provided by the game and no longer in the physical world, where the task is actually accomplished. This may explain the autotelic nature of flow during gaming.

The influence of flow on performance was not too strong. Nevertheless, the effect seems to be solid since the influence of flow on performance was found in three different gaming settings with three completely different performance measurements. As expected, flow also influences enjoyment. This could be shown in all studies. Whereas, the influence was not too strong in study 3, about one-quarter percent of variance was explained in studies 1 and 2. This refers to a strong effect. In line with previous assumption and findings (e.g., [3, 49, 50]), we found that gaming is more fun when a player is experiencing presence and flow during the actual media use. Thus, flow strongly contributes to gaming enjoyment. Voiskounsky et al. [5] as well as Klimmt [26] seem to be right when suggesting that flow is an important source of the attractiveness of computer games.

The relationship between presence, flow, enjoyment, and performance also seems to be dependent on the type of game. Even though, the results were quite similar, the influence of presence and flow on enjoyment was smaller within the jump and run game compared to the computer role-playing game and the racing game. In study 3, less than 10 percent of variance was explained. This might be because this game provided less vivid and elaborate spatial information what in turn may have led to lower presence ratings. Furthermore and in contrast to study 1 and 2, no indirect effect of presence on performance was observed in the jump and run game. Therefore, we conclude that presence plays a more important role in vivid and realistic games than in cartoon-like games with less vividness. This is in line with the assumptions of Tamborini and Skalski [50]. Since the effect of flow on performance was even stronger in the jump and run game compared to the other games, we assume that flow experiences are less depending on spatial aspects like the vividness of the game environment. Thus, the type of game rather seems to be of more importance for presence experiences than for flow experiences. However, further studies should be conducted to draw final conclusions about the role of presence in different gaming settings.

Our findings are of practical and especially of theoretical importance because they can—at least to a certain amount—help explaining the popularity of computer games. Enjoyment is a main gratification for playing games [51]. The studies, we accomplished, are of theoretical significance since they help explaining the sources of performance and—after all—enjoyment. Our results suggest that game players after all enjoy the gaming action when they experience presence and flow. Thus, game developers should design games in a way they evoke presence and especially flow. Our study also shows the importance of individual characteristics. Therefore, we conclude that prior assessment of a users' personality and motivation might effectively help in tailoring the most suitable environment for each user. This in turn could help to facilitate immersion and to enhance sensations of presence and flow. As a consequence, game designers could then increase the level of enjoyment, what is one of their main objectives (cf. [4]). Furthermore, our findings suggest that future research using computer games could consider presence and flow as relevant covariates. This could help to partial out the possibly confounding influences of presence or flow on the observed variables.

Since we used three different computer games for our studies, the external validity of our study is good and generalizations for other computer games seem reasonable. Further research could additionally investigate these issues for other media. Furthermore, since gamers are mostly male (cf. [1]), future studies are suggested to replicate this study using a sample with male participants as the majority. Even though no gender differences occurred within our studies, gender may still be a significant factor influencing gaming experience. Also, performance measures were assessed within nonspatial tasks. The results may have been different with performance measures that rather refer to spatial tasks. Future studies should therefore consider capturing spatial as well as nonspatial task performances.

7. Conclusion

We attempted to examine the relation between presence and flow. The results of exploratory as well as confirmatory factor provides empirical evidence that flow and presence

are distinct constructs, the first referring to the sensation of being involved in the gaming action, the latter referring to the sensation of being there. Furthermore, we could show within three different computer games that immersive tendency and the (pre)motivation contribute to presence and flow. Flow in turn influences enjoyment and performance. In addition, flow mediates the relationship between presence and enjoyment. In two of the three studies, flow also mediates between presence and performance.

Our study shows that flow is a central construct and may explain the popularity of computer games. Computer Games seem to be ideal to induce flow experiences. This might be because the difficulty level of a computer game is usually varying. As a consequence, it is likely that the balance between challenge and skills is rather given compared to other applications. However, this a mere speculation which should be tested in future studies.

References

[1] N. Yee, "The demographics, motivations, and derived experiences of users of massively multi-user online graphical environments," *Presence: Teleoperators and Virtual Environments*, vol. 15, no. 3, pp. 309–329, 2006.

[2] M. Lombard and T. Ditton, "At the heart of it all: the concept of presence," *Journal of Computer-Mediated Communication*, vol. 3, no. 2, 1997.

[3] W. Wirth, T. Hartmann, S. Böcking et al., "A process model of the formation of spatial presence experiences," *Media Psychology*, vol. 9, no. 3, pp. 493–525, 2007.

[4] J. L. Sherry, "Flow and media enjoyment," *Communication Theory*, vol. 14, no. 4, pp. 328–347, 2004.

[5] A. E. Voiskounsky, O. V. Mitina, and A. A. Avetisova, "Playing online games: flow experience," *PsychoNology Journal*, vol. 2, no. 3, pp. 259–281, 2004.

[6] D. Weibel, B. Wissmath, S. Habegger, Y. Steiner, and R. Groner, "Playing online games against computer- vs. human-controlled opponents: effects on presence, flow, and enjoyment," *Computers in Human Behavior*, vol. 24, no. 5, pp. 2274–2291, 2008.

[7] J. V. Draper, D. B. Kaber, and J. M. Usher, "Telepresence," *Human Factors*, vol. 40, no. 3, pp. 354–375, 1998.

[8] D. L. Hoffman and T. P. Novak, "Flow online: lessons learned and future prospects," *Journal of Interactive Marketing*, vol. 23, no. 1, pp. 23–34, 2009.

[9] G. Fontaine, "The experience of a sense of presence in intercultural and international encounters," *Presence: Teleoperators and Virtual Environments*, vol. 1, no. 4, pp. 482–490, 1992.

[10] K. E. Bystrom, W. Barfield, and C. Hendrix, "A conceptual model of the sense of presence in virtual environments," *Presence: Teleoperators and Virtual Environments*, vol. 8, no. 2, pp. 241–244, 1999.

[11] B. G. Witmer and M. J. Singer, "Measuring presence in virtual environments: a presence questionnaire," *Presence: Teleoperators and Virtual Environments*, vol. 7, no. 3, pp. 225–240, 1998.

[12] D. Weibel, B. Wissmath, and F. W. Mast, "Immersion in mediated environments: the role of personality traits," *Cyberpsychology, Behavior, and Social Networking*, vol. 13, no. 3, pp. 251–256, 2010.

[13] S. Engeser, F. Rheinberg, R. Vollmeyer, and J. Bischoff, "Motivation, flow-experience, and performance in learning settings

at universities," *Zeitschrift fur Pedagogische Psychologie*, vol. 19, no. 3, pp. 159–172, 2005.

[14] M. Csikszentmihalyi, "The flow experience and its significance for human psychology," in *Optimal Experience: Psychological Studies of Flow in Consciousness*, M. Csikszentmihalyi and I. Csikszentmihalyi, Eds., pp. 15–35, Cambridge University Press, Cambridge, UK, 1988.

[15] J. Steuer, "Defining virtual reality: dimensions determining telepresence," *Journal of Communication*, vol. 42, pp. 72–92, 1992.

[16] M. Slater and S. Wilbur, "A framework for immersive virtual environments (FIVE): speculations on the role of presence in virtual environments," *Presence: Teleoperators and Virtual Environments*, vol. 6, no. 6, pp. 603–616, 1997.

[17] A. Van Dam, A. S. Forsberg, D. H. Laidlaw, J. J. LaViola, and R. M. Simpson, "Immersive VR for scientific visualization: a progress report," *IEEE Computer Graphics and Applications*, vol. 20, no. 6, pp. 26–52, 2000.

[18] R. Tamborini, "The experience of telepresence in violent games," in *Proceedings of the Annual Conference of the National Communication Assosiation*, Seattle, Wash, USA, 2000.

[19] M. Csikszentmihalyi, *Beyond Boredom and Anxiety: Experiencing Flow in Work and Play*, Jossey-Bass, San Fransisco, Calif, USA, 1975.

[20] J. Bryce and J. Rutter, "In the game—in the flow: presence in public computer gaming," Poster presented at the computer games and digital textualities, Copenhagen, Denmark, March 2001, http://www.cric.ac.uk/cric/staff/Jason_Rutter/presence.htm.

[21] J. A. Ghani and S. P. Deshpande, "Task characteristics and the experience of optimal flow in human computer interaction," *Journal of Psychology*, vol. 128, no. 4, pp. 381–391, 1994.

[22] F. Rheinberg and R. Vollmeyer, "Flow experience in a computer game under experimentally controlled conditions," *Zeitschrift fur Psychologie*, vol. 211, no. 4, pp. 161–170, 2003.

[23] J. Webster, L. K. Trevino, and L. Ryan, "The dimensionality and correlates of flow in human-computer interactions," *Computers in Human Behavior*, vol. 9, no. 4, pp. 411–426, 1993.

[24] F. Rheinberg, S. Engeser, and R. Vollmeyer, "Measuring components of flow: the Flow-Short-Scale," in *Proceedings of the 1st International Positive Psychology Summit*, Washington, DC, USA, October 2002.

[25] F. Rheinberg, R. Vollmeyer, and S. Engeser, "Die Erfassung des Flow-Erlebens [Measuring flow experiences]," in *Diagnostik von Motivation und Selbstkonzept. Tests und Trends*, J. Stiensmeier-Pelster and F. Rheinberg, Eds., vol. 2, pp. 261–279, Hogrefe, Göttingen, Germany, 2003.

[26] C. Klimmt, "Computer-Spiel: Interaktive Unterhaltungsangebote als Synthese aus Medium und Spielzeug," *Zeitschrift für Medienpsychologie*, vol. 13, no. 1, pp. 22–32, 2001.

[27] D. L. Hoffman and T. P. Novak, "Marketing in hypermedia computer-mediated environments: conceptual foundations," *Journal of Marketing*, vol. 60, no. 3, pp. 50–68, 1996.

[28] T. P. Novak, D. L. Hoffman, and Y. F. Yung, "Measuring the customer experience in online environments: a structural modeling approach," *Marketing Science*, vol. 19, no. 1, pp. 22–42, 2000.

[29] D. Weibel, D. Stricker, and B. Wissmath, "The use of a virtual learning centre in the context of a university lecture: factors influencing satisfaction and performance," *Interactive Learning Environments*. In press.

[30] C. Heeter, "Being There: the subjective experience of presence," *Presence*, vol. 1, pp. 262–271, 1992.

[31] C. I. Teng, "Customization, immersion satisfaction, and online gamer loyalty," *Computers in Human Behavior*, vol. 26, no. 6, pp. 1547–1554, 2010.

[32] R. Weber, R. Tamborini, A. Westcott-Baker, and B. Kantor, "Theorizing flow and media enjoyment as cognitive synchronization of attentional and reward networks," *Communication Theory*, vol. 19, no. 4, pp. 397–422, 2009.

[33] T. B. Sheridan, "Musing on telepresence and virtual presence," *Presence*, vol. 1, pp. 120–126, 1992.

[34] World Medical Association, "Declaration of Helsinki," *Law, Medicine & Health Care*, vol. 19, pp. 264–265, 1991.

[35] BioWare Corp., "Neverwinter Nights [Computersoftware und Manual]," 2002, BioWare Corp., Edmonton, Canada.

[36] T. Kim and F. Biocca, "Telepresence via television: two dimensions of telepresence may have different connections to memory and persuasion," *Journal of Computer-Mediated Communication*, vol. 3, no. 2, 1997.

[37] S. G. Nicovich, G. W. Boller, and T. B. Cornwell, "Experienced presence within computer-mediated communications: initial explorations on the effects of gender with respect to empathy and immersion," *Journal of Computer-Mediated Communication*, vol. 10, no. 2, 2005.

[38] M. C. Green, T. C. Brock, and G. F. Kaufman, "Understanding media enjoyment: the role of transportation into narrative worlds," *Communication Theory*, vol. 14, no. 4, pp. 311–327, 2004.

[39] S. Knobloch and D. Zillmann, "Mood management via the digital jukebox," *Journal of Communication*, vol. 52, no. 2, pp. 351–366, 2002.

[40] H. F. Kaiser and J. Rice, "Little jiffy mark IV," *Educational and Psychological Measurement*, vol. 34, pp. 111–117, 1974.

[41] R. M. Baron and D. A. Kenny, "The moderator-mediator variable distinction in social psychological research: conceptual, strategic, and statistical considerations," *Journal of Personality and Social Psychology*, vol. 51, no. 6, pp. 1173–1182, 1986.

[42] Sony Computer Entertainment Europe, "Formula 1: Championship Edition (Version 1.0) [Computer Software]," London, UK, 2006.

[43] T. Schubert, F. Friedmann, and H. Regenbrecht, "The experience of presence: factor analytic insights," *Presence: Teleoperators and Virtual Environments*, vol. 10, no. 3, pp. 266–281, 2001.

[44] N. J. M. Smets, M. S. Abbing, M. A. Neerincx, J. Lindenberg, and H. van Oostendorp, "Game-based versus storyboard-based evaluations of crew support prototypes for long duration missions," *Acta Astronautica*, vol. 66, no. 5-6, pp. 810–820, 2010.

[45] R. C. Freire, M. R. De Carvalho, M. Joffily, W. A. Zin, and A. E. Nardi, "Anxiogenic properties of a computer simulation for panic disorder with agoraphobia," *Journal of Affective Disorders*, vol. 125, no. 1–3, pp. 301–306, 2010.

[46] Sega Corporation, "Sonic the Hedgehog [computer software]," Tokyo, Japan, 1991.

[47] P. Vorderer, W. Wirth, F. R. Gouveia et al., "MEC Spatial Presence Questionnaire (MEC-SPQ): short documentation and instructions for application," Tech. Rep. MEC (IST-2001-37661), European Community, 2004.

[48] A. Sacau, J. Laarni, and T. Hartmann, "Influence of individual factors on presence," *Computers in Human Behavior*, vol. 24, no. 5, pp. 2255–2273, 2008.

[49] C. Klimmt and P. Vorderer, "Media Psychology "is not yet there": introducing theories on media entertainment to the Presence debate," *Presence: Teleoperators and Virtual Environments*, vol. 12, no. 4, pp. 346–359, 2003.

[50] R. Tamborini and P. Skalski, " The role of presence in the experience of electronic games," in *Playing Computer Games: Motives, Responses, and Consequences*, P. Vorderer and J. Bryant, Eds., pp. 225–240, Erlbaum, Mahwah, NJ, USA, 2006.

[51] J. H. Wu, S. C. Wang, and H. H. Tsai, "Falling in love with online games: the uses and gratifications perspective," *Computers in Human Behavior*, vol. 26, no. 6, pp. 1862–1871, 2010.

8

Out of the Cube: Augmented Rubik's Cube

Oriel Bergig,[1] **Eyal Soreq,**[2] **Nate Hagbi,**[1] **Kirill Pevzner,**[1] **Nati Levi,**[1] **Shoham Blau,**[2] **Yulia Smelansky,**[2] **and Jihad El-Sana**[1]

[1] *Department of Computer Science, Ben-Gurion University of the Negev, P.O.B 653 Be'er Sheva 84105, Israel*
[2] *Screen-Based Arts, Bezalel Academy of Arts and Design, Jerusalem 91240, Israel*

Correspondence should be addressed to Oriel Bergig, bergig@gmail.com

Academic Editor: Suiping Zhou

Computer gaming habits have a tendency to evolve with technology, the best being ones that immerse both our imagination and intellect. Here, we describe a new game platform, an *Augmented Reality Rubik's cube*. The cube acts simultaneously as both the controller and the game board. Gameplay is controlled by the cube, and game assets are rendered on top of it. Shuffling and tilting operations on the cube are mapped to game interaction. We discuss the game design decisions involved in developing a game for this platform, as well as the technological challenges in implementing it. Ultimately, we describe two games and discuss the conclusions of an informal user study based on those games.

1. Introduction

Augmented Reality (AR), where computer-generated graphics is rendered and registered on the real world in real time, has existed as an academic field since the 60's. As anticipated by Bolter and Grusin [1], AR is now gaining wider public acceptance as AR applications are being demonstrated in art, entertainment, and gaming.

In 2007, the first commercial AR game was produced. In The Eye of Judgment (http://www.eyeofjudgment.com/) an AR game for the Sony Play Station, a special set of board and cards was designed. Since the Eye of Judgment saw light, a constantly increasing number of commercial AR games are developed every year, motivating research for AR game technologies.

In this work, we present a game technology that extends an existing game platform, a toy. While some game platforms are developed and tailored to support AR experiences (e.g., The Eye of Judgment game board), others can be based on existing ones. For example, augmenting regular cards may lay the foundations for a new game technology based on an existing game platform.

One of the advantages in exploiting an existing game platform (e.g., cards) to create new digital experiences lies in the fact that people are familiar with the underlying game mechanics (e.g., pile cards). In addition, although the game uses a tangible platform, distributing it becomes a simpler task. For example, the software for the game can be downloaded online.

Augmented Reality game technologies that revolve around familiar game platforms can exploit the interactions of the underlying platform. For example, piles of cards could translate to grouping models represented by those cards. In many cases, it seems natural to preserve the meaning of interactions in the underlying platform and map them to the AR experience. Furthermore, new game interactions are made possible with meaning only within the scope of the extended AR platform. For example, tilting a card to one side can cause an augmented model to slip aside.

In this work, we developed Out of the Cube (OOTC), an AR extension to the traditional Rubik's cube. To play the game, the player modifies the cube using our sticker kit. We define a set of interactions and provide a natural mapping between those interactions and events that take place in the digital world. One of the early design decisions was to make all of the interactions based on the cube itself, essentially creating a controller-free interface. The traditional meaning of "shuffling the cube" interaction is preserved across the AR experience and used for virtual puzzle solving. Additional interactions are only possible with the augmented cube as described later.

To explore Rubik's cube as an AR game platform, we designed and implemented two games. Figure 1(a) is screen shot from a puzzle game, which is organized in levels. The game was designed to advance the United Nations Millennium Development Goals (http://www.un.org/millenniumgoals) with the premise of aiding in the development of poor countries. In the game, virtual villages are augmented on the cube faces. These villages develop according to the resources they receive which are controlled by the arrangement of the cube. The goal is to reach equilibrium of resources across all villages. To achieve this, the player shuffles virtual assets between the villages. Figure 1(b) is a screen shot from our second game, which is a skill-based maze walking challenge. In this game, the player has to help a child reach his goal of education and happiness by tilting the cube and walking him carefully on a narrow path. Failing to navigate the character carefully may result in a free fall from the cube's face to the ground.

This work participated in Microsoft Imagine Cup and won the 1st place in the national phase in Israel and was demonstrated in the Imagine Cup International Expo in Cairo.

The rest of the paper is structured as follows. We begin by describing background work in Section 2. We then describe the design of OOTC. In Section 4, we describe the architecture and implementation of the game application. The conclusions of an initial and informal user study are described in Section 5. Section 6 proposes ideas for additional games. In Section 7, we conclude and present directions for future work.

2. Background

OOTC has emerged as a quest to combine the popular and addictive Rubik's Cube toy with the interactivity and immersiveness of AR games. We first describe the history of Rubik's Cube and its use as a platform. We continue by describing AR games based on cubical platforms and finally extend the discussion to AR tangible interactions and AR games.

2.1. Rubik's Cube Platform. Rubik's cube is a game mechanics invented in 1974 and sold commercially since 1980. As of January 2009, 350 million cubes have been sold worldwide, making it the world's top-selling puzzle game [2]. It is widely considered to be the world's best-selling toy [3].

The traditional Rubik's cube game mechanics has been used to develop new games extending the traditional puzzle game. The cube was extended to 4×4 and 5×5 cubes by Seven Towns Ltd, the company that owns the Rubik's cube brand. They also offer Rubik's Custom Sticker Kits (http://www.rubiks.com/shop) for people to create their own games. It comes with five sheets of A4 paper size blank stickers for use in a color printer. Different designs are used for promoting business, and special designs are sold commercially (e.g., NBA teams logo Cube). In this work, we created a sticker kit, very similar to those offered by Seven Towns Ltd. The symbols on our sticker kit allow pose estimation and identification of cubelet (one of the nine squares of a Rubik's Cube's face).

Electronic games based on the cube mechanics exist as well. Rubik's TouchCube (http://www.rubikstouchcube.com/) is an electronic cube with touch sensor technology. The challenge is faced by swiping a finger on the cube, rather than shuffling it. Rubik's Puzzle World is an abstract environment populated by cubelets which make up the game's DNA. A collection of games based on this world are available for the Nintendo DS and Wii game consoles. In this work, we developed electronic games based on the cube played in front of a computer with a webcam.

2.2. Cube Platforms Used in AR. Cube platforms have been used for creating AR games. Magic Cubes [4] is a research project seeking after unique user interfaces made of two cubes with markers in an AR environment. In Jumanji Singapore [5], the cubes are used as a dice and control tool for a monopoly-style game. The purpose of Jumanji is to take its users on a virtual three-dimensional tour of Singapore's attractions while playing a board game competition. LevelHead (http://ljudmila.org/~julian/levelhead/) is a spatial memory game using three small plastic cubes with a unique marker on each face. It creates the impression that a room is somehow inside each cube. Our work shares some interaction metaphors with all the above games. However, it is based on the traditional Rubik's cube where the shuffling interaction is used to solve an AR puzzle.

2.3. Related AR Interactions and Games. Some of the interactions available in OOTC are not entirely new. For example, occlusion-based interaction has been described in [6]. Tilting and moving markers to interact with augmented 3D content are described in [7]. Our goal is to explore the design decisions and implications involved in using them in a game based on Rubik's cube as a game platform.

Augmented Reality games that are real-world extensions of existing purely virtual games have been developed to extenuate different effects of the game environment. ARQuake [8] and Human Pacman [9] are augmented versions of Quake and Pacman that are played outdoors. Invisible Train [10] and Smart Memory [11] are based on popular game mechanics and played on handheld devices. Other AR games were designed to demonstrate interaction between virtual and physical objects. Neon Racer [12] allows players to steer vehicles with traditional gamepads while spectators (and players) can use real objects to influence the race. Monkey Bridge [13] demonstrates how virtual objects can react to events in the virtual and physical worlds. The physical world is a tabletop setup with physical objects like bricks and wooden blocks that take part in the game. In this work, the games were designed to demonstrate how Rubik's cube can be used to interact with virtual content.

AR parrot (http://ardrone.parrot.com/parrot-ar-drone/usa/) is a physical platform designed for AR games. It consists of a quadricopter equipped with two cameras, which can be controlled using a computer or a phone that display the live feed from the camera. In AR.Pursuit, the video is augmented with virtual content in a combat game.

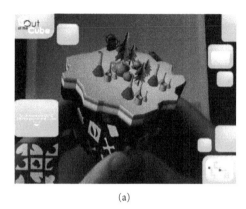
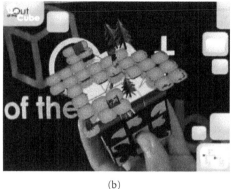

(a)   (b)

FIGURE 1: Augmented Reality games based on Rubik's Cube. (a) A village puzzle game and (b) a skill-based maze walking game.

3. Game and Technology Design

Designing AR games based on an existing game platform is challenging. Preserving the nature of underlying platform is usually preferred [14]. In this work, we harness the tangible interactions embedded in the design of Rubik's cube, while preserving the cube shuffling interaction (see Figure 2). We extend interactivity with additional AR interactions. Rubik's cube turns into an AR interface making it a platform for AR games.

In the village puzzle game (see Figure 1(a)), the player is responsible to the world that is literally in the palm of his hand. The playground of the game consists of a computer and a webcam. To play, the player modifies a Rubik's cube using an OOTC sticker kit and interacts with the cube by rotating and shuffling the cube. While manipulating the cube, the player sees his own hands holding a small village and its surroundings. The village and the assets around it change according to the cube combinations.

The village puzzle game is a 3D educational puzzle experience trusting the responsibility of developing poor villages in the hands of the player. The augmented space includes six villages tied in with different visual themes. Each village has its own unique story and environmental problems. The villages are overlaid in 3D on top of the Rubik's cube face. Each village is surrounded by the virtual assets that are necessary ingredients for its development. Through each level, the player has to distribute wisely different assets inside a village and between villages in order to find an arrangement that brings equilibrium. In some cases, it is necessary to combine two ingredients to make them more effective. In such cases, the two ingredients need to be placed one next to the other.

The maze game (see Figure 1(b)) is a skill-based challenge where a virtual character is controlled by tilting the cube to collect different assets. Two items are spread on the maze, and the character has to collect one item and bring it close to the other item. The challenge is to orient the movements of the character on a narrow path laid out in a maze structure. The path is organised in tiles that are hung in the air and stepping over the boundary results in free fall from the cube.

We magnified the experience by designing the maze as a minigame of the puzzle game. In the puzzle game, when two assets are placed nearby, they can have a stronger effect on the development of the village. To unlock the effect, the maze minigame has to be played. The virtual character has to pick one asset and bring it to the other one walking on the maze. For example, shuffling the cube to bring a lab resource and a laptop resource to the village assists each one on its own to the development of the village. However, if the two are placed next to each other and then carried one to the other by the character in the maze minigame, it will boost this village development.

The OOTC platform design enables interactions with virtual content augmented on a Rubik's cube. We designed and developed five different interaction metaphors (examples are depicted in Figure 3). These are (1) shuffling to change game assets, (2) tilting to move items around, (3) rotating faces to see different views, (4) hiding a cubelet, which is one of the nine squares of a Rubik's Cube's face, to press a button, and (5) hotspots to choose between menu items. These interactions are further detailed below.

Shuffling the cube is based on the traditional mechanics of the Rubik's cube for level solving. We preserve the familiar context of this mechanics by shuffling to spatially arrange virtual assets in order to solve the puzzle. Rotating the whole cube face reveals different views of the puzzle. Each face is augmented with one of six different villages sharing the available resources. It follows that shuffling the cube adds ingredients to one village but takes away ingredients from another. Rotating the whole cube, which changes the currently viewed and augmented cube face, is necessary to find out what is available for each village. The player seeks to find an equilibrium between villages while responding to unpredicted events, for example, a storm that demolishes the food reserves. This is similar to the Rubik's cube mechanics, as players constantly check the different faces to make sure that the last shuffle has not caused serious damage to one of the villages.

We borrowed existing AR interactions and mapped them to the cube, creating a self-contained platform. Tilting the cube causes virtual objects rendered on the cube to move

FIGURE 2: Shuffling the cube shuffles the assets arranged around the village accordingly. Here, shuffling the right side of the cube will cause the laptop and the lab assets to be replaced with other assets depending on the cube new arrangement.

around according to the tilt direction and magnitude. In our game it is used to direct a boy character on a maze and collect farm ingredients. Hiding a cubelet has an effect that is similar to pressing a button. When two complementary ingredients (augmented on cubelets) have been placed nearby, the player has to hide one of these cubelets with a finger which fires the described maze minigame. Finally, the screen corners can be used as hotspots and moving the cube to one of these corners is equivalent to choosing an action from the menu. For example, when the level is over, the player can choose to continue to the next level, open a relevant United Nations Millennium Development webpage, or contribute by donating a dollar. The last corner is used to save and exit the game.

4. Architecture and Implementation

4.1. Platform Architecture. Our architecture decouples platform and game implementation allowing various games to be developed on the same platform.

OOTC is organized in two layers. The core layer analyzes the live video feed and detects the pose of the cube at each frame. The reasoning layer keeps state history and maps core layer detections to game interactions. The core layer is developed using OpenCV, the open-source computer vision library (http://opencv.willowgarage.com/), and ARToolKit (http://www.hitl.washington.edu/artoolkit/), an open source library for marker-based AR. ARToolKit traditional markers are square black frames with symbols inside, and, here, we designed a sticker kit (see Figure 4) with a different appearance which required preprocessing the image before sending it to ARToolKit.

The reasoning layer analyzes and accumulates core layer detections received at every frame. It also stabilized registration and interactions. Supporting interactions require identifying the elements: viewable face, shuffling, hidden cubelets, and hotspots.

4.2. Identifying a Cube's Face. Determining the currently viewed face is performed by the core layer and forms the basis for other interactions as well. The sticker kit includes a unique sticker for each face's central cubelet. The sticker

design is preconfigured as a marker ID for the ARToolKit library. The stickers' background is white with a black symbol in the middle, while ARToolKit markers have black frames with a black symbol in the middle. We explored the possibility of using standard ARToolKit markers, but since the cube has thin black areas between cubelets which tend to merge with the black frame of the sticker, it made the tracking instable.

4.3. Pose Estimation and Tracking. Designing a sticker kit that can support robust registration and provide an appealing game design is a challenging task. We experimented with different sticker kit designs and chose a white background with a black symbol in the middle as the central cubelet. We first identify the white backgrounds and invert their color so that ARToolKit can process them. While black tends to be relatively preserved in different lighting conditions, white areas vary widely according to the lighting conditions and camera quality. Figure 5 depicts the difference between a white area in four lighting conditions of faces different angles. This results in wide variations in white color. To overcome these variations, we assume one of the six patterns is present in the image. The first step of ARToolKit is thresholding the image and a parameter can be used to control the threshold level. We, thus, try different numbers until one of the six patterns is found.

We experienced jittering and classification failures caused by the small size of the marker, the white background, and the webcam quality. We overcame these effects by keeping a short history of the poses in the reasoning layer. We then dropped outlier poses and smoothed inliers using DESP [15]. We now turn to describe the identification of the cubelets around the central one.

4.4. Identifying a Cube's Arrangement. Identifying the shuffle of the cube is performed using Shape Context signatures [16]. Shape Contexts are designed to identify shapes across Euclidian transformations, rather than projective ones. Hence, we first rectify the face image to restore its planar state. We then mask each of the eight cubelets around the center and proceed to match them to the set of eight cubelets learned through a calibration step.

4.5. Hidden Cubelets. The cubelets can be used as virtual buttons by hiding a single cubelet by a finger. The occlusion formed by a finger is identified by examining the Shape Context signatures. A finger might cover more than one cubelet at a time. Hence, if one, two, or three neighboring cubelets are not identified while all the others are, we conclude that the user is pressing a button. It follows that only one button can be pressed at a time.

4.6. Hotspots. Hotspots are areas on the screen that trigger an event when the cube is aligned to them. This can be easily determined using the homography's translation vector. The reasoning layer accumulates hotspot events with their ID's for several consecutive frames before invoking a callback with the pressed cubelet's ID.

(a) Shuffling

(b) Hiding cubelet

(c) Rotating face

(d) Hotspots

FIGURE 3: Interaction metaphors. (a) Shuffling to change game assets; (b) hiding a cubelet to press a button; (c) rotating faces to see different views; (d) hotspots to choose between menu items.

4.7. Technical Challenges. So far we described all the ingredients of the OOTC platform and our implementation and only lightly touched on the numerous attempts we made to realize it. One of the most time-consuming tasks was figuring out how to perform cube face detection and cubelet identification while supporting design decisions for the sticker kit.

While the final central cubelet marker is a black symbol on white background as explained earlier, our first attempt was using a black frame surrounding the entire cube face. It was straightforward to implement and covered the maximal possible face area resulting in stable pose estimation. The main caveat of this approach is that the cube itself is black and, when tilting the cube, the black frame printed on the stickers merges with the spaces between the cubelets. We hence turned to a single central cubelet solution. However, we required it to remain colored, as in the original design, to look better. However, robust color identification under different lighting conditions remains a challenging task and even a black pattern with white frame can be difficult to track as explained above and depicted in Figure 5.

Cubelet identification was initially planned to use ARToolKit rather than Shape Contexts. During implementation, we found that this constrained the stickers' design to relatively small symbols with dominant white background

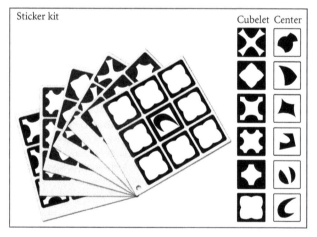

FIGURE 4: The OOTC sticker kits.

similar to the central cubelet. In addition, it introduces more patterns into the ARToolKit pattern set, which yields a higher ratio of identification error than with six patterns.

5. User Study

We developed a village puzzle game with a maze minigame to demonstrate the platform. The games were presented in

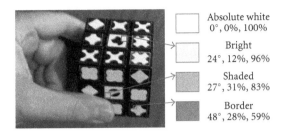

	Absolute white 0°, 0%, 100%
	Bright 24°, 12%, 96%
	Shaded 27°, 31%, 83%
	Border 48°, 28%, 59%

FIGURE 5: The appearances of white under different angles. Values are given in HSV.

FIGURE 6: Users trying the system at Imagine Cup Expo.

TABLE 1: Camera position.

Configuration	Number of users who succeeded	Average duration (in seconds)
Hat	2 of 10	123
Screen	6 of 10	82
Stand	10 of 10	79

TABLE 2: Determining tilt interaction speed.

Configuration	Average duration (in seconds)
Fixed speed	89
Two speeds	56
Continuous	96

TABLE 3: Number of users who preferred a configuration.

Hat	Screen	Stand	Fixed speed	Two speeds	Continuous speed
1/10	3/10	6/10	3/15	10/15	2/15

several events. At the Imagine Cup International Expo (see Figure 6), many attendees played the game and provided positive feedback.

We describe here results from user studies we performed at the design stage of the platform. We tested different interactions and possible hardware setups. We found that the positioning of the camera relative to the user and the screen meaningfully affects usability. Furthermore, the tilt interaction is not as trivial as expected and controlling direction and speed can be confusing. The "natural" orientation of the cube (which is mapped to "no movement" of the augmented character) is challenging, since the cube is held by the player. On the other hand, shuffling the cube was natural and required minimal practice to be used. Following are the main user studies we performed.

5.1. Camera Position. To explore the most natural camera setup, three camera positions were experimented with, where the camera was (1) fixed on a hat, (2) mounted to a laptop screen, and (3) fixed to a down-facing stand. We experimented with ten students selected randomly around the campus. The students had a chance to try the game with each of the camera positions for one minute. We performed an objective test where the mission is to make a character cross a simple maze augmented on top of a cube face. Success in the mission is crossing without falling off the path. Each time the character falls, the player has to start from the beginning. Table 1 summarizes the results. A fixed camera on a hat led to poor game experience. While users indicated the advantage of the eye view direction for the camera, their head movements created a too hard to control scenario. On the other hand, the camera mounted to the laptop screen generated constant confusion, regardless of our attempts to mirror and flip the image. Finally, we mounted a down-facing camera to a stand to make the bottom of the image reflect the player's direction. All players exhibited a shorter average time to complete the mission.

5.2. Determining Tilt Interaction Speed. We initially assumed that the speed of a character moving on a tilted cube should correspond to the magnitude of the tilt. However, our experiments reveled that it was hard to control the character movements. We created three tasks and asked fifteen students, picked at random around the university campus, to complete tasks in three different configurations. The tasks were (a) follow a virtual line, (b) cross a cube face on its two diagonals, and (c) go around the face following a square path. The objective was to perform the tasks as fast as possible. We measured the combined time it took the player to complete the three tasks experimenting with three different selections for character speed. (1) Fixed speed: the magnitude of the tilt was ignored; the character stands or walks in the direction of the tilt. (2) Two speeds: the character stands and either walks or runs depending on the tilt. (3) Continuous: character speed is a linear function of tilt magnitude. From Table 2 we conclude the two-speed configuration brought to shorter time for completing tasks.

Finally, we were interested in the subjective opinion of the players who participated in the experiments above and play our games for ten minutes. Table 3 summarizes the results we found. Most players preferred the camera mounted to a stand and the ability to toggle between standing, walking, and running. Some players spent a considerable amount of time trying to figure out the correct combination of the cube and asking for help indicating a deep level of involvement in the game. In the minigame, some players tried to catch the augmented character when it flipped over the cube.

6. Additional Games

To provide more support on how OOTC can be used as a game platform, we briefly describe three additional game concepts that were considered as alternative to the games we finally developed. The first game is aimed for toddlers and features an image puzzle game. The goal is to connect piece-to-piece six images of different animals on the cube's faces. Each animal image is broken to nine pieces, and the player has to shuffle the cube until the six images are complete. Once an image is fully assembled, a 3D model appears on top of the cube and interacts with the player. For example, feeding of the 3D animal is possible by moving the cube to a hotspot with food. Playing with the animal is possible by tilting the cube.

In another possible game, the goal could be to experiment with tweaked combination of animal. Animal images are broken to nine on the cubelets, and the arrangement of the cube implies a combination of the animal pieces. Morphed 3D models can then be created from the different pieces and augmented. Once an interesting creature is crafted, the player can share it with friends.

The third game is a skill-based challenge organized in levels. It is a maze defined dynamically by shuffling the cube, and the player has to control a character on this maze. The maze is made of tiles that carry collectable items, providing different rewards. The goal is to cross a cube face from point A to point B in limited time while collecting as many items as possible. Tiles may be missing, making crossing impossible without shuffling the cube. Rearranging the maze can also help earning rewards by revealing more items. While collecting as many points as possible, the player has to reach point B in time to complete the level.

7. Conclusion

In this work, we introduced OOTC, an Augmented Reality Rubik's Cube game platform. We developed several games to demonstrate the platform. We discussed design issues for games based on OOTC and described several design decisions taking limiting factors into account. We also explored the design and implementation of five interaction metaphors. The cube shuffling action preserves its original usage pattern from a Rubik's cube. Other interactions are borrowed from other tangible AR experiences and studies on the Rubik's cube environment.

We expect more games based on OOTC and would like to extend the user study with more players and a deeper investigation of the cube shuffle interaction.

Acknowledgments

This work was supported by the Tuman Fund and Kreitman Foundation Fellowships. The authors would like to thank the reviewers for their suggestions, which helped improving the paper. The authors would like to thank players who provided us with valuable feedback.

References

[1] J. D. Bolter and R. Grusin, *Remediation: Understanding New Media*, MIT Press, Cambridge, Mass, USA, 2000.

[2] L. A. William, "The Rubik's cube: a puzzling success," *Time*, 2009.

[3] A. Jamieson, "Rubik's cube inventor is back with Rubik's 360," *The Daily Telegraph*, 2009.

[4] Z. Z. Ying, C. A. David, L. Yu, and K. Hirokazu, "Magic cubes for social and physical family entertainment," in *Proceedings of the International Conference for Human-Computer Interaction (CHI '05)*, pp. 1156–1157, Portland, Ore, USA, 2005.

[5] Z. Z. Ying, C. A. David, C. Tingting, and L. Yu, "Jumanji Singapore: an interactive 3D board game turning hollywood fantasy into reality," in *Proceedings of the International Conference on Advances in Computer Entertainment Technology (ACM SIGCHI '04)*, 2004.

[6] G. A. Lee, M. Billinghurst, and G. J. Kim, "Occlusion based interaction methods for tangible augmented reality environments," in *Proceedings of the ACM SIGGRAPH International Conference on Virtual Reality Continuum and its Applications in Industry (VRCAI '04)*, pp. 419–426, June 2004.

[7] M. Billinghurst, H. Kato, and I. Poupyrev, "Tangible augmented reality," in *Proceedings of the ACM SIGGRAPH ASIA courses*, December 2008.

[8] B. Thomas, B. Close, J. Donoghue, J. Squirs, P. De Bondi, and W. Piekarski, "ARQuake: an outdoor/indoor augmented reality first person application," *Journal of Personal and Ubiquitous Computing*, vol. 6, no. 1, 2002.

[9] A. D. Cheok, S. W. Fong, K. H. Goh et al., "Pacman: a mobile entertainment system with ubiquitous computing and tangible interaction over a wide outdoor area," in *Proceedings of the 5th International Symposium Human-Computer Interaction with Mobile Devices and Services*, vol. 2795, pp. 209–223, Udine, Italy, September, 2003.

[10] D. Wagner, T. Pintaric, F. Ledermann, and D. Schmalstieg, "Towards massively multi-user augmented reality on handheld devices," in *Proceedings of the 3rd International Conference on Pervasive Computing*, pp. 208–219, May 2005.

[11] M. Rohs, "Marker-based embodied interaction for handheld augmented reality games," *Journal of Virtual Reality and Broadcasting*, vol. 4, no. 5, 2007.

[12] M. Weilguny, *Design aspects in augmented reality games*, Diploma thesis, 2006.

[13] I. Barakonyi, M. Weilguny, T. Psik, and D. Schmalstieg, "MonkeyBridge: autonomous agents in augmented reality games," in *Proceedings of the International Conference on Advances in Computer Entertainment Technology (ACM SIGCHI '05)*, 2005.

[14] S. Hinske and M. Langheinrich, "W41K: digitally augmenting traditional game environments," in *Proceedings of the 3rd International Conference on Tangible and Embedded Interaction (TEI'09)*, pp. 99–106, USA, February 2009.

[15] J. J. LaViola, "Double exponential smoothing: an alternative to Kalman filter-based predictive tracking," in *Proceedings of the Work-Shop on Virtual Environments*, pp. 199–206, 2003.

[16] S. Belongie, J. Malik, and J. Puzicha, "Shape matching and object recognition using shape contexts," *IEEE Transactions on Pattern Analysis and Machine Intelligence*, vol. 24, no. 24, pp. 509–522, 2002.

9

Determining Solution Space Characteristics for Real-Time Strategy Games and Characterizing Winning Strategies

Kurt Weissgerber, Gary B. Lamont, Brett J. Borghetti, and Gilbert L. Peterson

Department of Electrical and Computer Engineering, Graduate School of Engineering and Management,
Air Force Institute of Technology, Wright Patterson AFB, Dayton, OH 45433, USA

Correspondence should be addressed to Gary B. Lamont, cruisede@aol.com

Academic Editor: Alexander Pasko

The underlying goal of a competing agent in a discrete real-time strategy (RTS) game is to defeat an adversary. Strategic agents or participants must define an a priori plan to maneuver their resources in order to destroy the adversary and the adversary's resources as well as secure physical regions of the environment. This a priori plan can be generated by leveraging collected historical knowledge about the environment. This knowledge is then employed in the generation of a classification model for real-time decision-making in the RTS domain. The best way to generate a classification model for a complex problem domain depends on the characteristics of the solution space. An experimental method to determine solution space (search landscape) characteristics is through analysis of historical algorithm performance for solving the specific problem. We select a deterministic search technique and a stochastic search method for a priori classification model generation. These approaches are designed, implemented, and tested for a specific complex RTS game, Bos Wars. Their performance allows us to draw various conclusions about applying a competing agent in complex search landscapes associated with RTS games.

1. Introduction

The real-time strategy (RTS) domain [1] is of interest because it relates to real world problems, for example, determining a "good" military battlefield strategy or defining the "best" strategies for complex RTS video games. A participants/agent strategy is to develop a long-term plan using an agent's resources to win the game. Note that the RTS genre is different than games requiring only real-time tactics (RTT) which deal with making decisions on detailed resource use at each iteration of the game. RTT sometimes are considered a subgenus of real-time strategies. Another way of defining an RTS structure is to consider the terms *macro-management* referring to high-level strategic maneuvering and *micro-management* referring to RTT game interaction.

The objective of a competing agent in an RTS game is to defeat an adversary (or adversaries) by directly and indirectly moving and maneuvering resources in order to destroy the adversary's resources, capture and destroy the adversary, and secure physical regions of the environment [1]. In a gaming situation, it is desired to gather or destroy resources, build physical structures, improve technological development, and control other agents. This is a daunting set of strategic tasks for an RTS game player.

A comprehensive RTS game could include extensive models of information availability, relations (espionage, diplomacy, intrigue), politics, ingenuity, economics, control (stability), logistics (scarcity), risk management, synchrony, and the scope of complexity, space, and time (speed). To incorporate all of these strategic models into an RTS game or simulation is probably next to impossible! Thus, all may not be part of a contemporary RTS game. For example, games such as Ground Control or Company of Heroes do not require resource-gathering. On the other hand, the scope of time and space complexity for each RTS game characteristics are generic areas of interest that may present very difficult problem domains for a dynamic and adaptive RTS agent.

Nevertheless, an existing method for development of a *strategy-based agent* is to employ Artificial Intelligence (AI) techniques in learning while playing. Such an approach can include genetic algorithms, coevolution, and scripts via a variety of search techniques. Most such learning approaches involve defining an agent architecture, decision variable representation, explicit functional objectives, search exploration and exploitation algorithms, information collection, and a simulation implementation. Any AI architecture must permit an RTS agent to observe its environment and make decisions based on what it observes. An adversarial agent must take actions which allow it to defeat some opponent(s). Many current RTS approaches use AI learning agents, where the agent determines appropriate actions to take in a particular *state* through trial and error; that is, instantiating if-then-else rules or case-based reasoning [1]. The agent must determine some way to collect the required information about the environment and the opponent and then use this information effectively to "beat" the opponent via an action sequence.

We present an AI strategy-based agent which collects information and learns about an opponent by examining its past performance. Past performance can be captured through a collection of *game trace* records from the adversarial agent's state movements. Traces by definition consist of a vector of *snapshots* and each snapshot also contains the value of various types of *features* at a specific point in time. A vector of snapshots which encompass an entire RTS game can be used to reconstruct via search and learn the important strategic features of the game which can lead to victory.

Before the subject of agent generation can be approached, a reliable method of generating a classification model needs to be created. The RTS domain is relatively new; while many different AI search approaches have been applied to agent generation, little research has been done into determining the underlying characteristics of the domain. Are there many different feature combinations which lead to victory? Are they in close proximity to each other, or are they spread out around the domain? Is the solution space (fitness landscape) jagged, where good feature combinations are in very close proximity to bad feature combinations, or are the transitions between the two more gradual? By answering these questions, we can determine an algorithm to use which can leverage the characteristics of the domain to find the better solutions in a reasonable amount of time.

In this paper, related RTS investigations including RTS games are summarized in Section 2 which provides a background for our method. Section 3 formulates the RTS plan and the classification problem along with the generic solution space analysis and the selected information representation. Algorithmic learning techniques based upon deterministic and stochastic search are developed in Section 4 resulting in our AI strategy. The experimental design is provided in Section 5 with results and analysis reflected in Section 6. Conclusions and Future Work are presented in Sections 7 and 8, respectively.

2. Related Work

Related to the development of RTS games are appropriate contemporary RTS agent development methods, some

current applications, and supporting generic feature selection and class identification methods.

2.1. Current RTS Game Methods. Over the past three decades, there have been a variety of imperfect information (note that perfect information games include tic-tac-toe, checkers, chess, backgammon, and Go. RTS and RTT approaches have been applied to these games with some success depending upon depth of look-ahead search [2].) RTS games including The Ancient Art of War, Cytron Masters, Utopia, Supremacy, Carrier Command, SimAnt, Dune II. And then Total Annihilation, Age of Empires, Homeworld Cataclysm, Warcraft II & III, and Age of Mythology, Dragonshard, Star Wars: Empire at War, and StarCraft evolved. Newer strategy games include current versions of World in Conflict, Company of Heroes, Civilization 4, Sins of a Solar Empire, Medieval II, Supreme Commander, and the Rise of Nations. Each limits the generic definition of a general RTS game via the previous stated possible characteristic in Section 1. Also, many incorporate RTT templates. Various action and strategy games offer single and multiplayer options as well. Always important are the issues of visualization and animation features of each game regarding ease of use and understanding along with the associated computational and graphic requirements.

Distinct details of these games can usually be found by name via the internet. We address specific RTS game attributes that have a direct consideration in our "optimal" agent algorithmic approach: Case-Based Reasoning, Reinforcement Learning, Dynamic Scripting, and Monte-Carlo planning, along with available RTS software platforms.

A Case-Based Reasoning approach was used by Ontañón et al. [3] in WARGUS, which is an open source implementation of the Blizzard RTS game WarCraft II. They define a state as a 35-feature vector and execute the case in their database closest to the current state. Cases are extracted from expert game traces; humans that were proficient in WARGUS played the game and then annotated each action they took with the goal they were trying to achieve. Each goal is a case, and each action taken to accomplish it is added to the script executed when the case is selected. The AI approach was successful, although on a small scale of only nine games. Note that Ahal et al. [4] also used a Case-Based Reasoning technique for WARGUS which generated successful results.

A Hybrid Case-Based Reasoning/Reinforcement Learning approach was used by Sharma et al. [5] to develop an AI approach for a game called MadRTS, a "commercial RTS game being developed for military simulations". Their technique uses a set of features to determine a game state, such as the number of territories controlled by a given player and the number of units still alive for a given player. Additionally, they incorporate lessons learned from similar tasks to increase learning speed. The developed agent showed significant gains in achieving victory when allowed to transfer knowledge from other domains.

Graepel et al. apply extended Q-learning reinforcement in order to find "good" Markov decision policies for a fighting agent game [6]. The agents are trained using an on-policy algorithm (an on-policy learning algorithm for an agent interacts with the environment and updates the agent's policy based on current actions taken) for temporal difference learning that employs linear and neural network function approximators. Various selected rewards encourage aggressive or defensive agent behavior. Some acceptable agent policies using these reward functions are found for the author's particular AI game.

Continuous action model-learning in an RTS environment was addressed by Molineaux et al. [7]. They develop the Continuous Action and State Space Learner (CASSL). Their approach is an integrated Case-Based Reasoning/ Reinforcement Learning algorithm. Testing indicated that CASSL significantly outperformed two baseline approaches for selecting agent actions on a task from an RTS gaming environment.

Dynamic Scripting is a method developed by Spronck et al. [8] for third person role-playing games. The generic technique uses a set of rules to define a game state, and the value of these rules determines what actions are added to the script at each turn. This is a way of dealing with the huge decision space of RTS games. However, it prevents this approach from reasoning on actual game conditions. This research was extended to the RTS domain by Kok [9]. Reinforcement learning was used to determine appropriate actions based on states. Instead of using only rule values, the approach allowed use of some knowledge of the actual state which generally leads to success.

A Monte-Carlo planning approach was used by Chung et al. [10] in "Capture the Flag" (CTF) games. In a CTF game, the agent's objective is to obtain the opponent's flag and return it to its base before the opponent is able to do the same. Using a CTF game reduced the complexity of the state; resource collection was unnecessary, and complex strategic level plans were not required. At each step of the game, the designed agent would generate a number of plans (parameter passed to the function), evaluate their performance against the possible actions the opponent could take, and execute the best plan. The success of this approach of course was highly linked to the specific game conditions.

In general, these approaches for solving RTS games do generate acceptable nonoptimal but not robust RTS solutions. This situation is generally due to the characteristics of the highly dimensional RTS search space being jagged and very rough. Moreover, we show this characteristic empirically via more appropriate stochastic search.

Note that contemporary AI techniques in RTS games continue to be in the development stage but with limited implementation. Observe that currently all such RTS games can be beaten by a knowledgeable human opponent, thus, making RTS games quite interesting and one would hope playable. Also, no single AI or human approach has been shown to be better or show more promise than others; therefore, there probably is no generic robust RTS game strategy-based agent that leads to victory in all cases! One can think of this situation as a reflection of the no-free-lunch theorem [11].

2.2. Some Current RTS Platforms. There are a number of RTS platforms on which to implement an RTS game along with collection of algorithmic game data. For example, *Bos Wars* [12] which is an open-source RTS developed as a no-cost alternative to commercial RTS games. Another is *Spring Engine* [13] where perfect knowledge of the environment is not available so a *temporal difference learning* technique is employed. A physics engine called *Havok* Game Dynamics SDK is used in some other RTS games such Age of Empires III and Company of Heroes for realism. Another platform is the NERO game [14], which stands for Neuro-Evolving Robotic Operatives. For the NERO project, a specific neural-net evolutionary algorithm is designed called rtNEAT, real-time Neuro-Evolution of Augmenting Topologies. These RTS platforms operate under Windows or Linux and require high-speed CPUs and extensive graphical interfaces. which stands for Neuro-Evolving Robotic Operatives.

We choose to use the Bos Wars platform for determining general RTS search space characteristics. This choice provides an efficient and effective computational platform for gaining initial insight to the RTS search space. Knowing these characteristics, generic RTS platforms can be used later to explicitly search for RTS strategic solutions using appropriate stochastic AI algorithms.

2.3. General Feature Selection. The goal of generic feature selection is to find a *subset* of features from a data domain (game traces) in order to maximize some identification function a priori. This subset of features can then be used to classify given date at some epoch *(snapshot)*. In the RTS Feature Selection problem, the goal is to classify game states via this feature subset at each snapshot. An initial execution of a selected number of the same RTS game can determine the feature subset. The RTS optimization identification function is derived from a general classification problem; once the appropriate RTS subset features are determined through the RTS training data, game playing state data can be separated quickly with this subset into classes at each snapshot. Note that a method to generalize each class must be determined, so all game states can be classified as well. Those states classified as winning strategies are sought out of course. This is in general a very difficult computational problem. Of course, Generic Feature Selection and Classification continue to be open research areas in engineering and science.

A general overview of feature selection and classification methods is given by Blum and Langley [15]. Although the others listed would also be appropriate, Bos Wars was chosen for ease of analysis. Different ways of defining a *relevant* feature are discussed. One of the most basic is "feature x_i is relevant if there exists some example in the instance space for which twiddling the value of x_i affects the classification." For the remainder of this paper, the term "important" is used synonymously with the definition of relevant.

Blum and Langley [15] also discuss three different general methods of feature selection and classification: filter, wrapper, and embedded. In *filtering methods*, features are selected and then passed to a classification algorithm. This solves the entire problem as a two-step process. In a *wrapper approach*, the two problems are still separate, but multiple solutions are explored. A subset of features is chosen and passed to a classification algorithm, then a different subset is chosen and its performance in the classification algorithm is compared. This process is repeated many times leading to an acceptable classification. In an *embedded approach*, the two problems are solved concurrently via parallel interaction.

The algorithm designed in this paper takes an embedded approach to a priori feature selection and classification. In each method, possible class separability and clustering functions are based upon a distance function. Such metrics include error probability, interclass distance, k-means clustering, entropy, consistency-based feature selection, and correlation-based feature selection.

A good overview of the feature selection problem domain is presented by Jain et al. [16] in which they define some pertinent terms. "Pattern representation" refers to the number of classes, the number of available patterns, and the number, type, and scale of the features available to the clustering algorithm. Again, the goal of feature selection/classification is to find the specific pattern representation which maximizes (optimizes) the performance of a classifier, in our case, winning game strategies.

Collections of RTS game traces can be used to construct a generalization of a particular game given many runs. By using machine learning techniques, specifically the generation of classification models for the game traces, the feature value combinations which tend to lead to victory and the feature value combinations which tend to lead to defeat can be determined. These good and bad feature values can then be given to an agent that would seek to avoid the bad feature combinations and approach the use of good combinations in the temporal decision process of the game.

There are numerous approaches to feature selection, using many different algorithms and heuristics. For example, search algorithms include deterministic depth-first search and breath-first search (best-first search), and stochastic simulated annealing and genetic algorithm techniques. The Feature Selection problem is known to be NP-Complete [17], with a solution space of $O(n^n)$, where n is the number of possible features which could be selected. Thus, in large feature spaces, stochastic approaches are preferred generating acceptable solutions relatively quickly.

For example, to reduce the problem search space, Somol et al. [18] used heuristics to prevent the expansion of unproductive nodes. By predicting the value of a node instead of computing its actual value, they were able to reduce the amount of time spent evaluating each node. This led to reduced time spent on a search, as well as pruning off nonproductive areas of the search space.

As an example in the marketing domain, feature selection is used to determine customers who are likely to buy a product, based on the other products they have bought. Genetic algorithms were used by Jarmulak and Craw [19] to solve this problem. They assigned weights to each feature selected to take advantage of the relative importance of each feature. Simulated annealing was used by Meiri and Zahavi [20] to solve a similar marketing problem. Feature identification results in both cases were deemed acceptable. Historical motivation for simulated annealing use in optimization problems is discussed by Kirkpatrick et al. [21].

There are numerous examples of feature selection methods, in many different domains. However, feature selection is usually a domain specific problem; a feature selection algorithm which gives a good solution in one problem domain does not necessarily give the same quality of solution in a different domain. Our embedded algorithm uses a priori stochastic feature selection as motivated in the following sections.

2.4. Classification Methods. A classifier is a system created from quantitative labeled data which can then be used to generalize qualitative data. In a more general sense, building a classifier is the process of learning a set of rules from instances. These rules can be used to assign new samples to classes. In an AI taxonomy, classification falls into the realm of supervised machine learning [22]. Note that our *perception* is the process of attaining awareness or understanding of sensory information via classification.

A classifier is often generated from an initial dataset, called the training set. This training set is a series of samples of feature values, where a feature is some measurable aspect of a specific problem domain. Each sample has values for all the features and is labeled as to what class in the problem domain it came from.

There are numerous methods of generating classifiers. *Logic-based* algorithms construct decision trees or rule-based classifiers for games [23]. New data can be classified by following the decision tree from the root to a leaf node and classifying appropriately. *Perceptron-based* techniques (neural net) learn weights for each feature value and then compute a function value for all the training data. Instances are classified based on this function value. *Statistical learning* and *Probabilistic learning* algorithms generate probabilities that a sample belongs to a specific class, instead of a simple classification. Common examples of these techniques are linear discriminant analysis [24] and Bayesian networks, which were first used in a machine learning context in 1987 [25]. Note that various classifiers can come under a variety of learning algorithm definitions.

The family of *instance-based* learning algorithms are the most useful when developing an agent [26]. Instance based learning (IBL) algorithms assume that similar samples have similar classifications. They derive from the k-Nearest Neighbor (k-NN) classifier, which classifies a sample based on the k closest samples to it in the classifier. IBL algorithms represent each class as a set of exemplars, where each exemplar may be an instance of the class or a more generalized abstraction [27].

Two basic IBL exemplar models are *proximity* and *best-example*. A proximity model stores all the training instances with no abstraction, so each new instance is classified based on its proximity to all the samples in the training data. Best-example models only store the typical instances of each concept [28]. Best-example models can greatly reduce the subset size of features.

Another classification method based upon the K-NN approach is the K-winner machine (KWM) model [29]. KWM training uses unsupervised vector quantization and subsequent calibration to label data-space partitions.

A K-winner classifier seeks the largest set of best-matching prototypes agreeing on a test pattern and provides a local-level estimate of confidence. The result leads to tight bounds to generalization performance. The method maybe suitable for high-dimensional multiclass problems with large amounts of data. Experimental results on both synthetic and real domains confirm the approach's effectiveness.

One method of creating a best-example model from the training set is the *K-means clustering* algorithm. K-means is a two-step algorithm which takes N samples and assigns them to K clusters. Each cluster is represented by a vector over all the features called its mean. K-means is a two-step process: in the assignment step, each data point $n \in N$ is assigned to the nearest mean. In the update step, the means are adjusted to match the sample means of all the data points which are assigned to them. This process repeats until the change in the clusters approaches zero or some defined threshold [30]. Although a spectrum of classification techniques have been introduced for clarification, the classification method selected in the following sections is motivated by the desired to provide insight to RTS search space characteristics. In developing an efficient and effective classification process for a specific RTS game, consideration of the above approaches should be addressed.

3. The Problem

Our Real-Time Strategy Prediction Problem (RTSPP) is a classification problem which is formulated as a basic search problem. Any search problem definition including the RTSPP can be defined by its input, output, and fitness function.

3.1. Problem Definition. The input to the RTSPP is a set of game traces from RTS games. Each game trace consists of "snapshots" taken at constant intervals or epochs. Each snapshot contains the value of all the possible features which an agent can observe. In the RTS domain, features could be the number and type of units, the amount of energy or fuel, or the rate at which energy and fuel are collected or used. Features could also be the rate of change of any of the static features across some time interval. Each snapshot is labeled as to whether it came from a game which was won or lost from player one's perspective.

All features are defined as the difference between player one's value and player two's value. For example, if at some point in a game player one has two infantry units and player two has three, then the value of the infantry unit feature is negative one. Expressing features as a difference cuts the space required to store game traces in half.

The output (solution) of the RTSPP is a classifier: a subset of features, a set of winning *centers*, and a set of losing centers. The set of features determines which features are used in the classifier. Each center in the set of winning centers gives a set of values across the features which generally result in a winning game. The set of losing centers is the same concept, only from losing games.

The classifier is then used to predict the outcome of a game based on only the current state. During a game, the values for the features in the solution are measured. Then, the distance to each center in the sets of centers is measured. The closest center is determined. If this center is a winning center, then the game state is predicted to result in a win. If it is a losing center, then the game state should result in a loss.

The quality of a solution to the RTSPP can be measured by testing its classification performance. *Classification performance* is measured as a percentage of right answers to total samples over various games.

3.2. Formal Problem Definition. The RTSPP is formally defined to remove any ambiguity of understanding. There is a set F of features and a set S of snapshots. The input to the problem is a set of $n \times m$ data, where n is the number of features and m is the number of snapshots.

The output of the problem is a set of features F', where $F' \subseteq F$, and a set of centers C, where the winning centers are C_w and the losing centers C_l, so $C_w \cup C_l = C$ and $C_w \cap C_l = \varnothing$. Each center is a representative sample of a snapshot that is a mean of a cluster of minimizing samples.

The fitness of a solution can be determined by using it to classify all the samples in S. The function $\text{dist}(s, c)$ returns the Euclidean distance for example from a sample s to a center c, so the value of a prediction function $P(s)$ is

$$P(s) = \begin{cases} 1 & \min_{c \in C}(\text{dist}(s,c)) \cap C_w = c, \\ 0 & \min_{c \in C}(\text{dist}(s,c)) \cap C_w = \varnothing. \end{cases} \tag{1}$$

Next, a function which determines the accuracy of a prediction is needed. The function $g(s)$ returns one if the prediction is correct, zero if it is not. For ease of notation, the actual classification value of sample s is denoted by $P^*(s)$. $g(s)$ is formally defined as

$$g(s) = \begin{cases} 1 & P(s) = P^*(s), \\ 0 & P(s) \neq P^*(s). \end{cases} \tag{2}$$

Total fitness $G(S)$ is just the sum of g over all samples $s \in S$ divided by the number of samples:

$$G(S) = \frac{\sum_{i=1}^{m} g(s_i)}{m}. \tag{3}$$

The *objective* of the RTSPP is to find F' and C for which $G(S)$ is maximum.

3.3. RTSPP Solution Space Analysis. The concluding step in the problem definition is an analysis of the number of possible RTSPP solutions. This information is important because it determines the difficulty of the search.

In the RTSPP, there are two components to a solution: the features in the set F' and the centers in C. The number of possible feature subsets is $O(n!) \approx O(n^n)$.

Center solution space analysis is more complicated. If centers are restricted to being a sample $s \in S$, then the number of possible centers is $O(m!) \approx O(m^m)$. However, if center values are not restricted, then the solution space is much larger. If each feature is split into 1,000 possible values, then there are $O(1000^n)$ possible values for a single center. Since there is no reason to have more than m centers, the solution space for real valued centers is of order $O(1000^n \times m)$.

Combining the two solution spaces leads to a total solution space of $O(n^n \times 1000^n \times m)$.

One of the easiest reductions to the problem domain is to reduce the number of features in F' and centers in C. An overall objective of the RTSPP solution is to reduce the decision space for an agent. While keeping all the features/samples in a solution may lead to high fitness values, it does not accomplish this objective. Accordingly, the size of F' is limited to some constant j and the size of C is limited to some constant k, leading to these two formal constraints on a solution:

$$|F'| < j,$$
$$|C| < k. \tag{4}$$

The two constraints significantly reduce the size of the solution space. The feature selection portion is now $O(n^k)$. The center portion is $O(1000^j \times j)$ for real-valued centers and $O(m^j)$ when centers are subject to $C \subset S$. Total solution space size is $O(n^k \times 1000^j \times j)$ or $O(n^k \times m^j)$.

With the reduction based on the constraints, the solution space is polynomial in the number of features and samples in the input data.

4. Feature Subset Search Methods

Any search problem can be solved using one of two general search types: deterministic and stochastic [31]. A deterministic algorithm is not probabilistic. The next search state is only determined from the current search state (partial solution) and the chosen search algorithm. To generate an optimal solution via expanding partial solutions, the entire search space must be searched either explicitly or implicitly. This means that the problem domain could be relaxed to decrease the size of the search space so it can be searched in a reasonable amount of time. Thus, relaxing the problem domain dimensionally yields an optimal solution to a smaller problem.

In a stochastic search, the algorithm is a probabilistic search over the solution space. The next state (solution) of a stochastic search algorithm is not always the same. Instead, the search is guided towards profitable areas using some heuristic. A stochastic algorithm does not search the entire solution space; instead, it seeks to exploit characteristics of the problem domain to find good solutions. Stochastic search algorithms require the assumption that the search is allowed to run forever to guarantee optimality. This is clearly unrealistic. However, the solution yielded by a stochastic algorithm is a solution in the original problem domain which may be near optimal or at least acceptable.

In some problem domains, a near optimal solution to the original problem is better than an optimal solution. In others, the converse is true. One way to determine this is to test both approaches on the problem domain. To do this, the problem domain must be explicitly defined. Next,

a specific search algorithm can be developed and tailored to the problem. In this chapter, both deterministic and stochastic search algorithms are developed to solve the RTS classification problem. They are tested on a data set from an RTS application, and their performance is compared. Finally, a selection is made between the deterministic and stochastic families for further development. To appreciate the subtle aspects of these feature selection search techniques for RTS games, the following sections are provided.

4.1. Deterministic Feature Subset Search. In general, features work in combinations to determine the fitness of a given RTS state. To find a subset of features, deterministic search in the RTS domain faces an immediate problem because of the complexity and roughness of the solution space. There is no way to search the entire problem space in a reasonable amount of time, which would be required to guarantee an optimal classification solution. Moreover, classification, when conducted on a problem with dependent variables, does not lend itself to implicit searching. The RTSPP for example probably has dependent variables.

In problems with independent variables, a solution can be constructed by adding features to a solution one by one, adding the feature at each level which has the greatest positive effect on the classification accuracy of the model. Dependent variables provide no such guarantee; because they work in combinations, the addition or deletion of a feature from a solution can have a large and unpredictable effect on classification model accuracy.

Basically, this means there is no admissible heuristic [31] which can be used to trim the search space. An admissible heuristic by definition always generates an optimal solution. However, there are nonadmissible ways which can be used to guide the search. We present one such method, which we use to achieve two different goals: it decreases the solution space so that every possible solution can be tested in a reasonable amount of time, and it guides the search towards profitable areas of the search space. By examining the solutions generated through the use of a heuristic, we can determine characteristics of the solution space, which is one of our objectives. Of course, an admissible heuristic would be more appropriate, but for RTS games, good admissible heuristics are yet to be generated.

When reducing the size of the solution space via classification, we need to find a heuristic which preserves the high fitness solutions of the entire space, while discarding the solutions with low fitness. If we start with the solution space in Figure 1, we would like to find a heuristic which transforms this into the solution space in Figure 2, a desired relaxed or reduced dimensionally problem domain solution space (fitness landscape). The undesired transformed solution space in Figure 3 reflects the removal of some low fitness solutions, but the high fitness solutions have not been retained.

4.1.1. The Heuristic. One of the easiest ways to reduce solution space size is to determine a way to pair features with centers. If at each step a triple could be selected

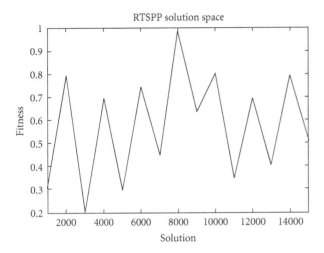

FIGURE 1: A hypothetical solution space.

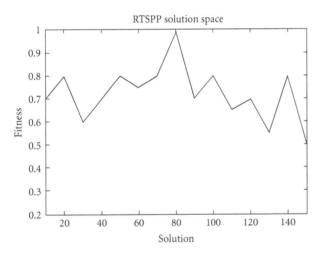

FIGURE 2: A hypothetical solution space which has been pruned through the use of a heuristic.

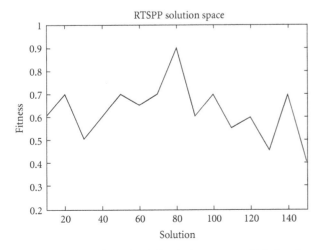

FIGURE 3: Another hypothetical solution space which has been pruned through the use of a heuristic.

which consisted of one feature, one winning center and one losing center, the number of combinations would be greatly reduced. This requires a means of determining good feature values when features are selected.

One way of determining good features involves the use of the *Bhattacharyya Coefficient (BC)* [32]. The BC can be used to determine the separability of two data sets. It computes the separability of two classes of data, based on a histogram of the data. Values for the coefficient for a feature are between 0 and 1, where values close to zero show the feature is very separable between the two classes, while values close to one show the feature is not very separable for these two classes. Therefore, the BC heuristic can be used to choose the feature with the most separability at each step. Each feature can be paired with a sample in its histogram. The BC finds data distributions that are as far apart as possible; centers should be chosen that best generalize each distribution. Therefore, *the median sample of the winning/losing distribution is chosen as the center for each feature.*

The BC is calculated by taking a histogram of all the data and determining the probability of a sample falling in a bin for both classes. The two probabilities for each bin are multiplied together and summed over the entire histogram. Formally, this is

$$BC = \sum_{i=1}^{I} P(W_i) \times P(L_i), \qquad (5)$$

where I is the number of bins in the histogram, W_i is the set of winning samples, L_i is the set of losing samples, and $P()$ is the probability of the samples being in the bin. Figure 4 is a visualization of this idea. The two curves are distributions over the winning and losing samples. The BC is a number between one and zero, expressing the amount of "overlap" of the two distributions; zero represents no overlap, while one represents complete overlap. On this graph, it is the space bounded by both curves. To pair a feature with a winning and losing center, we take the sample at the median of the respective distributions, symbolized by the lines W_i and L_i. We have expressed the win/loss samples for feature F_i as Gaussian distributions, but the BC can use any type of distribution.

The BC pairs each feature with two centers (one winning, one losing), so at each step of the *depth-first-search with backtracking (DFS-BT)* algorithm, the set of candidates contains a set of triples, each containing one feature and two centers. Because the BC drives a particular choice of center for each feature, the maximum size of the set of candidates is $|F|$.

Of course, BC is not an admissible heuristic. The optimization function (percent classified correctly) is not directly related to the BC. However, if the triple with the lowest BC is chosen at each step, it should drive the greatest improvement in classification accuracy because the overlap between the winning/losing sets is as small as possible. If the feature with the lowest BC remaining is selected and it does not improve the value of the optimization function, the next one picked should not do any better; the solution samples are close together.

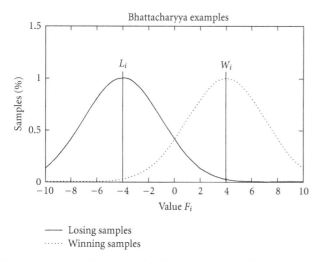

FIGURE 4: A visualization of the Bhattacharyya coefficient (BC) on feature F_i.

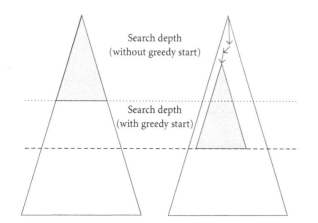

FIGURE 5: The increased space searchable with greedy search portion.

4.1.2. Choosing a Deterministic Search Algorithm. When choosing a search algorithm, we must keep in mind our goal: to determine the characteristics of the RTSPP solution space. We have a heuristic which we would like to test, the BC. A *best-first* algorithm would allow us to determine the effectiveness of the heuristic, as long as we search the entire domain. If the best solution found by the algorithm is found at the beginning, then the heuristic is good; it guided the search in a profitable direction. However, if the solution found is near the end of the search, then the heuristic is guiding us towards nonoptimal space.

Another way to test the effectiveness of the heuristic is to use a *greedy (DFS)* portion in our overall search. If this greedy portion is at the beginning of the search, then it allows us to increase the depth of our global search, as depicted in Figure 5. Again, the performance of this greedy search can be used to gauge the effectiveness of our heuristic. If better solutions are found when increasing the greedy search depth, then the heuristic guides us towards profitable areas of the search space.

The BC heuristic also prunes the search space. The BC pairs each feature with a center, as described. This significantly reduces the space, allowing us to completely search the space in a reasonable amount of time. However, we eliminate many possible combinations. To test the effectiveness of the heuristic from this perspective, some other method of search must be used which searches other possibilities missed by the deterministic search.

The best choice for a deterministic search algorithm is to begin with a greedy search which chooses some number of feature/center triples for a partial solution. Then, we begin a best first search which tries all the possible combinations of triples which can be used to form a solution, subject to the constraints on the number of features in a solution.

These algorithm choices lead to two different search parameters: the depth of the greedy search and the total number of features in a solution. By varying these parameters, we can gauge the effectiveness of the heuristic, as well as determine some characteristics of the solution space. But, because of the deterministic algorithm computational characteristics, a stochastic local search algorithm is selected.

4.2. Stochastic Feature Subset Search. It is assumed because of the combinatorics that the solution landscape of the RTSPP has many local maximum and minimum points. Most of these would exist in close proximity to each other; some features should be more closely related to the eventual outcome of a game. For instance, the total number of units for one player compared to the units for another player is one feature which would probably give good prediction accuracies, while the total amount of money or fuel which could possibly be stored is probably not in a solution. Local maxima should be near the global maximum, while local minima should be near the global minimum. As a result of these search landscape characteristics, a stochastic algorithm that is initially biased towards exploration, but then tends to exploitation is suggested.

This tentative analysis of the solution space shows the RTSPP may be responsive to a relatively simple stochastic algorithm like *simulated annealing (SA)* [33]. Simulated annealing is very similar to the deterministic search algorithm hill-climbing [31]. Hill-climbing starts with a solution and generates another solution in the neighborhood. If the fitness of this new solution is better, it becomes the solution and the algorithm repeats. If it is not better, then the generated solution is discarded and another solution is generated and tested.

In simulated annealing, the same approach is taken, but worse solutions can be accepted with some probability. Hill-climbing is subject to getting caught in a local maximum since it has no way of escaping. The probabilistic acceptance provided by simulated annealing allows the algorithm to possibly escape from a local maximum. The probability of selecting a worse solution is based on the current temperature, which changes based on a cooling parameter. At the beginning of the algorithm, the temperature is high so almost all solutions are accepted. As the search continues, the temperature falls such that lower quality solutions are accepted less frequently. By the end of the algorithm, SA becomes hill climbing.

Simulated annealing is easy to implement and runs quickly. It is a good choice to test the performance of a stochastic algorithm on the RTSPP.

4.3. SA Algorithm Domain Refinement.

In order to appreciate the important design evolution of our SA method, the SA algorithm refinement is presented. Initially, we need to consider a complete formal SA specification, which requires a solution form, fitness function, neighborhood function, and cooling function for the problem domain.

A solution to the RTSPP is a set of features along with a set of centers. There are $n = |F|$ features, so a solution to the feature selection portion of the RTSPP is an n-length binary string, where each feature is represented by a location in the string. A zero in the fth position of the string means feature f is not in the solution; a one means it is in the solution. Similarly, a solution to the center selection portion of the RTSPP is a binary string of length $|S|$, where a one in the sth position of the string means sample s is a center, while a zero means it is not. A total *chromosome* solution is a binary string of length $|F| + |S|$.

The fitness function is determined by the chromosome string representing the current solution z. The fitness value is of course $G(z)$, from (3).

To generate the next solution, the current solution may be *mutated* in two different ways. Either a bit in the solution is flipped or two bits of opposite value (a zero and a one) are swapped. The generic neighborhood function permits a slow exploration of the solution space (landscape) with the use of this mutation operator.

The cooling function is a geometric decreasing function defined by a parameter $0 < \alpha < 1$, where $T_{n+1} = \alpha \times T_n$. The probability of choosing a solution with lower fitness is the current temperature divided by the original temperature: T_n/T_0. Termination is when T_n reaches zero.

4.4. Program Specification.

The combination of the algorithm constructs and specification generates the program specification in Algorithm 1.

The algorithm complexity depends on the time it takes to compute the fitness function $G()$. As in the deterministic solution, this takes $O(k \times |S|^2)$. The stochastic algorithm examines a new solution at each step. Since the termination condition is $T_n = 0$, and the current temperature is selected to be a geometric cooling function based on α, SA tests $\ln(\epsilon)/\ln(\alpha)$ solutions, where ϵ is a very small number, say 0001. The overall problem solution space, from the problem definition, is $O(|F|^k \times |S|^j)$. The stochastic algorithm is not able to explore the entire solution space, but the SA initialization of solutions should "cover" all the various search space regions. The SA implementation should guide the search in good directions so the unexplored portions of the space should be uninteresting ones.

4.5. Program Specification Refinement.

The problem with the program as currently designed is in the neighborhood

---

$D_o = \varnothing$ "String Solution Domain"
$x = x_0$ "initial string"
$n = 0$
while $T_n > 0$ **do**
  Select $z \in N(x)$ "Select string in ngbr of x via mutation"
  if $g(z) > g(x)$ **OR** *random* $> (T_n/T_0)$ **then**
    $x = z$
  end if
  $T_{n+1} = T_n \times \alpha$
  $n = n + 1$
end while
$D_o = x$ "Final string solution"

ALGORITHM 1: SA RTSPP Initial Specification.

$$s = F_1 \cdots F_N \mid S_1 \cdots S_M$$
$$x = 0110 \mid 10010110$$
$$z_1 = 0101 \mid 10100101$$
$$z_2 = 1001 \mid 01101001$$

FIGURE 6: Proximity in solution space.

function. Allowing flipped bit s can potentially change the number of features/centers in a solution. Since the two constraints are limits on the number of features and centers, this means the algorithm may generate infeasible solutions. To deal with this problem, a repair function could be introduced to "fix" infeasible solutions, or the neighborhood function could be changed. Since one of the main concerns with the search is complexity, and introducing a repair function increases complexity, changing the neighborhood function is the best course.

Instead of allowing "flipped" bits, only swaps are allowed, and bits must be swapped in the same portion of the binary solution so a bit in the feature portion of the solution is not swapped with a bit in the center portion. Three swaps are made based upon problem insight: one in the feature portion and two in the center portion of the solution. For ease of notation, this function is called swap(). It takes the current solution x and returns a new solution z. An example of this swap is in Figure 6. s is a general solution; the first $|N|$ numbers are features, the next $|M|$ are samples. x is a possible solution; there are four features and eight samples in this example. The first four samples are winning; the last four are losing. z_1 is a possible nearby solution; one sample and two centers have been swapped. z_2 is not a nearby solution, two samples and four centers have been swapped out.

As already stated, the solution x is a binary string of length $|F| + |S|$. However, this is used to compute the fitness function $G(x)$. To reduce the complexity of this computation, there is a secondary implementation of the solution as three arrays of integers, one of l features and two of k centers. The feature array is F', the winning centers array is C_w, and the losing centers array is C_l. When a new solution is accepted, these three sets are updated in constant time by removing the value swapped out and adding the value swapped in.

```
x_best = 0 "Initial Best String Solution"
x = random
step = 0
while T_step > ε do
    if fitness(x) > fitness(x_best) then
        x_best = x
        z = swap(x)
    end if
    if fitness(z) > fitness(x) OR random < (T_step/T_0)
    then
        x = z
    end if
    T_step+1 = T_step × α
    step + +
end while
x_best = x "Final Best String Solution"
```

ALGORITHM 2: SA RTSPP Final Specification.

Additionally, the data array is used to compute the entire fitness function. Like in the deterministic solution, the data is stored in an array for fast access, the array *data*.

The best solution is x_{best}, and its value is $G(x_{best})$. As in the partial solution, this is a binary array of length $|F| + |S|$. In order to quickly print the best solution at the end of the program, the features and centers are stored in integer arrays like in the current solution: F'_{best}, C^{best}_w, and C^{best}_l.

Instead of having the user specify the initial solution, it is generated randomly by picking l features, $k/2$ winning centers, and $k/2$ losing centers.

The data structures lead to the final program refinement in Algorithm 2. The details of the integer array solutions, F', C_w, C_l, and their respective *best* values are left out; implementation can be done easily inside the swap() function. The algorithm is implemented, tested, and analyzed via experimental design.

5. Experimental Setup

RTS problem domain data is used to test the two designed classification search algorithms, the parameters used in each algorithm, and the performance metrics used to gauge their performance.

5.1. Data: Bos Wars Game. The algorithms are tested on data from the RTS platform *Bos Wars* [12]. Bos Wars is an open source RTS developed as a no-cost alternative to commercial RTS games. There are eight maps or game environments packaged with the game. In most maps, starting conditions for both players are similar. Each player has the same resource amount and the same access to resources and starts with the same number and type of units. Three different two-player maps are used: two have similar starting conditions and one had a line of cannons (defensive buildings) for one player. Bos Wars has a "dynamic, rate-based economy", making it somewhat different than most other RTS games. Energy (money) and magma (fuel) are consumed at a rate based on the number of units and buildings a player owns. As

the size of the player's army increases, more resources must be allocated to sustaining infrastructure. Additionally, Bos Wars has no "tech-tree", so all unit and building types can be created at the beginning of any game.

There are three scripted AI search techniques packaged with the development version of the game: *Blitz, Tank Rush, and Rush*. Blitz creates as many buildings and units as possible in the hopes of overwhelming the opponent. Tank Rush tries to create tanks as quickly as possible, using a strong unit to beat the weaker units normally created at the beginning of a game. Rush creates as many units as quickly as it can and attacks as soon as possible in order to catch the enemy off guard.

Additionally, there are three different difficulty levels for the game: *Easy, Normal, and Hard*. Changing the difficulty level allows the AI search to execute its script faster, so it progresses farther in its strategy in a given time period during a Hard game than a Normal game and Normal progresses further than Easy. As indicated, three Bos Wars maps or different environmental games are executed and evaluated: *Battlefield, Island Warfare, and Wetlands*.

To collect data, the Bos Wars source code is modified to take a snapshot of the game state at intervals of five seconds and output the feature values to a text file. *Each snapshot consists of thirty different statistics:* including Energy Rate, Magma Rate, Stored Energy, Stored Magma, Energy Capacity, Magma Capacity, Unit Limit, Building Limit, Total Units, Total Buildings, Total Razings, Total Kills, Engineers, Assault Units, Grenadiers, Medics, Rocket Tanks, Tanks, Harvesters, Training Camps, Vehicle Factories, Gun Turrets, Big Gun Turrets, Cameras, Vaults, Magma Pumps, Power Plants, and Nuclear Power Plants. Additionally, thirty delta values for all the features based on the snapshot taken 25 seconds before are created, so there are *sixty features*.

Altogether, *eighty-one games* are recorded. For the three maps, three iterations are run for selected combinations of the Bos Wars AI search techniques (Tank Rush Rush, Tank Rush Blitz, Rush versus Blitz) at each difficulty level, so each map has twenty-seven game traces.

Win/loss prediction is easier: the closer one gets to the end of the game, and almost impossible at the beginning. The goal of the RTSPP is to capture the important part of a game, where one player obtains an advantage over the other. To facilitate this, only game states in the third quarter of a game, the ones starting after 50% of the game had elapsed and before 75% of the game had elapsed, are used as input. The shortest game was about ten minutes long, while the longest was more than forty minutes. Predictions ranged from samples 2.5 minutes from the end of the game to 20 minutes from the end of the game. Table 1 gives the records of each scripted agent match on a specific map. Results are summed for each agent, no matter what difficulty level, since both agents have the same advantage. Table 2 shows the average standard deviation in game length for a specific agent combination at a specific difficulty level on a specific map. This standard deviation is an average of the standard deviation across the three difficulty settings. These statistics show the deterministic nature of the Bos Wars scripts. In a given agent combination on a given map, the

TABLE 1: Records for each agent combination on listed map (1st agent wins—2nd agent wins).

Map/Agent combination	Battlefield	Island Warfare	Wetlands
Rush versus Blitz	6–3	9–0	9–0
Tank Rush versus Blitz	9–0	9–0	9–0
Rush versus Tank Rush	0–9	2–7	9–0

TABLE 2: Average standard deviation in game length (seconds) for agent combinations on specific maps.

Map/Agent combination	Battlefield	Island Warfare	Wetlands
Rush versus Blitz	0.00	31.30	38.10
Tank Rush versus Blitz	0.00	0.00	34.78
Rush versus Tank Rush	0.77	30.41	0.26

TABLE 3: Number of winning samples for each fold of the Bos Wars Training Set and the number of winning samples in the Bos Wars Test Set.

Data set	Winning samples	Samples	Percentage
Fold One	311	998	31.2%
Fold Two	311	998	31.2%
Fold Three	310	997	31.1%
Bos Wars Test Set	452	1463	30.9%

same agent tends to win every time. The game length is almost the same every time.

Extracting all the third quarter samples from the game leads to a sample size of about 4500. This data is split into two portions: the first, of around 3000 samples, is used by both algorithms to develop classifiers. This data is referred to as the Bos Wars Training Set. The remaining 1500 samples are held out and used to compare the best classifiers found by the two algorithms. This data is referred to as the Bos Wars Testing Set. Holding out a portion of the data so neither algorithm is allowed to train on it leads to a fair comparison. The percentage of winning samples in each data set is presented in Table 3. When analyzing results, the win/loss bias of the data determines how good the accuracy is when compared to an uninformed algorithm which simply assigns the majority label to every sample.

When generating classifiers, both algorithms use 3-fold cross validation to develop their classifiers. In 3-fold cross validation, the data is split into three sections. The algorithm takes two of these sections to train a classifier and then uses the final third to test the performance of the classifier.

The Bos Wars Training Set is used to determine the best search parameters for each algorithm. Solutions obtained using the best search parameters on the Training Set are then tested on the Bos Wars Testing Set.

5.2. Deterministic Search Parameters. The developed deterministic algorithm is a *greedy, depth-first search with back-tracking* combined search. It has two search parameters which could be varied: the depth of the greedy jump start (i) and the max depth of the search (j). At each level, the

TABLE 4: Parameter combinations for testing of the stochastic search algorithm.

Parameter	Range	Step	Unique values
T_0	50–200	25	7
α	0.2–0.8	0.1	7
l	2–8	1	7

search adds a feature/center triple, created using a BC, to the solution. At the beginning of the DFS portion of the search, the solution contains i feature/center triples. At the end of the DFS, a full solution has $j = k$ feature/center triples, where j and k are the constraints set out in (4) and j is also the max depth of the search.

The depth of the DFS portion of the search is limited to values less than or equal to four because of computational complexity, or the constraint $j - i \leq 4$. Additionally, the goal of a solution to the RTSPP is to reduce the number of features in a solution, leading to the additional constraint $j \leq 8$. To test the performance of the algorithm, the search is run with all possible parameter combinations subject to these constraints, a total of *34 different test combinations*.

5.3. Stochastic Search Parameters. The chosen stochastic search algorithm is simulated annealing. The SA algorithm has three search parameters: the initial temperature T_0, the cooling parameter α, and the number of features in a solution l. In the developed SA algorithm, the total number of centers in a solution is equal to the number of features.

Table 4 gives the parameter combinations for the SA tests. Because this is a stochastic algorithm, performance is averaged across fifty runs for each parameter combination. The experimental setup is a full factorial design (every parameter combination is tested) across the three parameters, so there are 343 runs × 50 iterations × 3 folds = 51450 experiments for SA.

5.4. Performance Metrics. To assess the performance of each classification algorithm, two metrics are used: the fitness of the generated classifiers and the time to complete a search. The fitness of a classifier is its classification accuracy on the test set.

For the deterministic solution, every time the algorithm is run with the same parameter settings on the same data set, it finishes with the same solution. Repeated iterations are not required. For each parameter setting, the algorithm is run on each of the three folds in the data set. The best classifier found is tested on the appropriate fold, and the fitness across all three folds is averaged, giving an average classification accuracy for the parameter setting. The time to complete each search is expressed in seconds required for the search; this is also averaged across all three folds for the specific parameter setting.

In the stochastic search, subsequent runs of the algorithm do not necessarily result in the same answer, so one hundred iterations are run for each parameter combination on each fold. The average time required to complete one iteration is computed for each fold.

Finally, to compare the two algorithms, the classifiers for the top five parameter settings are tested on the Bos Wars Test Set. The average fitness for each parameter setting is computed and can be used for comparison of the performance of the two algorithms, along with the average time to complete a search.

6. Results and Analysis

This section displays the results of the deterministic and stochastic search algorithms and compares their performance. First, the best performing deterministic search parameters are determined by examining algorithm performance on the Bos Wars Training Set. The process is repeated for the stochastic search algorithm. Next, the classifiers generated using the best performing parameters are compared on the Bos Wars Training Set.

6.1. Deterministic Search. Deterministic search algorithm performance is measured in terms of time to search and classification performance. The chosen deterministic search algorithm was a Depth First Search with Backtracking (DFS-BT). *3-fold cross validation* was used on the Bos Wars data set. Table 5 shows an average and a standard deviation for search time and classification accuracy across all the folds. i is the greedy search depth and j is the full search depth. Fitness is the average classification accuracy for the solution found in the training data on the appropriate test set for each fold. Time is the average length of the search rounded to the nearest second. St Dev is the standard deviation for the three measurements which are averaged.

6.2. Effect of Deterministic Search Parameters. In the deterministic search, there are two parameters: the greedy search depth and the total search depth, i and j, respectively. DFS depth is equal to $j - i$. The two graphs in Figure 7 show the effect of the two search parameters on classifier performance.

In the first, the direct relationship between classification accuracy and DFS depth $j - i$ can be clearly observed. No matter what the greedy search depth, the classification accuracy of the solution increases when the DFS is allowed to search deeper.

However, the greedy search portion, which is reflected in the second graph, is not as effective. Although not as definitive, the trend in the classification accuracy as i increases but $j - i$ is held constant appears to be downward. This can be validated by looking at the best performing parameter sets, as determined by mean classification accuracy: the top four parameter sets are where the greedy search depth is zero or one.

The solutions with the best fitness are generated for the parameter values $j - i = 4$ and $i = 0$. The results of the classifiers determined with these parameter values are compared to the best stochastic algorithm solutions on a novel data set in Section 6.5.

6.3. The Bhattacharyya Metric. The Bhattacharyya Metric (BC) is computed for each training set in the Bos Wars

TABLE 5: Results for the DFS-BT across all folds on the Bos Wars Training Set.

i	j	Fitness	St Dev	Time (s)	St Dev
0	1	73.6%	0.039	<1	0.00
0	2	80.5%	0.050	1.33	0.58
0	3	86.7%	0.027	46.67	0.58
0	4	90.0%	0.004	1013.00	5.29
1	2	70.7%	0.060	<1	0.00
1	3	83.1%	0.046	3.00	0.00
1	4	85.6%	0.039	69.33	1.16
1	5	89.0%	0.019	1345.33	17.79
2	3	67.8%	0.060	<1	0.58
2	4	80.5%	0.040	3.33	0.58
2	5	83.6%	0.036	90.67	0.58
2	6	84.7%	0.008	1673.00	51.18
3	4	65.2%	0.050	<1	0.58
3	5	77.5%	0.020	4.67	0.58
3	6	80.9%	0.023	113.00	1.00
3	7	85.5%	0.022	1962.33	15.54
4	5	67.5%	0.010	<1	0.58
4	6	75.9%	0.031	6.00	0.00
4	7	83.4%	0.019	141.67	0.58
4	8	85.5%	0.009	2279.00	6.56
5	6	73.0%	0.017	1.00	0.00
5	7	83.4%	0.019	7.00	0.00
5	8	85.5%	0.009	164.00	0.00
6	7	72.9%	0.016	<1	0.58
6	8	83.1%	0.009	9.00	0.00
7	8	75.7%	0.082	<1	0.57

Data before beginning the deterministic search. In Figure 8, the value of the BC for each feature in the training set is displayed, in order of lowest to highest. The best BC for any set is 37%, which quickly rises. The BC determines separability of a feature: its high values lead to the conclusion that the Bos Wars data is not very separable.

As a heuristic for the greedy search portion of the deterministic algorithm, the BC is ineffective. In almost all cases, adding more levels to the greedy search decreased performance. However, using the BC to pair features with centers is effective: using these triples, the deterministic search is able to attain accuracies over 90% in some cases.

6.4. Stochastic Search. To fine-tune the simulated annealing stochastic algorithm, the effects of various parameters on solution fitness are explored. Figure 9 depicts the effect of the number of features in the solution l, the cooling parameter α and the initial temperature T_0 on both solution fitness and search time across all three folds of the Bos Wars data.

Both the number of features in a solution and the cooling parameter have a direct relationship with both classification accuracy and search time. For alpha values, the relationship appears to be linear. An increase of 0.1 in α results in an average fitness increase of 2%. Two-sample t-tests for

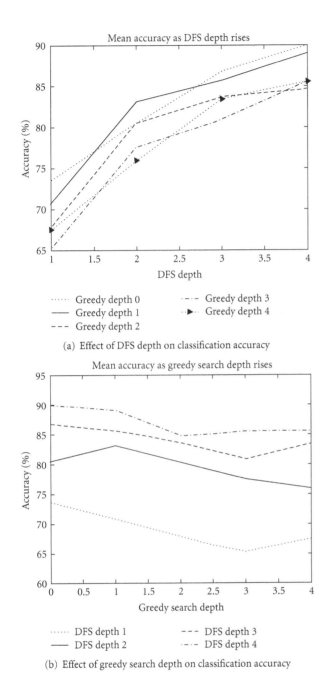

(a) Effect of DFS depth on classification accuracy

(b) Effect of greedy search depth on classification accuracy

FIGURE 7: Effect of search depth on classification accuracy, (a) and (b).

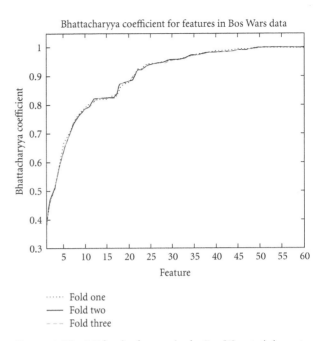

FIGURE 8: The BC for the features in the Bos Wars training sets.

comparisons of the average fitness values for different alpha values all yield very small P values, giving significant statistical evidence that these averages are different. However, the increase in search time looks exponential. Increasing alpha exponentially increases the number of iterations for the simulated annealing algorithm. In Section 4.4, the number of simulated annealing iterations is derived as $\ln(\epsilon)/\ln(\alpha)$, so the exponential relationship was to be expected.

The number of features in a solution has a large impact on fitness at the low ends, but less at the high ends. Again, two-sample t-tests yield P values of .000, giving significant statistical evidence of a difference in average fitness value for different feature values. The effect on search time is

linear. This was also expected. The complexity of the fitness computation is linear in the number of features, so an increase has a linear effect on complexity.

The *starting temperature* has a negligible effect on classification accuracy and search time due to α. Two-sample t-tests for the difference in average fitness are less definitive, with P values ranging from .6 to .000. The largest difference between average fitness is <3%, showing the starting temperature has little effect on overall fitness. This is because of the cooling function, which multiplies the current temperature by α to get the next temperature. For temperature to have a larger effect, the steps between values would have to be much larger. Basically, this would increase the number of iterations for the search. Since changing the value of α already does this, there is no real reason to adjust the starting temperature as well.

The detailed analysis of the effect of the parameter values leads to a selection of the best values for the Bos Wars data set. In this case, those values are $T_0 = 200$, $\alpha = 0.8$, and $l = 8$. In the next section, the results of the stochastic and deterministic algorithms are compared on the Bos Wars Test Set.

6.5. Comparing Deterministic and Stochastic Search. To choose whether to develop a deterministic or stochastic algorithm, we must compare the solutions found by each. For each algorithm, the best performing search parameters are determined. In the deterministic algorithm, these parameters are $i = 0$ (greedy search depth) and $j = 4$ (total search depth). For the stochastic algorithm, the parameters are $T_0 = 200$ (starting temperature), $\alpha = 0.8$ (cooling parameter), and $l = 8$ (number of features in solution).

Instead of comparing the results of the algorithms on the data sets already observed, they are tested on a different Bos Wars data set on which neither was allowed to train. The deterministic algorithm uses the three different solutions

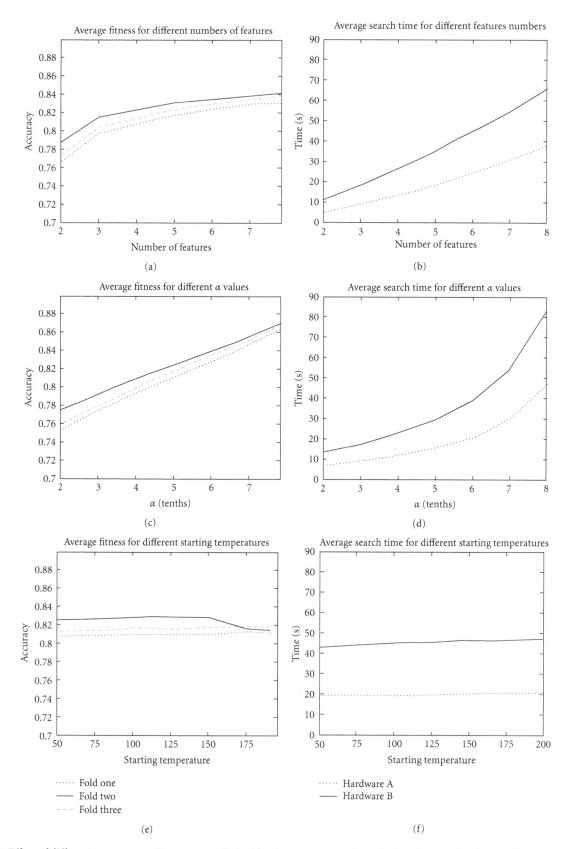

FIGURE 9: Effect of different parameter settings on overall classification accuracy and search time for Simulated Annealing on the Bos Wars data set.

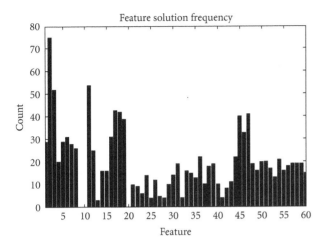

FIGURE 10: The frequency of each feature in the 150 SA solutions evaluated on the Bos Wars Test Set.

TABLE 6: Results for the solutions found with the best parameters by the deterministic and stochastic algorithms.

Algorithm	Accuracy	Search time
Deterministic	91.4%	1013.0
Stochastic	96.2%	75.0

developed for the parameter settings. Each solution is the result of a DFS on a different fold of the Bos Wars training set. The stochastic algorithm is run fifty times on each fold, so there are 150 different solutions for the best parameter set. All these solutions are tested on the novel data set.

The classification accuracy, along with the time which is required to generate each solution from the training data, is presented in Table 6. Accuracy is the average accuracy on the Bos Wars test data, on which neither algorithm is allowed to train. Search Time is the average time in seconds of an average search with the best performing parameters on Hardware Configuration A.

7. Conclusion

The results are unequivocal: the stochastic algorithm outperforms the deterministic algorithm on both performance metrics. In the RTSPP domain, a near-optimal solution to the original problem is better than an optimal solution to the reduced-dimension problem.

The simulated annealing solution gives good performance on this data set. However, simulated annealing is a simple stochastic search algorithm which was chosen for the ease with which it could be implemented. It would be more complicated to refine or tune the algorithm for a specific RTSPP search landscape.

On the other hand, the SA solution exposes information about the problem domain. Figure 10 shows the number of times each feature appears in one of the 150 SA solutions tested on the Bos Wars Test Set. Although some features are clearly used more than others, no single subset of features appears to dominate all the solutions. The standard deviation

of the fitness for each iteration is 0.000197, showing all the solutions found have similar fitness values.

We conclude there is *no single feature representation which is obviously better*. Good feature representations are spread out around the space, with many different local maximums which appear to have similar accuracy. While the exact difference between the fitness of these solutions and the fitness of the optimal solution is unknown, the max fitness is 100%, so they cannot be more than 5% below this value. Good solutions can be found in many different sections of the solution space since the RTSPP solution space landscape is jagged.

The failure of the BC metric to generate good classification accuracies for the deterministic solution indicates that the features are dependent. Features work in combinations to determine the outcome of an RTS game.

This study was conducted to determine the characteristics of the RTSPP. While the stochastic search method was able to find good classification accuracies that was not our main objective, instead, we used the results to determine the characteristics of the space, which allows us to develop a search algorithm tailored to our specific RTSPP problem.

The deterministic search tries to find a heuristic. In many searches, a heuristic is used to guide the search in profitable directions. If admissible, it can also be used to implicitly search much of the domain, using a best-first search strategy like A^* or Z^* [31]. The heuristic could reduce search time, allowing the entire domain to be explored in a reasonable amount of time through pruning.

In the RTSPP, we do not have that luxury. No admissible heuristic could be found. Instead, we used a heuristic to reduce the size of the solution space. Our hope was the heuristic would preserve the high fitness solutions in the space, while discarding the lower fitness solutions. For example, if the entire problem domain looked as in Figure 1, then the reduced solution space looks as in Figure 2. In this pedagogical example, we accomplish our goal. The heuristic makes it so the reduced solution space can be completely explored, and the reduced solution space retains all the high fitness solutions from the original solution space.

Our results show this does not work for the RTSPP. The stochastic algorithm is allowed to search the entire space. Even though it is only able to explore a small portion of solutions on each run, it finds solutions superior to those from the deterministic solution. Instead of the ideal reduced solution space, we have found a space looking more like Figure 3. We have removed some of the low fitness solutions, but have not retained the high fitness solutions.

The stochastic search results tell us the solution space is quite jagged and rough. However, it also tells us the fitness of the solution at the top of each *ridge* is similar. While we do not know the fitness of the optimal solution in the domain, we know we can use a simple hill climbing approach to find a high fitness solution. The solution found is composed of different features and centers on every iteration, but has a similar fitness, as demonstrated by the low standard deviation between the fitness of the SA solutions. In the RTS domain, this is an intuitive result: there are many different strategies which can be pursued to win an RTS game, each one equally valid!

8. Future Work

Our goal is to use the understanding of the solution space characteristics determined in this study and develop a more complicated RTSPP algorithm. This innovative generic RTSPP method would employ a hybrid genetic algorithm/ evolutionary strategy [34, 35]. This algorithm would be tested on the Bos Wars data as well as data obtained from the more complicated RTS game platform called *Spring* [13] or another available platform.

Specific to the RTS game domain, Bakkes et al. [13] created an evaluation function for the RTS platform called *Spring Engine*, where perfect knowledge of the environment is not available. *Temporal difference learning* is used to create an appropriate weighting for two features, "number of units observed of each type" and "safety of tactical positions". In [36], the same authors used five different features to accomplish the same basic goal. Like us, they hope to use their evaluation function to help drive improvements in adaptive RTS games. We hope to develop a more formal method of feature selection and allow this feature selection to correctly determine an appropriate strategy for an RTS game. Additionally, instead of temporal difference learning to determine appropriate weights for the features discovered, we desire to characterize winning/losing game states in terms of their location in n-space, where n is the number of features selected: a strategic approach. We would take classifiers generated for the Spring platform and use them as the foundation for a strategy-based agent which would generate and execute counter-strategies for a given opponent. Also, using a time-delay window of the past n snapshots should be address instead of the single snapshot.

Acknowledgment

This investigation is a research effort of the AFIT Center for Cyberspace Research (CCR), Director: Dr. Rick Raines.

References

[1] B. Geryk, *A History of Real-Time Strategy Games*, GameSpot, 2008.

[2] S. M. Lucas and G. Kendall, "Evolutionary computation and games," *IEEE Computational Intelligence Magazine*, vol. 1, no. 1, pp. 10–18, 2006.

[3] S. Ontañón, K. Mishra, N. Sugandh, and A. Ram, "Case-based planning and execution for real-time strategy games," in *Proceedings of the 7th International Conference on Case-Based Reasoning*, vol. 4626 of *Lecture Notes in Computer Science*, pp. 164–178, Springer, Berlin, Germany, 2007.

[4] D. W. Aha1, M. Molineaux, and M. Ponsen, "Learning to win: casebased plan selection in a RTS game," in *Proceedings of the 6th International Conference on Case-Based Reasoning (ICCBR '05)*, H. Muoz-Avila and F. Ricci, Eds., pp. 5–20, Springer, 2005.

[5] M. Sharma, M. Holmes, J. Santamaria, A. Irani, C. Isbell, and A. Ram, "Transfer learning in real-time strategy games using

[6] T. Graepel, R. Herbrich, and J. Gold, "Learning to fight," in *Proceedings of Computer Games: Artificial Intelligence, Design and Education (CGAIDE '04)*, Q. Mehdi, N. Gough, and D. Al-Dabass, Eds., pp. 193–200, 2004.

[7] M. Molineaux, D. W. Aha, and P. Moore, "Learning continuous action models in a real-time strategy environment," in *Proceedings of the 21th International Florida Artificial Intelligence Research Society Conference (FLAIRS '08)*, pp. 257–262, AAAI Press, May 2008.

[8] P. Spronck, M. Ponsen, I. Sprinkhuizen-Kuyper, and E. Postma, "Adaptive game AI with dynamic scripting," *Machine Learning*, vol. 63, no. 3, pp. 217–248, 2006.

[9] E. Kok, *Adaptive reinforcement learning agents in RTS games*, M.S. thesis, University Utrecht, Utrecht, The Netherlands, 2008.

[10] M. Chung, M. Buro, and J. Schaeffer, "Monte Carlo planning in rts games," in *Proceedings of the IEEE Symposium on Computational Intelligence and Games*, 2005.

[11] D. H. Wolpert and W. G. Macready, "No free lunch theorems for optimization," *IEEE Transactions on Evolutionary Computation*, vol. 1, no. 1, pp. 67–82, 1997.

[12] F. Beerten, J. Salmon, L. Taulelle, F. Loeffler, N. Mistry, and T. Penfold, "Bos wars. Open Source Software," 2008, http://www.boswars.org/.

[13] S. Bakkes, P. Kerbusch, P. Spronck, and J. van den Herik, "Automatically evaluating the status of an rts game," in *Proceedings of the Workshop on Reasoning, Representation, and Learning in Computer Games (IJCAI '05)*, 2005.

[14] R. Miikkulainen, B. D. Bryant, R. Cornelius, I. V. Karpov, K. O. Stanley, and C. H. Yong, "Computational intelligence in games," in *Computational Intelligence: Principles and Practice*, G. Y. Yen and D. B. Fogel, Eds., IEEE Computational Intelligence Society, Piscataway, NJ, USA, 2006.

[15] A. L. Blum and P. Langley, "Selection of relevant features and examples in machine learning," *Artificial Intelligence*, vol. 97, no. 1-2, pp. 245–271, 1997.

[16] A. K. Jain, M. N. Murty, and P. J. Flynn, "Data clustering: a review," *ACM Computing Surveys*, vol. 31, no. 3, pp. 316–323, 1999.

[17] M. R. Garey and D. S. Johnson, *Computers and Intractability: A Guide to the Theory of NP-Completeness*, W.H. Freeman, New York, NY, USA, 1979.

[18] P. Somol, P. Pudil, and J. Kittler, "Fast branch & bound algorithms for optimal feature selection," *IEEE Transactions on Pattern Analysis and Machine Intelligence*, vol. 26, no. 7, pp. 900–912, 2004.

[19] J. Jarmulak and S. Craw, "Genetic algorithms for feature selection and weighting," in *Proceedings of the Workshop on Automating the Construction of Case Based Reasoners (IJCAI '99)*, 1999.

[20] R. Meiri and J. Zahavi, "Using simulated annealing to optimize the feature selection problem in marketing applications," *European Journal of Operational Research*, vol. 171, no. 3, pp. 842–858, 2006.

[21] S. Kirkpatrick, C. D. Gelatt, and M. P. Vecchi, "Optimization by simulated annealing," *Science*, vol. 220, no. 4598, pp. 671–680, 1983.

[22] S. B. Kotsiantis, "Supervised machine learning: a review of classification techniques," *Informatica*, vol. 31, no. 3, pp. 249–268, 2007.

[23] A. Champandard, *AI Game Development: Synthetic Creatures with Learning and Reactive Behaviors*, New Riders, 2003.

[24] J. H. Friedman, "Regularized discriminant analysis," *Journal of the American Statistical Association*, vol. 84, no. 405, pp. 165–175, 1989.

[25] B. Cestnik, I. Kononenko, and I. Bratko, "Assistant 86: a knowledgeelicitation tool for sophisticated users," in *Proceedings of the 2nd European Working Session on Learning*, pp. 31–45, 1987.

[26] E. Larry Bull, *Advances in Learning Classifier Systems*, Springer, New York, NY, USA, 2004.

[27] R. L. de Mantaras and E. Armengol, "Machine learning from examples: inductive and lazy methods," *Data & Knowledge Engineering*, vol. 25, no. 1-2, pp. 99–123, 1998.

[28] E. E. Smith and D. Medin, *Categories and Concepts*, Harvard University Press, Cambridge, Mass, USA, 1981.

[29] S. Ridella, S. Rovetta, and R. Zunino, "K-winner machines for pattern classification," *IEEE Transactions on Neural Networks*, vol. 12, no. 2, pp. 371–385, 2001.

[30] D. J. C. MacKay, *Information Theory, Inference, and Learning Algorithms*, Cambridge University Press, Cambridge, UK, 2003.

[31] J. Pearl, *Heuristics*, Addison-Wesley, New York, NY, USA, 1984.

[32] F. J. Aherne, N. A. Thacker, and P. I. Rockett, "The Bhattacharyya metric as an absolute similarity measure for frequency coded data," *Kybernetika*, vol. 34, no. 4, pp. 363–368, 1998.

[33] E. Aarts and J. K. Lenstra, *Local Seach in Combinatorial Optimization*, Wiley, New York, NY, USA, 1997.

[34] K. Weissgerber, B. Borghetti, G. Lamont, and M. Mendenhall, "Towards automated feature selection in real time strategy games," in *GAMEON-NA Conference*, August 2009.

[35] K. Weissgerber, B. J. Borghetti, and G. L. Peterson, "An effective and efficient real time strategy agent," in *Proceedings of the 23rd Annual Florida Artificial Intelligence Research Society Conference*, 2010.

[36] S. Bakkes, P. Spronck, and J. van den Herik, "Phase-dependent evaluation in RTS games," in *Proceedings of the 19th Belgian-Dutch Conference on Artificial Intelligence*, pp. 3–10, 2007.

10

MovieRemix: Having Fun Playing with Videos

Nicola Dusi, Maria Federico, and Marco Furini

Department of Communication and Economics, University of Modena and Reggio Emilia, Via Allegri 9, 42100 Reggio Emilia, Italy

Correspondence should be addressed to Marco Furini, marco.furini@unimore.it

Academic Editor: Alexander Pasko

The process of producing new creative videos by editing, combining, and organizing pre-existing material (e.g., video shots) is a popular phenomenon in the current web scenario. Known as *remix* or video remix, the produced video may have new and different meanings with respect to the source material. Unfortunately, when managing audiovisual objects, the technological aspect can be a burden for many creative users. Motivated by the large success of the gaming market, we propose a novel game and an architecture to make the remix process a pleasant and stimulating gaming experience. MovieRemix allows people to act like a movie director, but instead of dealing with cast and cameras, the player has to create a remixed video starting from a given screenplay and from video shots retrieved from the provided catalog. MovieRemix is not a simple video editing tool nor is a simple game: it is a challenging environment that stimulates creativity. To temp to play the game, players can access different levels of screenplay (original, outline, derived) and can also challenge other players. Computational and storage issues are kept at the server side, whereas the client device just needs to have the capability of playing streaming videos.

1. Introduction

In the past few years the usage of video material has largely grown in popularity, fueled by an increasing number of websites designed to share video material. Watching, uploading, downloading, and sharing videos are nowadays common activities in the web scenario. The well-known YouTube, the third most visited website according to Alexa statistics [1], is coupled with several other video sharing sites like Vimeo, MetaTube, and Yahoo! Video, not to mention the high usage of videos in several social network sites like Facebook, MySpace, and Flickr. With no doubt, video applications generate the main source of traffic for the Internet backbone network: it accounts for 90% of the worldwide Internet data traffic [2], and several research studies predict that the popularity of all forms of video material (video on demand, Mobile, Internet, P2P, 3D, and HD) will continue to increase.

The gaming market experiences a similar success. Despite the current economic environment, the video game market continues to report promising results and is expected to have a significant growth in the next few years. Mainly due to the introduction of new devices (e.g., XBox's Kinect, Nintendo 3DS) and to the turnover of software sales, a research analysis of IDATE [3] predicts that, worldwide, the gaming market will increase from 38 billion EUR in 2010 to 52.3 billion EUR in 2014.

The combination of both scenarios would likely create a success and popular environment. To this aim, in this paper we want to make the editing of a video a gaming experience. Motivated by the large usage of video material, by the success of the gaming market, and by the increasing presence of active users in the Web 2.0, our goal is to propose a MovieRemix game and an architecture able to support it.

Video remix is a popular phenomenon in the current web scenario: several websites with remixed video material (e.g., http://www.totalrecut.com/) are appearing on line, and the word "Remix" returns more than 1.5 millions of videos when entered in the YouTube search box. It is worth noting that the remix practice is not a new phenomenon, but what is new is the scale: nowadays multimedia and web technologies allow people an easy access to video material.

Roughly, a remix video is an audiovisual content obtained by editing, combining, and organizing preexisting material (e.g., professional video contents like movies, previews, recaps, or commercials). The remix is usually a creative video with new meanings with respect to the original sources [4]. More generally, a remix may come from catalogs or libraries of music, images, and audiovisual and multimedial cultural products [5]. The author of the remix is a *bricoleur* [6], and he/she takes advantage of the advent of digital technologies that facilitate the remix practices in many scenarios. For instance, in popular music we have cover versions and remixes of golden oldies as well as new songs. The transformation of the original sources seems to have no limits. The same happens in the video scenario, where remix videos are made from copying or editing several different movies.

The success of the *Be Kind Rewind* (http://www.youtube .com/user/bekindrewind/) initiative highlights that users want to manipulate professional videos to create personal and customized clips. In essence, using many different sources and remixing them, creative users aim at creating new cultural and artistic products [4].

Unfortunately, when dealing with audiovisual material the technological aspect plays a critical role and can be a burden for many creative users who do not have a sufficient technological background. The raw material of a remixer is usually a set of video shots, and these are obtained either by personally shooting them or by copying them from different sources. The shooting requires a video camera and limits the amount of audiovisual material that can be used (i.e., it is difficult to use a New York background if you do not live in New York City), whereas the extraction of video material from other sources requires knowledge of video editing applications and of low-level video characteristics (e.g., sources may be encoded with different encoding technologies like MPEG, DivX, Flash, etc.), not to mention that copyright laws protect from unauthorized usage many materials available in the web scenario. However, assuming that a user can have access to several video clips, he/she has to edit/organize them in order to create the remixed video. Once again, this process requires knowledge that many users may not have. As a result, a relatively small number of users may express their creativity within the video remix phenomenon.

In this paper we propose a game and an architecture that make the remix experience easy, fun, and pleasant. Similarly to many video games where a user plays a role different from the real one (e.g., soccer player, airplane pilot, music director), our goal is to allow people to act like a movie director, but instead of dealing with cast, camera shot, and so on, our player deals with a catalog of pre-existing video shots and with a catalog of screenplays. The objective of the game is to create a video starting from a given screenplay. Different levels of screenplay (derived, original, and outline) are given to players in order to increase game difficulties. Through a developed graphical application, a player can select the preferred video shots from the MovieRemix catalog, can add music, and transition effects so as to create a new video. Once done, the remixed video can be uploaded, shared, and voted by other players. To temp to play the game, charts and challenges are also possible.

It is worth noting that, to play the game, users are simply required to be creative and to have Internet access: no special knowledge is required as all technical details (encoding format, compression mechanism, storage space, etc.) are

hidden from users. Similarly, the architecture is designed to keep computation and storage issues (i.e., encoding and storage of video material) at the server side, whereas the client device can be very simple (the only requirement is to play streaming videos).

To evaluate MovieRemix we set up an experimental scenario. The investigation involved a group of heterogeneous people that were asked to use MovieRemix and to answer several different questions about the proposed game. Using a mean opinion score evaluation, results confirmed that MovieRemix is considered an educational game and that players have almost no difficulties in understanding the given screenplay. Furthermore, results showed that MovieRemix is better using with news and music video remix.

The paper is organized as follows. Section 2 briefly describes related works in the area of video remix; Section 3 presents preliminaries whose reading facilitates the understanding of the proposed architecture; Section 4 introduces game and architecture details; prototype implementation is described in Section 5, whereas the experimental evaluation is shown in Section 6. Conclusions are drawn in Section 7.

2. Related Work

In the literature, several studies analyzed the practice of audiovisual remix from different points of view: sociological, philosophical, analytical, and technological (e.g., [7–12]). In the following, we present approaches related to the technological aspect, that is, proposals designed to facilitate the making of remixed videos.

Early works in the area of video remix propose systems developed to make up for a lack of adequate tools to support collaborative knowledge building around media material or creative thinking.

Pea et al. [11] present DIVER, a system which makes it possible to create an infinite number of new digital video clips and remix compilations starting from a single source video recording. The DIVER project was born at Stanford University to support collaborative analysis of learning and teaching video records in a distributed community of researchers and practitioners. DIVER works like a virtual camera which can zoom and pan through space and time within a video record. The virtual camera dynamically crops image clips to create a *dive* which is a set of reordable panels, each one containing a thumbnail that represents a clip as well as a text field that may contain an accompanying annotation. The user can upload the created dive to a website for interactive browsing searching and display of video clips and collaborative commentary on them.

Multisilta and Mäenpää [10] propose MoViE, a platform that enables users to create narrations and stories made with the mobile phone and for the mobile phone in a collaborative way and using narrative structures. Applying a narrative structure used in jazz music, a user defines a topic for the story and shoots a short video about this topic; then he/she uploads the video to the system and tags it with appropriate keywords. At this point, like in a jazz concert, another author watches the video using a mobile phone, and, using the video as an inspiration source, he shoots several clips (called solos) to express his ideas about the original video and story. Finally, the system automatically creates remixes of original video by randomly combining shots and solos based on tags to produce creative arts video stories. A slightly different version of MoViE appeared in [13], where the basic idea of the tool is the same, but in this version users can create remixes either manually (i.e., by selecting videos one by one and by adjusting their order and their start and end cues) or semiautomatically (i.e., by defining a list of tags that the system uses to search for corresponding clips and to create the remix).

Scheible et al. [12, 14] propose an urban storytelling game which combines a mobile client, a storytelling tool in the Web, and a large public display into a collaborative street art authoring system deploying ubiquitous multimedia. The aim of the game is the illustration of stories created by a web player (also by remixing sentences from a pool of already illustrated stories) in collaboration with mobile players. Selected best stories are displayed on a large public display. The design of the game triggers creativity in writing stories and taking photos and fosters collaboration and social interaction in the form of team play.

As video sharing becomes more and more widespread, the same happens with video remix designated for supporting users during the process of video editing. The market offers a wide range of professional video editing softwares like Adobe Premiere (http://www.adobe.com/products/premiere/), Apple's iMovie (http://www.apple.com/ilife/imovie/), and Windows Live Movie Maker (http://explore .live.com/windows-live-movie-maker?os=other). During the last years also a lot of online tools proliferated. Examples are JayCut (http://jaycut.com/), Eyespot and Jumpcut (the latter two online video tools were quite popular in the past few years, but has been recently shut down), which allow users to upload home videos and edit them on the Web, providing an alternative to simple desktop video editors. Others, like Cuts (http://www.cuts.com/) and Sweeney Todd Trailer Editor powered by GorillaSpot (http://research.yahoo.com/ Yahoo_Research_Berkeley), have been released to create video mashup and provide users with the ability of selecting preexisting contents to create personalized audiovisual material.

Diakopoulos et al. [7] present a qualitative case study of JumpCut, illustrating how collaborative authorship in remix culture is being affected by the composition of environmental constraints, which include legal codes, community and social norms, physical and architectural design, and economic factors. Authors suggest also some potential design implications based on their analysis. In particular, they say that tools to support creativity could be leveraged in the interface to enhance a remixer's ability to find interesting juxtapositions of clips by, for instance, providing a palette of suggested clips based on loosely related tags. Furthermore, reducing the time and efforts of searching for and importing contents would enhance the ability to rapidly test and evaluate creative remix ideas.

Same findings are reported by Shaw and Schmitz [15] from the analysis of the user behavior during a pilot deployment, in association with the San Francisco International Film Festival, of a web-based platform which allows users to select, annotate, and remix material from a shared media archive.

Cesar et al. [16] describe an architecture of an inherently more social approach to viewing and sharing media. Authors promote the introduction of advanced user features (e.g., facilities to fragment a video in one or more ranges of clips, or to add annotations to video and its fragments, or to enrich video adding subtitles, captions, remixing, repurposing, or voice to a baseline object) as a spontaneous activity in order to enhance social sharing of video.

A recent tool of video mashup which reflects many of the suggestions given in works cited above has been presented by Cardillo et al. [4]. The tool allows users to navigate and interrogate a video repository structured following an ontology which mirrors the personal cinematic world of the audience and returns as result of the user query an automatic editing of the requested clips exploiting metadata (high- and low-level features) and tags. This process provides the user with a collection of clips having semantic coherence and stylistic homogeneity. Once the requested clips have been found, users can modify the remixed video, for example, changing the order of the clips, their start and end points, or the audio properties of clips.

Finally, in the area of remix, it is worth noting a project initiative between Yahoo! and Research Berkeley (http://research.yahoo.com/Yahoo_Research_Berkeley). The partnership has a declared scope of exploring and inventing social media and mobile media technology and applications that will enable people to create, describe, find, share, and remix media on the web.

MovieRemix differs from the above proposals in several different ways. First of all, although it may recall a video editing tool, it is not, neither is a tool to promote creative thinking like Diver [11] nor a tool to support collaborative story narration as MoViE [10, 13] and Story Mashup [12, 14]. Conversely, MovieRemix has been designed with two main goals. First, it aims at creating an exciting environment where the production of creative videos has to be easy, fun, and pleasant; to this aim, MovieRemix exploits experiences of the several proposals in the field like [7] and [15]. Second, by giving players a real screenplay, it aims at improving competences and abilities of people who would like to act like a movie director. This means that MovieRemix allows players to produce remix of videos from scratch and therefore is different from proposals (like the one in [4]) that mainly focuses on automatic production of video remix.

3. Preliminaries

MovieRemix is designed to produce a creative video product called remix. This product is based on a given screenplay (original, outline, or derived); once received, a player has to find and organize video shots so as to meet the screenplay guidelines. In the following, we briefly describe what is a remix, a screenplay, and a derived screenplay. In addition, since this paper also proposes an architecture to support the game, in the following we also briefly review basics of the standards used in the architecture.

3.1. Remix. The advent of new digital technologies has opened up whole new world of replica (or remix) practices. For instance, in popular music we have cover versions and remixes of golden oldies as well as new songs. A similar trend is true for music videos and movies. In essence, the transformations of the myth of the "original" or source text seem to have no limits. According to Lessing [17] and Manovich [18] remix has nowadays a broad meaning of transformation, reediting, bricolage, junctioning, or overlapping the original with other pictures, sounds, videos, or music [19]. Remixing aims to create something new with practices of bricolage and recycle. Manovich [18] states that we are living in a remix culture society: music, fashion, design, art, user-generated contents, media sharing, and even food are mostly remix, mashup, and collage.

Roughly, we can define a remix as the art of reusing catalogs of music, images, audiovisual, and multimedial cultural products [5]. It is worth noting a difference between video remix and video mashup: the former is a whole rework of another video given as a single source, whereas a mashup is a rework of just some fragments of many existing videos.

It is inevitable that the practices of interpretation will revise known texts and generate new texts. This is easy to qualify as the multitude of films containing variations, or sequels, remixes, cover versions as in Von Trier's movie *The Five Obstructions.* Furthermore, some texts or parts of a text become a sort of "matrix" generating other texts, other versions and practices, new interconnections, and so on. For example, *Run Lola Run* (Lola rennt) by Tom Tykwer is a film about variations that invite us to compare the film proper with its teaser preview and video clip preview by putting both clips in the same DVD [20]. Texts can generate a variety of practices from "bastard pop" to "mashup" in music and from reworking to remaking in film and video. This is exactly what happens in *Be Kind Rewind* by Gondry (2008) which is a film about "how to swede" a movie, that is, how to make a remake [21]. The film gives details of the practice and so does the film's website, which shows lots of fans "sweeded" short films. Talking about repetition and internal variations, *Run Lola Run* has an incipit that becomes a matrix of invariants to provide three versions of the same narrative. Each version replicates the same forms of content and expression as the first one, changing only the representation and some moments of the action. Though different, each story is bound to the others: it employs the same logic of a videogame, and hence the three versions are a sort of implicit sequel, in which the hero is gaining new strength and new skills. Like the spectator, the hero is also learning in the repetition, so by the second and the third games Lola knows and takes advantage of what is about to happen. Also Gondry's *Be Kind Rewind* uses remake and remix practices as a subplot. A cult movie scene deals with a video tape from a rental store that does not work because it has been canceled. The whole story is exploited to lament the end of an era that started in the 1990s with the first DVDs. They talk about zero-budget short remakes. The movie exemplifies the homemade movie as a form of art, the reuse of some key scenes as a way to recreate the source film and the practice of the remix. Although neither *Be Kind*

Rewind nor *The Five Obstructions* shows a whole homemade remix, Gondry does make explicit references to the various original movies using markers like the source movie credits. It is thus still a postmodern aesthetic of fragments and variations. The film becomes a myth in the fan's affective memory, and the original movie is considered as a series of instructions of setting, costumes, characters, music, shots, and so forth. These instructions will be mixed with a clever bricolage to create new short movies. *Be Kind Rewind* has also a rich website, with video of instructions related to how to recreate "your own film." Anybody can shoot a digital short film and post it on this site. As a result, more and more people are making home-made remix videos.

3.1.1. Screenplay. A movie is scheduled through a screenplay and a shooting script. A screenplay may be described as a writing technique to plan and preview a movie. Its composition is unique because the screenplay is a text that must have expressive, dramatic, and aesthetic qualities as well as practical and functional utilities. A screenplay contains the dialogs the actors have to play but may also contain psychological and aesthetic aspects of the story that are necessary when playing particular scene as well as when preparing the set or the cast costumes. Shooting choices and other technical instructions could be given aside in a shooting script.

3.1.2. Screen-Derived Screenplay. After every possible variations given by actors and set problems or by other improvisations or choices that occur during the shootings there is the phase of editing and postproduction. When a spectator watches a movie, he/she does not know how different this is from the first outline and even from the final screenplay. That is the reason why scholars who analyze movie propose to write down an inferred or derived screenplay, which is a screenplay described directly from the screen and realized only after the movie release. Therefore, the original screenplay is written in the planning phase of the film, while the derived screenplay is an analytical rewrite after the film has found its final form, has reached its audience, and, perhaps, has become a classic. A derived screenplay is usually a transcription with two columns: in the left column are provided all descriptions concerning sound, dialog, voice-over, music, and so forth, whereas the right column usually presents the number of the shots, a brief description of images and actions, technical data such as the type of shot and the cinematic effects (like fade-in or fade-out), and every camera movement (like pan shots, dolly, etc.).

3.1.3. The MPEG7-MDS. From the technological point of view, to manage a media content, it is useful to use a representation language capable of describing with metatags the semantics of the contents. For instance, apart from video data, it is necessary to have additional information like title, author, initial and ending points of a video segment, and so forth. MPEG-7 Multimedia Description Schemes [22] have been designed to this aim. It is the core part of the MPEG7 standard and was proposed to describe multimedia contents with a set of textual tags. It is a markup description language

```
<VideoSegment>
  <title>DEAD POET'S SOCIETY: SEGMENT #23</title>
  <lable>"clip2"</label>
  <RelatedMaterial>
      <MediaLocator>
          <MediaUri>http://xxx.com</MediaUri>
      </MediaLocator>
  </RelatedMaterial>
  <MediaTime>
      <MediaTimePoint>00:04:30</MediaTimePoint>
      <MediaDuration>00:00:12</MediaDuration>
  </MediaTime>
  <screenplay>
    <FreeTextAnnotation>
      On the left is a life-sized mural depicting a group of young
      school boys looking up adoringly at a woman who represents
      liberty. On the right is a mural showing young men gathered
      around an industrialist in a corporate boardroom. Between the
      murals stands a boy.
    </FreeTextAnnotation>
  </screenplay>
  <tags>
    <FreeTextAnnotation>
      Drama; robin williams; Peter Weir; prep school; Welton Academy;
      tradition, honour, discipline and excellence;
      O Captain! My Captain!;
    </FreeTextAnnotation>
  </tags>
</VideoSegment>
```

FIGURE 1: The usage of MPEG7-MDS to describe a video shot.

based on XML Schema that allows producing a description of the spatial layout of different media objects (e.g., audio, video, text, graphics) as well as the temporal order in which these objects will be played out. The description is based on tags, which define the purpose of the media object description. A tag usually has attributes and values that define the media object aspect (e.g., position and color) and has the form <tag attribute=value> (with the exception of tags that do not have attributes).

Details of MPEG7-MDS are outside the scope of this paper, and we refer the readers to [22] for such details. However, to appreciate the power of MPEG7-MDS, we report in Figure 1 an example of MPEG7-MDS description, where a video segment is described with some basic information like title and time length and with some textual description like screenplay and tags.

3.1.4. The MPEG-4 Standard. The encoding mechanism is another important technological aspect, very important when dealing with video streaming. As earlier described, our proposal uses Internet to stream the video to the client. Therefore, we need an efficient coding mechanism that provides acceptable quality while offering low bitrates. With such constraints, MPEG-4 [23] is probably the most used coding algorithm. It is a standard defined by the Moving Picture Experts Group to handle audio/video material. It is composed of several parts that deal with different aspects of the audio/video encoding. In our proposal we consider Part 2 (encoding of video material) and Part 3 (encoding of audio material). The former has different profiles in order to accommodate needs of different applications (from low to high quality). For the purpose of this paper, we focus on Simple Profile, a profile designed to provide videos in

devices with limited system resources (e.g., cellphones and iPods). Part 3 (also known as Advanced Audio Coding) specifies audio encoding algorithms and provides higher quality with respect to previous released versions. Details of these encoding algorithms go beyond the scope of this paper (interested readers can refer to [23]).

4. Our Proposal

In this section we present details of the MovieRemix game and of the architecture we propose to support it. The main motivation behind MovieRemix is to create an environment able to stimulate the production of creative contents starting from pre-existing video material like professional or amateur video shots. MovieRemix creates a social space where general audience can produce creative videos. Needless to say, in addition to the game, it is necessary to design an architecture capable of supporting MovieRemix.

In essence, the goals of our proposal are to (i) create a game environment where the making of a video is easy, fun, and pleasant, (ii) stimulate creativity by providing different levels of game complexity, (iii) avoid the need to have special or particular devices (a device with an Internet access is sufficient), and (iv) design an architecture that keeps all the technological issues at the server side (and hide them from users).

Before presenting details of our proposal, let us depict a possible scenario.

Paul is fond of technology, and one of his favorite hobbies is to create new videos starting from pre-existing video shots. He gets videos from the Internet and uses a video editing application to extract video shots from long videos, to combine them in a particular order, and to add sound effects

```
...
Camera traveling back up to find out the street sign:
SUNSET BOULEVARD, stenciled on a curbstone.
Traveling back shooting the asphalt of the road.
SUPERIMPOSED on all this are the CREDIT TITLES, in the stenciled
style of the street sign.
Pan shot up to frame all the Sunset Boulevard
DISSOLVE (FADE OUT)
...
```

FIGURE 2: Derived screenplay example.

```
Now the CAMERA leaves the sign and MOVES EAST, the gray asphalt
of the street filling the screen. As speed accelerates to around
40 m.p.h., traffic demarcations, white arrows, speed-limit warnings,
man-hole covers, and so forth, flash by.
SUPERIMPOSED on all this are the CREDIT TITLES, in the stenciled style
of the street sign.
```

FIGURE 3: Original screenplay example.

and a soundtrack. When Paul is satisfied with his creation, he uploads his video to popular video sharing websites in order to make it visible to other people. Alice is a journalist, and she uses a computer everyday, both for work and for fun. She loves watching remixed video from YouTube, and she would like to create her own videos, but unfortunately, she does not know how to use a video editing application. She tried, but never succeeded. One day she finds a game called MovieRemix. The challenge is exciting: make a movie following a given screenplay, using an easy-to-use video editing application. The game provides her with a library of video shots, each one described with high-level features (like title and actors), low-level features (like number of colors and time length), screenplay details, and users' tags. She decides to play, and she gets an outline screenplay of what to do. MovieRemix gives her just a theme: "Bicycle in the traffic." She starts searching for video shots using several different keywords: *"bicycle," "traffic," "New York City,"* and *"critical mass."* After a while, she finds what she needs, combines them with transitions, music, title, and credits, and she uploads her final work to the MovieRemix video gallery. The day after, her remixed video results the most viewed video. One day she decides to play the "challenge" mode. The game server selects two players and gives them the same screenplay. Alice plays against Paul with the goal of making a video based on the theme "Plastic bottle." After a while, they both upload their creative works and wait for other players' responses.

Although simple, the above scenario is common in the current Web 2.0 scenario, where users want to play an active role. The contribution of this paper is to remove most of the technological burdens that may cut off a portion of our society. By coupling the architecture with a novel game that stimulates the production of creative videos, our proposal aims at creating an exciting environment where people can have fun playing with videos.

4.1. The Game. To stimulate users in the production of creative videos, we set up a game with three different complexity levels. As mentioned the game's goal is to create a remix from preexisting video shots. The production guidelines are given to each user in the form of screenplay (original, derived, or outline). The three levels are the following.

(i) *Director.* The player is provided with a derived screenplay. The player acts like a movie director and is required to follow the guidelines of the derived screenplay. Therefore, he/she has to select carefully different video shots stored in the MovieRemix catalog depending on the characteristics specified in the derived screenplay. Figure 2 shows an example of a derived screenplay.

(ii) *Apprentice Director.* The player is provided with an original screenplay. The player can introduce a subjective interpretation of the screenplay, and therefore he/she is more free to express his/her creativity. Figure 3 shows an example of an original screenplay.

(iii) *Bricoleur.* The player is provided with an outline screenplay (e.g., a simple theme or a movie title); therefore, he/she is free to create the remix as he/she does not have detailed guidelines to follow. Figure 4 shows an example of an outline screenplay.

After selecting the game level, a player may select the *challenge* option to play "against" another player. If so, the same subject is given to two different players (randomly selected by the game or specified by one player). During the remix process, MovieRemix allows applying transitions effects between video shots, soundtrack, title, and credits. When satisfied with the remix, a player can upload it to the MovieRemix gallery. If playing in the *challenge* mode, the two videos are compared one against the other and the winner will be the most voted by the MovieRemix community.

4.2. The Architecture. Figure 6 shows the architecture we designed to support MovieRemix. It is composed of a *Game Server*, a *Game Client*, a *Streaming Server*, and a *Movie and Screenplay database* where video shots and movie descriptions are stored.

The architecture is designed to keep all the complexity processes (e.g., video encoding, video retrieval, video

```
Genre: Drama/Film Noir
Shots on Sunset Boulevard. A voice over start to tell what's
happening.
Arrival of police motorbikes and cars, with reporters and
photographers into a villa in Sunset Boulevard.
They discover a body of a dead young man floating face downward.
```

FIGURE 4: Simple theme example.

```
<VideoSegment>
  ...
  <transition>
    <FreeTextAnnotation>
      Dissolve (clip1, clip2, 10)
    </FreeTextAnnotation>
  </transition>
  ...
</VideoSegment>
```

FIGURE 5: The usage of MPEG7-MDS to describe a transition between two consecutive shots.

description) at the server side. In this way, no technological skills are required to players, and members of the MovieRemix community are free to express their creativity.

Before entering into details of the architecture, it is worth recalling here that our proposal uses standard techniques to manage video editing and to produce *portable* Remix videos. Portability is an important characteristic as it ensures that the produced file can be used over several different devices. To achieve portability our proposal uses MPEG7-MDS for describing and organizing audiovisual data. Similarly, to encode video data, our proposal uses MPEG-4, a standard largely used in the Internet scenario to manage audio and video data.

In the following, we present details of the MovieRemix architecture.

4.2.1. Movie and Screenplay Database. Video material and screenplays are stored in a database accessible both to the Game Server and to the Streaming Server. Each video (e.g., video shots, short videos, and remix video) is coupled with textual information to better define the video contents. In particular, each video is provided with an MPEG7-MDS description of its high- and low-level features:

(i) *High-level features.* Title, director, cast, and screenplay are entered by who releases the video and makes it available to the Movie and Screenplay database.

(ii) *Low-level features.* Number of colors, resolution, duration, and number of frames per second are automatically extracted from each video shot when it is released to the Movie and Screenplay database.

(iii) *Tags.* Keywords that describe video content may be entered by both who releases the video to the database and by players who watch the video. Note that tags may be very useful in describing multimedia contents as high- and low-level features may not completely describe the video content and a taxonomy-based approach could be too rigid for video browsing.

(iv) *Thumbnails.* A set of keyframes that represent a sort of static summary. In this way, when browsing the video catalog, a player can understand the video content by simply hovering the mouse on the video shot, instead of watching it entirely.

Figure 7 depicts the information associated with every video shot stored inside the MovieRemix catalog. Note that textual information is described through MPEG7-MDS as shown in Figure 1.

4.2.2. Streaming Server. A streaming server, or a farm of streaming servers, is in charge of retrieving and streaming a requested video to the client. We recall here that the proposed architecture does not allow clients to download video. From the client point of view, when a video (or a video shot) is played in streaming, it is indistinguishable from an ordinary media file stored in the local computer device. By using this approach, all the video operations are done at the server side, whereas everything stored and managed at the client side is text based. This choice is twofold: it avoids unauthorized storage (and possible unauthorized redistribution) of video material, and it does not require clients' devices to have huge storage space to keep video material at the client side. As previously mentioned, all the video material MPEG-4 encoded.

4.2.3. Game Client. The game client interacts with game and streaming servers and creates an environment where the production of remixed video is easy and fun to play. In addition, the game client has to provide the following facilities.

(i) *Authenticate.* At startup every player needs to login to the game server; after that the MovieRemix game can begin with the downloading of a screenplay (derived, original, or outline).

(ii) *Search and Browse.* Every player should be able to look for specific video shots by entering textual keywords. The game server should reply with a list of video shots that the player should browse in an easy way.

(iii) *Retrieve.* Once an interesting video shot is identified, it should be easily added to the personal bin of video shots for a possible usage in the remixed video. Note that video shots should be virtually added to the personal bin, as they physically remain at the database side.

(iv) *Edit.* Different video operations should be available: extraction of a part of a long video by specifying an

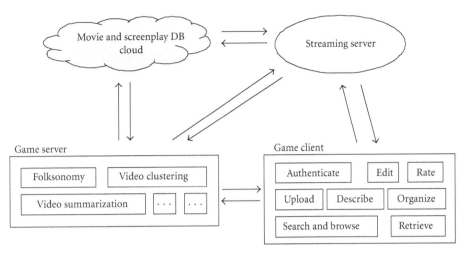

FIGURE 6: MovieRemix architecture.

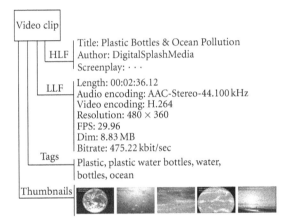

FIGURE 7: Example of information associated to each video shot stored in the MovieRemix catalog: high- and low-level features are coupled with a set of tags and a set of thumbnails to better describe the content of the video shot.

initial and an ending point; availability of tools to facilitate the creation of titles, credits, and subtitles; availability of several possible transitions to be used when a video shot ends and another one begins; availability of a tool to add soundtrack.

(v) *Describe.* The player should be able to define and add his/her own tags for every video when playing it.

(vi) *Organize.* The player should be provided with a storyboard, simple and easy to organize.

(vii) *Rate.* The player should be able to rate a video remix and to view a video remix chart.

(viii) *Upload.* The player should have the capability of uploading his/her remix to the MovieRemix gallery in order to make it visible to other MovieRemix players (Figure 5).

Note that all complex and time-consuming operations (e.g., encoding and visual effects) are done at the server side. The client simply needs to describe the operations that

the server has to perform. For instance, let us suppose that a player applies a dissolve transition effect of 10 frames between clip 1 and clip 2. The client will simply write into the remix file an instruction like Dissolve (clip1, clip2, 10), and the streaming server will do all the necessary work.

4.2.4. Game Server. The game server is the core of the MovieRemix architecture: it interacts with the game client and gives instructions to the streaming server of how and where to find specific videos. In particular, the game server is in charge of the following tasks.

(i) *Authenticate.* When a player performs the login process, the game server has to check whether the player is registered to play the game. If ok, the game server sends the client the screenplay (derived, original, or outline).

(ii) *Summarize.* Every video stored in the MovieRemix catalog needs to be summarized. This allows players to save time when browsing the video catalog. In essence, by watching a video summary (either static or dynamic) players may avoid wasting time watching entire (and eventually) useless videos.

(iii) *Extract.* Every video stored in the MovieRemix catalog needs to be described through low-level features. This allows a better description of the video material and facilitates the retrieval process.

(iv) *Group.* When players ask for video shots, the game server may present "similar" video. This can be done by grouping together similar videos. If grouped according to low-level features, clustering algorithms are usually employed. If grouped according to players' tag, algorithms based on folksonomy are usually employed.

(vi) *Retrieve.* When players look for videos, they enter textual keywords: the goal of the game server is to retrieve the most relevant videos according to the specified keywords. Keywords can be screenplay words, high- or low-level features, or tags.

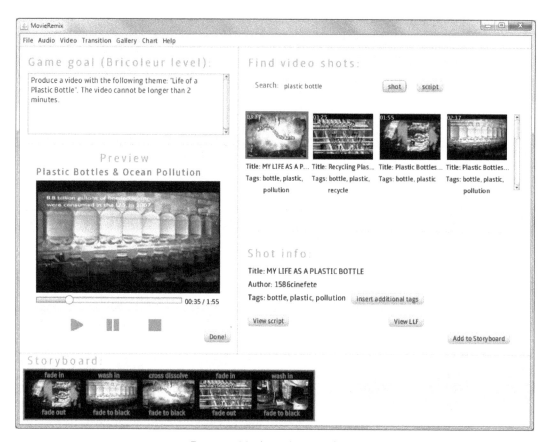

FIGURE 8: MovieRemix game client.

(vii) *Communicate.* The game server interacts with the streaming server to facilitate the stream of the requested video towards the game client.

(viii) *Update.* Players can introduce additional tags to every video shot. Therefore, the game server needs to update the information associated with every video shot.

5. Prototype Implementation

In this section we present a prototype implementation of MovieRemix.

5.1. Streaming Server. The goal of a streaming server is to stream a video toward the game client. Several applications (either proprietary or public) are available to this aim. In our prototype we use AviSynth (http://www.avisynth.org/) for three main reasons: (i) it is released under GNU GPL license, (ii) it has a powerful and scalable scripting language that can be used to provide transition and video effects, and (iii) it is simple to use as it takes a text file (written with AviSynth scripting language) in input and creates a video file that can be read through any media player.

5.2. Game Client. The Game Client is developed in JavaFX (http://javafx.com/), a platform for creating cross-platform media applications that can easily provide media playback in

the desktop window, within a web page, or on the mobile device. Based on an object-oriented scripting language, JavaFX is extremely practical with the development of graphical applications.

MovieRemix game client allows users to select, describe, and remix material from the MovieRemix Video Catalog.

Figure 8 shows the interface. The top menu allows players to select a specific medium of the remixed video (Audio, Video, Transitions) and to operate on it (e.g., the submenu Video contains the *extract* feature that allows extracting a video shot from a long video), to browse the MovieRemix Galleries (one for each game level), and to explore the MovieRemix charts (one for each game level).

On the left side, the *Game goal* box contains the screenplay (original, derived, or outline), whereas the *preview* box provides all the standard video player controls a player might need.

The right side presents two boxes: *Find video shots* and *Shot info.* The former allows players to search video shots by entering textual keywords. When a player hovers the mouse pointer over a remix, a set of thumbnails appear one after the other. By selecting a shot among the ones returned by the game server, players can access detailed information about the video shot. This additional information is presented in the *Shot info* box and includes high- and low-level features and tags.

The storyboard is located at the bottom side: here players can organize video shots and can add video shot

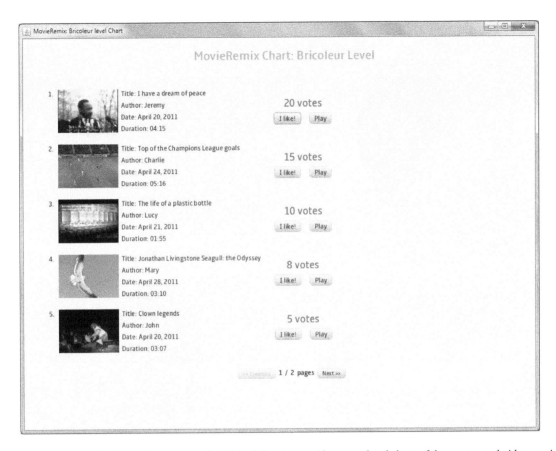

FIGURE 9: MovieRemix Chart: for any game level MovieRemix provides an updated chart of the most voted video remix.

transitions (choosing them from the submenu *Transition*), can introduce title and credits (through an option of the submenu *Video*), and can add soundtrack to the remixed video (through the submenu *Audio*). Note that to preclude any possible conflict between soundtrack and shot audio, the audio of each video shot can be silenced.

Figure 9 shows a MovieRemix chart (in particular, the one of the Bricoleur level). Members of MovieRemix can play and vote the preferred video remix. Once again, to save players' time, when a player hovers the mouse pointer over a remix, a set of thumbnails representing the video summary appear one after the other.

5.3. Game Server. As previously mentioned, the game server is the core of the MovieRemix architecture and is in charge of several tasks. In the current version of the prototype, the game server uses a simple algorithm to extract thumbnails from a video shot. These thumbnails are taken at video cuts (i.e., when two consecutive video frames are very different) identified using a combination of luminance and chrominance values. Also low-level features are taken using a simple algorithm that retrieves such information from the header file. With respect to the grouping algorithm, in the current version of the prototype, grouping is available only according to players' tag, that is, an algorithm based on folksonomy is employed; the grouping according to low-level features is not currently implemented.

6. Experimental Evaluation

To assess our proposal we set up an experimental scenario where a group of people were asked to play with MovieRemix. We used a mean opinion score (MOS) technique, which is widely employed in testing products or services. Roughly, it works as follows: evaluators need to rate several questions with a scale expressed from 1 to 5. This type of test can be considered effective as long as the obtained results do not present a large statistical difference. Our experimental scenario consisted of 16 people with different backgrounds (computer science and social sciences) and different work experiences (academic and private employees).

We asked them to answer several questions with respect to the MovieRemix experience. It is to note that the obtained MOS results did not present a large statistical difference.

Figure 10 presents the different game levels selected by players. Most of the players chose the *Bricoleur* mode, whereas few of them played in the *Director* mode. To better understand the reason for this behavior, we asked them the motivations that led to such choice. Figure 11 highlights that two were the main reasons: one is the difficulties of playing with the other levels, whereas the other is the easiness of translating the proposed screenplay into video. Figure 12 shows that personal creativity is another important reason for the game level selection. As showed, most of the players

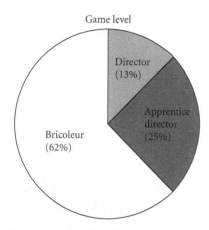

Game level

FIGURE 10: Percentage of preferred game level selected by players.

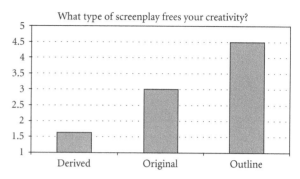
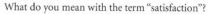

FIGURE 12: Type of screenplay that frees players' creativity.

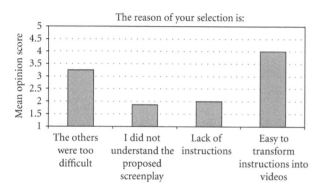
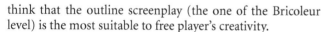

FIGURE 11: Reasons that brought players to choose a specific game level.

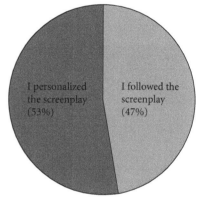

FIGURE 13: Players' reason of being satisfied with the produced remix video.

think that the outline screenplay (the one of the Bricoleur level) is the most suitable to free player's creativity.

Figure 13 presents results obtained from asking players when they are satisfied with their work, meaning when they consider their remixed video done. Most of them like to personalize the given screenplay. Although this may be surprising, it is not. Indeed, many movie directors like to change the given screenplay according to their inspiration.

At the end of the game, we asked players what the main difficulties they encountered were. Figure 14 shows that players had no problem in understanding the given screenplay and also highlights that there are two main burdens in making a remix video: one is related to the technological aspect (either editing the different media streams or browsing the video catalog), whereas the other is more semantic as it is related to the translation of the given screenplay into video.

Figure 15 presents results obtained from asking players the genre of video that is more suitable to produce with MovieRemix. Players are happy with all types of videos, with a slight preference for music and news videos.

Figure 16 presents results obtained from asking players how they would improve the video retrieval. Sample videos (i.e., related videos suggested by the systems) seem to be very

important for players when looking for video clips to use in the video remix. Tagclouds and moving videosummaries are considered equally important.

Figure 17 presents results obtained from asking players what type of game is MovieRemix. Players considered MovieRemix both an educational and a serious game, which confirms the goal of our proposal.

7. Conclusions and Future Directions

MovieRemix is both a novel educational game and an architecture that supports the production of video remix. It allows players to deal with real screenplays and to use them as a movie director. Through a developed prototype we evaluated the proposed approach and results showed that players like to use MovieRemix to produce different types of video (e.g., movies, documentaries, news, music, commercials, and recaps). An interesting result was that players had almost no difficulties in understanding screenplays. On the contrary, the main burdens were related to the technological (e.g., browsing the video catalog) and to the semantic (e.g., translating the given screenplay into videos) aspects. Players also pointed out possible improvement of MovieRemix by suggesting a more deep usage of sample videos (e.g., videos

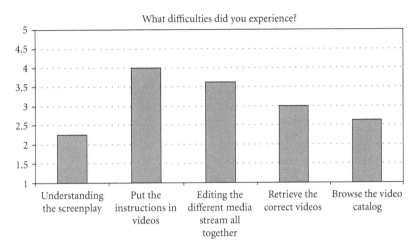

FIGURE 14: Difficulties encountered during the MovieRemix experience.

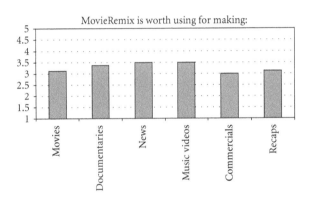

FIGURE 15: Type of videos worth using with MovieRemix according to players' responses.

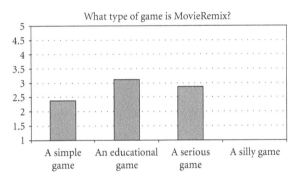

FIGURE 17: Players' definition of the MovieRemix game.

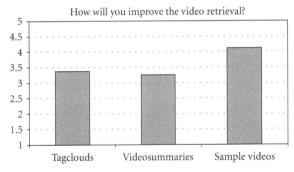

FIGURE 16: Players' suggestions to improve the video retrieval process.

related to the given screenplay and suggested by the system), of tagclouds, and of moving videosummaries.

Acknowledgments

The authors wish to thank all the people who helped doing the subjective evaluation. The work of M. Federico has been partially supported by Disabled Students Services under the project. Design and Analysis of Mechanisms to Improve Multimedia Contents Accessibility within the Learning Scenario.

References

[1] "Alexa top sites," http://www.alexa.com/topsites.

[2] G. Kim, "Video dominates global traffic," *Business Video*, January 2011.

[3] IDATE, "World video game market," *IDATE Consulting and Research*, September 2010.

[4] D. Cardillo, A. Rapp, S. Benini et al., "The art of video MashUp: supporting creative users with an innovative and smart application," *Multimedia Tools and Applications*, vol. 53, no. 1, pp. 1–23, 2011.

[5] N. Dusi and L. Spaziante, *Remix-Remake. Pratiche di Replicabilità*, Meltemi, 2006.

[6] C. Levi-Strauss, *The Savage Mind*, University Of Chicago Press, 1968.

[7] N. Diakopoulos, K. Luther, Y. Medynskiy, and I. Essa, "The evolution of authorship in a remix society," in *Proceedings of the 18th ACM Conference on Hypertext and Hypermedia, (HT '07)*, pp. 133–136, New York, NY, USA, 2007.

[8] L. V. Kuleshov, *Kuleshov on Film: Writings*, University of California Press, 1975.

[9] L. Lessing, *Free Culture: How Big Media Uses Technology and the Law to Lock Down Culture and Control Creativity*, Penguin Press HC, 2004.

[10] J. Multisilta and M. Mäenpää, "Mobile video stories," in *Proceedings of the 3rd International Conference on Digital Interactive Media in Entertainment and Arts, (DIMEA '08)*, pp. 401–406, New York, NY, USA, 2008.

[11] R. Pea, M. Mills, J. Rosen, K. Dauber, W. Effelsberg, and E. Hoffert, "The diver project: interactive digital video repurposing," *IEEE Multimedia*, vol. 11, no. 1, pp. 54–61, 2004.

[12] J. Scheible, V. H. Tuulos, and T. Ojala, "Story mashup: design and evaluation of novel interactive storytelling game for mobile and web users," in *Proceedings of the 6th International Conference on Mobile and Ubiquitous Multimedia, (MUM '07)*, vol. 284, pp. 139–148, New York, NY, USA, 2007.

[13] J. Multisilta and M. Suominen, "MoViE: mobile video experience," in *Proceedings of the 13th International Academic MindTrek Conference: Everyday Life in the Ubiquitous Era, (MindTrek '09)*, pp. 157–161, New York, NY, USA, 2009.

[14] V. H. Tuulos, J. Scheible, and H. Nyholm, "Combining web, mobile phones and public displays in large-scale: Manhattan story mashup," in *Proceedings of the 5th International Conference on Pervasive Computing, (PERVASIVE '07)*, vol. 4480 LNCS, pp. 37–54, Springer, Berlin, Germany, 2007.

[15] R. Shaw and P. Schmitz, "Community annotation and remix: a research platform and pilot deployment," in *Proceedings of the 1st ACM International Workshop on Human-Centered Multimedia, (HCM '06)*, pp. 89–98, New York, NY, USA, 2006.

[16] P. Cesar, D. C. A. Bulterman, D. Geerts, J. Jansen, H. Knoche, and W. Seager, "Enhancing social sharing of videos: fragment, annotate, enrich, and share," in *Proceedings of the 16th ACM International Conference on Multimedia, (MM '08)*, pp. 11–20, ACM, New York, NY, USA, 2008.

[17] L. Lessing, *Remix: Making Art and Commerce Thrive in the Hybrid Economy*, Penguin Press HC, 2008.

[18] L. Manovich, "Software takes command," 2008, http://lab.softwarestudies.com/2008/11/softbook.html.

[19] J. L. Kincheloe, "Describing the bricolage: conceptualizing a new rigor," *Qualitative Inquiry*, vol. 7, no. 6, pp. 679–692, 2001.

[20] N. Dusi, "The internal variant. modularity and repetition in audiovisual epitexts," *Cinema Scope Magazine*, 2005.

[21] C. Tryon, *Reinventing Cinema. Movies in the Age of Media Convergence*, Rutgers University Press, 2009.

[22] J. Hunter, "An overview of the MPEG-7 description definition language (DDL)," *IEEE Transactions on Circuits and Systems for Video Technology*, vol. 11, no. 6, pp. 765–772, 2001.

[23] MPEG4, "Overview of the MPEG-4 standard," Research Report, MPEG Group, 2002, http://mpeg.chiariglione.org/standards/mpeg-4/mpeg-4.htm.

11

Using Game Development to Teach Software Architecture

Alf Inge Wang and Bian Wu

Norwegian University of Science and Technology, Sem Sælandsv. 7–9, 7491 Trondheim, Norway

Correspondence should be addressed to Alf Inge Wang, alfw@idi.ntnu.no

Academic Editor: Jihad El-Sana

This paper describes a case study of how a game project using the XNA Game Studio from Microsoft was implemented in a software architecture course. In this project, university students have to construct and design a type of software architecture, evaluate the architecture, implement an application based on the architecture, and test this implementation. In previous years, the domain of the software architecture project has been a robot controller for navigating a maze. *Robot controller* was chosen as the domain for the project, as there exist several papers and descriptions on reference architectures for managing mobile robots. This paper describes the changes we had to make to introduce an XNA game development project to the software architecture course, and our experiences from running a software architecture project focusing on game development and XNA. The experiences described in this paper are based on feedback from the course staff, the project reports of the students, and a mandatory course evaluation. The evaluation shows among other things that the majority of the students preferred the game project to the robot project, that XNA was considered to be suitable platform for a software architecture project, that the students found it useful to learn XNA and C#, and that some students were carried away when developing the game in the software architecture project.

1. Introduction

Games have been used in education for many years mainly focusing on teaching children in an interesting and motivating way. Research shows that integrating games within children's classroom can be beneficial for academic achievement, motivation, and classroom dynamics [1]. Teaching methods based on educational games are not only attractive to schoolchildren, but can also be beneficial for university students [2]. Research on game concepts and game development used in higher education is not unique, for example [3–5], but we believe there is an untapped potential that needs to be explored. By introducing games in higher education lecturers can access teaching aids that promote active students, provide alternative teaching methods to improve variation, enable social learning through multiplayer learning games, and motivate students to work harder on projects and exercises.

Games can mainly be integrated in higher education in three ways. *First,* traditional exercises can be replaced by games motivating the students to put extra effort in doing the exercises, and giving the course staff an opportunity to monitor how the students work with the exercises in realtime [6, 7]. *Second,* games can be used within a traditional classroom lecture to improve the participation and motivation of the students through knowledge-based multiplayer games played by the students and the teacher [8, 9]. *Third,* game development projects can be used in computer science (CS) or software engineering (SE) courses to learn specific CS or SE skills [10, 11]. This paper focuses on the latter, where a game development project was introduced in a course to teach CS and/or SE skills. The motivation for bringing game development into a CS or SE course is to utilize the students' fascination for games and game development to stimulate the students to put extra effort in the course project. Many students dream of making their own games, and game development projects allow the students to use their creativity in contrast to, for example developing a more traditional web-based application. Game technologies and game user interfaces are now being more commonly used in serious applications [12–14], and the market for serious games is growing. This makes it important for students to learn how to develop games even the students do not target to work in the game industry.

In this paper, we describe a case study of how a game project was integrated with a software architecture course. From the perspective of a game developer, knowledge and skills about how to develop appropriate software architectures are becoming increasingly important. As games are growing bigger and becoming more complex, well-designed software architectures are needed to cope with variations in hardware configurations, functional modifications, and network real-time constraints [15]. From the perspective of a software architect, games are interesting due to the inherent characteristics of the domain including real-time constraints, changing and varying functionality, and user-friendliness. In addition, games are interesting from the perspective of a software architect, as there exist no real functional requirements that stem from the users. Typical user requirements for games are that the game should be fun to play, it should have enough variety, and it should be engaging.

The case study presented in this paper describes how a software architecture course was adapted to include a game development project. The paper describes the parts of the course and syllabus that had to be changed to make game development a natural part of the course, and how XNA was used as a game development platform in the course. Further, we present an evaluation of how the game development project was perceived by the students and the course staff compared to the robot project. The data of this evaluation is based on the students' responses to the final course evaluation, the feedback from the students during the project, and the student project reports.

The rest of the paper is organized as follows. Section 2 describes related work. Section 3 describes the software architecture course. Section 4 describes how the course was changed to adapt to the game project. Section 5 presents experiences we learned from running a game development project along with the robot development project in a software architecture course, and Section 6 concludes the paper.

2. Related Work

This paper describes experiences from introducing an XNA game development project in a software architecture course. The main benefits from using XNA to teach software architecture is that the students get more motivated during the software development project. As far as we know, there are only few papers (presented here) that describe usage of XNA to teach CS or SE, and only few papers that contain case studies of games used in CS and SE education (also described here). In this section, we will also briefly describe alternative game development frameworks to XNA that can be used in CS and SE education.

Youngblood describes how XNA game segments can be used to engage students in advanced CS education [16]. Game segments are developed solution packs providing the full code for a segment of a game with a clear element left for a student to implement. The paper describes how XNA was used in an artificial intelligence course where the students were asked to implement a chat bot, motion planning,

adversarial search, neural networks, and flocking. Finally, the paper describes seven design principles for using game segments in CS education based on lessons learned. The approach described by Youngblood could also be used in a software architecture course, where the students can put together parts of the game (game segments) based on their designed architecture. However, this approach is very limiting as the architectural freedom will be very restricted and the students will not get the chance to design their own software architecture of their own game.

El-Nasr and Smith describe how modifying or modding existing games can be used to learn CS, mathematics, physics, and ascetic principles [10]. The paper describes how modding of the WarCraft III engine was used to teach high school students a class on game design and programming. Further, they describe experiences from teaching university students a more advanced class on game design and programming using the Unreal Tournament 2003 engine. Finally, they present observations from student projects that involve modding of game engines. Although the paper claims to teach students other things than pure game design and programming, the focus is on game development in contrast to CS or SE. Modding existing games is not very useful in a software architecture course, as the focus of the course is the structure of software components and not game content nor game engine scripts.

Sweedyk and Keller describe how they have introduced game development in an introductory SE course [17]. The students learn principles, practices, and patterns in software development and design through three projects. In the *first* project, the students develop a campus life 2D arcade game over four weeks with the educational focus on gaining familiarity with UML tools, learn and use a variety of development tools and gain understanding of game architecture and the game loop. In the *second* project, the students should build a one-hole miniature golf game over five weeks with the educational focus on learning and practicing evolutionary design, prototyping and refactoring, usage of UML design tools, usage of work management tools, and design and implementation of a test plan. In the *third* and final project, the students can develop a game of their own choice over five weeks with educational focus on reinforcing the practices and principles learned in two previous projects, learn to apply design patterns, and practice management of complex software projects. The students' response to this SE course has according to the authors been extremely positive. They argue that game projects allow them to better achieve the learning objectives in the SE course. Their main concern is related to gender, as women are less motivated to learn SE through game development projects. The main difference with Sweedyk and Keller's approach and ours is that they have introduced three projects instead of one, and the SE focus is different. For our purpose, more than one project would take away the focus on the software architectural educational goals and miss the opportunity to follow the evolution of the software architecture through a complete development cycle.

K. Calypool and M. Calypool describe another SE course where a game development project was used to engage the students and make the course more fun [18]. In this course, the students worked with one game project where the students had to go through all the phases in a software development process. The preliminary results of comparing the game-based SE course with a traditional SE course showed that the game version had higher enrollment, resulted in average higher grades, a higher distribution of A grades, and had a lower number of dropouts. The feedback from the students was also very positive. The approach described in this paper is very similar to our approach. The main difference is that in our course the students carry out the various phases in a software process from a software architecture perspective focusing on quality attributes, software architecture design, and software architecture evaluation.

Volk describes how a game engineering course was integrated into a CS curriculum [19] motivated by the fact that game development projects are getting more and more complex and have to deal with complex CS and SE issues. The experiences from running this course showed that it was a good idea handle the game engineering course more in a form of a real project, that the students were very engaged in the course and the project, that the lack of multidisciplinary teams did not hinder the projects, that the transition from preproduction to production was difficult (extracting the requirements), and that some student teams were overambitious for what they wanted to achieve in their project. In our software architecture course, we experienced some of the same issues as described in this paper, namely difficult extraction of requirements and overambitious teams.

Linhoff and Settle describe a game development course where the XNA platform was used to allow the students gain experience in all aspects of console game creation [20]. The course focuses on creating of fonts, icons, 3D models, camera and object animation paths, skeletal animations, sounds, scripts, and other supporting content to the XBOX 360 game platform. In addition, the students are required to edit the source code of a game to change variables, and copy-and-paste code. The student response to the course was positive. The results also showed that students with programming background did better in the class. The students did not learn any CS or SE skills.

Zhu et al. describe how games can be introduced in SE courses to teach typical SE skills [21]. The paper describes how the two games SimSE and MO-SEProcess were used to give students an opportunity to practice SE through simulations to learn the complex cause and effect relationships underlying the process of SE. MO-SEProcess is a multiplayer online SE process game based on the SimSE in 3D implemented in Second Life. In this game, the players should collaborate with other developers to develop a system by giving out tasks and following up tasks. Although the models and simulations in SimSE are much more extensive than the ones in MO-SEProcess, the usage of Second Life bring some advantages such as better support for group sharing and collaboration, and the possibility to create interactive learning experiences that would be hard to duplicate in real life. This approach is very different from ours and does not fit with our educational goals.

Rankin et al. describe a study on how game design project impact on students' interest in CS [22]. In a Computer Science Survey course, the students are given the task to apply SE principles in the context of game design. The pre and post survey results reveals that game design project can have both a positive and a negative impact on students' attitudes about enrollment in a game design course, pursuit of a CS degree, further development of programming skills and enrollment in additional CS courses.

Leutenegger and Edgington argue that the course assignment and example content is more important than whether a introductory programming course should focus on procedural versus object-oriented approach [23]. Their paper describes an introductory programming course focusing on game programming. The results showed that the students improved their understanding basic programming concepts, and the students were satisfied with the course.

Coller and Scott describe an interesting approach for teaching mechanical engineering through game programming [24]. In a numerical methods course, the students are asked to program the behavior of a car in the Torcs open racing car simulator. The students must use numerical methods to program acceleration, steering, gearshifts, and breaking. A comparison with a traditional version of the course showed that for the game-based course the students on average spent roughly twice as much time on the course, and that the students achieved deeper learning as the students were more interested, more engaged, and invested more in learning the material.

We have found the XNA was a perfect fit for our game project as it provides a high-level API, the framework is mature and well supported, and the students are motivated by the fact that XNA makes it easy to develop for XBOX 360. There are also other alternative game frameworks that can be used. The *Labyrinth* [25] is implemented in Java and is a flexible and easy-to-use computer game framework. The framework enables instructors to expose students to very specific aspects of CS courses. The framework is a finished game in the Pac-Man genre, highly modular, and it lets the students change different aspects of the game. The *JIG (Java Instructional Gaming)* project [26] has the aims to build a Java Instructional Game Engine suitable for a wide variety of students at all levels in the curriculum, to create a set of educational resources to support the use of the game engine at small, resource-limited, schools, and to develop a community of educators that use and help improve these resources. The *DXFramework* [27] is a game engine written in C++ targeted specifically for 2D games to be used in game programming education. The *SAGE* [28] game engine is also written in C++ and is targeted for game programming educational use focusing on 3D games. *GEDI* [29] game engine is another alternative for 2D games in C++ designed with game programming educational use in mind. For business teaching, *Arena3D* [30] is a game visualization environment with animated 3D representations of the work environments, simulation of patients queuing at the front desk, and interacts with the staff. IBM has also produced a business game called *INNOV8* [31], which is "an interactive, 3D business simulator designed to teach the fundamentals of business process management and bridge the gap in understanding between business leaders and IT teams in an organization".

Of the related work described in this section, the work by Kajal and Calypool is closest to the work described in this paper. The main difference with our approach is that we focus on software architecture methods and processes and not only software engineering topics in general. The students' responses to our course are very similar to the studies described in this section, characterized by higher motivation, higher enrollment, and more effort spent on the course.

3. Software Architecture Course

The software architecture course is a postgraduate course offered to CS and SE students (not mandatory) at the Norwegian University of Science and Technology (NTNU). The course is taught every spring, its workload is 25% of one semester, and about 70–80 students attend the course every spring. The students in the course are mostly of Norwegian students (about 80%), but there are also 20% foreign students mostly from EU countries. There are about 10% female students. The textbook used in this course is the "Software Architecture in Practice, Second Edition," by Clements et al. [32]. Additional papers are used to cover topics that are not sufficiently covered by the book such as design patterns, software architecture documentation standards, view models, and postmortem analysis [33–37].

The education goal of the course is: "the students should be able to define and explain central concepts in software architecture literature, and be able to use and describe design/ architectural patterns, methods to design software architectures, methods/techniques to achieve software qualities, methods to document software architecture and methods to evaluate software architecture."

The course is taught in three main ways:

(1) ordinary lectures given in English,

(2) invited guest-lectures from the software industry,

(3) a software development project with emphasis on software architecture.

The software architecture course at NTNU (course code TDT4240) is taught in a different way than at most other universities, as the students also have to implement their designed architecture in a project. The motivation for doing so is to make the students understand the relationship between the architecture and the implementation, and to be able to perform a real evaluation of whether the architecture and the resulting implementation fulfill the quality requirements specified for the application. The architecture project in the course has similarities with projects in software engineering courses, but everything in the project is carried out from a software architecture perspective. Throughout the project, the students have to use software architecture techniques, methods, and tools to succeed according to the specified project requirements and the document templates. The development process in the project will also be affected by

the focus on software architecture, as the development view of the architecture will specify how the teams should be organized and how they should work. The main disadvantage of this approach is that the students get less time dedicated to do the architectural design, as they have to spend time on the implementation. The main advantage is that the students are learning software architecture through doing a whole project where they can see the results of their architectural design as a product.

The TDT4240 software architecture course has been rated as one of the most useful and practical courses offered at the Deptartment of Computer and Information Science in surveys conducted among exstudents now working in the IT industry. The course staff has also seen the benefits of making the students implement the architecture, as the students have to be aware of the developing costs of fancy and complicated architectural designs.

30% of the grade awarded to the software architecture course relate to the evaluation of the software architecture project all students have to do, while 70% is awarded for the results of a written examination. The goal of the project is for the students to apply the methods and theory in the course to design and fully document a software architecture, to evaluate the architecture and the architectural approaches (tactics), to implement an application according to the architecture, to test the implementation related to the functional and quality requirements, and to evaluate how the architectural choices affected the quality of the application. The main emphasis when grading the projects is on the quality of the software architecture itself, but the implementation should also reflect the architecture and the architectural choices.

The project consists of the following phases.

(1) *Commercial Off-the-Shelf (COTS)*. Learn the development platform/framework to be used in the project by developing some simple test applications.

(2) *Design Pattern*. Learn how to utilize design patterns by making changes in two architectural variants of an existing system designed with and without design patterns.

(3) *Requirements and Architecture*. Describe the functional and the quality requirements, describe the architectural drivers, and design and document the software architecture of the application in the project including several view points and views, stakeholders, stakeholder concerns, architectural rationale, and so forth.

(4) *Architecture Evaluation*. Use the Architecture Trade-off Analysis Method (ATAM) [32, 38, 39] to evaluate the software architecture in regards to the quality requirements.

(5) *Implementation*. Do detailed design and implement the application based on the designed architecture and based on the results from the evaluation. Test the application against both functional and quality requirements specified in phase 3, evaluate how well the architecture helped to meet the requirements,

and evaluate the relationship between the software architecture and the implementation.

(6) *Project Evaluation.* Evaluate the project using a Post-Mortem Analysis (PMA) method [34]. In this phase, the students will elicit and analyze the successes and problems during the project.

In the two first phases of the project, the students work on their own or in pairs. For the phases 3–6, the students work in self-composed teams of four students. The students spend most time in the implementation phase (6 weeks), and they are also encouraged start the implementation in earlier phases to test their architectural choices (incremental development). During the implementation phase, the students continually extend, refine, and evolve the software architecture through several increments.

In previous years, the goal of the project has been to develop a robot controller for a robot simulator in Java with emphasis on an assigned quality attribute such as availability, performance, modifiability, or testability. The functional aim of this project was to develop a robot controller that moves a robot in a maze collecting balls and bringing them to a light source. Robot controller was chosen as a case for the software architecture project, as the problem of software architecture is well defined within this domain. For the robot controller domain there exist several examples of software architecture patterns or reference architectures that can be applied, such as Control loop [40], Elfes [41], Task Control [42], CODGER [43], Subsumption [44], and NASREM [45].

4. How the Course Was Changed?

This section presents the changes we made to the course to integrate an XNA game development project with the software architecture course.

4.1. Course Preparations. Half a year ago we integrated the game development project with the software architecture course, we initiated a master research project, named XQUEST, to explore how XNA could be used and integrated with the course. The goal of this project was to answer the following questions.

(Q1) How well is the XNA framework suited for teaching students software architecture?

(Q2) What resources must be in place to quickly get up to speed developing games using the XNA framework?

(Q3) How should XNA be introduced to the students?

The first question (Q1) was decomposed into three sub-questions. *First*, the XQUEST project investigated which software/game components were required to allow the students to stay focused on the software architecture during the their project. This work resulted in an implementation of a game library named XQUEST framework [46] to provide a high-level sprite animation framework, a game object management framework, and some additional helper classes (audio, input, text out, and texture store) on top of XNA to ease

the development. *Second*, the XQUEST project investigated how difficult it was for the students that only knew Java to learn the C# programming language. They found that it took about three days to learn the most essential features of C# for a postgraduate student with average Java skills. *Third*, the XQUEST project investigated what limitations or restrictions that should be put on a game development project in a software architecture course. The conclusion was to limit the projects to 2D games, and only to focus on the two quality attributes modifiability and testability. 2D games were preferred to 3D games, as the students should not spend too much time on 3D graphics and focus on the structure of the software. We also considered the quality attributes performance and usability for the project. *Performance* was dropped because the XNA framework handles most of the performance issues and it is hard to make architectural design that actually will affect this quality attribute. Further, *usability* was dropped because this quality attribute is rather hard to measure without extensive usability tests (not within the scope of the software architecture course).

The necessary resources to quickly develop games in XNA (Q2) was found to be C# and XNA tutorials, XNA examples, XNA documentation, libraries of graphical art (sprites, tiles, etc.), a high-level API on top of XNA, and making course staff available that could answer specific XNA or C# questions. Although XNA provides a high-level API, the XQUEST framework was found necessary to provide an even higher API to help the students get going faster.

The conclusion of final question (Q3) was that XNA should be exposed to the students through a mixture of lectures, an XNA resource webpage and continues technical support through the semester. It was found to be very important to give an introductory lecture in XNA to learn the tools, environments, and the core concepts of XNA, and give an overview of the differences between Java and C#.

4.2. Changes to the Syllabus. It was rather difficult to change the syllabus of the software architecture course to include more the literature about software architecture in games. Good books and papers that give an in-depth insight into game architectures and game architecture patterns are to our knowledge non-existent. There are several papers that describe architectures of specific games such as [47, 48] or books that give a brief overview of game architecture [49, 50], but none that looks at the typical abstractions (architectural patterns) you can observe in game software development. The syllabus ended up with including some chapter from the book "Game Architecture and Design" [50] to describe the initial steps of creating a game architecture, and two self-composed sets of slides on (1) *software architecture and games* and (2) *architectural patterns and games*. The *former* was a one hour lecture on motivation software architecture design in games [15], architectural drivers within game development [51], challenges related to software architecture in games [52], and the main components of game architectures [53]. The *latter* was a one-hour lecture describing architectural patterns that are common and useful for games, such as model-view controller, pipe-and-filter, layered architecture, and hierarchical task trees.

4.3. Changes of the Project. The course staff decided to let the student teams themselves choose between the robot and the game project. This meant that the main structure of the project had to remain the same, and that we had to make two variants of the project. For the robot project the students had fixed requirements, while for the game project the students should define their own requirements (design their own game). However, the documents to be delivered were the same for both types of projects based on the same templates, and the development process was also to be the same.

To evaluate and grade the software architecture project, we posted some project evaluation criteria in the beginning of the semester that stated *how* the project should be documented, *what* should be *documented*, *what* should be *delivered* (such as documents, source code, complied code, etc.), *completeness* of robot controller or game, and an implementation that *reflects* the architecture. The main difference between the game and the robot versions of the evaluation criteria was how the implementation was to be evaluated. For the XNA projects, we required the game to have a certain level of complexity (at least five classes organized in a structure), the game should be easy to install and run. For a top grade (A), the game should be impressive in some way (fun, nice, creative, or original). For the robot controller, the implementation should similarly have a certain level of complexity, but it had to adhere to the given functional requirements. For a top grade (A), the robot should be able to solve the task efficiently.

Another thing we had to change was the quality attributes the various teams should focus on during the project. The teams that chose the robot projects were assigned to focus on safety of the robot (not get stuck in the maze), modifiability (easiness of changing the robot controller software), and testability (easiness of testing the robot software). For the game projects, we ended up with modifiability (easiness of changing the game software) and testability (easiness of testing the game software).

The main change of the project assignments was to add XNA game variant of the COTS introexercise (phase 1, see Section 2). The COTS intro exercise for the robot controller asked the students to do simple navigation and make to robot pick up balls. In the XNA game variant of this exercise, the students were asked to perform the following four tasks.

(1) Draw a helicopter sprite on the screen and make it move around on its own (computer controlled).

(2) Move around the helicopter sprite from previous task using the keyboard or a game controller, change the size of the sprite, rotate the sprite, and write the position of the sprite on the screen.

(3) Animate the helicopter sprite using several frames and do sprite collision with other sprites.

(4) Create the classical Pong game (2D from-above tennis game).

4.4. Changes of the Staff and the Schedule. The main change to staffing was that two last year master students were hired to give technical support for student during the project (both robot and XNA). The main tasks of the technical support staff were to give lectures on the COTS, to be available for technical questions on email, to be available two hours a week in a lecture halls for questions, and to evaluate the implementation of the final project delivery (testing the games and the robots).

The main changes that were made to the course schedule were:

(i) Changing the motivation of the software architecture project to also include the game project. An extra bonus for the teams that chose the game project was that they could register for the Norwegian Game Awards competition [54]. This is an open national game developer competition for the all universities and colleges in Norway.

(ii) Added an extra two-hour COTS introduction lecture to give an introduction to the robot simulator, C#, and XNA.

(iii) Adding an extra two-hour technical support lecture on COTS every week (both for robot and XNA).

(iv) Changing a one-hour lecture on architectural patterns to also include architectural patterns on games.

(v) Added a one-hour lecture on software architecture in video games.

(vi) Changing the project workshop where selected teams presented their work to give room to show more demos (mostly games and some demos of robots).

5. Experiences and Results

This section presents experiences and results from running the course. The experiences presented here are collected from course staff interviews and notes, final course evaluation, the project reports, student feedback by email, and feedback during lectures. The students doing game development projects used version 2.0 of XNA Game Studio (the most recent version at that time).

5.1. Staff Experiences. In the first weeks of the semester, we were faced with a problem introduced by allowing students to choose between a robot and a game project. In previous years, the students did not have to make any decisions (e.g., forming teams, etc.) regarding the project before week 7, as this was the start of the main project (phase 3, see Section 3). By introducing two variants of the project, the students had to choose in week 3 if they were going to do the robot or the game project (before they had formed the teams) due to the two variants of the COTS exercise. As a result, some students ended up doing an exercise on the robot and later did the game project and vice versa.

The course staff was exited to see the distribution the number of student that chose the robot versus the game project. When we introduced the project to the students in the beginning of the semester, we admitted that this was the first time running a game project in the software

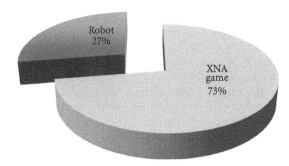

FIGURE 1: Distribution of project selection.

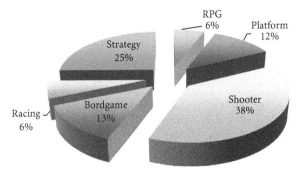

FIGURE 2: Distribution of game genres in student projects.

architecture course, and that the robot version of the project was better supported through previous experience, examples, the literature, and software architecture patterns. The result was that 6 teams chose the robot project while 16 teams chose the game project (see the distribution in Figure 1). The percentage of teams choosing the game project was much higher than we expected (almost 3 out of 4). The results show that students are attracted to games, and it indicates that games can be a motivation for choosing a course or for putting extra effort into projects.

During the semester, the students receive feedback on their part-deliveries from the course staff. The most notably difference between the part-deliveries made by robot, and game project teams were found in phase 3 of the project (Requirements and Architecture, see Section 3). For many game project teams, it was hard to create proper requirements documentation. This was not unexpected, as these teams first had to specify some gameplay element and then translate these into functional requirements. The course staff suspected that it also would be harder to specify the software architecture in the game projects due to less available literature and architectural patterns. This was, however, not the case. For the final delivery of the project, there was no noticeable difference in the quality of documentation, requirements, design, architecture, and implementation between the two variants (robot versus game). The implementation of some teams (both robot and game) suffered for being too ambitious resulting in unfinished implementations. For teams implementing a robot controller, the main challenge was to implement an intelligent maze navigator. For teams implementing a game, the main challenge was to implement advanced game logic.

The educational approach for our software architecture course is to force the students to use the theory described in the textbook during the project by applying the methods and theoretical framework described. To make this work, the course schedule is heavy on theoretical presentations in the first part of the semester. At the same time, the students have to learn the COTS through exercises (phase 1 and 2). Phase 3 is really the start of the project, where the students will document the requirements and do the architectural design. Although the students at this stage should know the COTS and all the software architectural theory required to describe the requirements and to the design, we discovered that the students were lacking both knowledge of the COTS

and the theory. This was true for both types of projects, and we did not discover any differences between robot and game teams. Based on feedback from the course staff and from another student team evaluating the project using ATAM, the software architectures improved significantly in terms of quality and quantity in the implementation phase of the project. The teams discovered problems with their architectural design mainly due to wrong assumptions about the COTS. Both XNA and Khepera put constrains on how to design the architecture, and the students discovered this through trial and error. The XNA teams struggled to make this work due to the complexity of the COTS, while for the Khepera simulator the main problem was lack of documentation. The students learned most during the implementation phase of the project, as they in this phase had to put everything together, reflect on their choices, make changes to make it work, and do the final documentation including updating documentation from previous phases. The course staff also noticed that the students worked a lot the last couple of weeks to be able to finish in time, and put everything together.

One noticeable difference for the course staff after introducing the game project was that the software architecture workshop, where a selected number of teams presented their work, was much more interesting and exciting. In previous years, these workshops have not been very interesting, since most all the students had worked with the same domain (robot). The game projects brought new life to the workshop, and it was very interesting to learn from creative game projects.

5.2. The Games Developed. In total, 16 different 2D games were developed. The type of games varied in several dimensions like number of players, game genre, network support, real-time versus turn-based games, and so forth. The distribution of the game genres implemented by the students is shown in Figure 2. From the figure, we can see that most students chose to implement a variant of a shooter game including a bee-shooter, space shooters, balloon-shooter, tank-shooter, and so forth. The other major game genre was the strategy games that included trading games, and turn-based worm clones.

The student projects also varied in support for multiplayer and network, and usage of the XQUEST-framework as

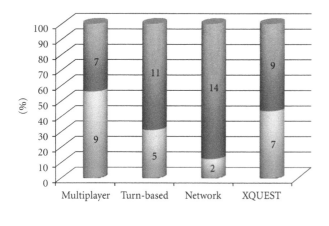

FIGURE 3: Distribution of game characteristics.

shown in Figure 3. More than 56% of the games developed supported multiplayer, 31% were turn-based, and only two games supported playing over network. About 44% of the games used the XQUEST framework that was developed for this course to simplify the development in XNA.

None of the games developed were groundbreaking in terms of gameplay or graphics, but several of the games had new twists in gameplay or graphics (like including the two most known buildings in the local city—Trondheim). The most novel game was a two-player split screen death-match shooting game, where two players were navigating in an environment that was hand-drawn using colored pencils. One of the levels in the game was actually architectural drawings of the implementation of the game itself. Figure 4 shows a screenshot of this game named BlueRose.

Some of the teams have continued to develop their games after the course ended.

If we look further into differences between how the robot teams and the game teams in terms of the implementation, we found that the projects varied in complexity and size. Although the APIs of XNA and Khepera framework is about at the same abstraction level, the game projects on average had more complex architectures. The architecture of game teams on average consisted of 12 classes compared to 9 for robot teams. We also noticed that the robot teams had a standard deviation of about 3 classes compared to 4 classes for game teams. We found the same tendency for lines of code where robot teams wrote in average 1800 lines of code (without comments), while game teams wrote 3400 (about 90% more lines of code). Another finding was that there was much more variation in number of lines code in game teams compared to robot teams. For robot teams, the most productive team wrote about 2500 lines of code (less than the average for game teams), and the least productive 850 lines of code. For game teams, however, the most productive team wrote about 12000 lines of code and the least productive about 800 lines of code. From analyzing the code, we found that the game teams that produced most lines of code really got carried away with programming the game

with less attention to the software architecture. We also compared the final grade of students doing game projects versus students doing robot projects and did not find any significant difference in the final grade. However, we noticed a tendency that students from game teams got a better grade on the project compared to the final written examination, and the students from the robot teams the opposite. An extensive analysis of the differences between the two projects is described in [55].

5.3. Lessons Learned from the Students. This section describes experiences described in the students' lessons learned section of the teams' final reports.A striking difference between students that did a game versus students that did a robot project was how they experienced using the COTS. None of the robot students said anything positive about the Khepera framework. The students that did the game projects described XNA and C# to be easy to learn and work with, that the tools were user-friendly and helpful, that the XNA framework provided the most important functionality including the game loop, and that the game project was very interesting. The students also wrote that it was very valuable to learn XNA and C#, and that XNA and the XQUEST library let them focus on the logic of the video game thus saving a lot of time.

There were several comments both from robot and game teams about the negative experiences from using the chosen COTS. For the students working with the robot simulator, the main problems were related to random and unpredictable behavior of the robot, that the robot simulator performed differently on different PCs, that it was difficult to implement the designed architecture using the API, and that the implementation forced the students to think too much on AI issues instead of software architecture. The random and unpredictable behavior of the robot simulator is a built-in feature to simulate unpredictable sensors in the real worlds. This issue caused a lot of frustration among the students. The different performance of the robot simulator on different PCs is due to problems of real-time execution in Java and real-time performance on different virtual machines. The negative experiences from using XNA was insufficient audio support (only support uncompressed audio files), no support for network testing of two instances on the same machine, limitations of the provided network API in XNA, and that more knowledge of the XNA framework was required to do a good architectural design.

Another topic that was covered by many teams in the lessons learned was their experience with the software architecture domain. Both robot and game teams found that they had learned a lot about software architecture through the design and implementation of the software architecture. One game team said that especially the XQUEST put some major restrictions on the architecture as it was tightly coupled to XNA. This made it difficult to implement a layered architectural pattern. Their conclusion was that the team should have spent more time in the beginning discovering the architectural limitations of the COTS. Another XNA team found that the COTS enabled a proper balance between the game

FIGURE 4: Screenshots from the BlueRose XNA game.

functionality and the software architecture, which resulted in a smooth implementation. Finally, an XNA team described that they did not do an attempt to separate game logic and graphics beyond what was done in XNA, and that this was a big mistake that cause a lot of problems later in the project. For the robot teams, one team said that they used an inappropriate amount of time on the implementation and that the software architecture was therefor, put in the background. One robot team discovered that having a well-planned architecture before starting to implement made it a lot easier to divide the work and make changes during the project. Another robot team explained that they in the beginning only had considered the top-level architecture without examining the architecture of the major modules, which caused a lot of problem. Finally, yet another a robot team admitted that they should had thought more about splitting different classes into packages, as they ended up with code that was hard to modify and manage.

The overall lessons from the students doing a robot project were a mixture of positive and negative issues. The robot simulator itself frustrated the students, and they had nothing positive to say about the COTS. Many students found the robot simulation domain to be fascinating, but they thought it was too difficult to implement the logic of the robot. However, the students had many positive comments about learning software architecture through such a project and designing a software architecture for a robot controller. They also mentioned that they had many reference architectural patterns they could use as a starting point. The hard part was implementing the architecture and the logic for the robot controller.

The overall lessons learned from the students doing an XNA game project were very positive about introducing a game project in a software architecture course. Some

students felt that learning C# and XNA in addition to the syllabus was a bit too much, but generally most students said that to learn XNA and C# did not take much time. Some students said that the XNA architecture put major restrictions on their architecture. This is of course true, but this is also the case in most commercial software development projects, as they often use some kind of framework that the architecture must adhere to. The main challenges of using XNA in the software architecture project was to spend enough time learning the framework before designing the architecture, and doing the design and implementation. The identified issue of lacking support for other audio format than wav was resolved in XNA Game Studio 3.0. From the reports we could also see that our own XNA extension (XQUEST) limited the choices of architecture more than only using XNA. The main benefit of using XQUEST was a simpler interface to some of the most useful game functionality.

5.4. Student Evaluation Feedback. After completing the project, all students had to fill in a final course evaluation and write responses to three questions: what has been good about the course, what has been not so good, and what would you like to change to next year?

The responses regarding *what had been good* about the course can be categorized into main areas the project, learning, practical work, and group dynamics. Both students from robot and game teams stated that the project had been good, but students from game teams were overall happier with the project and described it to be cool, interesting, fun, and motivating. Also both categories of students described that they learned a lot from the project in that they got to try out the theory from the lectures in practice. They also gave concrete example of theory that they got to try out in the project such as architectural and design patterns and how the software architecture is represented in code. Many students from game teams also wrote that the project was a fun way of learning software architecture and that it was useful to learn about the interplay of game and architectural approaches. Regarding the practical work, students from game teams mentioned that it was really useful to learn C# as it is commonly used in industry and that it was easy to learn because of its similarities with Java. Both robot and game students gave positive comments about the fact that the course forced the students to do practical work. Finally, it was mentioned that it was useful to learn from other teams through the final workshop. The responses from the students taking the course were overall very positive. The feedback from game team students was generally more positive than the feedback from the robot controller projects. Typical positive feedback we received from students doing a game project was that they felt they learned a lot from the game project, that they liked the practical approach of the project and having to learn C#, and the interaction between the teams (both ATAM and the project workshop). The students doing a robot project were pleased with learning software architecture through practical work, and thought it was very interesting to learn about software architecture in general.

The responses regarding *what had been not so good* about the course mainly concerned the COTS. Both students from robot and game teams complained about the lack of technical support during the project and sufficient introductory lecture on the COTS in the beginning of the course. Further, both categories of students complained that the COTS took away focus from software architecture in the course. Few students on game teams complained that learning C# took so much time that they did not have enough time to study software architecture. Some other students on game teams said that the focus on the game itself keep them from focusing on the software architecture, and that the game domain limits the choice of architecture too much. Students on robot teams complained that the difficulty of implementing the robot controller took the focus away from architectural design, and that the workload of the project was way too high. The main negative feedback from students doing game projects focused on the lack of XNA technical support during the project, and that some student felt that there was too much focus on C#, XNA and games and too little on software architecture. The students doing a robot project also complained about not sufficient technical assistance, and that the robot simulator and the robot domain were very difficult to master.

On the final question in the course evaluation, *what would you have changed* for next year's course; we received various course improvement suggestions. Game team students suggested to allocate more time to develop the game, to make the project count 50% of the grade, to give a better C# introduction, to provide better technical support, and to put more restrictions on game-type to ensure that the teams choose games suited for the course. The robot team students suggested to either give better information on how to program the robot or drop the robot project all together, provide better technical support during the project, and split the project into several smaller exercises. One robot team student said that he rather would choose the game project if he could start all over again. The suggestions to improve the course were mainly according to the negative feedback namely to improve teaching and technical support related to the COTS (XNA and robot simulator), and to adjust the workload of the project.

6. Conclusion

In this paper, we have described how we changed a software architecture course to include a game development project. The main motivation for introducing such a project was to motivate the students to put extra effort into the project and motivating for higher course enrollment. Some parts of the syllabus were changed to include game development as a natural part of the software architecture course. A challenge we discovered was to find the appropriate literature on design of software architecture for the game domain, which we are still looking for. It is not very hard to motivate for why game developers can benefit from learning more about software architectures as games are becoming increasingly more complex (especially massively multiplayer online games). From a software architecture perspective, games are interesting since they introduce relevant challenges such as dealing with continues changes of functional requirements (modifiability), and hard real-time requirements both for hardware and network.

Our experience from running a game development project in a software architecture course is very positive. The course staff noticed an increasing interest and motivation for the project in the course. From the course evaluation, we also notice that students choosing the game project were more positive towards the project compared to those who chose the robot project. Robot team students complained more about the project while game team students generally expressed that the project was fun and engaging. Game development projects are also very positive for the group dynamics, as other that CS and SE skills are required (e.g., creative and artistic skills). The main negative effect of introducing a game development project was that some teams focus more on developing the game than on the software architecture of the game. This effect was not a major issue, as most teams did a good job of designing the architecture and then implementing it. There will always be some students that do not like to do a project on games. When we looked at the demographics to see if there were any various in choosing game projects, we only found minor variations between male (73%) and female (71%). Actually, the difference was larger between Norwegians (74%) and foreign students (70%). One challenge for some students was that they had to learn C#. Most students did not think this issue was negative thing, as to know C# is useful for later in the career and it is not very different from Java. Another challenge using XNA as a development platform was that it only runs on the Microsoft Windows platform. This is a major problem as more and more students have laptops running Mac OS X and Linux. To compensate for this problem, we provided a computer lab where 10 PCs running Microsoft Windows with XNA Game developer studio 2.0 installed. Unfortunately, these PCs did not have proper graphics cards, making game development slow and tedious. To compensate for this problem in the future, we might offer game projects on other platforms such as Android and iPhone. Apart from the lack of support for other operating systems, we were very pleased with using XNA as a game developer platform. The high-level APIs in XNA makes it possible to be productive with little effort. Also XNA is flexible in terms of what games can be implemented and how the architecture can be designed. For the students, the opportunity to develop XBOX 360 games is very tempting. Only few of the teams tried to run their games on the XBOX 360 mainly due to time pressure. In XNA Game Studio 4.0, it is also possible to develop for Windows Phone, extending the target platform even more. This can give more variety of what kind of projects the students can develop in future projects.

Acknowledgments

The author would like to thank Jan-Erik Strøm and Trond Blomholm Kvamme for implementing XQUEST and for their inputs to this paper. They e would also like to thank Richard Taylor at the Institute for Software Research (ISR) at University of California, Irvine (UCI) for providing a stimulating research environment and for hosting a visiting researcher from Norway. The Leiv Eriksson mobility program offered by the Research Council of Norway has sponsored this work.

References

[1] R. Rosas, M. Nussbaum, P. Cumsille et al., "Beyond Nintendo: design and assessment of educational video games for first and second grade students," *Computers and Education*, vol. 40, no. 1, pp. 71–94, 2003.

[2] M. Sharples, "The design of personal mobile technologies for lifelong learning," *Computers and Education*, vol. 34, no. 3-4, pp. 177–193, 2000.

[3] A. Baker, E. O. Navarro, and A. Van Der Hoek, "Problems and programmers: an educational software engineering card game," in *Proceedings of the 25th International Conference on Software Engineering (ICSE '03)*, pp. 614–619, Irvine, Calif, USA, May 2003.

[4] L. Natvig, S. Line, and A. Djupdal, "Age of computers: an innovative combination of history and computer game elements for teaching computer fundamentals," in *Proceedings of the 34th Annual Frontiers in Education: Expanding Educational Opportunities Through Partnerships and Distance Learning*, pp. F-1–F-6, Trondheim, Norway, October 2004.

[5] A. O. Navarro and A. Hoek, "SimSE: an educational simulation game for teaching the software engineering process," in *Proceedings of the 9th Annual SIGCSE Conference on Innovation and Technology in Computer Science Education (ITiCSE '04)*, p. 233, ACM Press, New York, NY, USA, 2004.

[6] G. Sindre, L. Natvig, and M. Jahre, "Experimental validation of the learning effect for a pedagogical game on computer fundamentals," *IEEE Transactions on Education*, vol. 52, no. 1, pp. 10–18, 2009.

[7] B. A. Foss and T. I. Eikaas, "Game play in engineering education—concept and experimental results," *International Journal of Engineering Education*, vol. 22, no. 5, pp. 1043–1052, 2006.

[8] A. I. Wang, O. K. Mørch-Storstein, and T. Øfsdahl, "Lecture quiz—a mobile game concept for lectures," in *Proceedings of the 11th IASTED International Conference on Software Engineering and Application (SEA '07)*, November, 2007.

[9] A. I. Wang, T. Øfsdahl, and O. K. Mørch-Storstein, "An evaluation of a mobile game concept for lectures," in *Proceedings of the 21st Conference on Software Engineering Education and Training, (CSEET '08)*, pp. 197–204, April 2008.

[10] M. S. El-Nasr and B. K. Smith, "Learning through game modding," *Computers in Entertainment*, vol. 4, no. 1, pp. 45–64, 2006.

[11] B. Wu and A. I. Wang, "An evaluation of using a game development framework in higher education," in *Proceedings of the 22nd Conference on Software Engineering Education and Training, (CSEET '09)*, pp. 41–44, Hyderabad, India, February 2009.

[12] A. Sliney and D. Murphy, "JDoc: a serious game for medical learning," in *Proceedings of the 1st International Conference on Advances in Computer-Human Interaction, (ACHI '08)*, pp. 131–136, February 2008.

[13] F. Mili, J. Barr, M. Harris, and L. Pittiglio, "Nursing training: 3D game with learning objectives," in *Proceedings of the 1st International Conference on Advances in Computer-Human Interaction, (ACHI '08*, pp. 236–242, Rochester, NY, USA, February 2008.

[14] L. V. Ahn, "Games with a purpose," *IEEE Computer Magazine*, vol. 39, no. 6, pp. 92–94, 2006.

[15] J. Blow, "Game development: harder than you think," *ACM Queue*, vol. 1, no. 10, pp. 28–37, 2004.

[16] G. M. Youngblood, "Using XNA-GSE game segments to engage students in advanced computer science education," in *Proceedings of the 2nd Annual Microsoft Academic Days Conference on Game Development*, February, 2007.

[17] E. Sweedyk and R. M. Keller, "Fun and games: a new software engineering course," *ACM SIGCSE Bulletin*, vol. 37, no. 3, pp. 138–142, 2005.

[18] K. Claypool and M. Claypool, "Teaching software engineering through game design," in *Proceedings of the 10th Annual SIGCSE Conference on innovation and Technology in Computer Science Education (ITiCSE '05)*, pp. 123–127, Caparica, Portugal, June, 2005.

[19] D. Volk, "How to embed a game engineering course into a computer science curriculum," in *Proceedings of the Conference on Future Play: Research, Play, Share*, pp. 192–195, Toronto, Canada, November, 2008.

[20] J. Linhoff and A. Settle, "Teaching game programming using XNA," in *Proceedings of the 13th Annual Conference on innovation and Technology in Computer Science Education (ITiCSE '08)*, pp. 250–254, Madrid, Spain, June-July 2008.

[21] Q. Zhu, T. Wang, and S. Tan, "Adapting game technology to support software engineering process teaching," in *Proceedings of the 3rd International Conference on Natural Computation, (ICNC '07)*, pp. 777–780, Haikou, China, August 2007.

[22] Y. Rankin, A. Gooch, and B. Gooch, "The impact of game design on students' interest in CS," in *Proceedings of the 3rd International Conference on Natural Computation (ICNC '07)*, pp. 777–780, Miami, Fla, USA, February-March 2008.

[23] S. Leutenegger and J. Edgington, "A games first approach to teaching introductory programming," *SIGCSE Bulletin*, vol. 39, pp. 115–118, 2007.

[24] B. D. Coller and M. J. Scott, "Effectiveness of using a video game to teach a course in mechanical engineering," *Computers and Education*, vol. 53, no. 3, pp. 900–912, 2009.

[25] J. Distasio and T. Way, "Inclusive computer science education using a ready-made computer game framework," in *Proceedings of the 12th Annual Conference on Innovation and Technology in Computer Science Education*, pp. 116–120, June 2007.

[26] Washington State University Vancouver and University of Puget Sound, "2008 The Java Instructional Gaming Project," June 2008, http://ai.vancouver.wsu.edu/jig/.

[27] C. Johnson and J. Voigt, "DXFramework," June 2008, http://www.dxframework.org.

[28] I. Parberry, "SAGE: a simple academic game engine," June 2008, http://larc.csci.unt.edu/sage.

[29] R. Coleman, S. Roebke, and L. Grayson, "GEDI: a game engine for teaching videogame design and programming," *Journal of Computing Science in Colleges*, vol. 21, no. 2, pp. 72–82, 2005.

[30] Rockwell Automation Inc, "Arena Simulation Software," June 2008, http://www.arenasimulation.com.

[31] IBM, "INNOV8—a BPM Simulator," June 2008, http://www-304.ibm.com/jct03001c/software/solutions/soa/innov8.html.

[32] P. Clements, L. Bass, and R. Kazman, *Software Architecture in Practice*, Addison-Wesley, 2nd edition, 2003.

[33] J. O. Coplien, "Software design patterns: common questions and answers," in *The Patterns Handbook: Techniques, Strategies, and Applications*, pp. 311–320, Cambridge University Press, New York, NY, USA, 1998.

[34] A. I. Wang and T. Stålhane, "Using post mortem analysis to evaluate software architecture student projects," in *Proceedings of the 18th Conference on Software Engineering Education and Training (CSEET '05)*, pp. 43–50, April 2005.

[35] D. P. Perry and A. L. Wolf, "Foundations for the study of software architecture," *ACM Sigsoft Software Engineering Notes*, vol. 17, no. 4, pp. 40–52, 1992.

[36] IEEE, "IEEE recommended practice for architectural description of software-intensive systems," *Software Engineering Standards Committee of the IEEE Computer Society*, 2000.

[37] P. B. Kruchten, "The 4+1 view model of architecture," *IEEE Software*, vol. 12, no. 6, pp. 42–50, 1995.

[38] R. Kazman, M. Klein, R. Kazmani et al., ""The architecture tradeoff analysis method," engineering of complex computer systems," in *Proceedings of the Fourth IEEE International Conference on Engineering Complex Computer Systems (ICECCS '98)*, vol. 0, 1998.

[39] A. BinSubaih and S. C. Maddock, ""Using ATAM to evaluate a game-based architecture", workshop on architecture-centric evolution," in *Proceedings of the 20th European Conference on Object-Oriented Programming (ECOOP '06)*, Nantes, France, July 2006.

[40] T. Lozano-Pérez, *Autonomous Robot Vehicles*, Springer, New York, NY, USA, 1990.

[41] A. Elfes, "Sonar-based real-world mapping and navigation," *IEEE Journal of Robotics and Automation*, vol. 3, no. 3, pp. 249–265, 1987.

[42] R. G. Simmons, "Concurrent planning and execution for autonomous robots," *IEEE Control Systems Magazine*, vol. 12, no. 1, pp. 46–50, 1992.

[43] S. A. Shafer, A. Stentz, and C.E. Thorpe, "An architecture for sensor fusion in a mobile robot," in *Proceedings of the IEEE International Conference on Robotics and Automation*, pp. 2002–2011, April 1986.

[44] D. Toal, C. Flanagan, C. Jones, and B. Strunz, "Subsumption architecture for the control of robots," in *Proceedings of the 13th Irish Manufacturing Conference (IMC-13)*, pp. 703–711, 1996.

[45] R. Lumia, J. Fiala, and A. Wavering, "The NASREM robot control system and testbed," *The International Journal of Robotics and Automation*, no. 5, pp. 20–26, 1990.

[46] A. I. Wang and B. Wu, "An application of game development framework in higher education," *The International Journal of Computer Games Technology*, 2008.

[47] C. Vichoido, M. Estranda, and A. Sanchez, "A constructivist educational tool: software architecture for web-based video games," in *Proceedings of the 4th Mexican International Conference on Computer Science (ENC '03)*, Apizaco, Mexico, September 2003.

[48] J. Krikke, "Samurai romanesque, J2ME, and the battle for mobile cyberspace," *IEEE Computer Graphics and Applications*, vol. 23, no. 1, pp. 16–23, 2003.

[49] S. Rabin, "Introduction to game development," in *Course Technology Cengage Learning*, 2008.

[50] A. Rollings and D. Morris, *Game Architecture and Design—A New Edition*, New Riders, 2004.

[51] G. Booch, "Best practices in game development," IBM Presentation, March 2007.

[52] A. Grossman, *Postmortems From Game Developer*, Focal Press, 2003.

[53] R. Darken, P. McDowell, and E. Johnson, "Projects in VR: the delta3D open source game engine," *IEEE Computer Graphics and Applications*, vol. 25, no. 3, pp. 10–12, 2005.

[54] NGA, "Norwegian game awards 2011—home," April 2011, http://www.gameawards.no.

[55] A. I. Wang, "Extensive evaluation of using a game project in a software architecture course," *Computers & Education*, vol. 11, pp. 1–28, 2011.

12

Affect and Metaphor Sensing in Virtual Drama

Li Zhang[1] and John Barnden[2]

[1] School of Computing, Teesside University, Middlesbrough TS1 3BA, UK
[2] School of Computer Science, University of Birmingham, Birmingham B15 2TT, UK

Correspondence should be addressed to Li Zhang, l.zhang@tees.ac.uk

Academic Editor: Abdennour El Rhalibi

We report our developments on metaphor and affect sensing for several metaphorical language phenomena including affects as external entities metaphor, food metaphor, animal metaphor, size metaphor, and anger metaphor. The metaphor and affect sensing component has been embedded in a conversational intelligent agent interacting with human users under loose scenarios. Evaluation for the detection of several metaphorical language phenomena and affect is provided. Our paper contributes to the journal themes on believable virtual characters in real-time narrative environment, narrative in digital games and storytelling and educational gaming with social software.

1. Introduction

In our previous work, we have developed virtual drama improvisational software for young people age 14–16 to engage in role-playing situations under the improvisation of loose scenarios. The human users could be creative at their roleplays. A human director normally monitors the improvisation to ensure that the human actors have kept the general spirit of the scenarios. In order to reduce the burden of the human director, we have developed an affect detection component, EMMA (emotion, metaphor, and affect), on detecting simple and complex emotions, meta-emotions, value judgments, and so forth. This affect sensing component has been embedded in an intelligent agent, which interacts with human users and plays a minor role with the intention to stimulate the improvisation. In one session, up to 5 characters are involved in. The affect sensing component can detect 25 affective states in our previous development [1].

Metaphorical language has also been intensively used to convey emotions and feelings in the collected transcripts during the testing. The work presented here reports further developments on metaphor interpretation and affect detection for several particular metaphorical expressions with affect implication, which include affects as physical objects metaphor ("anger ran through me," "fear drags me down"), food metaphor ("X is walking meat", "Lisa has a pizza face",

and "you are a peach"), animal and size metaphor ("X is a fat big pig", "shut ur big fat mouth") and anger metaphor ("she exploded completely", "he fired up straightaway", and "she heated up just as fast"). Size metaphor also plays an important role in indicating affect intensities. We have detected these several metaphorical language phenomena using decision tree, naïve Bayes classifier, and support vector machine with the assistance of syntactic parsing and semantic analysis. WordNet and WordNet-affect domains have also been used to detect affect from the identified figurative language phenomena.

Also, several loose scenarios have been used in our study, including school bullying and Crohn's disease. The animation engine adopts the detected affect implied in users' text input to produce emotional gesture animation for the users' avatars. The AI agent also provides appropriate responses based on the detected affect from users' input in order to stimulate the improvisation.

In school bullying and Crohn's disease scenarios, the AI agent plays a minor role in drama improvisation. For example, it plays a close friend of the bullied victim (the leading role) in school bullying scenario, who tries to stop the bullying and a close friend of the sick leading character in Crohn's disease scenario who tries to give support to his friend with the decision on his friend's life-changing operation.

We have also analysed affect detection performance based on the collected transcripts from user testing by calculating agreements via Cohen's Kappa between two human judges, human judge A/the AI agent and human judge B/the AI agent, respectively. A corpus extracted from the collected transcripts and other similar sources has also been used to evaluate the metaphorical phenomena recognition based on various machine learning approaches.

The content is arranged in the following way. We report relevant work in Section 2 and the new developments on metaphor, affect, and affect intensity detection for the processing of affect, food, animal, size, and anger metaphor in Section 3. Brief discussion on how the detected affects contribute to the emotional animation is provided in Section 4. Evaluation results of the metaphor and affect detection component are reported in Section 5. Finally, we summarize our work and point out future directions in Section 6.

2. Relevant Work

Textual affect sensing is a rising research branch for natural language processing. ConceptNet [2] is a toolkit to provide practical textual reasoning for affect sensing for six basic emotions, text summarization, and topic extraction. Shaikh et al. [3] provided sentence-level textual affect sensing to recognize evaluations (positive and negative). They adopted a rule-based domain-independent approach, but they have not made attempts to recognize different affective states from open-ended text input.

Although Façade [4] included shallow natural language processing for characters' open-ended utterances, the detection of major emotions, rudeness, and value judgements is not mentioned. Zhe and Boucouvalas [5] demonstrated an emotion extraction module embedded in an Internet chatting environment. It used a part-of-speech tagger and a syntactic chunker to detect the emotional words and to analyse emotion intensity for the first person (e.g., "I" or "we"). Unfortunately the emotion detection focused only on emotional adjectives and did not address deep issues such as figurative expression of emotion (discussed below). Also, it seems to have limited the system's functionalities on affect interpretation by focusing purely on first-person emotions. There has been relevant work on general linguistic cues that could be used in practice for affect detection (e.g., Craggs and Wood [6]).

There is also well-known research work on the development of emotional conversational agents. Egges et al. [7] have provided virtual characters with conversational emotional responsiveness. Elliott et al. [8] demonstrated tutoring systems that reason about users' emotions. They believe that motivation and emotion play very important roles in learning. Virtual tutors have been created in a way that not only having their own emotion appraisal and responsiveness, but also understanding users' emotional states according to their learning progress. Aylett et al. [9] also focused on the development of affective behaviour planning for the synthetic characters. Cavazza et al. [10] reported a conversational agent embodied in a wireless robot to provide suggestions for users on a healthy living lifestyle. Hierarchical Task Networks (HTNs) planner and semantic interpretation were used in this work. The cognitive planner played an important role in assisting with dialogue management, for example, giving suggestions to the dialogue manager on what relevant questions should be raised to the user according to the healthy living plan currently generated. The user's response was also adopted by the cognitive planner to influence the change of the current plan. The limitation of such planning systems was that they normally worked reasonably well within the predefined domain knowledge, but their performance became worse when open-ended user input going beyond the planner's knowledge was used intensively during interaction. The system we present here intends to deal with such challenge.

Moreover, metaphorical language has drawn researchers' attention for a while since it has been widely used to provide effective vivid description. Fainsilber and Ortony [11] commented that "an important function of metaphorical language is to permit the expression of that which is difficult to express using literal language alone". Metaphorical language can be used to convey emotions implicitly and explicitly, which also inspires cognitive semanticists [12].

Indeed, the metaphorical description of emotional states is common and has been extensively studied (Fussell and Moss [13]), for example, "he nearly exploded" and "joy ran through me," where anger and joy are being viewed in vivid physical terms. Such examples describe emotional states in a relatively explicit if metaphorical way. But affect is also often conveyed more implicitly via metaphor, as in "his room is a cess-pit"; affect (such as "disgust") associated with a source item (cess-pit) gets carried over to the corresponding target item (the room). There is also other work conducting theoretical research on metaphor in general (see, e.g., Barnden et al. [14]; Barnden [15]), which could be beneficial to our application as a useful source of theoretical inspiration.

Our work is distinctive in the following aspects: (1) metaphor and affect detection in figurative expressions; (2) real-time affect sensing for basic and complex affects, meta-emotions, value judgments and so forth, (including 25 affective states) from improvisational open-ended user input; (3) expressive animation driven by the detected affective states from users' input.

3. Metaphor and Affect Sensing

Before we introduce the new developments on affect, food, animal, size, and anger metaphor, we briefly introduce our previous work on affect detection and responding strategy development for the AI agent. As mentioned earlier, our original system has been developed for age 14–16 secondary school students to engage in role-play situations in virtual social environments. Without predefined constrained scripts, the human users could be creative in their role play within the highly emotionally charged scenarios. The AI agent could be activated to interact with human actors by playing a minor bit-part character in the two scenarios.

We have used responding regimes for the conversational AI agent in order to stir up the discussion and stimulate the improvisation. For example, the responses can be activated when its confidence on interpreting affect from users' input is high.

The language used by the secondary school students during their roleplay is highly diverse with various online chatting features. Thus, before affect detection processing, we have implemented preprocessing procedures including spelling checking, abbreviation checking, and Metaphone algorithm dealing with letter repetitions in interjections and onomatopoeia in order to recover the standard user input. The recovered user input is sent to the Rasp parser to obtain syntactic information. We have particularly focused on users' input with potential emotional implication, such as diverse imperatives ("Lisa, go away", "you leave me alone", "Dave bring me the menu", and "do it or I will kill u") and statements with a structure of "first-person + present-tense verb" ("I like it", "I hate u", and "I enjoy the meal"). In addition, the approach followed for the detection of affect intensity was limited to checking punctuation (e.g., repeated exclamation marks) and capitalization in users' input.

Overall, we have adopted rule-based reasoning, robust parsing, pattern matching, and semantic and sentimental profiles (e.g., WordNet and a semantic profile [16]) in our approach. Jess, the rule engine for Java platform, has been used to implement the rule-based reasoning while Java has been used to implement other algorithms and processing with the integration of the off-the-shelf language processing tools, such as Rasp and WordNet.

In this study, we have made further developments on affect detection especially from several different types of metaphorical expressions—size, affect, food, animal, and anger metaphor. Affect intensity has been further explored on size metaphor, size adjectives, and degree adverbs. Especially, these several metaphorical language phenomena will also be detected by several machine learning approaches (classifiers) based on our previous rule-based development.

The machine learning approaches have also been trained by 400 extracted examples of these several metaphorical phenomena and literal expressions which are represented by the identified extracted semantic and syntactic structures. The implementation detail is presented in the following.

3.1. Size Metaphor and Affect Intensity. In our study, size adjectives are often used to emphasize the affect conveyed in the users' literal and metaphorical input ("shut ur big fat mouth", "u r a big bully"). As degree adverbs, they could be used to measure intensity of the affect conveyed. In our previous work, affect intensity is simply judged by punctuations and repeated letters, syllables in interjections and ordinary words, and so forth. We now employ size adjectives and degree adverbs to reason about intensity. In order to facilitate our study, we have created our own semantic dictionary. It contains not only size adjectives and degree adverbs with their corresponding semantic tags but also emotional and affective terms, food terms, animal names, and so forth. The semantic annotations used in our

TABLE 1: Size adjectives and degree adverbs and their corresponding semantic tags.

Size adjectives and degree adverbs	Semantic tag
Maximizer adjectives (e.g., huge)	n3.2++
Booster adjectives (e.g., "big", "massive", and "fat")	n3.2+
Diminisher adjectives (e.g., "little", "small", and "tiny")	n3.2−
Maximizer adverbs (e.g., "completely")	a13.2
Booster adverbs (e.g., "greatly")	a13.3
Approximator adverbs (e.g., "almost")	a13.4
Compromiser adverbs (e.g., "pretty")	a13.5
Diminisher adverbs (e.g., "slightly")	a13.6
Minimizer adverbs (e.g., "hardly")	a13.7
Frequency minimizer adverbs (e.g., "rarely").	n6−

semantic dictionary have been borrowed from Wmatrix [17], which facilitates users to obtain corpus annotation with semantic and part-of-speech tags to compose dictionary. For example, for size adjectives, since "n3.2" represents measurement, size according to Wmatrix, a semantic tag "n3.2++" is used to label maximizer adjectives such as "huge", with "n3.2+", used to indicate booster adjectives such as "big", "massive", and "fat", and "n3.2-" used to mark diminisher adjectives such as "little", and "small", "tiny". For degree adverbs, Wmatrix uses "a13" to represent degree generally with "a13.x" to indicate a particular type of such adverbs. "N6-" is used to indicate frequency minimizer adverbs (e.g., "rarely"). After the metaphorical phenomena and affect detection using various methods reported in the following with the assistance of sentence types information obtained from Rasp, the system checks for these intensity indicators (size adjectives and degree adverbs) to reason about affect intensities. Table 1 lists all types of size adjectives and degree adverbs that have been considered in our paper.

First of all, at the beginning of metaphor and affect detection, Rasp is used to obtain the sentence type information from user input. It also reports part-of-speech information for each word in the user input. Then after affect is detected from user input, all the adjectives and adverbs (indicated by their part-of-speech tags) from the user input are attached with their corresponding semantic tags provided by the semantic dictionary mentioned above. If maximizer and booster size adjectives (e.g., "huge", "big", "fat" etc,) and degree adverbs (e.g., "completely", "greatly", and "extremely") are detected, then we conclude that the affect intensity is strong (e.g., "u r completely a big idiot" and "keep your big mouth shut"). If approximator and compromiser adjectives and adverbs (e.g., "almost", "nearly", "rather", "quite", and "pretty") are presented, then we believe that the user input implies affect with medium intensity ("u r quite cool", "fear nearly kills me"). Otherwise, if diminisher size adjectives (e.g., "little", "small", and "tiny") and degree adverbs (e.g., "slightly") are found, the system believes that the intensity of the affect expressed in user input is weak (or minor) (e.g., "u r just a little idiot"). Finally, if minimizer degree and frequency adverbs (e.g., "hardly", "rarely", and "seldom") are detected, the affect detected from the user input is discounted (e.g., "Lisa hardly is a pizza/freak", "fear rarely controls me"). Although the intensity processing could be fooled by user input with complex syntactic structures, our current processing is effective enough in dealing with intensity detection in sentence-level conversational interaction.

From the collected transcripts, there is also one particular phenomenon of theoretical and practical interest, that is, physical size is often metaphorically used to emphasize evaluations, as in "you are a big bully", "you're a big idiot", and "you're just a little bully." The bigness is sometimes literal as well. Sharoff [18] indicates that "big bully" expresses strong disapproval and "little bully" can express contempt, although "little" can also convey sympathy or be used as an endearment.

3.2. Affect Metaphor Interpretation. Affect terms have been used intensively during online interaction. Besides they have been used literally to convey users' emotional states (e.g., "I am angry", "I get bored"), affect terms have been mentioned in affective metaphorical language. One category of such metaphorical expression is "Ideas/Emotions as Physical Objects" [12, 19], for example, "joy ran through me", "my anger returns in a rush", "fear is killing me", and so forth. In these examples, emotions and feelings have been regarded as external entities. The external entities are often, or usually, physical objects or events. Therefore, affects could be treated as physical objects outside the agent in such examples, which could be active in other ways [19]. Implementation has been carried out to provide the affect detection component with the ability to deal with such affect metaphor.

In order to effectively detect such metaphorical expressions, their general semantic and syntactic structures have to be identified, so that these metaphorical expressions could be converted into these structures (to train the classifiers for future recognition). Thus, Rasp has been used to detect statements with a structure of "a singular common noun subject + present-tense/past-tense lexical verb phrase" or "a singular common noun subject + present-tense copular form + -ing form of lexical verb phrase". A syntactic annotation for each word in the user input has also been provided by Rasp.

Various user inputs could possess such syntactic forms, for example, "the girl is crying", "the big bully runs through the grass", and so forth. Our special semantic dictionary has been employed to recover corresponding semantic tags for the singular common noun subjects. As mentioned earlier, the semantic dictionary created consists mainly of emotion and affect terms, food terms, animal names, measureable adjectives (such as size), special verbs (e.g., explode, fire, heat) and so forth, with their corresponding semantic tags due to the fact they have the potential to convey affect and feelings. For example, if the main subject is an affective term ("joy"), then its corresponding semantic tag ("e4.1+") will be recovered. If it is not recorded in the semantic dictionary ("girl"), then the syntactic part-of-speech tag obtained from Rasp for the main subject is retained ("nn1").

Thus, with the assistance of the semantic and syntactic analysis, the user input with affect terms as main subjects will be converted into the following structure: "the semantic tag for the main subject + the part-of-speech tag (obtained from Rasp) for the lexical main verb + the part-of-speech tag for the object". The step-by-step analysis is listed in the following for the user input "anger runs through me":

(1) Rasp recognizes the input with a structure of "nn1 (a singular common noun subject: anger) + vvz (present-tense lexical verb phrase: runs) + ppio1 (object: me)";

(2) the subject noun term, "anger", has been sent to the semantic dictionary;

(3) then the input is interpreted as a semantic syntactic structure of "e3- (semantic tag: anger) + vvz (runs) + ppio1 (me)".

From such an expression, the system realizes that an emotional state has been used as a subject which carries out an activity indicated by the verb phrase(s). It has been noticed that this extracted structure could be at least extended to other similar expressions belonging to "affects as external entities" metaphor such as "a terrible rage began to seize hold of me", "blind waves of panic swept over and over him", and "joy runs through me". Thus, we need to train the system to regard any new input with such a semantic and syntactic structure as affective metaphor belonging to the category of "affects as entities". Therefore, we have gathered 80 examples of such metaphorical expressions not only from the collected transcripts from the previous testing but also from an online metaphor databank [19] and represented these examples in the above semantic syntactic structures. Since quantifiers (e.g., "completely", "almost", and "hardly") play an important role in the interpretation of the affect conveyed in the user input as mentioned earlier, they have also been incorporated in the extracted structure represented by their semantic annotations. Moreover, sentence types sometimes also may become affect indicators. For example, imperatives may contain potential emotional implication, especially without softeners such as "please". Thus, sentence types have been taken into our study.

Thus, these examples have been served as (part of) the training data for several chosen classifiers including decision tree, naïve Bayes classifier, and support vector machine, in order to provide our system with the ability of detecting such a metaphorical language phenomenon effectively and distinguishing these figurative expressions from other types of metaphors and literal expressions. The chosen classifiers have also been trained with examples of other metaphorical phenomena (such as food, animal, and anger metaphor) and literal expressions. Some training examples for affect metaphor are presented in Table 2.

In our processing, we allow the quantifiers to be present at any position within the sentence. For any new input, Rasp informs the system of any input with a structure of "a singular common noun subject + present-tense/past-tense lexical verb phrase" or "a singular common noun subject + present-tense copular form + -ing form of lexical verb

TABLE 2: Affect metaphor training examples (s represents a statement sentence).

Sentence type	Subject	Quantifiers	Verb	Object	Category
s	E3-("anger")	null	VVZ ("runs through")	PPIO1 ("me")	Affect metaphor
s	E3-("anger")	A13.4 ("almost")	VVZ ("hits")	PPIO1 ("me")	Affect metaphor
s	E5-("panic")	A13.2 ("completely")	VVZ ("sweeps over")	PPHS1 ("him")	Affect metaphor

phrase". With the assistance of the semantic dictionary, the semantic annotation of the singular common noun subject is derived as discussed above. The semantic syntactic structure is sent to the classifiers, which are trained by examples from several different language phenomena. Generally the classifiers perform reasonably well for the detection of such affect metaphor although they could be challenged by its variations (e.g., "I stare at her, fighting a rising tide of disbelief"). The evaluation detail is presented in Section 5.

Further processing has also been conducted to sense affect from the identified affective metaphorical expressions. Although the semantic annotation for the main subject has suggested that the subject belongs to emotional states, and the overall user input has been recognized as affect (as entities) metaphor, further processing is needed in order to recover the appropriate affect conveyed in the user input.

WordNet-affect domain (part of WordNet-domain 3.2) [20] has been used in our application. It provides an additional hierarchy of "affective domain labels", with which the synsets representing affective concepts are further annotated. Thus the singular common noun subject is sent to WordNet-affect in order to obtain the hierarchical affect information. For example, if the subject is the affective term "panic", then the hierarchical affect information obtained from WordNet-affect is "negative-fear → negative-emotion → emotion → affective-state → mental-state". A further processing based on the hierarchical affect result leads to the exact affective state conveyed in user's input—fear (negative emotion). If such an input has a first-person object, "me" (e.g., "panic is dragging me down"), then it indicates the user currently experiences fear. Otherwise if such input has a third-person object, "him/her" (e.g., "panic is sweeping over and over him"), it implies that it is not the user who currently experiences "fear", but another character. The step-by-step analysis is listed in the following for the new input "panic is dragging me down", which is not included in the training examples for the classifiers.

(1) With the assistance of Rasp and the semantic dictionary, the input becomes "e5- (emotional state: panic) + vvg (-ing form of lexical verb: dragging) + ppio1 (me)" (by the procedure described as in the above training example).

(2) The classifiers deduce and conclude that the input = an affects as entities metaphor.

(3) The main subject (panic) → WordNet-affect.

(4) WordNet-affect → the hierarchical affect information → panic: fear (negative emotion).

Obviously the quantifiers may influence the detected affect from the user input as mentioned above. For example,

"hardly" may dismiss the detected affect from the input although it could be recognized as a metaphorical expression (e.g., "anger hardly touches him"); "completely" may emphasize the affect conveyed in the input (e.g., "sorrow completely hits him").

Moreover, if the user input is literal (e.g., "Lisa hits me", "the boy sweeps the floor"), the classifiers will not regard it as a metaphorical expression but literal. Thus, other suitable processing methods (e.g., checking syntactic information and affect indicators etc) are adopted to extract affect. On the whole, such processing on metaphor interpretation is indeed at a very initial stage. However, it provides a useful way to recognize affect and affect metaphor in which emotions are used as external entities.

3.3. Food and Animal Metaphor Interpretation. Food has been used extensively as metaphor for social position, group identity, and so forth. For example, food could be used as a metaphor for national identity. British have been called "roastbeefs" by the French, while French have been referred to as "frogs" by the British. It has also been used to indicate social hierarchy. For example, in certain Andean countries, potatoes have been used to represent poor rural farmers of native American descent and white flour and bread have been used mainly to refer to wealthy European descent. In our school bullying scenario, the big bully has called the bullied victim (Lisa) names, such as "u r a pizza", "Lisa has a pizza face" to exaggerate that fact that the victim has acne. Another most commonly used food metaphor is to use food to refer to a specific shape. For example, body shape could be described as "banana", "pear", and "apple". In our application, "Lisa has a pizza face" could also be interpreted as Lisa has a "round (shape)" face. Therefore, insults could be conveyed in such food metaphorical expression. We especially focus on the statements of "second-person/a singular proper noun + present-tense copular form + food term".

In our application, Rasp informs the system of the user input with the following structure: "second-person/a singular proper noun + present-tense copular form + noun phrases" (e.g., "Lisa is a pizza", "u r a hard working man", and "u r a peach"). The noun phrases are examined in order to recover the main noun term. Then its corresponding semantic tag is derived from the composed semantic dictionary if it is a food term, or an animal-name and so forth. Syntactic annotations for the user input are also obtained from Rasp. For example, "u r a peach" has been regarded as "ppy (second-person) + vbr (present-tense copular form) + f1-l3 (semantic tag for food terms but also plants)", while the input "Lisa is a pizza" is described as "np1 (singular proper noun) + vbz (present-tense copular form) + f1 (semantic tag for food terms)".

TABLE 3: Food and animal metaphor training examples.

Sentence type	Subject	Quantifiers	Verb	Object	Category
s	PPHS1 ("she")	null	VBZ ("is")	F1-L3 ("peach")	Food metaphor
s	NP1 ("Lisa")	A13.2 ("completely")	VBZ ("is")	F1 ("pizza")	Food metaphor
s	NP1 ("Lisa")	null	VBZ ("is")	L2 ("pig")	Animal metaphor
s	PPY ("you")	N3.2- ("little")	VBR ("are")	L2y ("bunny")	Animal metaphor

TABLE 4: Anger metaphor training examples.

Sentence type	Subject	Quantifiers	Verb	Object	Conjunction	Category
s	PPHS1 ("she")	A13.4 ("nearly")	E3- ("exploded")	null	null	Anger metaphor
s	PPHS1 ("she")	A13.2 ("completely")	O4.6+/a2.1 ("heated up")	null	CS ("when")	anger metaphor
s	NP1 ("Lisa")	A13.7 ("hardly")	O4.6+/a2.1 ("fires up")	null	null	Anger metaphor

Also, in common sense, calling someone a baby animal name may indicate affection, while calling someone an adult animal name may convey insults. Thus, we have put animal names in our own newly created semantic dictionary with the semantic tag—"l2" to indicate living creatures generally for adult animal names [17] and the semantic tag—"l2y" to indicate young living creatures for baby animal names (e.g., "puppy", "bunny", "kitten" etc). According to the processing described above, for example, the user input "Lisa is a pig" is also converted into "np1 (singular proper noun) + vbz (present-tense copular form) + l2 (semantic tag for adult animal names). Thus, we collected 80 training examples for each of the two metaphorical language phenomena from the collected transcripts and converted them into the above identified semantic and syntactic structures to train the classifiers. Examples are listed in Table 3.

The classifiers are trained on these examples and deduce if any new user input belongs to these two metaphorical phenomena. Once an input has been recognized as an animal metaphor, then it carries affectionate if the semantic tag for the object indicates a young animal name. Otherwise the input conveys insulting if the object implies an adult animal name.

If the input is identified as a food metaphor, WordNet has been employed in order to get the synset of the food term. If among the synset, the food term has been explained as a certain type of human being, such as "beauty" and "sweetheart". Then another small slang-semantic dictionary collected in our previous study containing terms for special person types (such as "freak", "angle") and their corresponding evaluation values (negative or positive) has been adopted in order to obtain the evaluation values of such synonyms of the food term. If the synonyms are positive (e.g., "beauty"), then we conclude that the input is affectionate with a food metaphor (e.g., "u r a peach" → deduced as a food metaphor → "peach" is sent to WordNet → synonyms of peach from WordNet: beauty and sweetheart → from slang-semantic profiles: beauty is positive → the input is affectionate).

3.4. Anger Metaphor Interpretation. There are several anger metaphors that have also been widely used, such as "anger is the heat of a fluid in a container" [12] (e.g., "she nearly exploded", "he fired up straightaway", and "she heated up just as fast") and "anger is giving birth" [21] (e.g., "he had a baby when he heard what happened" and "don't have a cow! It's no big deal"). They all depict an attack of anger. As Kövecses [12] suggested, the above examples of the first anger metaphor imply the conceptualization of the "release of pressure". The second anger metaphor indicates the similarity of the behaviour during labour to the behaviour expressed during an attack of anger. We are particularly interested in the metaphor "anger is the heat of a fluid in a container" in this study.

In order to train the classifiers, Rasp is used to detect user input with a structure of "a singular proper noun/second person/a third-person singular pronoun + past-tense or present-tense lexicon verb phrase" (e.g., "Lisa hits me", "Peter needs the operation", "she exploded completely", and "Lisa likes school") and provide part-of-speech tags for the user input. Then the adverb and the base form of the main verb (identified by their part-of-speech) are sent to the semantic dictionary. If the verb is among those verbs with strong affective implication (e.g., "fire", "heat", "explode", "toast", "steam" etc), then its semantic annotation is derived. Otherwise, its part-of-speech tag remains.

For example, Rasp converts the input "she nearly exploded" into "pphs1 (she) + rr (nearly) + vvd (exploded)". With the assistance of the semantic dictionary, the input becomes "pphs11 (she) + a13.4 (semantic tag for quantifiers: nearly) + e3- (semantic tag for verbs indicating emotional states—Calm/Violent/Angry: explode)". Examples such as "she heated up completely when she heard the news" are interpreted as "pphs1 (she) + a13.2 (semantic tag for quantifiers: completely) + o4.6+/a2.1 (semantic tag for verbs indicating Temperature/Affect: heat) + rp (up) + cs (when)". The example training data of this language phenomenon are presented in Table 4.

Conjunctions are considered since our study shows that they tend to be used in such affective metaphorical expressions. The classifiers have also been trained by 80 examples of such a language phenomenon represented in the above structures in order to equip themselves with the ability to detect such expressions effectively and improve future performance.

When dealing with any new user input, Rasp informs the system about any input with the desired structure: "singular proper noun/second person/third-person singular + past-tense or present-tense lexicon verb phrase". After the semantic annotations for the adverb and the main verb derived from the semantic dictionary, the derived semantic and syntactic representation of the input is sent to the classifiers to identify if it is an anger metaphorical expression or not. If it is, then the quantifier is employed to measure the affect intensity. For example, for the new input (not included in the training samples), "she fired up completely when she heard the news", the processing detail is provided in the following:

(1) Rasp recognizes the input with a syntactic structure: "pphs1 (she) + vvd (fired) + rp (up) + rr (completely) + cs (when)" and recognizes the input as a statement sentence;

(2) since "completely" has a syntactic tag, "RR", indicating it is a general adverb, it is sent to the semantic dictionary to recover its corresponding semantic tag, "a13.2". In a similar way, the base form of the verb, "fire", is sent to the semantic dictionary to derive its corresponding semantic tag, "o4.6+/a2.1";

(3) the user input has been interpreted as "pphs1 (she) + o4.6+/a2.1 (main verb: fire) + a13.2 (quantifier: completely) + cs (conjunction: when)";

(4) the above derived structure has been sent to the classifiers. It has been recognized as an anger metaphor ("anger is the heat of a fluid in a container");

(5) the quantifier, a13.2 (completely), indicates the input implying "anger" with a strong intensity.

In general, we have made some initial attempts on the interpretation and detection of several metaphorical language phenomena and the implied affect in such expressions. The overall component on affect and metaphor sensing is integrated with the conversational intelligent agent. The component is implemented in Java, integrated with Rasp, WordNet-affect, WordNet, and the APIs for the classifiers (decision trees, naïve Bayes, and support vector machine) embedded in Weka, which is a well-known data mining tool and incorporates many machine learning approaches together for various classification and clustering tasks.

The approaches we have taken provided some flexibility in the processing and recognition of metaphorical expressions. However, our processing could also be challenged by various variations of these several language phenomena (e.g., "I couldn't bear to touch the memories", "he felt his anger rising step by step", "he was red with anger. I could see the smoke coming out of his ears", "she was filled

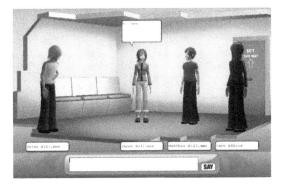

FIGURE 1: Emotional animation.

with joy" etc), and there are also other figurative language phenomena such as irony, humor, and simile that we have not even touched. But our work points out a potential positive direction for affect and metaphor interpretation and detection for figurative language processing.

4. Emotional Animation

The detected affective states from users' open-ended text input play an important role in producing emotional animation of human players' avatars. The emotional animation mainly includes emotional gesture and social attention (such as eye gazing). The expressive animation engine, Demeanour (Gillies and Ballin [22]), makes it possible for our characters to express the affective states detected by EMMA. When EMMA detects an affective state in a user's text input, this is passed to the Demeanour system attached to this user's character and a suitable emotional animation is produced.

The Demeanour system has also used character profiles, particularly including personality traits and relationships with other characters, to provide expressive animation for other avatars when the "speaking" avatar experiences affect. For example, Figure 1 shows a screen shot of user interaction at the beginning of Crohn's disease scenario. Briefly, in Crohn's disease scenario, Peter has had Crohn's disease since the age of 15. Crohn's disease attacks the wall of the intestines and makes it very difficult to digest food properly. The character has the option to undergo surgery (ileostomy) which will have a major impact on his life. The task of the role-play is to discuss the pros and cons with friends and family and decide whether he should have the operation. The other characters are Mum, who wants Peter to have the operation, Matthew (younger brother), who is against the operation, Dad, who is not able to face the situation, and David (the best friend), who mediates the discussion.

In Figure 1, from left to right, the characters are Peter (with Crohn's disease and needs to go through another life-changing operation), Janet (Peter's mum who approves the idea of operation), Matthew (Peter's younger brother who is against the operation idea since Peter could be bullied because of the side effects of the operation) and Dave (Peter's best friend who tries to mediate the discussion). The character suffering from the disease (Peter) tends to

FIGURE 2: Emotional animation and the AI character.

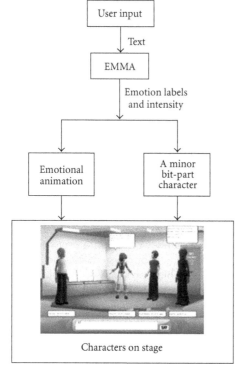

FIGURE 3: Affect detection and the control of characters.

feel uncomfortable and sad. Demeanour makes this type of personality trait expressed by a default, low-level emotional state (see Peter in Figure 1).

Figure 2 shows an interface of emotional interaction and animation with the same order of the characters as shown in Figure 1 in Crohn's disease scenario. The mum character, Janet, expressed her anger towards Matthew (her ather son, Peter's younger brother) by saying "shut it matt, stop talking like that 2 Dave". Since Matthew and Janet had a positive relationship (mother and son), Matthew showed a mild emotional response of acceptance of Janet's suggestion by gesture. Dave, played by EMMA, had also provided a conversational response, "Could we all tone down our language a bit? ppl (people) r (are) watching...", in order to mediate the discussion. All the characters shared

social attention as well by looking at the angry "speaking" character, Janet.

Figure 3 gives an overview of the control of the expressive characters. Users' text input is analyzed by EMMA in order to detect affect in the text. The output is an emotion label with intensity derived from the text. This is then used in two ways. Firstly, it is used by the minor bit-part character (played by EMMA) to generate a response. Secondly, the label and the intensity are sent to the emotional animation system (via an XML stream) where it is used to generate animation.

As disucssed earlier, the main intention of Dave's (the AI agent) responses is to stimulate the improvisation. For example, Dave may tune down the argument, or he may also stir up the discussion by mentioning emotionally charged sensitive topics such as "Arnold, u (you) r (are) family to Peter and he needs ur (your) support", "Arnold, Peter is ur (your) son and you can't just ignore it", when Dave detected that Arnold (the Dad character) was "embarrassed" to talk about Peter's disease in public ("Peter we know about it. Stop talking about it"). Since in our previous pilot user testing, EMMA was commented by the testing subjects (14–16 years old school children) that its responses were different from theirs, we have also used abbreviations, acronmys and slang language in the construction of EMMA's responses in order to simulate the language style used by school children. More discussion on user testing and EMMA's performance on affect sensing and drama improvisation is provided in the following section.

5. Evaluation

We carried out user testing with 220 secondary school students from Birmingham schools and Education Village in Darlington for the improvisation of school bullying (SB) and Crohn's disease scenarios. Briefly, the methodology of the testing is that we had each testing subject have an experience of both scenarios, one including the AI minor character only and the other including the human-controlled minor character only. Such arrangement could not only enable us to measure any statistically significant difference to users' engagement and enjoyment due to the involvement of the AI minor character but also provide us the opportunity to compare the performance of the AI minor character with that of the human-controlled one. After the testing, sessions, we obtained users' feedback via questionnaires and group debriefings. Improvisational transcripts were automatically recorded during the testing so that it allows further evaluation of the performance of affect detection component.

Moreover, in order to identify the following several particular metaphors—affect, food, animal, and anger, we used 400 different language phenomena examples (80 samples for each metaphorical phenomenon and 80 for literal expressions) for the training of the classifiers. We have collected a small test set to evaluate the performance of the classifiers, with 50 examples for each category (most from the collected transcripts, which were produced by the testing subjects and automatically recorded during the testing, and

TABLE 5: Detailed recognition results for metaphorical and literal test expressions using decision tree learning.

Metaphorical and literal expressions	Results for decision tree learning		
	Precision	Recall	F-Measure
Affect metaphor	1	1	1
Food metaphor	0.929	1	0.963
Animal metaphor	1	0.813	0.897
Angry Metaphor	1	1	1
Literal expression	0.667	0.667	0.667

TABLE 6: Detailed recognition results for metaphorical and literal test expressions using naïve Bayes.

Metaphorical and literal expressions	Results for Naïve Bayes		
	Precision	Recall	F-Measure
Affect metaphor	1	1	1
Food metaphor	0.929	1	0.963
Animal metaphor	0.933	1	0.966
Angry Metaphor	1	0.917	0.957
Literal expression	0.667	0.667	0.667

a small portion from an online chatting transcripts database on travel (http://akayoglu_s.web.ibu.edu.tr/webheads.htm)). All the chosen classifiers obtained reasonably good results for the metaphor sensing. Decision tree, naïve Bayes, and support vector machine achieved more than 90% of the accuracy rates for the recognition of these four types of metaphorical expressions. Since the training samples for the literal expressions are dramatically less than those for metaphorical expressions, the recognition results of such expressions are generally worse than those of the figurative phenomena, with the *F-Measure* 0.667 for both decision tree and naïve Bayes, and 0.333 for the support vector machine. Detailed evaluation results including *Precision*, *Recall*, and *F-Measure* obtained from Weka have been presented in Tables 5, 6, and 7 for the recognition of literal and metaphorical expressions using the three approaches, respectively. (The *True Positive (TP)* rate provided by Weka is the proportion of examples which were classified as class *x*, among all examples which truly have class *x*, that is, how much part of the class was captured. It is equivalent to *Recall*, while the *Precision* is the proportion of the examples which truly have class *x* among all those which were classified as class *x*. According to Weka, the *F-Measure* is produced in the following way: 2*Precision*Recall/(Precision+Recall), that is, a combined measure for precision and recall. Overall, although there is room for further improvements, the evaluation results for the three approaches are generally promising.

We also noticed that some of the testing metaphorical examples collected from our recorded transcripts showed much resemblance to some of the training data although they have been produced by different testing subjects in different testing sessions. Therefore, we need to adopt a bigger size sample in order to evaluate the classifiers fully and choose the most effective approach for further development.

Also, we provided Cohen's Kappa in order to evaluate the efficiency of the affect detection processing for the detection of 25 affective states. The following formula was used for the interagreement calculation: Kappa = (the number of actual agreed annotation − the number of agreed annotation by chance)/(the total number of annotation − the number of agreed annotation by chance).

As indicated in the formula, we have removed the effects of producing agreement between annotators purely by chance in interagreement calculation. Two human judges (not involved in development) have been employed to annotate part of the recorded transcripts of the SB scenario (72 turn-taking user input) filed from the testing. The interagreement between human judge A and B is 0.896. The agreements for human judge A/the AI agent and human judge B/the AI agent are, respectively, 0.662 and 0.729. Although improvement is needed, the AI agent's affect detection performance is acceptable and could achieve satisfactory level in good cases (e.g., in good cases, the interagreement between the human judge B and the AI agent is close to that between two human judges).

Inspection of the transcripts collected indicates that the AI agent usefully pushed the improvisation forward on various occasions. Box 1 shows an example about how the AI actor contributed to the drama improvisation in Crohn's disease scenario. In it, Dave was played by the AI actor, which successfully led the improvisation on the desirable track. In another scenario (school bullying) used for the testing, example transcripts have also shown that the AI actor has helped to push the improvisation forward.

Other evaluation results were also provided for the performance of the AI character. Generally the results indicated that the involvement of the AI character has not made any statistically significant difference to users' engagement and enjoyment with the emphasis of users' notice of the AI character's contribution throughout. Figure 4 also shows some evaluation results from a "within-subjects" analysis looking at the difference made PER SUBJECT by having

TABLE 7: Detailed recognition results for metaphorical and literal test expressions using support vector machine.

Metaphorical and literal expressions	Results for support vector machine		
	Precision	Recall	F-Measure
Affect metaphor	1	0.857	0.923
Food metaphor	1	1	1
Animal metaphor	0.833	0.938	0.882
Angry Metaphor	0.923	1	0.96
Literal expression	0.333	0.333	0.333

Peter Williams: I'M THE ILL ONE
Dave Atkins: Arnold, Peter needs ur support and u can't just ignore it.
Janet Williams: nobody cares peter
Arnold Williams: we know peter now stop talking about it
Peter Williams: yes I need your support
Dave Atkins: Hey guys, lets all calm down a bit.
Arnold Williams: we will discuss it later
Janet Williams: well you have got time
Peter Williams: help me daddy
Arnold Williams: not now son

Box 1: *Example transcripts; Crohn's disease scenario; Dave: the AI character.* Part of an example transcript produced in the user testing.

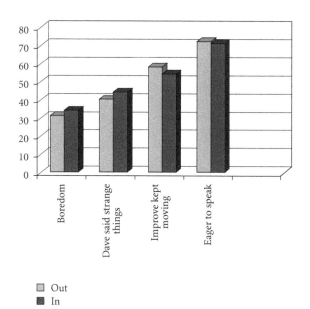

■ Out
■ In

FIGURE 4: Statistical results for "boredom," "Dave said strange things", "improvisation kept moving", and "eager to make own character speak" when EMMA is OUT of or IN an improvisation.

EMMA IN (= playing Dave, in either scenario) or OUT. When EMMA is out, the overall boredom is 31%. When EMMA is in, it changes to 34%. The results of "human Dave and EMMA Dave said strange things", respectively are 40% and 44%. When EMMA changes from in to out of an improvisation, the results of "improvisation kept moving" are, respectively, 54% to 58% and the results of "the eagerness to make own character speak" are, respectively, 71% to 72%. Although the measures were "worsened" by having EMMA in, in all cases the worsening was numerically fairly small and not statistically significant.

The preliminary results from statistical analysis also indicate that when the AI actor is involved in the improvisation, users' abilities to concentrate on the improvisation are somewhat higher in Crohn's disease scenario than school bullying scenario. When the AI actor is not involved in the improvisation, users' abilities to concentrate on the improvisation are a lot higher in school bullying than Crohn's disease. This seems very interesting, as it seems to be showing that the AI actor can make a real positive difference to an aspect of user engagement when the improvisation is comparatively uninteresting.

Moreover, as we mentioned earlier, the AI agent's responses are mainly directed based on the detected affect from users' input and at the beginning of the testing, we also concealed the fact that one character was computer controlled in order to get some fair results for the testing of the AI agent. In the debriefing sessions, it surprised us that no testing subject realized that sometimes one character was computer controlled. Generally, our statistical results gathered from the analysis of the questionnaires indicated that our AI agent performed as good as another 14–16-year-old school pupil. Analysis results also indicated that improvement is needed for negative affect detection (e.g., using context information). In our future development, we intend to employ context-based emotional modeling (e.g., using hidden Markov models) and psychological and linguistic contextual indicators to deduce affect conveyed in the input with the assistance of user profiles.

6. Conclusions

Metaphorical affective expressions have been employed to provide powerful vivid descriptions when literal expressions seem weak and unlikely to describe a feeling effectively. Such metaphorical expressions also challenge any natural language processing system if accurate semantic and sentiment interpretations are exploited. In our study, we have made a step towards automatic metaphor and affect sensing from several metaphorical figurative phenomena, including size, affect, food, animal, and anger metaphor. Although our system mainly focused on the interpretation of a few variations of the above metaphors, the study has been used as a test application and shows inspiration for theoretical metaphor studies and research. However, there is still a long way to go in order to successfully process the rich diverse variations of metaphorical language and other figurative expressions, such as humor, lies, and irony. Also, context information sometimes is very crucial for textual affect detection. These indicate that our strength needs to lie in the future development. We also intend to make the AI agent capable of recognizing and generating metaphor using metaphor ontologies to stimulate the improvisation and conduct autonomous learning of new concepts.

Overall, our work provides automatic improvisational agents for virtual drama improvisation situations. It makes a contribution to the issue of what types of automation should be included in human-robots interaction, and as part of that the issue of what types of affect should be detected and how. It also provides an opportunity for researchers to explore how emotional issues embedded in the scenarios, characters, and open-ended metaphorical expressions can be represented visually without detracting users from the learning situation. Finally, the automated conversational AI agent and the emotional animation may contribute to improving the perceived quality of social interaction.

We envisage that there is great potential for the use of our system in education in areas such as citizenship, PHSE, and drama. Beyond the classroom, our system can be easily customised for use in professional training, where face-to-face training can be difficult or expensive, such as customer services training and e-learning in the workplace.

References

[1] L. Zhang, M. Gillies, K. Dhaliwal, A. Gower, D. Robertson, and B. Crabtree, "E-drama: facilitating online role-play using an AI actor and emotionally expressive characters," *International Journal of Artificial Intelligence in Education*, vol. 19, no. 1, pp. 5–38, 2009.

[2] H. Liu and P. Singh, "ConceptNet: a practical commonsense reasoning toolkit," to appear in *BT Technology Journal*.

[3] M. A. M. Shaikh, H. Prendinger, and I. Mitsuru, "Assessing sentiment of text by semantic dependency and contextual valence analysis," in *Proceedings of the 2nd International Conference on Affective Computing and Intelligent Interaction (ACII '07)*, vol. 4738 of *Lecture Notes in Computer Science*, pp. 191–202, Lisbon, Portugal, 2007.

[4] M. Mateas, *Interactive drama, art and artificial intelligence*, Ph.D. thesis, School of Computer Science, Carnegie Mellon University, 2002.

[5] X. Zhe and A. C. Boucouvalas, "Text-to-emotion engine for real time internet communication," in *Proceedings of International Symposium on Communication Systems, Networks and DSPs*, pp. 164–168, Staffordshire University, Stafford, UK, July 2002.

[6] R. Craggs and M. Wood, "A two dimensional annotation scheme for emotion in dialogue," in *Proceedings of AAAI Spring Symposium: Exploring Attitude and Affect in Text*, 2004.

[7] A. Egges, S. Kshirsagar, and N. Magnenat-Thalmann, "A model for personality and emotion simulation," in *Proceedings of Knowledge-Based Intelligent Information and Engineering Systems (KES '03)*, vol. 2773 of *Lecture Notes in Computer Science*, pp. 453–461, Springer, Berlin, Germany, 2003.

[8] C. Elliott, J. Rickel, and J. Lester, " Integrating affective computing into animated tutoring agents," in *Proceedings of Workshop on Intelligent Interface Agents (IJCAI '97)*, pp. 113–121, 1997.

[9] R. Aylett, S. Louchart, J. Dias et al., "Unscripted narrative for affectively driven characters," *IEEE Computer Graphics and Applications*, vol. 26, no. 3, pp. 42–52, 2006.

[10] M. Cavazza, C. Smith, D. Charlton, L. Zhang, M. Turunen, and J. Hakulinen, "A 'companion' ECA with planning and activity modelling," in *Proceedings of the 7th International Conference on Autonomous Agents and Multi-Agent Systems*, pp. 1281–1284, Estoril, Portugal, 2008.

[11] L. Fainsilber and A. Ortony, "Metaphorical uses of language in the expression of emotions," *Metaphor and Symbolic Activity*, vol. 2, no. 4, pp. 239–250, 1987.

[12] Z. Kövecses, "Are there any emotion-specific metaphors?" in *Speaking of Emotions: Conceptualization and Expression*, A. Athanasiadou and E. Tabakowska, Eds., pp. 127–151, Mouton de Gruyter, New York, NY, USA, 1998.

[13] S. Fussell and M. Moss, "Figurative language in descriptions of emotional states," in *Social and Cognitive Approaches to Interpersonal Communication*, S. R. Fussell and R. J. Kreuz, Eds., Lawrence Erlbaum, 1998.

[14] J. Barnden, S. Glasbey, M. Lee, and A. Wallington, "Varieties and directions of interdomain influence in metaphor," *Metaphor and Symbol*, vol. 19, pp. 1–30, 2004.

[15] J. A. Barnden, "Metaphor, semantic preferences and context-sensitivity," in *Words and Intelligence II: Essays in Honor of Yorick Wilks*, K. Ahmad, C. Brewster, and M. Stevenson, Eds., pp. 39–62, Springer, Dordrecht, The Netherlands, 2007.

[16] A. Esuli and F. Sebastiani, "Determining term subjectivity and term orientation for opinion mining," in *Proceedings of the 11th Conference of the European Chapter of the Association for Computational Linguistics (EACL '06)*, pp. 193–200, Trento, Italy, 2006.

[17] P. Rayson, *Matrix: a statistical method and software tool for linguistic analysis through corpus comparison*, Ph.D. thesis, Lancaster University, 2003.

[18] S. Sharoff, "How to handle lexical semantics in SFL: a corpus study of purposes for using size adjectives," in *Systemic Linguistics and Corpus*, Continuum, London, UK, 2005.

[19] "ATT-Meta Databank: Examples of Usage of Metaphors of Mind," July 2008, http://www.cs.bham.ac.uk/~jab/ATT-Meta/Databank/.

[20] C. Strapparava and A. Valitutti, "WordNet-affect: an affective extension of WordNet," in *Proceedings of the 4th International Conference on Language Resources and Evaluation (LREC '04)*, pp. 1083–1086, Lisbon, Portugal, 2004.

[21] D. Glynn, "Love and anger: the grammatical structure of conceptual metaphors," *Style*, vol. 36, no. 3, pp. 541–574, 2002.

[22] M. Gillies and D. Ballin, "Integrating autonomous behavior and user control for believable agents," in *Proceedings of the 3rd International Joint Conference on Autonomous Agents and Multiagent Systems (AAMAS '04)*, pp. 336–343, Columbia University, New York, NY, USA, July 2004.

13

Immersion and Gameplay Experience: A Contingency Framework

Daniel Örtqvist[1] and Mats Liljedahl[2]

[1] *Department of Business Administration and Social Sciences (IES), Luleå University of Technology, 971 87 Luleå, Sweden*
[2] *Interactive Institute, Sonic Studio, Acusticum 4, 941 28 Piteå, Sweden*

Correspondence should be addressed to Mats Liljedahl, mats.liljedahl@tii.se

Academic Editor: Michael Katchabaw

The nature of the relationship between immersion and gameplay experience is investigated, focusing primarily on the literature related to flow. In particular, this paper proposes that immersion and gameplay experience are conceptually different, but empirically positively related through mechanisms related to flow. Furthermore, this study examines gamers' characteristics to determine the influence between immersion and gameplay experiences. The study involves 48 observations in one game setting. Regression analyses including tests for moderation and simple slope analysis are used to reveal gamers' age, experience, and understanding of the game, which moderate the relationship between immersion and gameplay experience. The results suggest that immersion is more positive for gameplay experience when the gamer lacks experience and understanding of the game as well as when the gamer is relatively older. Implications and recommendations for future research are discussed at length in the paper.

1. Introduction

To date, gaming research has covered multiple disciplines including psychology and pedagogy as well as information and communication sciences, management and business, and different disciplines of engineering. Such broad interest has influenced the diversity of the research questions and the focus of the existing studies. One area that has recently drawn significant attention is the interactive nature of the game setting, focusing in particular on gamers' experiences and their consequences. As suggested by Ermi and Mäyrä, "The act of playing a game is where the rules embedded into the game's structure start operating, and its program code starts having an effect on cultural and social, as well as artistic and commercial realities. If we want to understand what a game is, we need to understand what happens in the act of playing, and we need to understand the player and the experience of gameplay" [1]. Following this statement, the current research specifically focuses on the nature of gameplay experiences.

One powerful gaming experience is immersion, which has been mentioned by gamers [2], designers [3], and game researchers [4] alike as an important experience of interaction. Research on gaming has examined the assumption of a strong relationship between immersion and gameplay experience, such that immersion is intertwined with gameplay experience—either by conceptual overlap or through a strong, positive, and linear relationship. Consequently, studies have been conducted on the antecedents of immersion in an attempt to more fully understand how to influence consumers of games (i.e., gamers) so that they experience both immersion and subsequent gameplay experience. Studies have found that immersion is related to the realism of the game world [5] as well as environmental and contextual sounds [6]. Immersion is also said to have depth [2]. Thus, the experience of immersion—which can be benefitted or harmed by game characteristics—has been deemed critical to game enjoyment. Yet little evidence supports such a strong relationship between immersion and gameplay experience. Indeed, only a few studies have truly investigated immersion's contribution (if any) to the gameplay experience. Therefore, the current study aims to investigate the nature of the relationship between immersion and gameplay experience as well as investigate contingencies influencing the relationship between immersion and gameplay experience.

In this paper, we discuss the ways in which the gameplay experience can be conceptualized, provide a model that organizes some of its fundamental components, and conclude with an assessment of the model, including some directions for further research. It should be noted that this study is exploratory in nature. As such, the goal is to generate new areas of discussion rather than propose results that are perfectly generalizable over different settings. The paper concludes with an analytical generalization in relation to results of previous studies in similar and different settings, offering proposals and guidance for future studies.

2. Theory and Hypotheses

Gameplay experience is one of the most central targets in the development of any game. The current study focuses on the temporal gameplay experience rather than players' weighted experience based on peer influence, game reviewers, or other social references. Gameplay experience is thus defined as "an ensemble made up of the player's sensations, thoughts, feelings, actions, and meaning making in a gameplay setting" [1]. As such, at the high end gameplay experience can be fun, challenging, and victorious. Our argument that follows is that gameplay experience is an attitude directed towards the game, which serves as a general opinion about the experience from the game.

A central component in understanding the gameplay experience is the influence of immersion [7]. Immersion has been studied both in the literature on games and also in the literature examining virtual reality. Studies focusing on virtual reality have, like studies on games, focused on contextually defining immersion, attempting to understand its antecedents and its relationship to enjoyment, and also to measure immersion. We have especially reviewed the literature on immersion related to games, and we do put forth some influential studies in Table 1. These studies have some common implications for our understanding of immersion and gameplay experience. First, while many studies have viewed immersion and gameplay experience as two very close conceptual constructs, we follow results from the literature review to argue that gameplay experience is a distinct construct from immersion. Gameplay experience relates to the gamer's development of attitudes toward the game whereas immersion is rather a synonym for presence when engaging in the game [8]. Similar studies reported in Table 1 have also viewed immersion (or presence) as generally separated from enjoyment (read gameplay experience). While separate, we do expect a strong, positive, and causal relationship between immersion and gameplay experience. The experience of being present in a game is generally perceived as a positive experience; hence, such an experience should result in the gamer developing positive attitudes for the game. As such, we believe that being immersed will lead to a certain gameplay experience.

Another general finding among the studies presented in Table 1 is that there are similarities between immersion and flow experiences. We here follow Csikszentmihalyi [14–17] when conceptualizing flow as a holistic experience that people feel when they act with total involvement. We also believe that flow-like experiences could bridge the sense of being immersed to the positive evaluation leading to a sense

TABLE 1: Literature review of immersion.

Reference	Main results/implications
Brown and Cairns [8]	Analyzed players' feelings towards their favourite game and led them to propose three gradual and successive levels of player immersion: engagement, engrossment, and total immersion.
Ermi and Mäyrä [1]	Subdivided immersion into three distinct forms: sensory, challenge-based, and imaginative immersion.
Nacke and Lindley [9]	Forwarded that the experience of immersion is very close to what Csikszentmihalyi describes as a flow experience.
Douglas and Hargadon [10]	Used schema theory to understand immersion in different media. Examined antecedents to immersion in interface design, options for navigation, and other features of game. Adopted flow for understanding the consequences of immersion.
Paras and Bizzocchi [11]	Argued that educational games need to be immersive to be well functioning. The main rationale was that immersion involves an acceptance and submission to rules and conditions that create and drive the participation in the virtual environment.
Reid et al. [12]	Found a positive correlation between immersion and enjoyment. Argued immersion to be temporal, but influences gamers over time as they trigger attitudes as enjoyment.
Weibel et al. [13]	Found presence (compare immersion), flow, and enjoyment (compare gameplay experience) to be different but yet related concepts in a statistical test of two groups with about 40 participants in each.

of gameplay experience. We return to this argument in the development of hypotheses in the study.

One central point of a conceptual separation of immersion and gameplay experience is the potential to allow their relationship to be dependent on contingent influences. According to a contingency framework, the gamer's characteristics moderate the relationship between immersion and gameplay experience such that immersion is expected to actually lead to different levels of gameplay experience. We draw from the literature related to flow to explain why a perceived presence in a game (i.e., immersion) can render different attitudinal developments (i.e., gameplay experience) depending on the characteristics of the person playing the game.

Gameplay experience is largely dependent on the perceptual interpretation of the gamer (labeled gamer characteristics) interacting with the immersion. Thus, we propose

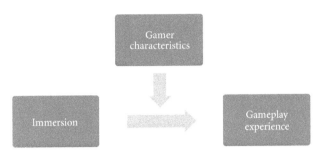

FIGURE 1: Research framework.

a model (see Figure 1) in which immersion is related to gameplay experience, but the magnitude of this influence is dependent on the characteristics of the gamer. This implies that immersion can evoke highly pleasant gameplay experiences for some gamers, but possibly even unattractive gameplay experiences for other gamers [18]. The following subsections introduce the rationale for a positive relationship between immersion and gameplay experience and discuss how gamers' age, experience, and game understanding influence the magnitude by which immersion influences gameplay experience.

2.1. Immersion and Gameplay Experience. Although the concept of immersion is frequently addressed by researchers and practitioners (i.e., players and game designers), the precision in the conceptual definition has been questioned [8]. Some have defined immersion as "the sensation of being surrounded by a completely other reality [· · ·] that takes over all of our attention, our whole perceptual apparatus" [19]. Immersion has also been defined as the "extent to which a person's cognitive and perceptual systems are tricked into believing they are somewhere other than their physical location" [20]. Overall, immersion refers to the success in a game to create an experience of escapism for the gamer. Following studies conducted on media, we refer to immersion as a psychological experience of nonmediation [21], which implies that significant immersion would relate to an experience of being in a world that is perceived to be generated by the computer instead of just using a computer [22].

Many studies treat immersion as a construct conceptually close to gameplay experience. We argue that these constructs are conceptually different, but empirically strongly related. Immersion is conceptually rooted in one's presence in the game while gameplay experience is an attitudinal evaluation of the experience of the game. Although the presence and the attitudinal evaluation are likely strongly related empirically, the conceptual foundation for immersion and gameplay experience is fundamentally different.

Researchers arguing that immersion is similar to presence often highlight that immersion is conceptually linked to Csikszentmihalyi's [14] conceptualization of flow. Following such trends, immersion has been labeled as "microflow" [18] and "gameflow" [23] to mention a few. The strong link between immersion and flow comes from the shared similarities in that both are interrupted when the task at hand is distracted; consequently, both require attention, alter one's sense of time, and lead to the sense of self being lost [8]. The conceptual arguments related to flow were developed to account for the pleasure found by immersion in everyday activities [15–17]. Although not explicitly developed to explain gameplay experience, conceptualizations of flow resonate well with reports of causes of gameplay experience and can explain how immersion and gameplay experience are different as well as why immersion is linked to rewarding gameplay experiences.

In essence, we suggest that the mechanism that transfers immersion to gameplay experience is based on flow. The flow-like experience of immersion triggers a powerful sense of gratification that is manifested in a rewarding gameplay experience (i.e., an experience that creates an attitude). In accordance with Csikszentmihalyi [17], the escape from the real world through fantasy behavior creates arousing and relaxing sensations, which in turn influence the attitudinal evaluation of the gameplay experience. As such, we propose the following hypothesis.

Hypothesis 1. Immersion is (a) conceptually different from but (b) positively related to gameplay experience.

2.2. Age. The first situational contingency is related to the gamer's age. Immersion is generally positively related to the gameplay experience, yet the level of gameplay experience developed from a certain level of immersion is dependent on the gamer's age. We argue in our theorizing that older gamers will experience more rewarding gameplay experiences from increases in immersion than younger gamers.

Much research has shown that a difference exists in the appraisal of rewards depending on age. In media work, Rettie [24] found that younger respondents did not experience the same rewards when engaging in activities on the Internet, where they were exposed to challenges perceived as stressful and irritating instead of evaluating the immersion as a rewarding state. Similar arguments have been posted in studies examining flow. For instance, Csikszentmihalyi [25] argued that with age immersion-like experiences become increasingly rare; therefore, each experience of immersion adds to the development of positive attitudes (i.e., gameplay experience in this case). Thus, we suggest that age has a moderating influence on the relationship between immersion and gameplay experience.

Hypothesis 2. Age moderates the relationship between immersion and gameplay experience such that increases in immersion more positively influence the gameplay experience for gamers who are older compared to gamers who are younger.

2.3. Experience. The second situational contingency is related to the gamer's experience of gaming. In specific, we suggest that the level of gameplay experience developed from a certain level of immersion will be dependent on the gamer's experience of gaming. We argue in our theorizing that gamers with low gaming experience will experience more rewarding gameplay experiences from increases in immersion than gamers with high gaming experience.

Gamers with higher gaming experience will not experience the same reward effects from yet another flow-like experience; rather, they are more used to the transitions between the real and the created reality [25]. As such, the emotional influence triggering the attitudinal evaluation of the gaming experience would likely be deemed as less rewarding for a more experienced gamer compared to a novice gamer. Indeed, Novak et al. [26] examined online experiences and found that "the degree to which the online experience is compelling appears to decrease with years of experience online." As such, it is possible to assume that—although experiencing a presence—gamers with significant experience would consider the fact that they were facing challenges below their skill threshold when evaluating and forming their attitudes of gameplay experience. Hence, we propose that experience moderates the influence of immersion on gameplay experience.

Hypothesis 3. Gaming experience moderates the relationship between immersion and gameplay experience such that increases in immersion more positively influence the gameplay experience for gamers with low gaming experience compared to gamers with high gaming experience.

2.4. Game Understanding. The third situational contingency is related to the gamer's understanding of the game, suggesting that the level of gameplay experience developed from a certain level of immersion will be dependent on the gamer's understanding of the game. We argue that gamers with a limited understanding of the game will experience more rewarding gameplay experiences from increases in immersion compared to gamers with a higher level of understanding of the game.

Gamers with a comparably lower understanding of the game, but who still feel a presence in the game (i.e., immersion), will likely use their senses to a greater degree to fill in information when they do not understand the situation. This type of presence would likely positively influence the attitudinal evaluation of the gameplay experience, as it requires the gamer to be alert and emotionally intertwined with the game to a greater extent than a gamer who does not need to understand or learn in order to complete the game. Thus, it is more likely that a person who does not extensively use all the senses relies on less concentration, which has been proven to interrupt flow-like situations and lead to a more negative evaluation of the experience [27]. In addition, experienced challenges are positively related to flow-like experiences, transforming into rewarding attitudinal evaluations (see, for instance, Kim et al. [28]), such as evaluations of gameplay experience. Based on this argument, we propose that game understanding moderates the relationship between immersion and gameplay experience.

Hypothesis 4. Game understanding moderates the relationship between immersion and gameplay experience such that increases in immersion more positively influence the

gameplay experience for gamers with less game understanding than gamers with more game understanding.

3. Research Methods

The present study employed an experimental approach to test the nature of the relationship between immersion and gameplay experience and to investigate contingencies to this relationship. We used a single game setting—Beowulf—as our experimental vehicle (see next sub-section for an introduction to Beowulf). One advantage of sampling from a single game setting compared to multiple settings is reduced external variance, as universal factors are deemed to be more prominent in isolation. All gamers experienced the same game and played for the same length of time, thereby reducing alternative explanations for findings. Also, our selected game was audio based and developed for short gaming sessions. The plot and layout of the game was simple enough for the surveyed gamers to quickly get started with the game. These features of the game provided advantages given that we needed to do the study with individuals who played the game for only a short while. While the game setting has its unique characteristics, it still has common features for how to relate to the game (even if this is driven more by sound compared to graphics). We believe the game to be representative in how immersion and gameplay experience relate and are influenced by gamers' characteristics. The following subsections describe the research setting (i.e., the game), the sample and data collection, and the technique for measuring the phenomena under study.

3.1. Research Setting. Beowulf [29] is a heroic epic poem that experts believe was written sometime between 700 and 1000 A.D. It is sometimes referred to as England's national epic. In the Beowulf game used in the current study, one small episode of the long poem is lifted out and translated into a gameplay scenario. The episode in the poem narrates how the Scandinavian hero Beowulf defeats the monster Grendel in its lair.

In the game, Grendel lurks in a dark system of caves and tunnels inhabited not only by the monster itself, but also by wolverines, snakes, bats, and a host of potential dangers. As our hero enters the first cave, a gust of wind blows out his torch and darkness descends. The player, as Beowulf, must now completely trust in his/her hearing to navigate a route to the monster, with only minimal help from a simple revealing map. The task is to successfully navigate the hazards lying between the cave entrance and the monster. The player interprets the myriad of sounds that fill the environment both for navigation and for confrontational combat situations. Finally, the monster must be located and dispatched with a well-timed swing of Beowulf's sword.

A majority of the output stimuli from the game are sounds; indeed, gameplay is driven almost entirely by audio, with only sparse and coarse-grained visuals. This approach is called an "audio mostly game." An audio mostly game is not a game for visually impaired persons; rather, it is a game for hearing, possibly sighted persons who have various reasons for requesting the shift from eye to ear. In this sense, the

Beowulf project is different from the numerous audio-only game projects for persons who are visually impaired.

A nondetailed map represents the game world graphically. This map shows only the parts of the cave system that the player has visited so far. The map slowly reveals the game world as the player progresses through and explores it. Figure 2 shows one example of what this revealing map can look like after a couple of minutes of play.

Navigating and moving in the game world are controlled using the arrow keys on the computer keyboard in the same way as in the Sleuth game [30]. The blue triangular arrow in Figure 2 shows both the players' current position and current direction: north, south, east, or west. The right arrow key turns the current direction 90 degrees clockwise; the left arrow key turns the current direction 90 degrees anticlockwise. If the current direction is "east," as in Figure 2, pressing the right arrow key will alter the current direction to "south" while pressing the left arrow key will alter the current direction to "north." The up arrow key moves the current position one "map point" step in the current direction. In the situation illustrated by Figure 2, pressing the up arrow key will move the player one step east (right). If the player tries to move to a map point that does not exist, the blue arrow is not advanced, and a "bump" sound is played, indicating that the player hit a wall.

Having reduced the visual support to merely a simple revealing map, the soundscape perceptually takes several steps forward and becomes crucial in moving around the game world and handling the challenges and situations encountered. The soundscape is three dimensional. Players localize items and find directions by listening, moving, and turning, using the same stereophonic principles as in real life. Headphones ensure that players experience the necessary stereo sound experience.

Beowulf is a first-person listener game in which the player hears through Beowulf's ears. Very little visual information is provided to guide the player's perception. Instead Beowulf's soundscape takes over most of the responsibility for communicating the properties of the game world, traditionally done through graphics. For this to work, all sounds have to be very realistic, of high quality, and carefully implemented.

3.2. Sample and Data Collection Procedures.
Data were collected from a quota sample consisting of 48 individuals in an experimental setting. Four settings were used to collect data in order to ensure that sufficient variance existed in the data; thus, the data collection design was similar to a stratified sample. Each of the four groups comprised 12 respondents. Group 1 was made up of music conservatory students who were 20 to 25 years old. Group 2 was high school students from southwest Sweden who were 13 to 15 years old. Group 3 was art and design students who were 20 to 25 years old. Group 4 was high school students from northeast Sweden who were 13 to 15 years old. This type and size of sample is quite common in similar studies examining immersion. Similar studies have even addressed similar research questions with similar analytic methods using 25 respondents [9].

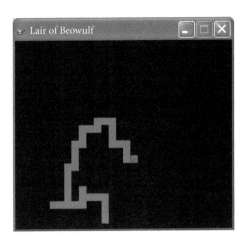

FIGURE 2: The revealing map.

Data were collected in an experiment setting in which respondents were asked to first try out the game and then give immediate feedback. As accuracy in filling out questionnaires decreases with time, we found it important that the respondents be able to discuss flow in an environment both physically and temporally close to their experience. During the test, the subjects first got a short introduction to the game, its background, and the Beowulf story as well as instructions on how to navigate in the game using the arrow keys on the computer keyboard. The test situation was conducted on identical laptops (Apple MacBook Pro), with all subjects using Koss Portapro headphones to ensure consistent audio parameters.

After having played the game for approximately ten minutes, the subjects started to fill out the questionnaire (described in Section 3.3). The test session was ended once the questionnaire was completed. Each session lasted approximately 30 minutes and was supervised by one of the authors.

3.3. Measurement.
A questionnaire was developed and administered to the sample in the gaming setting. The respondents were asked to complete the questionnaire after they had played the game for about ten minutes. The questionnaire contained in total 24 questions using a 7-point Likert scale with the same anchors (1 = strongly disagree, and 7 = strongly agree) and 6 open-ended questions in which the respondents could provide more qualitative data on the experiences with the game.

3.3.1. Gameplay Experience.
Gameplay experience was measured using three items on a seven-point Likert scale. The items were related to experiences of the game, including the gamers' attitude to the time it took to experience the game as interesting, the number of challenges in the game, and the amount of time needed to complete the game. A typical item was worded "It took very long time to play the game" (reversed scored). Gamers who expressed that they quickly became emotionally engaged in the game, that they were interested in more challenges, and that the game ended too fast were interpreted as exhibiting a high gameplay

experience. The average gameplay experience was 5.24, with a standard deviation of 1.20.

3.3.2. Immersion. Immersion was measured as a composite construct from two items, both assessed on a seven-point Likert scale. The items were related to the gamers' sense of being completely engaged in the game as well as how easy it was to grasp their presence in the gaming world. A typical item was worded: "I was completely engaged in the game". The average immersion in the sample was 5.24, with a standard deviation of 1.18.

3.3.3. Age. The study was conducted on a sample with two age categories: younger gamers (i.e., gamers between 12 and 18 years of age) and slightly older gamers (i.e., between 19 and 25 years of age). Due to the within-group homogeneity of the responses, age was categorized as a dichotomous variable in which the younger group was coded as 1 and the older groups as 2. Half (50%) of the sample were younger gamers.

3.3.4. Gaming Experience. Gaming experience was comprised of a single item assessed on a seven-point Likert scale. Gamers were asked to respond to a statement about how frequently they play games (i.e., "I often play computer games"), which was used as a proxy for gaming experience. The average response was 4.33, with a standard deviation of 2.06.

3.3.5. Game Understanding. Game understanding was measured using four items assessed on a seven-point Likert scale. The items related to the gamers' experience—namely, they found it easy to know when to use items embedded in the game, easy to understand what to do in the game, easy to understand when things happened, and easy to know how to act when things happened. A typical item was worded: "I immediately understood when I was under attack in the game". The average response was 4.46, with a standard deviation of 1.42.

3.4. Methods for Analyses. Hypotheses were tested by employing regression analyses following recommendations for evaluation of moderation. To retain statistical power due to the number of observations, the hypotheses were tested in isolation.

4. Results

First, we evaluated the psychometric properties of the variables adopted to test the hypotheses. Table 2 presents the descriptive statistics and the correlations of the variables in the study. We found initial support for our hypothesis as the measure of immersion was positively related to gameplay experience. The threat of multicollinearity is low: the highest correlation coefficient is about .39. To reduce multicollinearity among the independent variables and the interaction terms, the variables used to compute interaction terms were standardized. Reliability estimates (i.e., Cronbach's alpha)

TABLE 2: Descriptive Statistics.

	Min	Max	Ave	St.D.	1	2	3	4	5
(1) Gameplay experience	1.67	7.00	5.24	1.20	1.00				
(2) Immersion	2.00	7.00	5.24	1.18	.35*	1.00			
(3) Age	1.00	2.00	1.52	0.50	.24	.27	1.00		
(4) Experience	1.00	7.00	4.33	2.06	.22	.08	.07	1.00	
(5) Game understanding	1.50	7.00	4.46	1.42	.38**	.39**	.17	.07	1.00

$N = 48$, ***$P < .001$, **$P < .01$, *$P < .05$.

were acceptable (i.e., $\alpha > .70$) in relation to recommended levels (Nunnally [31]; Fornell and Larcker [32]).

After establishing initial support (i.e., by correlational analyses) for hypothesized relationships and support for the psychometric properties of the studied variables, we continued by examination of the hypotheses. First, we tested the argument that immersion and gameplay experience are two distinct constructs which are positively related. Second, we tested the moderation by gamers' characteristics (i.e., age, experience, and game understanding). In order to retain statistical power due to the sample size we tested the moderating influences in separate models. We followed general guidelines for how to test categorical and continuous moderation effects (Aiken and West [33]; Baron and Kenny [34]).

4.1. Immersion and Gameplay Experience. We argued in the first hypothesis that immersion is (a) conceptually different from and (b) positively related to gameplay experience. To test the first part of the hypothesis we performed a simultaneous principal component analysis with Oblimin Kaiser normalization of the items (i.e., variables) measuring immersion and gameplay experience. If the factor analysis extracts two factors with eigenvalues above one, and where loadings of items are according to measurement, then the first part of the hypothesis is supported. Secondly, to test whether immersion and gameplay experience are positively related, we performed a simple regression analysis where immersion is the independent variable and with gameplay experience is the dependent variable.

A principal component analysis with Oblimin Kaiser normalization (four rotations) revealed two distinct factors with eigenvalues over one (see Table 3). The first factor—immersion—contained two items which both related to the immersion factor with loadings between .77 and .85, and with simultaneous low loadings to the gameplay experience factor (i.e., loadings below .10). Similarly, the three items measuring gameplay experience revealed loadings between .67 and .85 on gameplay experience, and simultaneous loadings below .15 on the immersion factor. This supports the first part of the hypothesis, that immersion is conceptually different from gameplay experience.

The second part of the hypothesis concerned the influence by immersion on gameplay experience. Regression analysis reveals that immersion explains 10% of the variance in gameplay experience according to the adjusted R

TABLE 3: Principal component analysis.

Factors	Variables	Factor	
		Gameplay experience	Immersion
Immersion	Variable 1	,070	**,766**
	Variable 2	−,057	**,848**
Gameplay experience	Variable 3	**,727**	−,091
	Variable 4	**,674**	,149
	Variable 5	**,850**	−,008

TABLE 4: Regression results.

	Unstandardized coefficients		Standardized coefficients	T	Sig.
	B	Std. Error	Beta	B	Std. Error
(Constant)	5,236	,164		31,984	,000
Immersion	,412	,165	,345	2,491	,016

[a] Dependent variable: gameplay experience.

square value. Further, the regression model is significant ($F = 6,21^*$), and immersion is a significant predictor of gameplay experience with a standardized coefficient of .35 (see Table 4). This supports the second part of the hypothesis that immersion is positively related to gameplay experience. Overall, we found support for hypothesis one, and thereby we found support for a chain reaction which sets of in the flow-like experience of being immersed, which in turn will render positive attitudes, and finally be positively related to gameplay experience. As we found support for our central hypothesis, we continue by examining if this influence is dependent upon characteristics of the gamer.

4.2. Age. We next examine the role of the gamers' age as a moderating variable on the relationship between immersion and gameplay experience. We found the model including the interaction term to explain 17% of the variance in gameplay experience, which should be compared to the 10% explained by immersion only. The regression model is significant ($F = 4.19^*$) and the interaction term (immersion × age) is significant (see Table 5), which implies that the relationship between immersion and gameplay experience is dependent on the gamers' age, in accordance with the second hypothesis. As such this test strongly supported hypothesis two as the inclusion of the interaction term explained substantially more variance in the dependent variable and since the interaction term was significant. We continue by examining the support for hypothesis two by examining the nature of the interaction effect. First we plot the interaction effect, and thereafter we perform simple slope analyses.

Figure 3 plots the relationship between immersion and gameplay experience at the two age groups studied. We have followed guidelines for plotting moderation effects including categorical variables. As obvious from the plot, both slopes are positive but the slope for the older group is steeper suggesting that immersion is more important for the older group, and that the younger group still rates the gameplay

TABLE 5: Regression results.

Coefficients	Unstandardized coefficients		Standardized coefficients	T	Sig.
	B	Std. Error	Beta	B	Std. Error
(Constant)	5,335	,164		32,505	,000
Immersion	,482	,175	,403	2,756	,008
Age	,155	,166	,130	,933	,356
Immersion × Age	−,377	,179	−,297	−2,103	,041

[a] Dependent variable: gameplay experience.

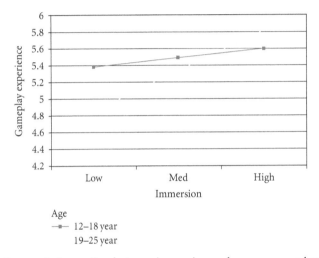

FIGURE 3: Interaction between immersion and age on gameplay experience.

TABLE 6: Simple slope analysis.

	Categorical moderator	
	12–18 years	19–25 years
Simple slope	0,105	0,482
Standard error	0,207	0,176
T-value	0,506	2,738
Significance	0,615	0,009
Degrees of freedom	44	

experience higher (compared to the older group) when immersion is low.

Further analysis of these slopes (as can be viewed in Table 6) shows that the slopes are differently positive (.11 for the younger group and .48 for the older group). However, only the older group is significant (T-value > 1.96; $P <$ .05). Therefore, it is not possible to state that immersion has any influence whatsoever for the gameplay experience of the younger group, while we provide evidence for the importance of immersion for the older group. Hence, the results are in line with our arguments that with age the flow-like experience of immersion adds more to the development of positive attitudes (i.e., gameplay experience in this case). As such we find support for hypothesis two.

TABLE 7: Regression results.

	Unstandardized coefficients		Standardized coefficients	T	Sig.
	B	Std. Error	Beta	B	Std. Error
(Constant)	5,257	,159		33,061	,000
Immersion	,332	,165	,277	2,012	,050
Gaming experience	,235	,161	,197	1,465	,150
Immersion × Gaming experience	−,288	,167	−,237	−1,726	,091

[a] Dependent variable: gameplay experience.

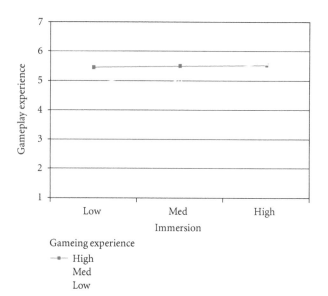

FIGURE 4: Interaction between immersion and gaming experience on gameplay experience.

TABLE 8: Simple slope analysis.

	Continuous Moderator		
	Low	Med	High
Simple slope	0.620	0.332	0.044
Standard error	0.207	0.213	0.259
T-value	3.000	1.562	0.170
Significance	0.005	0.126	0.866
Degrees of freedom		44	

4.3. Experience. We next examine the role of gaming experience as a moderating variable on the relationship between immersion and gameplay experience. The theoretical logic underpinning this argument is that increases in immersion more positively influence the gameplay experience for gamers with low gaming experience compared to gamers with high gaming experience. As such, we expect gamers with low gaming experience to have the most positive effect (i.e., the highest slope) of immersion on gameplay experience. We found the model, including the interaction term, to explain 16% of the variance in gameplay experience, which should be compared to the 10% explained by immersion only. The regression model is significant ($F = 3.89^*$), but the interaction term is marginally significant (i.e., $P < .10$). As such, we find but partial support for the moderating relationship of gaming experience on immersion-gameplay experience relationship (see Table 7 for more details on the results). Since the interaction term is at least marginally significant, we continue by examining the support for hypothesis three by examining the nature of the interaction effect. First we plot the interaction effect, and thereafter we perform simple slope analyses.

Figure 4 plots the relationship between immersion and gameplay experience at three levels of gamers' experience, low corresponds to one standard deviation below average, med stands for average, and high is one standard deviation above average. We have followed guidelines for plotting moderation effects including continuous variables. As obvious from the plot, all three slopes are positive, but the slope for gamers with lower experience is more steep compared to the other slopes. In fact, the slope for the experienced gamers seems almost to indicate no relationship between immersion and gameplay experience.

Further analyses (as can be viewed in Table 8) reveal all three slopes to be positive. However, only the simple slope for the gamers with low experience is significant (T-value > 1.96; $P < .05$). Therefore, it is not possible to state that immersion has any influence whatsoever for the gameplay experience of the gamers with average or high experience, while we provide evidence for the importance of immersion for the group with low experience. Hence, we find partial support for hypothesis three as the interaction term was marginally significant and the slopes behaved as predicted in the hypothesis.

4.4. Game Understanding. We next examine the role of the gamers' understanding for the game as a moderating variable on the relationship between immersion and gameplay experience. We found the model including the interaction term to explain 23% of the variance in gameplay experience, which should be compared to the 10% explained by immersion only. The regression model is significant ($F = 5.76^{**}$) and the interaction term is significant, which implies that the relationship between immersion and gameplay experience is dependent on gamers' understanding for the game, in accordance with the fourth hypothesis. As such, this test strongly supported hypothesis four as the inclusion of the interaction term (immersion × game understanding) explained substantially more variance in the dependent variable and since the interaction term was significant (see Table 9 for full details). We continue by examining the support for hypothesis four by examining the nature of the interaction effect. First, we plot the interaction effect, and thereafter we perform simple slope analyses.

Figure 5 plots the relationship between immersion and gameplay experience at three levels of game understanding, low corresponds to one standard deviation below average, med stands for average, and high is one standard deviation above average. We have followed guidelines for plotting moderation effects including continuous variables. As obvious

TABLE 9: Regression results.

	Unstandardized coefficients		Standardized coefficients	T	Sig.
	B	Std. Error	Beta	B	Std. Error
(Constant)	5,356	,159		33,605	,000
Immersion	,395	,173	,330	2,280	,027
Game understanding	,251	,171	,210	1,474	,148
Immersion × Game understanding	−,315	,133	−,318	−2,367	,022

[a] Dependent variable: gameplay experience.

TABLE 10: Simple slope analysis.

	Continuous moderator		
	Low	Med	High
Simple slope	0,710	0,395	0,080
Standard error	0,249	0,171	0,184
T-value	2,851	2,314	0,434
Significance	0,007	0,025	0,667
Degrees of freedom		44	

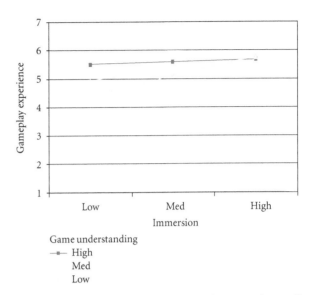

FIGURE 5: Interaction between immersion and game understanding on gameplay experience.

from the plot, all three slopes are positive, but the slope for the gamers with low game understanding is more steep compared to the other slopes. In fact, the slope for gamers' experiencing a high game understanding seems almost to indicate no relationship between immersion and gameplay experience.

Further analyses (as can be viewed in Table 10) reveal all three slopes to be positive. However, the simple slope for gamers with low and average game understanding is positive and significant (T-value > 1.96; $P < .05$). Therefore, it is not possible to state that immersion has any influence for the gameplay experience of gamers' with high understanding for the game, while we provide evidence for the importance of immersion for the group with low and average game understanding. Hence, we find support for hypothesis four as the interaction term was significant, and the slopes behaved as predicted in the hypothesis.

5. Discussion and Conclusions

The aim of this study was to examine the relationship between immersion and gameplay experience. Specifically, this study conceptually differentiated between immersion and gameplay experience and examined contingencies influencing the magnitude of influence between immersion and gameplay experience. We found support for our arguments based upon arguments related to flow; moreover, we determined that immersion is a separate, although empirically related construct to gameplay experience. Finally, several individual characteristics influenced the magnitude by which immersion influences gameplay experience.

Specifically, this study supports the claim that immersion can create a flow-like sense which in turn fosters a positive attitude (i.e., gaming experience) towards the gaming situation. We also established that the characteristics of the gamer can influence how likely it is that flow-like states are actually achieved. As such, we proposed and found support for the moderating role of age: older individuals experienced more impact on gameplay experience from immersion. This study also found marginally significant support for the moderating role of experience, implying that individuals with limited gaming experience perceived larger effects from immersion on gameplay experience. This study also found support for the moderating role of game understanding, such that individuals with less game understanding experienced larger effects from immersion upon gameplay experience. Interestingly, in some of the settings, it seemed that immersion did not influence gameplay experience at all.

The separation of immersion and gameplay experience in modeling, together with tests of moderation effects, makes possible a deeper understanding of the role and impact of creating immersion in games. In fact, the effect of immersion is not always positively and strongly related to gameplay experience. To a large extent, it depends on gamers' characteristics (i.e., age, experience, and understanding). This implies that game development is much more complex than merely creating senses of escapism for the gamer; rather, it is about combining the game plot with the characteristics of the intended segment of gamers.

Further, the present study holds implications for research on human-computer interaction as it highlights that gaming follows what has been labeled "the pleasure principle" [10]. That is, individuals who become immersed in their interaction with the game will experience affective pleasures and hence evaluate the game experience positively. The conceptualizations and empirical tests also strengthens recent developments in gaming literature that supports that flow can be used to understand the affective reactions of gamers, and that immersion is a core central experience for developing these affective reactions [9]. Further, by following developments in flow literature we also learn that the characteristics of the gamer influence the magnitude by which immersion actually triggers flow-like states that influence and develop affective pleasures and thereby gameplay experience.

As with any study, limitations do exist. The sample in the current study was rather limited and specific, meaning it may be difficult to generalize the results to other contexts. However, analytical arguments do not suggest that this sample is specific in any way; thus, further testing of these results in other samples should be conducted in order to generalize findings. Another potential limitation is related to the very specific game setting studied. While choosing a specific game setting has several advantageous (as it for instance reduces external variance and noise) it could also provide differences which make the results difficult to generalize for other games. Although our current belief is that the results from this study have potential to transfer to similar settings, as they are based on sound conceptual arguments and relate well to previous literature, they should still be replicated to examine the full potential of generalizability from the study. In addition, although the study design had several advantages, it actually proposed a limitation in terms of the potential to test causality. Although it is likely that immersion influences gameplay experience rather than the opposite, future studies should test a cross-lagged design to examine whether the relationship between immersion and gameplay experience takes the nature of regular, reversed, or reciprocal causation.

We also acknowledge that other factors could be relevant to include in a study on gameplay experience besides those used in this study. Our goal was to produce a very restricted set of insights to clarify points from the well-known and established literature. As such, we only needed constructs that captured immersion, gamers' characteristics, and gameplay experience. Of course, other constructs related to gamers' characteristics should be examined in future research, as those adopted here are only examples.

Despite the limitations, we believe the merit of this study is that it makes a number of contributions to the emerging literature on gameplay experience. Specifically, it clarifies the distinction and relation between immersion and gameplay experience, which most studies seem to have neglected. We also use several analytical techniques to evaluate the robustness of our findings.

References

[1] L. Ermi and F. Mayra, "Changing views: worlds in play," in *Proceedings of the 2nd International Conference on Digital Games Research Association (DiGRA '05)*, S. de Castell and J. Jenson, Eds., pp. 15–27, Vancouver, Canada, June 2005.

[2] T. Chown, "Review: Championship Manager 00/01," 2000, http://www.gamesdomain.co.uk/gdreview/zones/reviews/pc/nov00/cm001.html.

[3] E. Swing, "Adding immersion to collaborative tools," in *Proceedings of the 5th Symposium on the Virtual Reality Modeling Language (VRML '00)*, pp. 63–68, February 2000.

[4] A. Radford, "Games and learning about form in architecture," *Automation in Construction*, vol. 9, no. 4, pp. 379–385, 2000.

[5] F. Housten, "Review: Thief: The Dark Project," 1998, http://gamesdomain.com/gdreview/zones/pc/dec98/thief.html.

[6] D. Benge, "Review: Sanatorium," http://www.gamesdomain.co.uk/gdreview/zones/reviews/pc/jun98/sanity.html.

[7] L. Nacke and C. A. Lindley, "Flow and immersion in first-person shooters: measuring the player's gameplay experience," in *Proceedings of the Conference on Future Play: Research, Play, Share*, pp. 81–88, Toronto, Canada, 2008.

[8] E. Brown and P. Cairns, "A grounded investigation of game immersion," in *Extended Abstracts on Human Factors and Computing Systems (CHI '04)*, pp. 1297–1300, ACM Press, Vienna, Austria, April 2004.

[9] L. Nacke and C. A. Lindley, "Flow and immersion in first-person shooters: measuring the player's gameplay experience," in *Proceedings of the Conference on Future Play: Research, Play, Share, Future Play*, pp. 81–88, November 2008.

[10] Y. Douglas and A. Hargadon, "The pleasure principle: immersion, engagement, flow," in *Proceedings of the 11th Conference on Hypertext and Hypermedia*, pp. 153–160, 2000.

[11] B. Paras and J. Bizzocchi, "Game, motivation, and effective learning: an integrated model for educational game design," in *Proceedings of the 2nd International Conference on Digital Games Research Association (DiGRA '05)*, Vancouver, Canada, June 2005.

[12] J. Reid, E. Geelhoed, R. Hull, K. Cater, and B. Clayton, "Parallel worlds: immersion in location-based experiences," in *Extended Abstracts on Human Factors in Computing Systems (CHI '05)*, pp. 1733–1736, Portland, Ore, USA, 2005.

[13] D. Weibel, B. Wissmath, S. Habegger, Y. Steiner, and R. Groner, "Playing online games against computer- vs. human-controlled opponents: effects on presence, flow, and enjoyment," *Computers in Human Behavior*, vol. 24, no. 5, pp. 2274–2291, 2008.

[14] M. Csikszentmihalyi, *Flow: The Psychology of Optimal Experience*, Harper Perennial, New York, NY, USA, 1990.

[15] M. Csikszentmihalyi, "The future of flow," in *Optimal Experience: Psychological Studies of Flow in Consciousness*, M. Csikszentmihalyi and I. S. Csikszentmihalyi, Eds., pp. 364–383, Cambridge University Press, New York, NY, USA, 1988.

[16] M. Csikszentmihalyi, "The flow experience and its significance for human psychology," in *Optimal Experience: Psychological Studies of Flow in Consciousness*, M. Csikszentmihalyi and I. S. Csikszentmihalyi, Eds., pp. 15–35, Cambridge University Press, New York, NY, USA, 1988.

[17] M. Csikszentmihalyi, *Finding Flow: The Psychology of Engagement with Everyday Life*, Basic Books, New York, NY, USA, 1997.

[18] M. Blythe and M. Hassenzahl, "The semantics of fun: differentiating enjoyable experiences," in *Funology: From Usability to Enjoyment*, M. A. Blythe, K. Overbeeke, A. F. Monk, and P. C. Wright, Eds., pp. 91–100, Kluwer Academic Publishers, Dordrecht, The Netherlands, 2003.

[19] J. Murray, *Hamlet on the Holodeck: The Future of Narrative in Cyberspace*, The MIT Press, Cambridge, UK, 1997.

[20] E. Patrick, D. Cosgrove, A. Slavkovic, J. A. Rode, T. Verratti, and G. Chiselko, "Using a large projection screen as an alternative to head-mounted displays for virtual environments," in *Proceedings of the SIGCHI Conference on Human Factors in Computing Systems*, pp. 478–485, The Hague, The Netherlands, 2000.

[21] D. Freeman, "Creating emotion in games: the craft and art of Emotioneering," *Computers in Entertainment*, vol. 2, no. 3, pp. 15–15, 2004.

[22] M. Lombard and T. Ditton, "At the heart of it all: the concept of presence," *Journal of Computer-Mediated Communication*, vol. 3, no. 2, 1997.

[23] A. Järvinen, S. Heliö, and F. Mäyrä, "Communication and community in digital entertainment services: prestudy," Tech. Rep. Hypermedia Laboratory Net Series 2, University of Tampere, Tampere, Fla, USA, 2002, http://tampub.uta.fi/tup/951-44-5432-4.pdf .

[24] R. Rettie, "An exploration of flow during internet use," *Internet Research*, vol. 11, no. 2, pp. 103–113, 2001.

[25] M. Csikszentmihalyi, *Flow and the Psychology of Discovery and Invention*, Harper Perennial, New York, NY, USA, 1997.

[26] T. P. Novak, D. L. Hoffman, and Y. F. Yung, "Measuring the customer experience in online environments: a structural modeling approach," *Marketing Science*, vol. 19, no. 1, pp. 22–42, 2000.

[27] M. Csikszentmihalyi, *Beyond Boredom and Anxiety*, Jossey-Bass, San Francisco, Calif, USA, 1975.

[28] Y. Y. Kim, S. Oh, and H. Lee, "What makes people experience flow? Social characteristics of online games," *International Journal of Advanced Media and Communication*, vol. 1, no. 1, pp. 76–91, 2005.

[29] M. Liljedahl, N. Papworth, and S. Lindberg, "Beowulf—an audio mostly game," in *Proceedings of the International Conference on Advances in Computer Entertainment Technology (ACE '07)*, vol. 203, pp. 200–203, 2007.

[30] T. Drewes, E. Mynatt, and M. Gandy, "Sleuth: an audio experience," in *Proceedings of International Conference on Auditory Display (ICAD '00)*, Atlanta, Ga, USA, April 2000.

[31] J. C. Nunally, *Psychometric Theory*, McGraw-Hill, New York, NY, USA, 1978.

[32] C. Fornell and D. F. Larcker, "Evaluating structural equation models with unobservable variables and measurement error," *Journal of Marketing Research*, vol. 18, no. 1, pp. 39–50, 1981.

[33] L. S. Aiken and S. G. West, *Multiple Regression: Testing and Interpreting Interactions*, Sage, Newbury Park, Calif, USA, 1991.

[34] R. M. Baron and D. A. Kenny, "The moderator-mediator variable distinction in social psychological research. Conceptual, strategic, and statistical considerations," *Journal of Personality and Social Psychology*, vol. 51, no. 6, pp. 1173–1182, 1986.

14

Automatic Real-Time Generation of Floor Plans Based on Squarified Treemaps Algorithm

Fernando Marson and Soraia Raupp Musse

Graduate Programme in Computer Science, PUCRS, Avenue Ipiranga, 6681, Building 32, Porto Alegre, RS, Brazil

Correspondence should be addressed to Soraia Raupp Musse, soraia.musse@pucrs.br

Academic Editor: Rafael Bidarra

A novel approach to generate house floor plans with semantic information is presented. The basis of this model is the squarified treemaps algorithm. Previously, this algorithm has been used to create graphical representations based on hierarchical information, such as, directory structures and organization structures. Adapted to floor plans generation, this model allows the creation of internal house structures with information about their features and functionalities. The main contributions are related to the robustness, flexibility, and simplicity of the proposed approach to create floor plans in real-time. Results show that different and realistic floor plans can be created by adjusting a few parameters.

1. Introduction

Considering the game titles released in the last decade, the increase in visual complexity of Virtual Environments (VE) used as scenarios is noticed. Huge cities can be found in games like the GTA franchise (http://www.rockstargames.com/IV), Assassin's Creed (http://assassinscreed.us.ubi.com), and Left 4 Dead (http://www.l4d.com) which is remarkable. Apart from the cities, it may be necessary to create whole worlds, as in the case of Massively Multiplayer On-line Games (MMOGs), represented by World of Warcraft (http://www.worldofwarcraft.com) and Perfect World (http://www.perfectworld.com). As a consequence, the cost and time to develop a game are also increased.

The creation of a VE requires previous knowledge in several areas of expertise. Hence, it is necessary to allocate a team of professionals to create, maintain, and reuse large VEs. Some of the main problems faced when developing interactive virtual environments are described in [1] as the nonextensibility, limited interoperability, poor scalability, monolithic architecture, among others.

A possible solution to these problems is the use of procedural generation techniques [2], which allow the creation of

VE content just by setting input parameters. Such approaches may be used to generate terrains, buildings, characters, items, weapons, quests, and even stories adding a broad range of elements, but in a controlled way. A perfect example to illustrate the potential use of procedural contents generation is the game Spore (http://www.spore.com) . In this game, procedural techniques are used to create characters, vehicles, buildings [3], textures [4], and planets [5]. Even the music is created using this kind of technique.

There are some academic and commercial solutions that provide the creation of buildings with great realism. Nevertheless, there are few studies that focus on the generation of building interiors. Our model proposes a novel solution to generate floor plans of buildings using just a few parameters and constraints. After the floor plan generation, it creates a three-dimensional representation of the construction. In all generated rooms in the floor plan; semantic information is included to allow simulations involving virtual humans.

The remainder of this paper is organized as follows: in Section 2 we discuss some work found in literature, while in Section 3 we describe our model to generate floor plans. Section 4 discusses some obtained results, and the final considerations are drawn in Section 5.

2. Related Work

The process of creating large virtual cities can take considerable time and resources to be accomplished. Parish and Müller [7] present a model that allows the generation of a three-dimensional city from sociostatistical and geographical maps. The method builds the road network using an extended L-Systems. After creating the streets, the system extracts the information about blocks. Through a subdivision process, lots are created. A building is placed at each lot, generated by another module based on L-Systems. With this information, the system generates the three-dimensional geometric model of the city, and textures are added to provide greater realism to the final model.

A method to generate procedural "pseudoinfinite" virtual cities in real-time is proposed by Greuter et al. [8]. The area of the city is mapped into a grid defined by a given granularity and a global seed. Each cell in the grid has a local seed that can be used to create building generation parameters. A print foot is produced by combining randomly generated polygons in an iterative process, and the building geometries are extruded from a set of floor plans. To optimize the rendering process, a view *frustrum* is implemented to determine the visibility of virtual world objects before their generation, so that only visible elements are generated. Besides the generation of the environment, the appearance of the buildings can be improved. In this context, Müller et al. [9] propose a shape grammar called CGA Shapes, focused on the generation of buildings with high visual quality and geometric details. Using some rules, the user can describe geometric shapes and specify the interactions between hierarchical groups in order to create a geometrically complex object. In addition, the user can interact dynamically in all stages of creation.

The techniques presented previously are focused on the external appearance of buildings, without concerning their interior. Martin [10] introduces an algorithm to create floor plans of houses. The process consists of three main phases. In the first step of the procedure, a graph is created to represent the basic structure of a house. This graph contains the connections between different rooms and ensure that every room of house is accessible. The next step is the placement phase, which consists of distributing the rooms over the footprint. Finally, the rooms are expanded to their proper size using a Monte Carlo method to choose which room to grow or shrink.

An approach to generate virtual building interiors in real-time is presented by Hahn et al. [11]. The interiors are created using eleven rules that work like a guideline to the generation process. Buildings created by this technique are divided into regions connected by portals. Only the visible parts of the building are generated, avoiding the use of memory and processing. When a region is no longer visible, the structure is removed from the memory. The generation process also provides a persistent environment: all changes made in a given region are stored in a record that is accessed through a hash map when necessary.

Horna et al. [12] propose a method to generate 3D constructions from two-dimensionalarchitectural plans. Additional information can be included to the two-dimensional plans in order to support the creation of three-dimensional model. It is possible to construct several floors using the same architectural plan.

A rule-based layout approach is proposed by Tutenel et al. [13]. Their method allows to solve the layout and also to distribute objects in the scene at the same time. From an initial layout, the algorithm finds the possible locations of a new object based on a given set of rules. The relations between objects can be specified either explicitly or implicitly. The method uses hierarchical blocks in the solving process, so that if a set of elements are solved, they are treated as single block.

Besides the definition of appearance and geometry of objects, it is also necessary to specify their features and functionalities. Semantic information can be used to enhance the environment of games and simulations. This can be done by specifying features of a given actor or object, as well as functionality, physical or psychological attributes and behaviors. Tutenel et al. [14] list three levels of semantic specification: object semantics, object relationships, and world semantics. These levels can be used to create and simulate an environment. For example, information such as the climate of a region can be used to define the kind of vegetation, and the weight of an object can be used to decide if an agent can carry it or not.

The main contribution of this paper is to provide a framework for real-time procedural modeling of floor plans of houses, generating geometric and semantic information in a robust way, where all rooms can be accessible from outside the environment. Virtual agents can use the provided information, so that behavioral animation can be performed. Squarified treemaps [6] are used to generate rooms which aspect ratios approach 1. Section 3 presents the proposed model.

3. Creating Floor Plans

A common drawback in procedural generation of environments is the creation of a component that is not accessible from any other component. For instance, in a virtual city, one problem is the generation of buildings that are not accessible from the streets. Concerning internal structures of buildings, a similar problem happens when one room is not connected with any other. As far as we know, neither of the proposed procedural models to generate floor plans can solve such type of situation. Our proposed method treats this problem by adding corridors into the generated floor plan, similarly to what occurs in real life.

Our method for generating floor plans is based on Squarified Treemaps, proposed by Bruls et al. [6]. A treemap [15] is an efficient and compact form to organize and to visualize elements of hierarchical structures of information, for instance, directory structures, organization structures, family trees, and others. In general, treemaps subdivide an area into small pieces to represent the importance of each part in the hierarchy. The main difference between treemaps and squarified treemaps is how the subdivision is performed. In squarified treemaps, authors propose a subdivision method that takes into account the aspect ratio of generated regions, trying to achieve the value 1. Figure 1 shows on the left the result of the original treemap method and on the right the squarified treemap. Both models are discussed next.

3.1. Treemaps and Squarified Treemaps. The original treemaps approach [15] uses a tree structure to define how information should be used to subdivide the space. Figure 2 shows an example. Let us consider that each node in the tree (Figure 2(a)) has an associated size (e.g., in Figure 2 the name of node is *a* and its size is 20). The treemap is built using recursive subdivision of an initial rectangle (see Figure 2(b)). The direction of subdivision alternates per level (horizontally and vertically). Consequently, the initial rectangle is subdivided in small rectangles. Further details about treemaps can be found in [15].

This method can originate subdivisions like the one illustrated in Figure 3. In this case, it is possible to see that aspect ratios of generated rectangles are very different from 1. Consequently, this approach is not adequate to tackle the problem that we want to deal with in this paper.

Squarified treemaps were proposed by Bruls et al. [6] and have the main goal of maintaining the aspect ratios of generated rectangles, defined as max(height/width, width/height), as close to 1 as possible. Their method is implemented using recursive programming and aims to generate rectangles based on a predefined and sorted list containing their desired areas (from larger to smaller areas). Then, the aspect ratio of the region to be subdivided is considered in order to decide whether to divide it horizontally or vertically. Also, the aspect ratio of generated regions in a specific step t is compared to step $t + 1$, being possible to ignore later computing regions in $t + 1$ and reconsider data from step t. Figure 4 illustrates the generation process of squarified treemaps presented by Bruls et al. [6]. We discuss this example in this paper since the understanding of our model is very dependent of squarified treemap method.

The list of rectangular areas to be considered in the example of Figure 4 is: 6, 6, 4, 3, 2, 2, 1. In step 1, the method generates a rectangle with aspect ratio = 8/3 in vertical subdivision. So, in step 2 the horizontal subdivision is tested, generating 2 rectangles with aspect ratio = 3/2 which are close to 1. In step 3, the next rectangle is generated, presenting aspect ratio = 4/1. This step is ignored, and step 4 is computed based on rectangles computed in step 2. The algorithm (described in detail in [6]) presents rectangles which aspect ratios are close to 1. In our point of view, this method is more adequate to provide generation of floor plans than original treemaps, due to the fact that rooms in real houses present aspect ratios not very different from 1. However, other problems may occur, as shown in the next sections.

3.2. The Proposed Model. The pipeline of the proposed model to build floor plans is presented in Figure 5. The process begins with the definition of construction parameters and layout constraints.

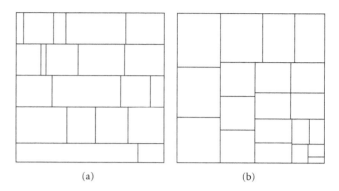

(a)   (b)

FIGURE 1: Original treemap (a) and squarified treemap (b).

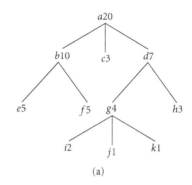

(a)

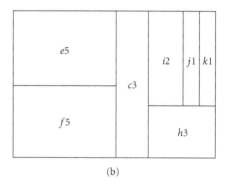

(b)

FIGURE 2: Tree diagram (a) and related treemap (b).

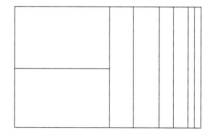

FIGURE 3: Example of treemap subdivision generating rectangles with aspect ratio different from 1.

TABLE 1: Possible connections between rooms.

	Outside	Kitchen	Pantry	Laundry room	Living room	Dining room	Toilet	Bedroom	Master bedroom	Bath room	Secondary room
Outside		X			X						
Kitchen	X		X	X	X	X					
Pantry		X		X							
Laundry room		X	X								
Living room	X	X					X	X	X	X	X
Dining room		X			X		X	X	X	X	X
Toilet					X	X					
Bedroom					X	X				X	
Master bedroom					X	X				X	
Bathroom					X	X		X	X		X
Secondary room					X	X				X	

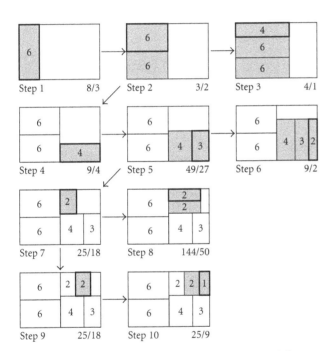

FIGURE 4: Example of squarified treemap process [6].

To create a floor plan, some parameters such as, height, length, and width of the building are required. It is also necessary to know the list of desired dimensions for each room and their functionalities. The functionality specifies how a particular area of residence should be used. There are three distinct possibilities: social area, service area, and private area. The social area can include the living room, the dining room, and the toilet. In the service area we can have the kitchen, the pantry, and the laundry room. At last, the private area can embrace the bedroom, the master bedroom, the intimate bathroom, and a possible secondary room that can be used in different ways, for example, as a library. This list is not fixed and can be customized by the user, and the proposed categorization is made to group the common areas.

The division of the residence area occurs in two different steps. At first, we compute the area of each one of three parts of the building (i.e., social, service, and private), and secondly, apply the squarified treemap in order to define three regions where rooms will be generated. This process generates an initial layout, containing three rectangles, each one for a specific area of the building (see Figure 6(a)).

After obtaining the positions of the polygon that represents a specific area, each polygon serves as input to run again squarified treemap algorithm in order to generate the geometry of each room. It is important to notice that we use original squarified treemap to generate each room in the building. Figure 6(b) shows the generated rooms.

With the result of the room subdivision, two more steps are required to complete the floor plan generation. Firstly, connections among rooms should be created. Secondly, rooms that are not accessible should be treated, since our environments should be used for characters animation. These two steps are further discussed in next sections.

3.3. Including Connections among the Rooms. With all the rooms generated as previously described, connections (doors) should be created among them. These connections are created using as criteria the functionalities of each room, that is, some rooms are usually not connected, for example, the kitchen and the bedroom. All the possible connections are presented in Table 1, which has been modeled based on a previous analysis of various floor plans commercially available. In this table, we consider the entry door of the floor plan as a connection from outside and two possible rooms: kitchen and living room. However, it is important to note that another set of connections can be defined by the user, to represent another style of architecture.

Geometrically, the door is created on the edge shared by two rooms that keep a possible connection. For instance, it is possible to have a connection between the kitchen and the living room, where a door can be created. The size of the doors is predefined, and their center on the edge is randomly

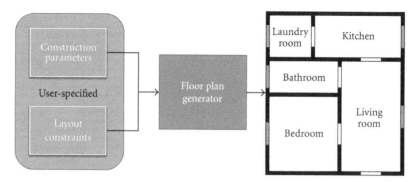

FIGURE 5: The generation process of floor plans. Construction parameters and layout constraints are provided by the user as input to floor plan generator.

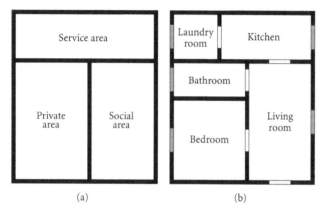

(a)   (b)

FIGURE 6: Dividing the total space of the house in three main areas (a): private, social, and service area. Example floor plan generated by the model (b).

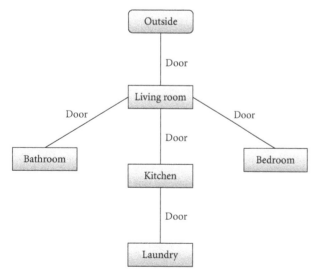

FIGURE 7: Connectivity graph for a generated floor plan.

defined. A similar process happens with the generation of windows, but ensuring that they are placed on the external edges. Figure 6(b) illustrates a generated floor plan, containing windows (dark rectangles) and doors (white rectangles).

After the connections between rooms are processed, a connectivity graph is automatically created (Figure 7), representing the links among the rooms. It allows checking if there is any room that is not accessible. Also, buildings and houses created with our method can be used to provide environment for characters simulation. The graph always starts from outside and follows all possible connections from the accessed room.

If any room is not present in the graph, it is necessary to include corridors. This situation can happen when there are no possible connections between neighboring rooms (rooms which share edges). This process is described in the next section.

3.4. Including Corridors on the Floor Plans. The generation of corridors is necessary in order to maintain the coherence of the generated environment and to provide valid space for characters navigation. Firstly, the rooms without access from the living room are selected. These rooms are flagged with an X, as illustrated in Figure 8(a). The main idea is to find possible edges shared by nonconnected rooms to be used to create the corridor.

The corridor must connect the living room (marked with an L in Figure 8(a)) with all X rooms. The proposed solution uses the internal walls of the building to generate a kind of circulation "backbone" of the space, that is, the most probable region to generate the corridor in the floor plan. The algorithm is very simple and has three main steps. Firstly, all external walls are removed, as corridors are avoided in the boundary of the floor plan (Figure 8(b)).

Secondly, we remove all internal segments (representing walls) that belong to the living room (Figure 8(c)). The remaining segments (described through their vertices) are used as input to the graph creation. Vertices are related to nodes, and segments describe the edges in the graph (Figure 8(c)). In order to deal with the graph, we use the A* algorithm [16], which is a very known algorithm widely used in path-finding and graph traversal. In our case, the graph is explored to find the shortest path that connects all rooms without connectivity to the living room. A room is considered connected if the graph traverses at least one of its edges. Finally the shortest path is chosen to create the corridor (Figure 8(d)).

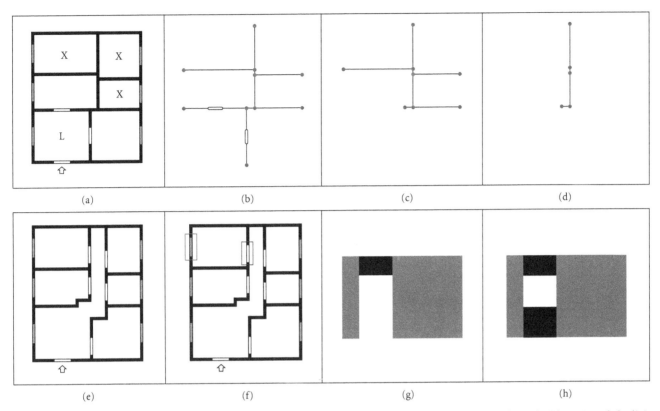

FIGURE 8: Steps to end the building generation. (a) Original floor plan with rooms without connectivity flagged with an X and the living room is marked with L. (b) Floor plan after external edges removed. (c) Internal walls that do not belong to living room. (d) The shortest path linking all rooms without connectivity to the living room. (e) Final 2D floor plan. (f) The red and blue rectangles highlight, respectively, the representation of a window and a door in the floor plan. Creation process of windows (g) and doors (h).

FIGURE 9: Three-dimensional model of 2D floor plan illustrated in Figure 8(e).

The "backbone" is the set of edges candidates to be used to generate the corridor. After the "backbone" generation, we should generate the polygons which represent the corridor, which is initially composed by a set of edges/segments. These segments must pass through a process of 2D extrusion in order to generate rectangles, allowing agents to walk inside the house. Indeed, the size of the corridor is increased perpendicularly to the edges. However, this process can cause an overlap between the corridor and some rooms, reducing their areas. If the final area of any room is smaller than the

minimum allowed value, the floor plan undergoes a global readjustment process to correct this problem, as shown in 1

$$area_{house} = area_{private} + area_{social} + area_{service} + area_{corridor}.$$
(1)

After obtaining the final floor plan (Figure 8(e)), two simple steps should be followed to generate the final building. Initially, each 2D wall represented on the floor plan is extruded to a given height H defined by the user. Generated walls can have doors (between two rooms) (blue rectangle in Figure 8(f)) and windows (red rectangle in Figure 8(f)), that should be modeled properly. The last step of process is to add an appropriate type of window to each room, according to its functionality, from a set of models. A three-dimensional view of a 2D floor plan (Figure 8(e)) is presented in Figure 9.

4. Results

In the following floor plans, we explicitly present the parameters used in their generation, and also show the geometric and semantic information generated. In addition, the connectivity graph is shown for each house or building.

Figure 10(a) shows a floor plan generated using our model. The list of rooms and their respective areas are as follows: living room ($9\,m^2$), two bedrooms ($8\,m^2$ and $7\,m^2$),

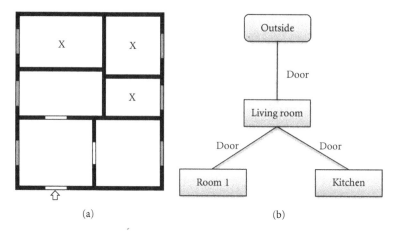

(a)   (b)

FIGURE 10: Example of floor plan (a) containing 2 nonconnected rooms (labeled with X) and its respective connectivity graph (b).

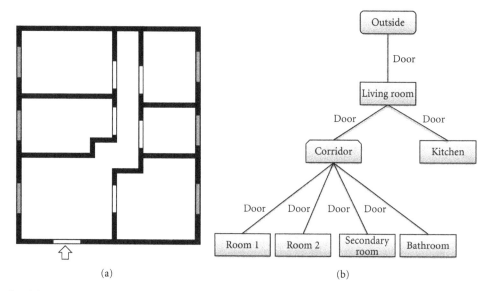

(a)   (b)

FIGURE 11: Example of floor plan of Figure 10 (a) containing corridors and all rooms are connected to the living room and its respective connectivity graph (b).

secondary room ($6\,m^2$), bathroom ($4\,m^2$), and kitchen ($8\,m^2$). The dimensions of the house are 6 meters wide, 7 meters long, and 3 meters high. The connectivity graph can be seen in Figure 10(b). Both the bathroom and the secondary room do not have connection with any other room. This situation is corrected by adding a corridor (Figure 11(a)). The new connectivity graph is shown in Figure 11(b). All rooms are now connected, being accessible from the outside or from any other internal room.

Another case study is illustrated in Figure 12(a). This house has 84 squared meters (12 m long × 7 m wide, being 3.1 m high). The list of rooms and their respective areas are as follows: living room ($22\,m^2$), two bedrooms (both with $14\,m^2$), a secondary room used as home office ($12\,m^2$), bathroom ($10\,m^2$), and kitchen ($12\,m^2$). For this specific configuration, the connectivity graph that can be seen in Figure 12(b) was generated. Both bedrooms and the bathroom are not accessible from any other room. The

solution is presented in Figure 13(a). Using the corridor, the new connectivity graph looks like the one presented in Figure 13(b). A generated 2D floor plan can be saved to disk and used as input to a home design software. Figure 14 shows the result of same floor plan when adding some 2D furniture.

In addition, we compared the floor plan of Figure 14 with an available real floor plan. As it can be seen in Figure 15, such real floor plan could generate exactly the same connectivity graph (see Figure 13(b)). Furthermore, the total dimension of the real plan is $94\,m^2$, while virtual plan has $84\,m^2$, and still generating rooms of similar size.

In Figure 16 we can observe a 3D model of floor plan visualized with textures.

It is important to note that for these results we determine parameters values in order to provide specific floor plans, and even compare with available houses, existent in real life. However, one can imagine having our method integrated into a game engine, and generating different floor plans in

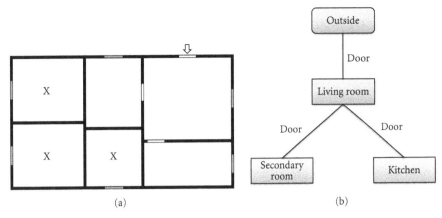

(a)   (b)

FIGURE 12: Example of floor plan (a) containing 3 nonconnected rooms (labeled with X) and its respective connectivity graph (b).

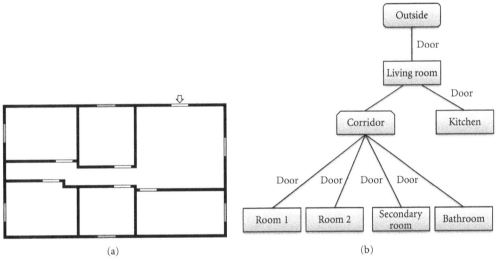

(a)   (b)

FIGURE 13: Example of floor plan of Figure 12 (a) containing corridors and all rooms are connected to the living room and its respective connectivity graph (b).

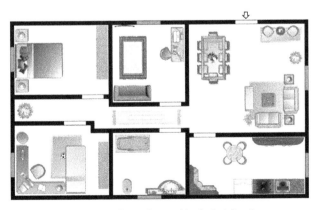

FIGURE 14: Our floor plan and included furnitures.

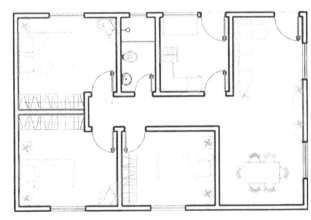

FIGURE 15: Real floor plan.

a dynamic way. For instance, using random functions and intervals for areas and a random number of rooms, our method is able to generate different floor plans automatically.

So, during the game, the player can visit different buildings and have always different floor plans, without previous modeling.

FIGURE 16: Three-dimensional model of a generated floor plan.

5. Final Considerations

We present a technique to provide floor plans for houses in an automatic way. The relevance of this method is the ability to generate real-time buildings for games and simulations. The generated environments are realistic as they could easily be found in real life. Besides geometric information, the technique also generates semantic information which is very useful to allow virtual humans simulation.

We compared a generated floor plan with an available commercial house in order to verify the similarity between the distribution of generated rooms and real ones. Furthermore, this work contributes to generate a connection graph which determines the navigation graph in the environment. Corridors could be created to solve problems of nonconnected rooms.

Currently there are some limitations that should be worked out later. The first concern relates to the general appearance of generated houses. Due to the squarified treemaps algorithm, created floor plans will present always a square or a rectangular shape. Depending on the initial division in social area, service area, and private area, possibly some parts may present an aspect ratio far away from 1. A possible improvement would be to change the order of the initial division of the three areas mentioned. Regarding the corridors generation, a few unnatural angles may occur due to the insertion of corridors. A possible way to solve this issue could be to align parallel straight lines of the backbone if the distance between them is smaller than a certain threshold. Probably the impact in each room area could be despicable, but this needs further investigation.

From an architectural perspective, both neighborhood and environmental factors (e.g., topography and solar orientation) should be considered when defining the house position and the apertures position (doors and windows). The introduction of a few parameters could help to generated a floor plan connected to the environment.

Future work should be focused on providing a procedural model of objects into each room (like furnitures), as well as data that allow easily behavioral simulation. For instance, we can codify in each room possible behaviors to be adopted by agents in different rooms and depending on their internal status and needs. Another issue that will be investigated is the extension of the proposed method in order to generate floor plans of an entire building or homes with more than one floor.

Acknowledgment

This work was supported by the brazilian research agency FINEP.

References

[1] M. Oliveira, J. Crowcroft, and M. Slater, "An innovative design approach to build virtual environment systems," in *Proceedings of the Workshop on Virtual Environments (EGVE '03)*, pp. 143–151, ACM, New York, NY, USA, 2003.

[2] D. S. Ebert, K. F. Musgrave, D. Peachey, K. Perlin, and S. Worley, *Texturing & Modeling: A Procedural Approach*, The Morgan Kaufmann Series in Computer Graphics, Morgan Kaufmann, San Francisco, Calif, USA, 3rd edition, 2002.

[3] L. Choy, R. Ingram, O. Quigley, B. Sharp, and A. Willmott, "Rigblocks: player-deformable objects," in *Proceedings of the International Conference on Computer Graphics and Interactive Techniques (SIGGRAPH '07)*, p. 83, ACM, New York, NY, USA, August 2007.

[4] D. DeBry, H. Goffin, C. Hecker, O. Quigley, S. Shodhan, and A. Willmott, "Player-driven procedural texturing," in *Proceedings of the International Conference on Computer Graphics and Interactive Techniques (SIGGRAPH '07)*, p. 81, ACM, New York, NY, USA, August 2007.

[5] K. Compton, J. Grieve, E. Goldman et al., "Creating spherical worlds," in *Proceedings of the International Conference on Computer Graphics and Interactive Techniques (SIGGRAPH '07)*, p. 82, ACM, New York, NY, USA, August 2007.

[6] M. Bruls, K. Huizing, and J. van Wijk, "Squarified treemaps," in *Proceedings of the Joint Eurographics and IEEE TCVG Symposium on Visualization*, pp. 33–42, 2000.

[7] Y. I. H. Parish and P. Müller, "Procedural modeling of cities," in *Proceedings of the 28th Annual Conference on Computer Graphics and Interactive Techniques (SIGGRAPH '01)*, pp. 301–308, ACM, New York, NY, USA, 2001.

[8] S. Greuter, J. Parker, N. Stewart, and G. Leach, "Real-time procedural generation of 'pseudo infinite' cities," in *Proceedings of the 1st International Conference on Computer Graphics and Interactive Techniques in Australasia and South East Asia (GRAPHITE '03)*, pp. 87–94, ACM, New York, NY, USA, 2003.

[9] P. Müller, P. Wonka, S. Haegler, A. Ulmer, and L. Van Gool, "Procedural modeling of buildings," in *Proceedings of the International Conference on Computer Graphics and Interactive Techniques (SIGGRAPH '06)*, pp. 614–623, ACM, New York, NY, USA, August 2006.

[10] J. Martin, "Procedural house generation: a method for dynamically generating floor plans," in *Proceedings of the Symposium on Interactive 3D Graphics and Games*, 2006.

[11] E. Hahn, P. Bose, and A. Whitehead, "Persistent realtime building interior generation," in *Proceedings of the ACM SIGGRAPH Symposium on Video Games (Sandbox '06)*, pp. 179–186, ACM, New York, NY, USA, 2006.

[12] S. Horna, G. Damiand, D. Meneveaux, and Y. Bertrand, "Building 3D indoor scenes topology from 2D architectural plans," in *Proceedings of the 2nd International Conference on Computer Graphics Theory and Applications (GRAPP '07)*, pp. 37–44, Setúbal, Portugal, March 2007.

[13] T. Tutenel, R. Bidarra, R. M. Smelik, and K. J. de Kraker, "Rule-based layout solving and its application to procedural interior generation," in *Proceedings of the CASA Workshop on 3D Advanced Media in Gaming and Simulation (3AMIGAS '09)*, Amsterdam, The Netherlands, 2009.

[14] T. Tutenel, R. Bidarra, R. M. Smelik, and K. J. D. De Kraker, "The role of semantics in games and simulations," *Computers in Entertainment*, vol. 6, no. 4, pp. 1–35, 2008.

[15] B. Johnson and B. Shneiderman, "Tree-maps: a space-filling approach to the visualization of hierarchical information structures," in *Proceedings of the 2nd Conference on Visualization (VIS '91)*, pp. 284–291, IEEE Computer Society Press, Los Alamitos, Calif, USA, 1991.

[16] P. Hart, N. Nilsson, and B. Raphael, "A formal basis for the heuristic determination of minimum cost paths," *IEEE Transactions on Systems Science and Cybernetics*, vol. 4, no. 2, pp. 100–107, 1968.

15

Time and Space in Digital Game Storytelling

Huaxin Wei, Jim Bizzocchi, and Tom Calvert

School of Interactive Arts and Technology, Simon Fraser University, 250-13450 102 Avenue, Surrey, BC, Canada V3T 0A3

Correspondence should be addressed to Huaxin Wei, huaxinw@sfu.ca

Academic Editor: Abdennour El Rhalibi

The design and representation of time and space are important in any narrative form. Not surprisingly there is an extensive literature on specific considerations of space or time in game design. However, there is less attention to more systematic analyses that examine both of these key factors—including their dynamic interrelationship within game storytelling. This paper adapts critical frameworks of narrative space and narrative time drawn from other media and demonstrates their application in the understanding of game narratives. In order to do this we incorporate fundamental concepts from the field of game studies to build a game-specific framework for analyzing the design of narrative time and narrative space. The paper applies this framework against a case analysis in order to demonstrate its operation and utility. This process grounds the understanding of game narrative space and narrative time in broader traditions of narrative discourse and analysis.

1. Introduction

Thanks to the rapid innovation in computational technologies, interactive media are becoming more and more dominant in communication and entertainment. As technical limitations disappear, artists and designers feel more at ease using interactive media as their vehicles for expression. Storytelling has found a new home in interactive media implemented in multimedia, websites, hypertexts, interactive fictions and films, as well as digital games. Among these forms, digital games have undoubtedly received most attention and popularity, and have become the most successful application of interactive narrative. Despite the debate that has centred on the potential conflict between interactivity and the experience of narrative, the past decade has seen increasing effort applied to creating meaningful and engaging stories in interactive media, especially digital games. This effort has quietly addressed the issue and has significantly advanced the power of storytelling to enhance the audience's experience. This can be seen in such successful commercial titles as the *Assassin's Creed* series, the *Prince of Persia* series, and the *Fable* series, as well as Mateas and Stern's noncommercial title *Façade*. Wolf has pointed out that "[a]s the video game's use of space and time grew more complex and graphics grew more representational, the

medium became increasingly narrative based" [1]. Indeed, in the construction of any kind of narrative, time and space play a crucial role, not only in the process of narrative authoring, but also in the process of narrative comprehension. Between the two, narrative comprehension is especially linked to a player's experience of a game. As Bridgeman put it: "[t]o read a narrative is to engage with an alternative world that has its own temporal and spatial structures" [2], the temporal and spatial design of a game, therefore, determines the ways that players engage with the game. Critical analyses of narrative implications of the construction of time and space in games can facilitate an understanding of the mechanism of interactive storytelling, for today's narrative-based games demonstrate the most sophisticated design and technology for digital interactive storytelling systems. This understanding will support more effective approaches in future narrative design and provide an objective basis for analyzing interactive narratives.

Time and space are equally important for storytelling in digital games. Through a look at past game studies, we can see contributions to both aspects and arguments promoting both. Game space has probably been explicitly recognized by more researchers and designers in the field. It is obvious that in order to design a game it is necessary to design a space. This strong recognition can be summarized by

Aarseth's claim: "The defining element in computer games is spatiality. Computer games are essentially concerned with spatial representation and negotiation; therefore the classification of a computer game can be based on how it represents or, perhaps, implements space" [3]. Along this line, there exist various classifications of game space. For example, Wolf identifies eleven spatial structures based on the dichotomy of on-screen and off-screen space used by film theory [4]; Boron takes a historical view and describes fifteen types of game space [5]; Jenkins directly connects game space to narrative experience and suggests four ways in which the structuring of game space can facilitate narrative experience. As Jenkins states: "spatial stories can evoke pre-existing narrative associations; they can provide a staging ground where narrative events are enacted; they may embed narrative information within their mise-en-scene; or they provide resources for emergent narratives" [6]. Using a player's experiential point of view to examine game time, Nistche concludes that the mapping of game time onto the game world can only be done with spatial reference thanks to the continuity of space [7]. The implication here is that time in games can be stopped, reversed, or altered in other ways, which can cause trouble when we try to denote a specific time point in a game; spatial reference is relatively more stable. Incorporating architectural approaches into the study of video game space functionality, Nitsche identifies such spatial structures as tracks/rails, labyrinths/mazes, and arenas. Similar to Jenkins, he observes that evocative narrative elements can be organized or placed according to the spatial structure; the player's experience is hence driven by the spatial structure.

Game time is just as important as game space in the understanding of game design and game experience. Digital games are a temporal medium—where players drive the gameplay forward to completion while the game narrative unfolds over time. Such frequently discussed topics in game narrative as repetition, pacing, dramatic arc, and closure, as well as such mechanics as deceleration and the ticking clock [8], all fall into the realm of temporality. Games do inherit certain temporal design conventions from older media like film. However, due to the dynamic nature of ludic gameplay, augmented by the power of computation, time in digital games also has unique characteristics that facilitate or mediate both the gameplay and the associated narrative.

Time and space can be seen as separate—but not unconnected—aspects of game design and experience. As Arsenault and Perron argue, "[w]e should not forget that the temporal dimension of gameplay prevails on its spatial characterization," since gameplay occurs through a series of interactions that take place in patterns of reflexive and cyclic progression [9]. In our construction of a story world, time and space are two aspects that complement and reference each other. While the literature mentioned above tackles time or space from various angles, there is no systematic account of how time and space are structured in game narratives. In previous work, spatial analyses have not gone much beyond the classification of topological spatial structures. Temporal analyses, similarly, have been limited to identifying a few typologies of time schemes or frames, such as Juul's dual

structure (play time and fictional time) [10] and Zagal and Mateas's four frames (real-world time, gameworld time, coordination time, fictive time) [11].

Compared with this largely undefined area of game narrative, time and space have been studied extensively in broader narrative theory. Both have mature descriptive frameworks that have been tested and refined in the long practice of narrative analysis. A mindful adaptation of narrative theory for game studies will help us understand game storytelling better and help build up context-specific principles for game narrative design. As Ryan concludes, "[t]he inability of literary narratology to account for the experience of games does not mean that we should throw away the concept of narrative in ludology; it rather means that we need to expand the catalog of narrative modalities beyond the diegetic and the dramatic, by adding a phenomenological category tailor-made for games" [12]. To do this, we pay special attention to the interactive nature of game storytelling. Our starting point is to examine how time and space are structured in narrative in general, then incorporate insights from the field of game design and game studies, and finally reach a game-specific description of the structural aspects of time and space in game narratives. After an overview of the foundational concepts we use for game narrative analysis, we will delineate in detail how these aspects characterize narrative time and space in games, and how time and space converge in the construction of the plot. The analysis is illustrated and supported with relevant game examples. In our discussion, despite the focus on game storytelling, we will always place the concepts and approaches in the bigger context of interactive storytelling systems. Occasionally we will draw in other interactive narrative examples in an effort to demonstrate the applicability of our game-specific framework to general interactive storytelling systems.

2. Analyzing Time and Space in Game Narrative

In narrative theory, there has been more discussion on temporality than spatiality. Stories are commonly framed as sequences of events (hence temporality is the ruling aspect) and space as a mere static description interspersed into narration. This opinion about time/space opposition, however, has been challenged by many who consider that time and space are closely bound together in narrative. Bakhtin was the most famous scholar who challenged the time/space opposition and proposed the concept of *chronotope*, i.e., the space-time complex, to refer to the connectedness of temporal and spatial relationships in narrative [13]. Zoran is another scholar who criticizes the opposition [14]. Taking a cognitive perspective, Herman considers narrative comprehension "a process of (re)constructing storyworlds on the basis of textual cues and in the inferences that they make possible" and promotes the notion of storyworld as an integrated view of narrative, with time and space being two important and complementary aspects [15]. The cognitive process of narrative comprehension is analogous to what a player goes through during gameplay. Through this process, as Jenkins observes, players, like film spectators, form their "mental maps of the narrative action and the story space" and act upon those mental maps "to test them against the game world itself" [6]. Nitsche also argues that players understand the space and movement in games by way of narrative comprehension. His study of video games views narrative as "a form of understanding of the events a player causes, triggers, and encounters inside a video game space" [16]. A focus on audiences' mental process will broaden the scope of narrative defined by the traditional mimesis (story as acted) and diegesis (story as told) and thus potentially gives room to develop a user-centric approach to games as suggested by Ryan quoted earlier, which addresses story as *generated* from a phenomenological perspective [12]. In this work, we adapt Herman's notion of *storyworld* to refer to the world a digital game creates through textual, visual, auditory, and haptic cues, where players draw inferences and drive the game to completion through a series of events. A game's storyworld will not be complete without players' mental (re)construction activities that help bridge the gaps left in the computer-generated virtual world. Time and space, consequently, are two important aspects in the reconstruction of a storyworld.

2.1. Story Time, Operational Time, and Fuzzy Temporality. In narrative theory, most of the approaches to time depart from the basic distinction of two temporalities in narrative: story time and discourse time. To put it simply, story is about *what* is depicted in a narrative and discourse is about *how* it is told. As story is the basic sequence of events, story time is considered the chronological time when the events happened. Discourse time, on the other hand, can be understood differently under different contexts. As Bridgeman points out, in oral narratives, discourse time can be the time of telling; whereas in written narratives, since we cannot access the act of writing, discourse time can be generally referred to as the time of reading [2]. In some narratives, story and discourse times are simply matched, but in many narratives, these two can be very different. The temporal relationships between the two schemes thus produce many interesting narrative effects. These relationships are best classified by Genette as *order, duration,* and *frequency* [17]. These three categories have been very popular and adopted by numerous works in narrative analysis; however, they are all based on the assumption that the relation between story time and discourse time can be determined. Studies of many recent narrative texts have seen the indeterminacy of temporality. Herman uses "fuzzy temporality" to describe a subtype of temporal relations that involve "temporal sequencing that is strategically inexact, making it difficult or even impossible to assign narrated events a fixed or even fixable position along a timeline in the storyworld" [15]. He uses "polychrony" to cover all types of narration with fuzzy temporality, including both temporal indefiniteness (i.e., events are partially ordered) *and* temporal multiplicity (i.e., events are ordered in multiple sequences). "Polychrony" is related to the notion of "achrony" but with bigger scope. The latter notion is originated from Genette's idea of "timelessness" regarding those "unplaceable" events; it is used by later narrative theorists like Bal. However, the notion of achrony does not

address the multiple ordering. We will include more details in a later section. This fourth category thus complements Genette's three categories, forming a coherent set of temporal relations in a narrative. We will use these four categories as our departure point for temporal studies of games.

Previous studies of game time have considered similar ideas yet using different perspectives. Eskelinen's early game studies work contrasts game with narrative. He argues that games only have one necessary time scheme, namely, "the movement from the beginning to the winning or some other situation," and "in cases where another time scheme is invented, it is not as important as the first one" [18]. While the dominant temporal relation in traditional narratives is the one between story time and discourse time, the dominant temporal relation in games, according to Eskelinen, lies between *user time* and *event time*. User time is the time taken by the player to perform actions whereas event time is the period for the "happenings" of the game. However, since user time and event time are durations (or time frames) based on one single time scheme, Genette's temporal categories are simply not effective here; hence Eskelinen's discussion of temporal relations only borrows the terms from narratology without the real spirit. Different from Eskelinen, Juul tries to distinguish his study from the narratological approach, even though he agrees that the two approaches are comparable to certain extent. Juul proposes two time schemes for games: *play time* and *fictional time* [10]. It is worth noting that in his previous version of this study [19], Juul called fictional time event time, which is coincident with Eskelinen's term. Play time is the time taken by a player to play a game and fictional time denotes the time of the events in the game world. Juul then used the term *projection* to describe the link between play time and fictional time; however, projection is the one and only temporal relation Juul looks at in games. Later studies follow the same thread but confuse time scheme with time frames (i.e., different periods within one scheme). For example, based on Juul's study, Hitchens extends, modifies, and presents a new model for game time, including playing time, game world time, engine time and game progress time [20]. Tychsen et al. further extend that model, in the context of multiplayer role playing games, into a seven-layer model, including such new layers as server time, story time and world time (derived from the original "game world time"), and perceived time [21]. Another work on game temporality is part of Zagal and Mateas's work for the Game Ontology Project. They proposed four temporal frames for games: real-world time (events taking place in the physical world), gameworld time (events within the represented gameworld, including events associated with gameplay actions), coordination time (events that coordinate the actions of players and agents), and fictive time (applying sociocultural labels to events, as well as narrated event sequences) [11].

A closer look at these works in game studies will tell us that these somewhat arbitrary concepts are not clearly defined. Some works create temporal frames based on one time scheme (e.g., Eskelinen's); some other works create double or more time schemes (e.g., Juul's); yet some create a mix (e.g., Hitchens's and Zagal's). Nevertheless, it is critical to be certain about which time scheme the discussion is based upon when setting up a clearly defined model for time. We therefore believe that it is beneficial to return to narrative theory and to start our analysis from the terms clearly defined there and adapt them to games with necessary modifications. In digital games, players do more than reading; instead, they participate in the events in the story and play a part in the telling of the story, too. While story time remains similar, discourse time becomes more complex for games. From the player's perspective, it should refer to both "reading time" and "acting time". Thus, we use the term *operation* to refer to the running process of a game driven by both the player's actions and the game's autonomous mechanisms. A game *story*, on the other hand, is the coherent story reconstructed during and/or after the gameplay by the player, which consists of a succession of events in chronological order. Therefore, *narrative time* in games concerns the relationships between two time schemes: *story time* and *operational time*. In our analysis of time in games, we will study the three temporal categories—order, duration and frequency—based on the relationships between story time and operational time. We will follow some recent narrative theorists (e.g., Bal [22] and Prince [23]) and use narrative *speed* to replace *duration*, which makes it more of a relative notion operating between story time and operational time. In addition, we will also study the existence of fuzzy temporality in games to exhaust all the possible temporalities. Although game storytelling is often accused of being simple and linear, we will show the exceptions to this as well as those unique temporal devices games employ.

2.2. Space in Time: An Integrated Approach to Game Narrative Space. The approaches to space in narrative theory are not as consistent as those to narrative time because of the lack of a rigorous model like Genette's. Following the approach to time, early narratology works have attempted to make inferences from the relationships between *story space* and *discourse space*, but this method did not go too far due to the multiple understandings of what is discourse space. It is unclear whether it is the space on the book pages, the space of the screen, or the space where the act of narrating occurs. When extending the analysis from written narratives to film, Chatman points out that discourse space "can be defined as *focus of spatial attention*"; "[i]t is the framed area to which the implied audience's attention is directed by the discourse" [24]. In this sense, story space and discourse space simply exist on the same plane. To comprehend the narrative space, the audience works on the mental construction of the *storyworld*. In digital games, players not only look at the space but also understand the space through navigation and interaction. Therefore, we consider *game narrative space* the space of the *game's storyworld*, a term that has been defined earlier in this section. Our later discussion will reveal the characteristics that qualify narrative space in games.

As mentioned earlier, spatial analysis in previous game studies has not gone much beyond classifying the topographic structures of game space. Nitsches' book *Video Game Spaces* is one of the few exceptions, providing a comprehensive study of game space framed under structure, presentation and functionality [16]. Discussion under "structure" looks at how textual qualities of games are reshaped by 3D game space; topics under "presentation" focus on the roles of moving images and sound in game space; "functionality" addresses the player's interactive access to the game space. By attempting to include all possible dimensions, this book touches on so many peripheral topics that it, in a way, loses its focus when it comes to the ultimate question of how to describe the structural aspects of game narrative space. The key characteristic of game space is that it is dynamic and can be interacted with. Unlike written narratives that can have less precise spatial information and films that can effectively use camera frame to guide the audience's view of the entire space, today's digital games, equipped with more advanced technology like 3D graphics and faster engines, provide expansive visual spaces for players to explore. These spaces cannot be represented without explicit spatial information conveyed via visual, auditory and haptic cues. In a literature of spatial analysis using narrative theory that often treats space as the static "setting" of story, Zoran's work stands out by going beyond this narrow understanding and recognizing that the structure of space influences the reconstructed storyworld in more than one way. In order to discover how the spatial structure affects the storyworld, he goes on to study the inherent structure of space and develops a model that distinguishes three levels of spatial structuring. These three levels are *the topographical level* (space as a static entity), *the chronotopic level* (space imposed with events and movements), and *the textual level* (space imposed with verbal signs) [14]. This model aptly embraces key aspects of narrative space and "anticipates many of the issues explored by subsequent researchers" [15].

There are both parallels and differences between Nitsche's study and Zoran's model. First, they are both created on the premise that understanding space and movement is done through reconstructing the storyworld (i.e., narrative comprehension). Second, the two frameworks overlap in some ways; for example, they both investigate the topographic structures of the space and relations between the textual signs and representations of the space. On the other hand, the most prominent difference between the two works, other than them working with different media, is that Zoran emphasizes the connectedness between space and time so much that he introduces a special level of analysis to track and understand their dynamic relationship. In addition, Zoran's model is solidly built on narrative theory, more clearly defined, and more concentrated on the ways space exists in the reconstructed storyworld. We therefore believe that Zoran's model, though originally created for written narratives, can inform the analysis of *narrative space* in games. We thus adapt Zoran's model to the interactive context of games and develop three views on game narrative space based on his three levels, which represent three types of inherent structure of space in its three existing modes.

The *topographical view*, which is Zoran's original first level, treats space as a static entity with fixed spatial reference and separated from temporal reference. Such terms as *layout*, *spatial organization*, and *spatial structure* used in game design or game analysis are all related to the topography of game space and thus belong to this view. In this view, maps can be drawn with such geographical reference as locations and landmarks, or references based on other ontological principles like treasure chests. Zoran borrows Bakhtin's notion of chronotope to address the role that time plays in space; hence, at the chronotopic level, space is structured by events and movements, which are all time-referenced. Zoran's level of textural structure investigates how textual (verbal in written narratives) patterns are imposed on the organization of space. In games, where the story is generated on the fly, player actions influence the storyworld through (non-prescribed) events and movements, which in turn causes changes in the on-screen and off-screen spaces (including acoustic space). This calls for a modification of the scope of Zoran's two levels and one possible solution is to define an *operational view* and a *presentational view*. In the operational view, the story unfolds (i.e., it is cogenerated by players) over time through events, taking places at one location after another; the space of the storyworld is thus revealed through movements. As a result, game operations impose movement and interactive patterns on the structure of space. In the presentational view, the dynamic presentation of the storyworld imposes its patterns of visual, auditory and haptic cues (i.e., the language of game as a medium) on the structure of space. This distinction between the operational and presentational views helps to isolate issues of how players navigate through and interact with the space from those regarding the visual/auditory display and game interface.

Zoran suggests that there are no clear boundaries between his three levels and in the audience's eyes; "they are always perceived together, one through the other" [14]. Our three views, consequently, are on a spectrum with shifting foci, from the textual (or representational, if we migrate from verbal to visual media) patterns, most immediate to the audience, to the reconstructed world as an existence itself, detached from all the activities that can happen within it.

3. A Closer Look at Game Narrative Time

In this section, we examine temporal relationships in games following the most frequently used categories *order*, *speed*, and *frequency*. As previously discussed, these relationships dwell in the dynamics between story time and operational time. We also look at the ways the aforementioned polychrony exists in game storytelling and how it affects the gaming experience indirectly through reducing the linearity and increasing the replayability. In the discussion, we also observe that when integrated into the game mechanics, time can play a significant role in gameplay. This operationalized use of time marks a fundamental difference between digital games and other narrative media.

3.1. Order. In narrative theory, order concerns the relation between the order of events in the presented narrative (i.e., in discourse time) and their chronological sequence in the story constructed by the reader or viewer (i.e., in story time). Correspondingly, in games, *order* is the relation between the ordering in operation and the ordering in story.

When these two orderings are consistent, we get a linear story. Traditional narratives often play with the sequential ordering to "draw attention to things, to emphasize, to bring about aesthetic or psychological effects, to show various interpretations of an event, to indicate the subtle difference between expectation and realization, and much else besides" [22]. Earlier games were often accused of having stories that were too linear, which can constrain player interactions. However, linear stories and nonlinear stories both have their own disadvantages. As Adams points out, linear stories can have more narrative power and greater emotional impact on players, but the cost is a corresponding loss in player agency [25]. Among the traditional narrative devices to manipulate the order, flashback is sometimes seen in games but flash-forward is quite rare. In a 2002 study that analyzed 130 digital games, the result returned a 6% of the investigated games use flashbacks and 2% flash-forwards [26]. We believe that the use of these two devices is higher in games that are more recent. Another common nonlinear technique is branching plotlines—commonplace in games and hypertexts because they are easily implemented computationally. As the use of branching plotlines gives the entire game operation multiple orderings, we will discuss it in a latter section that concerns fuzzy temporality.

A good example of manipulation of temporal order can be found in *Prince of Persia: The Sands of Time*. The game uses voice-over narration to feature the Prince telling a story to a person, whom we will only know at the end. The whole narration is in past tense even though at the same time the player is playing through the Prince's supposedly past adventure. Only at the end—when story time meets with operational time—does the player realize that the whole adventure was narrated in a flashback. Another well-known example of flashback with the player's involvement is the prologue of *Max Payne*. The game begins with a flashback where the protagonist Max Payne came home three years ago and found his wife and child had just been killed despite the fact that he had chased and shot the killers (enacted by the player). The game then continues with Max Payne carrying out his tasks as an undercover cop to hunt down the Valkry drug traffickers.

A comparison between the two examples cited above shows that the difference lies in the *span* of the flashback. The duration of the retroversion is an important characteristic of flashbacks. The duration of the flashback played at the opening of *Max Payne* is only a few minutes, which is typical in film storytelling. The style of the flashback is consistent with the genre of "sophisticated film-noir thriller" and thus helps set the mood [27]. In the example of *Prince of Persia: The Sands of Time*, on the other hand, the flashback spans over the entire game story; in this case, players, after a little while, will usually start feeling that nothing special is happening, similar to what Bal observes in literary works. Yet in the game, the voice-over narration using past tense is interspersed throughout the entire game reminding players that they are still in the flashback, which creates a hypermediated and slightly cynical or even comic effect. Mechner, writer of this game, openly admits that using voice-over narration as a framing device and nesting the entire story in a flashback is a design choice with the intent of combining game genres—making a "survival horror" game ostensibly a "swashbuckling acrobatic action-adventure" [28]. While in both examples the flashback is interactive, in many cases flashbacks can be done in such noninteractive forms as cut-scene, prescripted dialogue, or even on-screen captions. Juul believes that "interactive flashbacks" are problematic because "[t]he player's actions in the past may suddenly render the present impossible" [10]. Interestingly, this is exactly the case in *Prince of Persia: The Sands of Time*. When the player character accidentally dies, the voice-over narration will say: "Wait, what did I just say? That did not happen. Let me back up a bit." The player will then be given another chance to try. This method only intensifies the comic effect of the game narration. To keep the "suspension of disbelief," flashbacks players' interactions are often limited; even if they are not limited, the game may simply reset when players make "illegal" moves.

Moreover, games have one distinct use of temporal order that is not found in other narrative forms, that is, to use order as the answer of a puzzle. Eskelinen gives *Doom* as an example in this, where the player must find the right event sequence in order to continue [18]. Many adventure games (such as in *God of War* and *Lara Croft* titles) contain ordering puzzles—where players need to trigger a set of switches in the right order to open a gate,. Other narratively inflected puzzle games use this mechanism as well, in particular a number of online puzzle games (e.g., Samorost (http://www.amanita-design.net/samorost-1/.)) This practice effectively conjoins the narrative concept of order with the dynamics of ludic play.

3.2. Speed. In narrative theory, *speed* concerns the relation between the duration of the events that happened in the story and duration of the discourse that tells the story. The narrative speed of a game, correspondingly, is the relation between the duration of the operation of an event and the duration of the happening of that event in the story (i.e., in real-world time). As speed is a relative concept and there is no absolute means to measure it, based on previous theorists, Bal summarizes five canonical tempi that can be used as relative measurements: ellipsis, summary, scene, stretch, and pause, going from fast to slow, respectively [22]. The key to distinguishing one tempo from another is to compare two time schemes, and it does not matter which two they are. Therefore, if discourse time is replaced with operational time, the five tempi can be applied to measure the narrative speed of games.

The most common tempo in games, especially in action sequences, is the *scene* where events take place in operational time in the same speed as they do in story time. In film, since real people act out the actions in a scene, a perfect "scene" speed can be created; in games, however, where all the actions are computationally presented on the screen, there is not necessarily an absolute "scene" speed. A series of fighting actions, depending on which game is being played, can take slightly different durations. For example, in the 3D game *Fable II* on XBox360, the duration of in-game fighting actions is roughly the same as that in real world whereas in

the 2D game *The Legend of Zelda: Phantom Hourglass* on Nintendo DS, it feels a lot faster than in the real world as players speed up by tapping the stylus as quickly as they can. The duration of an action sequence is also related to the scale of the game space provided. As long as the sequence takes place within a reasonable range of duration considering the scale of the game, we can consider its speed as scene. Thus, scene is the most used speed when the game progresses in a normal state. Occasionally, we see a game like *Animal Crossing*, where the game is synced with real-world time so that the game story has the same seasons, holidays and so on as in the real world. Kelly suggests that this game design "intentionally draws on the passage of time to create both emotional resonance and economic value in the gameworld"; this design also encourages players to visit the game storyworld regularly in order to fully experience different events happening at different times of the day and even the year [29].

Summary happens when the duration of an event in the operational time is shorter than that in the story time. This tempo is used when the author wants the time point to make a major leap without showing the details of the happenings in between. For example in *Fable II*, in the "Birth of a Hero" chapter, the player character grows up into a young adult after a short cut-scene showing the rapid change of seasons accompanied by a voice-over narration; in this way, 10 years of story time is collapsed into 30 seconds of operational time in the game.

The opposite of summary is *stretch*, when an event takes longer to happen in the operational time than it does in story time. An often-cited example is "bullet time," where the usually very small duration of a bullet's flight is greatly elongated and presented in a slow motion. This effect was made famous by the film *Matrix* and latter adopted by the game *Max Payne*. In the game, bullet time goes beyond a representational effect and become an example of game mechanics that gives the player an advantage over enemies. When bullet time is triggered by hitting a key on the keyboard, it slows down the operational time so that the player is able to aim (when shooting) and react (when dodging the bullet). Ruffino comments that the innovative use of bullet time as a game mechanic is "a magnified satisfaction of a yearning that lies behind much computer game playing: the dream of control over time." Yet, it is not just added control, but something more for the player's ludic and aesthetic pleasure; it "transforms fights into quasi-ballets," where "every step of the fight determines and is determined by the steps of the other "dancers"" [30].

When games use *ellipsis*, there is a skip of story events in operational time. For example, in *Fable II*, the player character worked in the Tattered Spire as a labourer for 10 years in an effort to find the right timing to recruit Garth, the Hero of Will. Events happening in such a long story time are presented in a short operational time using ellipsis. The game only selects three moments, from Week 1, Week 38, and Week 137, to present. When the selected events in Week 1 are completed by the player, the game shows the caption "Week 38" and continues events from there so that things in between are entirely omitted. This tempo is very common in games. What is more, the commonplace gameplay device "teleporting" is essentially an ellipsis. When players go to the teleporter, they will be transported instantly to another location.

Lastly, when a story event is paused and the operation is taking care of something else, a *pause* occurs. This tempo is rarely used in games except in the form of a brief orientation cut-scene in some games. For example, in *Prince of Persia: The Sands of Time*, there will be a pause when the prince enters a new environment: a quick cut-scene with a camera pan will occur to show players the whole picture of the space and hint to them where the target is. Similarly in *Assassin's Creed II*, whenever players are about to solve a platforming puzzle in the tomb, a very quick cut-scene will be displayed to show the order of the spatial points players need to be at in order to pull a trigger before the timer is off. In addition, in most games players can pause the game, adjusting game settings or taking a break. This type of pause makes the game more user-friendly, but is not central to the experience or the analysis of game narrative.

3.3. Frequency. *Frequency* deals with the relation between the number of times an event "really" happened in the story and the number of times it is presented in the operation. The most common relationship is a *singular* presentation of an event occurring only once. When an event in a story occurs only once but in operation, it is presented more than once, *repetition* happens. When an event that took place multiple times in the story is only presented in the operation once, *iteration* happens. Iteration is found mostly in verbal narration, where a repetitive series of events can be summarized verbally (e.g., "for three years, he practices his sword skills every day"). Hence, it is not surprising when we see iterations in the verbal part of the game narration, such as in voice-overs, dialogues and diaries. Aside from being presented verbally, iterative narration is very hard to realize otherwise in a visual medium like film or game, although we do not exclude the possibility of using indirect means to implement iterations. Kinder has done a detailed discussion of iterations in films, where she considers iteration not being necessarily a temporal notion. There are some indirect ways to present iterative events visually in films, which she dubbed "pseudo-iterative." One way is to foreground the singular protagonist within a crowd in a habitual event to imply the iterative nature (e.g., in the hiring scene *Bicycle Thief*) [31].

Repetition is very common in games, but it is mostly employed as a game mechanic rather than a narrative device. The most common repetition is to help players overcome challenges. When players fail to complete a task, they get to repeat the task until done. In this type of repetition, events in operation may vary (e.g., each fight is different) but story events remain the same. The range of the segment that can be repeated and the maximal number of repetitions allowed are dependent on the design of the game. This type of repetition helps the player master gaming skills but is less relevant to the narrative experience.

Another type of repetition is at the player's choice. In many games, players are allowed to move back and forth. They may revisit a certain game section and repeat what they have done before. In this case, some games are able to offer variations for the repeated section; for example, the enemies may be spawned in different locations than the previous time. This type of repetition due to revisiting adds to a player's experience in both gameplay and narrative.

The third type of repetition is the result of a player's ability to reverse time. In *Prince of Persia: The Sands of Time*, the Dagger of Time is both a gameplay and a narrative device that can be used by players to turn back time to a point of their choice. At the gameplay level, the Dagger of Time allows players to rewind the game and so redo a task that they failed last time. At the narrative level, the Dagger of Time is so powerful that it can even turn over the story outcome, although in cut-scenes. As part of the prescribed story, after the nonplayer character (NPC) Princess Farah has died and the Dagger has been put into the Hourglass, marking the climax of the game, a cut-scene brings the time all the way back to the beginning, as a result of the Dagger returning to the Hourglass where it belongs. The Prince then starts to tell a story to Farah about the past adventure.

Finally, repetition also occurs at a low level, which can be seen in examples such as an NPCs' repetitive motions (e.g., the forever-swiping motions of the street cleaner in *Assassin's Creed II*) or a player character's "grinding" activities in order to access a new feature or gain a new status.

3.4. Polychrony and Narrative Variation. The concept of *fuzzy temporality* is developed by Herman to expand Genette's temporal study that is solely based on the relation between story time and discourse time. When one or more events cannot be assigned to an exact position in a story's timeline, it is no longer meaningful to look at the relation between the two time schemes. Inspired by the concept of "fuzzy logic" that opposes the bivalent logic having only true and false values, Herman rejects the bivalence of previous temporal studies that simply consider narrative time to be either determinable or indeterminable. Citing Margolin's notes, Herman states that a given set of events can be ordered in four ways. In the *full* ordering, for any two events "it is possible to decide whether one is earlier, later, or contemporaneous with the other." In the *random* ordering, "all mathematically possible arrangements are equally probable." In *alternative* or *multiple* ordering, the probability of one ordering can be higher than that of another. In *partial* ordering, some events can be "uniquely sequenced relative to all others, some only relative to some others, and some relative to none" [15]. Herman goes on to use *polychronic* narration to entail a system, which consists of three values— Earlier, Later, and Indeterminate, covering the entire range of fuzzy temporality. In a polychronic narrative, events can be inexactly *ordered* (i.e., as in the last three types of ordering mentioned above), or inexactly *coded* (i.e., being inexactly positioned on the timeline), or both.

Herman's discussion of fuzzy temporality can shed a light on temporal studies of games. One key strategy to make narrative interactive—that is, to let players have an impact on the story through interactions—is to generate variations for different readings (i.e., variation in plot) [32]. This is also related to what "breaking the linearity" is about in game designers' terms. The most common approach to the creation of a "nonlinear" story is to allow varied orderings to occur for each play of the game. To ensure that the game still follows the overarching story, foldback structure is very popular and is used to balance the freedom at a local level and the overarching narrative at a global level; as Adams points out, it is often adopted by modern story-driven adventure games like *The Secret of Monkey Island* [25]. In a foldback story, the entire game narrative is broken into several parts (or chapters) and accommodates multiple plot variations. Within each part, players can go through a different set of events *and/or* in a different order during each play. At the intersections between parts, inevitable events occur. These inevitable events usually follow a fixed order and occur at relatively fixed positions on the overall timeline of the game story. This structure can be seen in such recent examples as *Assassin's Creed* and *Fable II*, where the overarching mission or quest is the same, but players have the freedom to pick the side tasks or quests to complete in their favoured order. For "linear" games where there is no narrative variation, because players still interact at a local level, each prescripted (and inevitable) story event possesses a different position on the timeline due to individual pacing of the game. Hence, it is perhaps safe to conclude that digital game storytelling is all polychronic due to its more or less fuzzy temporality. We will explain further through analysis of an example in a later section of this paper. It is also worth mentioning that digital games have unique ways to create narrative variations, or fuzzy temporality in general. Apart from employing temporal devices, spatial structure can also be utilized to facilitate temporal design, which we will discuss in the next section.

4. A Closer Look at Game Narrative Space

In this section, we examine in detail narrative space in games from the three views that have been introduced earlier. These three views describe three different modes of how narrative space exists and functions in digital games. To iterate, in the first mode, space is considered as static and independent of both plot enactment and screen representation; it is the topographical structure of narrative space, which forms the underlying spatial reference of the storyworld. In the second mode, space is a space-time complex that encompasses plot enactment, that is, the storyworld as revealed through the operation of the game. In other words, space is structured through events and movements occurring in the operation. In the third mode, space is the presentation of storyworld. The presentational structure determines the visual and auditory manifestations of the game world and shapes players' perceptions and thoughts. Although these three modes are differentiated for the purpose of analytical clarity, we need to remember that it is the combination of the three modes working together that make the design and experience of a game's narrative space effective and satisfying.

4.1. Topographical Structure. The *topographical view* treats space as a static entity with fixed spatial reference and separated from temporal reference. The topographical structure can be perceived as a map or any mental conception that features the spatial relations between locations or entities. A map of a story certainly cannot exhaust all the topographical information; so "blanks" are unavoidable. It is often up to the audience whether the picture of the storyworld is clear; when it is unclear, they will attempt to fill in the blanks with imagination. As Zoran suggests, the mental conception can include not only locations but also the quality of things based on different ontological principles; in this case, "landmarks" and "regions" can be used to mark important locations or areas. Hence, there are all sorts of reader-constructed cognitive maps for reading purposes as well as in-game or player-drawn game maps and sketches aimed at enhancing player performance in different ways. Among all the characteristics relevant to topographical structure, layout and oppositions are two major considerations for structuring the space.

4.1.1. Topographical Layouts. The study of space has always involved typologies of spatial models based on topographical features. This is important because "[e]ven if players gain access to the space-generation process, some structure has to be provided either from the player or the system" [16]. Indeed, for interactive narratives and games, the discussion and classification of spatial models is always related to spatial navigation. For example, Murray discusses two structures of spatial navigation for interactive narrative: the maze and the rhizome [33]. Nitsche also proposes several distinct spatial forms: tracks and rails, labyrinths and mazes, and arenas. Since these forms define the spatial logic in their own way, their structures shape paths, edges, and regions, which in turn determine the ways of player navigation [16].

In the game design field, the layout of the game space is often created as part of the level design. Adams considers a successful layout needs to be "appropriate for the storyline and to achieve the atmosphere and pacing required to keep players engaged in the game world" [25]. Adams gives a list of 7 common patterns of layouts that we believe to be a practical typology of game spatial layouts. An *open layout* represents the outdoors and gives the player the freedom to wander about. When the player goes indoors or underground, as Adams observes, the layout often switches to a *network* or *combination layout*. Examples of open layout are role-playing games like the *Fable* series, war games like *Battlefield 1942*, and action adventure games like *Assassin's Creed*. The settings mimic their corresponding worlds in real-life and thus have few, if any, visible spatial boundaries. A *linear layout* is not bound to any particular shape, but it does ensure a fixed sequence for the player to experience. This is similar to Nitsche's concept of *tracks and rails* [16]. A *parallel layout* is a variation of the linear layout. It is like tracks with switches that allow the player to switch from one track to another. A *ring layout* makes the player's path return to the starting point, which is often used by racing games. A *network layout* provides more ways of connecting spaces and gives the player more freedom compared with a layout with tracks. A *hub-and-spoke* layout starts the player from a hub in the centre. The player can go out of the hub to a space but will have to return to the hub before heading out to another space.

Different layouts provide different qualities for player navigation. For instance, the hub-and-spoke structure is claimed by game designer Steve Gaynor to be "the most common high-level organizational strategy". He cites the Medical Pavilion hub in *BioShock* as an example of such structure, where "minor spaces are always closer to major spaces than they are to other minor spaces—the player always passes through the hub to get to another spoke" [34]. In contrast to a full open layout, the hubs and spokes give the player reorienting spatial references so that the comprehension and thus navigation of the game space become easier. Adams also reminds us that designers are not confined to just one layout for their game space. Some games have a combination of various layouts, either at the same level or in more complexly nested combinations across multiple levels.

4.1.2. Spatial Oppositions. In a thoughtful narrative design, spatial oppositions of all sorts can be used to structure the story world and thus create the desired story effect. In her discussion of location as a fabula element, Bal stresses that "[o]ppositions are constructions; it is important not to forget that and "naturalize" them" [22]. Similarly, Zoran considers that the map of a topographical structure "is based on a series of oppositions" [14]. Spatial oppositions are typically physical, for example, inside and outside, center and periphery, city and country, and so forth [14, 22]. They can be endowed with meanings or experiences, following, creating, or playing with conventions. In the *Assassin's Creed* series, for example, the rooftop space is open and relatively safe since the protagonist is out of sight of most of the guards whereas in the ground-level space he needs to be careful about his actions; players thus can take advantage of this opposition-based spatial convention to adjust their own pacing. This example illustrates how the design of narrativized space can affect ludic play.

Other than shaping the gameplay experience, spatial oppositions can also offer a way to group narrative elements and thus simplify complex content for players. Let us take a look at the map of Masyaf town (Figure 1) in *Assassin's Creed*. The upper part represents the mountain fortress and the lower part the village. Aside from being geographically separated, these two spaces also contrast with respect to population and infrastructure density. Naturally, in the village players will raise their alert level when surrounded by villagers as well as soldiers. In contrast, the mountain fortress serves as a *home region* where the player just gets instructions and training. Thus, the convention created via spatial opposition helps players adapt to the environment more easily and adjust their alert level and pacing accordingly. Again, the narrativized space serves to nuance ludic decision-making. It is worth noting that this type of opposition is reused in *Assassin's Creed II*, between the Monteriggioni villa, serving as the home region, and other cities, although on a much larger geographical scale.

The boundary or the transitory place between two opposed locations often functions as a mediator, as Bal also suggests [22]. In Masyaf, the passage between the mountain fortress and the village is the gateway for the player avatar to

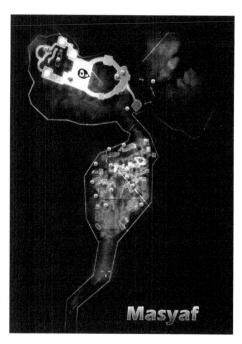

FIGURE 1: Masyaf town in *Assassin's Creed* (source: Ubisoft, 2007; image from IGN.com, used with permission).

step into the other part of the game world, either reporting to his master or going to carry out his missions. On this passage, the player often gets instructions from an NPC. A transitory place allows the player to take a break between missions (or levels) and get ready for the next adventure that will take place in yet another location in the game world.

4.2. Operational Structure. As defined earlier, the operational view sees the storyworld revealed through events and movements over time while the story unfolds. The operational structure is formed by characteristics that shape game spatial operations by regulating and patterning movements. The view of operational structure corresponds with Zoran's level of chronotopic structure, which addresses "what may be defined by an integration of spatial and temporal categories as movement and change" [14]. The chronotopic structure has a significant impact on the plot, which is not just a temporal structure but also includes "routes, movement, directions, volume, simultaneity, and so forth" [14]. In games, since the protagonist is often (en)acted by the player, the shaping of the plot is dependent on both predesigned plot structure and the ways the player navigates and interacts. In this sense, game plot becomes a set of all possible narrative instances, consistent with Manovich's conception of a "database narrative" [35]. We call this set of plot instances a *plot set*. When looking at the game retrospectively after one play, the player has gone through only one instantiation of the plot set. We thus consider this traversing act as an *operation* to differentiate it from chronotope. This section will explore the spatial qualities that characterize the operational structure of narrative space in games. One of the fundamental characteristics is the mobility of characters and objects, which is the key factor to identify a change of the state of the plot. Other characteristics characterize movements over the course of the operation. Our approach to the operational characteristics is inspired by Zoran. He suggests that synchronic and diachronic relationships are the two main concerns for the level of chronotopic structure. The former detects motion and rest whereas the latter characterizes the movement through directions, axes, and powers. Here we selectively adapt his suggestions to games and draw in some considerations specific to games as well.

4.2.1. Mobility of Characters and Objects.

4.2.1. *Mobility of Characters and Objects.* At any given moment, characters and objects in a game are in one of the two spatial states: movement or rest. Here the focus is on their general mobility. Some characters or objects move between spaces while others stay in one space. Hence we can replace the account of mobility with a question like "what is attached to one particular space, what not?"

Those characters attached to one space become the "background" of the space, that is, part of the context, especially when not interacting with the player. In this case, characters play the same role as other environmental objects. When players interact with these characters, the plot can change locally. The range of a character's mobility and interactivity often determines the significance of the change. Many NPCs are designed to attach to one location or one subspace. They are either enemies or background characters. This is very common in a game like *Fable II*, where, for example, the archaeologist can always be found in the same spot and the blacksmith always belongs to his shop. For "attached-to-space" characters, their qualities can be coordinated with the space. For example, on a difficult game level, an enemy character can be tough and hard to defeat.

Characters that are able to move with greater range from one space to another can play a more significant role in plot development. Hence, they are often the main characters that grow with the plot, along with the player character. The dog in *Fable II* is such a character that follows the player avatar all along. In general, the more highly mobile the characters, the more complex the plot is. In *Heavy Rain*, all four main characters are playable and highly mobile, which makes the plot intriguing and full of suspense. Similarly, some objects in games that have a high mobility can play an important role in the game operation and thus the plot development. For example, in *Prince of Persia: The Sands of Time*, the Dagger of Time is such an object with mobility. Once obtained, it follows with the player avatar and performs the magic of time reversal on request. The use of the dagger by the player contributes to the construction of the plot.

There are also characters and objects that are mobile within a certain range. Horses in *Assassin's Creed* series are one such example. They are located outside city gates and can be ridden by the player avatar all around in countryside but not into the city. In this way, they speed up the protagonist's movements between cities and yet make the scale of distance feel real.

4.2.2. *Paths and Axes.* A path between locations can be unidirectional or bidirectional; in the latter case, the movement is reversible. Axes are the principal paths surrounding which major events and actions take place. Axes help organize narrative content and form the operational structure for the space, especially for those plots that are driven by character movements.

For role-playing games, while players must move along the axis in order to progress in the game by pursuing the main quest, they are also allowed to explore the world and make social interactions on side quests that follow paths branching out from the axis. This is often realized in a rhizome structure, which is a "tuber root system in which any point may be connected to any other point" [33]. The tuber represents the axis, or the path for the main quest whereas the roots are the paths of other side quests. For example, the role-playing game *Planescape Torment*, as Diane Carr finds, uses such structure that "sends its multitasking players in rhizomic circles, deviations and side-quests in search of lost memories and fragmented histories" [36]. Such operational structure featuring one axis is, in a strict sense, still a linear structure. As Carlquist observes, even given all the player choices, games like *Planescape Torment* are still linear games because the player "still has to follow the main plot in a certain way" while pursuing the main quest in a linear order [37]. *Fable II* is another role-playing game that follows the rhizome structure.

The mobility and interactivity of characters and objects, directions for paths, existence of axes, as well as other spatial features work together to form the operational structure for games. They construct the storyworld for the player to navigate through and interact. The game mechanics are also embedded within the same structure, which therefore supports both narrative experience and ludic experience. This sharing of the operational structure between narrative and game mechanism allows for the deeper integration of game story within the gameplay.

4.3. *Presentational Structure.* The notion of presentational structure is mainly derived from Zoran's level of textual structure. Here we extend the scope of narrative text to cover visual narratives including films and games. The presentational structure concerns how the patterns of visual, auditory, textual, haptic and other cues (i.e., the language of game as a medium) are imposed on the dynamic presentation of the storyworld. Hence, the analysis on this level focuses on the ways and materials through which the game world is presented, as well as how the presentation incorporates player actions. The presentational view of game narrative space contains a large variety of aspects ranging from the organization of information to low-level representational techniques. These aspects have considerable commonality with those of films.

4.3.1. *On-Screen and Off-Screen Space.* While the topographic and operational structure can reveal the major spatial reference and movement potentials of the game world, detailed information on the space remains unclear to the player in these two views, and needs to be structured during the presentation of the game. The selection of the spatial information to reveal on the screen is probably the first thing at issue when presenting the story space. For complex games with a 3D story world, the on-screen space is different from the "shot space" of a film although it applies many cinematic techniques. In films, the view is constrained by the laws of optics and physics; in games, the view is computational and dynamic. The game's screen image is depicted by a "virtual camera," which extends far beyond the functionality of an actual camera. For example, a virtual camera can follow fast moving objects to create the "bullet time" effect, which manipulates not only the perceived space but also the perceived time of the player. Fly-through, originally used in the field of architecture, is yet another virtual cinematic technique to give the player a view of the space ahead of time from a predefined perspective, where the camera is "flying" or circling around the space. *Prince of Persia: The Sands of Time* and *Assassin's Creed II* both use this technique extensively. Another different use of on-screen space of a game is to display the screen interface of the game, which will be discussed latter.

For games that limit or disallow players to change the camera view, the on-screen space can be seen as a relatively independent space. In this case, it is close to the "shot space" of a film, where the screen composition conventions from film are selectively applied. In the controlled presentational space, the on-screen and off-screen spaces are not necessarily connected. In *God of War*, the camera angle will usually adjust or follow when the player character enters a less visible spot. When the player avatar enters a new subspace, there is usually an establishing shot of the space and then the camera closes up. Shot/reverse shot, a common camera convention used for two-person scenes, however, is only selectively employed by *God of War*: it is used in conversations but not in most of the fight scenes. In many combat scenes the on-screen space is enclosed with clear boundaries and thus cut off from off-screen space; thus, the on-screen and off-screen spaces are not necessarily continuous. Another example is *Heavy Rain*, which features discontinuous or limited continuous space because the on-screen space is heavily "edited" with restricted player control of the camera angle. In these cases, the designers need to decide how to transition from one on-screen space to another, which we will discuss in the following subsection.

4.3.2. Acoustic Space. While visual factors dominate the presentation in many games, in others auditory factors play an equally important role in the construction of the game space. As in film, sound is used to set the mood, create tension, and help to enhance the realism of the game world. In *Fable II*, the ambient sound helps to define the environment and shape the emotional tenor of the progress through the game space. When the player avatar is exploring a town, the background music is quiet and peaceful. When he or she is on the road or in the cave where bandits and monsters are nearby, the music becomes loud and ominous. When combat begins, drumbeats kick in to intensify the fighting mood. This dynamic design of musical soundtrack

effectively creates both narrative and gameplay tensions that intensify the player's experience of the game.

Game sound also has functions unique to the medium. For example, sound provides feedback for player interactions (e.g., footsteps made by the player avatar) and hints for players' next moves (e.g., a sound coming from off-screen suggesting the direction of an approaching enemy). Such auditory cues help players perceive the 3D game space and imagine the off-screen space. Grimshaw and Schott maintain that "sound functions as an acoustic ecology" consisting of both the players and their soundscapes. In their study of such ecology of first-person shooters, they discover that sophisticated use of sound "aids in imaginative immersion through the provision of virtual resonating spaces and paraspaces" [38]. In music/rhythm games like *Rock Band* and *Dance Dance Revolution*, sound goes even further to become part of the core gameplay mechanic.

4.3.3. Spatial Segmentation. In the operational view, game space is structured and presented in a temporal continuum. How spatial information is segmented and how the player gets passed from one segment of space to the next are two questions relevant to the spatial organization. What is more, according to Zagal et al., spatial segmentation "results from the division of the gameworld into different spaces that also partition gameplay" [39]. Although Zagal's original study is based on vintage arcade games, we find the notion applicable to digital games in general. Since digital games have overcome technical barriers and evolved from earlier 2D platforms to current complicated 3D game worlds, setting the boundaries becomes an important part of the design strategy to create rich gaming experiences. Hence, a game world is divided into distinct subspaces, each of which has different spatial features or even game rules. The question of how to segment the space also triggers the question of how to make the player have a fluid experience navigating through the subspaces. When the subspaces are disconnected topographically, they can be displayed in the form of episodes or scenes cut from one to the next; otherwise, they may be connected and form the entire game space in the structure of a tree or a network in graph theory terms, or, a maze or a rhizome in Murray's terms [33]. In the latter case, players simply "walk" into the next subspace.

There are four common styles for the transition from one subspace to another that is not directly connected: direct cut, fly-through (or orientation cut-scene), cut-scene, and caption. In *Prince of Persia: The Sands of Time*, for instance, when finishing one session, the player-avatar is often simply brought to a new setting to start a new session; this transition is a direct cut. Sometimes to make up for the possible loss of orientation, the game will play a "fly-through" video sequence to familiarize the player with the new subspace. Cut-scenes are another transitional means prevalent in games where a video sequence is played to introduce background information. Captions are often seen in text heavy games that simply tell players they are to enter a new subspace. *Fable II* is one such example. Another function of cut-scenes and caption screens is to occupy the player during the game loading time, which is often needed for transitions between spatial segments.

4.3.4. Perspective. "Perspective" exists in any form of narrative. The notion of perspective, or point of view, can refer to two possible layers of meaning. One is the psychological point of view that locates attitudes and emotions; the other is the optical point of view that refers to the visual positioning of the frame. The source of the perspective in both cases can be either subjective (from a particular character) or objective (from an external narrator or a neutral viewer). The psychological and visual layers are often intertwined—a "first-person" visual can reinforce the psychological perspective of the protagonist. The points of view of different sources can structure the story world on the presentational level. In films, camera angle and optical point of view can be used to reinforce either subjective (character-driven) or objective (neutral and observational) psychological perspectives. For games that employ virtual cameras, the player is simply assigned either the protagonist point of view as in first-person games, or a bird's eye view as in third-person games. It is very hard to find an instance in games where the psychological point of view is separated from the physical one, a case that is common to films. Even when the two perspectives are separated, it is often realized through voice-over narration. In *Prince of Persia: The Sands of Time* and *Max Payne*, for instance, the player controlled protagonist would occasionally talk to the player and comment on what has happened.

Unlike film viewers, game players sometimes are given the freedom of shifting their camera view. In *Prince of Persia: The Sands of Time*, the third-person camera view is fully controlled by the player and it can be switched to the player avatar's first-person view. Having the two kinds of view *Prince of Persia* possesses, *Assassin's Creed* also has an "eagle vision" as an option that offers the player a filtered vision that foregrounds the identity of targeted characters (e.g., guards or informants). As Adams summarizes, the first-person perspective is only used by avatar-based games, where the camera assumes the position of the avatar's eyes. The third-person perspective, most prevalent in 3D action and action-adventure games, has a more flexible camera view. In a normal state, the camera follows the avatar at a distance from a slightly higher angle; during combat, the camera cranes up and tilts down to enable the player to see more of the environment, as in the case of *God of War*. The aerial perspectives feature top-down camera views from different angles and are widely adopted by party-based battle games and strategy games [25].

Other than presenting players the view based on their avatars' in-game movement, the camera can also contribute to the game's interactive mechanism by guiding the player's attention to those interactive elements. This is usually done by a direct cut to a zoom-in view of an object or a space, implying what or where the player's next step is to be (e.g., picking up an item or going to that space).

4.3.5. The Screen Interface. For film, the screen is a presentational medium. For games, the screen has a second role—the interface between the game and the player. In our terms, the game's screen functions on both the operational level (supporting navigation and decision making) and the presentational level (presenting the game and its space as it is dynamically traversed). This duality corresponds to Manovich's distinction of the interactive screen as both a control device and a presentation device [35]. This double role can complicate the screen, layering the spatial information with interface information (control menu, dialogues, character status, game statistics, help information, etc.). The layering of information is realized in a screen layout that takes the form of a windowed view, an overlaid view, or a combination of the two, as Adams observes [25]. In a windowed view, the main window displays the game world, while interface information is shown in a separate window on the side, the bottom or the top of the main window. Many strategy games and some role-play games use this layout. This layout can potentially lessen the sense of immersion but it delivers interface information in an easy way. In an overlaid view, the interface information is imposed onto the main view in an opaque or semitransparent fashion. Aside from the two ways Adams observes, there is the third way to enable the screen to assume the double role. For games that strive to provide an immersive environment, they present a relatively clean full screen view displaying the game world but are willing to switch to a menu view at the player's request. *Assassin's Creed* and *Fable II*, for example, both have such interface for players to check maps and resources.

Besides the above use of the screen, there is another technique—split screen—that presents multiple spaces in the same screen. Split screen is not uncommon in modern films. It is typically employed when two or more characters take actions simultaneously; they can be in different places or the same place but viewed from different perspectives. *Heavy Rain*, for instance, uses split screen for such occasions. Split screen is also used in multiplayer games. Wolf's spatial structure type 10—"multiple, nonadjacent spaces displayed on-screen simultaneously"—refers to this technique [4]. He cites the racing game *High Velocity* as an example where players can see both their own view and the opponent's view on-screen. This helps players strategize their moves although it might distract their attention in the meanwhile.

5. Time, Space, and Plot: From Analysis to Design

In previous sections, we have developed a rich descriptive framework for analyzing time and space in game storytelling. How players experience a game is always influenced by the way the game is designed, and how players interpret a game story is always influenced by the way the game plot is organized and arranged. Time and space converge in the plot and together shape the structure of the story experience. Bridgeman describes how we perceive a plot: "our image of a work can involve the paths of the protagonists around their world, bringing together time and space to shape a plot" [2]. As we have discussed in a previous section, the plot of a game is an instance of the plot set that players go through during one play. On first examination, game plot might be seen as a function of time since, like a flowchart, it consists of events connected with decision points. In his discussion of interactive narrative, Meadows relates the notion of "plot" to the concept "use-case scenario" in software engineering, which consists of "the function, flow, time, and interaction between a user (or reader) and a particular piece of software" [40]. There are four interactive narrative structures most often cited by game designers, (admittedly without hard and distinct boundaries between the categories): the linear structure, the branching structure, the foldback structure, and the open structure [25]. The linear, foldback and open structures also correspond with Meadows' nodal, modulated, and open plot structures of interactive narratives including games [40].) These four narrative structures in turn support four structures for the gameplay and associated temporal design. All games' interactive narrative structures encompass polychrony—the key to making the story interactive—in one way or another. The fuzzy temporality brought by polychrony helps create interactive space: the indeterminate parts on the timeline are the gaps for players to fill and to create their emergent narrative. For example, in *Grand Auto Theft III*, as Rouse observes, although the main narrative arc consists of prescribed missions and cut-scenes, players are allowed to choose the missions they want to complete and follow their own order to complete them [41].

The above classification of structures frames the *plot set* in a collective view of an interactive narrative. From the audience or player's point of view, each reading or play is an integral experience of one plot instance. While most plots are constructed by a sequence of events that follow a temporal order or causal logic, other sequencing orders are possible. For examples, the events can be sequenced based on thematic changes, or on the portrayal of one key character after another, or based on one location after another. Nonetheless, no matter what principle is at work for the sequencing of events, many narratives carefully sequence and time the story events so that the dramatic tension is built into a strong emotional arc. These plots are based on the classical Aristotelian model and consist of three acts, which typically follow a rising action, a climax and a falling action, forming the dramatic arc. The dramatic arc seems to "achieve its effects without the audience's conscious awareness" [42].

In interactive storytelling systems, designers and developers use planning algorithms to sequence events based on their tension levels in order to ensure a strong dramatic and emotional tension arc. In the interactive drama *Façade*, the plot is divided into two levels of units. On a high level, the drama manager sequences a bag of dramatic *beats* based on the causal relation between major events. *Façade*'s beats are crafted based on traditional dramatic writing—where the dramatic beats represent the smallest units of dramatic action. On a low level, each beat contains a bag of *joint dialog behaviors* (jdbs); in response to player interactions, the beat dynamically selects and sequences a subset of jdbs. The system keeps track of the tension value for each beat and selects the next unused beat with the right tension value as well as other preconditions to ensure "an author-specified story tension arc" [43]. While some interactive narratives like *Façade* maintain a high level of authorial

control over the plot, other systems focus more on player characters' goals and actions. Barros and Musse created a prototype interactive storytelling system called Fabulator, which is based on the "riddle" master plot [44]. Their tension arcs model assumes that the tension will rise when the player acquires more knowledge to move closer to the truth. The plot climaxes when the player is just one clue away from solving the riddle and ends when the riddle is solved. In order to shape the tension arc to the desired level, the system dynamically adjusts the level of difficulty through participation by NPCs (i.e., helping or not helping the player character) [44]. To cater more to the player's preference, Thue et al. propose a player modelling approach via their interactive storytelling system PaSSAGE [45]. Their system creates the player model by automatically learning the style of play preferred by the player. It then uses the model dynamically to select the events and deliver an adapted story. To ensure the dramatic arc, events are grouped into phases of Joseph Campbell's Monomyth structure so that at runtime the system will select an event from the right phase.

As discovered in our spatial analysis, the spatial layout of the storyworld also affects how players traverse the game because the spatial structure is imposed on players' experience of time (e.g., one needs to reach room A via room B). This is especially true for spatial stories (or travel narratives) that are driven by a character's movement across a map. For spatial stories, as Jenkins argues, "organizing the plot becomes a matter of designing the geography of imaginary worlds so that obstacles thwart and affordances facilitate the protagonist's forward movement towards resolution." In this way, spatial exploration aids in the plot exploration. For games featuring spatial stories, successful plot design goes beyond the formulation of a sequence of events. Rather, it is based on the creation of a "compelling framework" where players can have some freedom at a local level without "totally derailing the larger narrative trajectory." As Jenkins rightfully points out, in order to more effectively reach this goal, game designers need to "develop their craft through a process of experimentation and refinement of basic narrative devices, becoming better at shaping narrative experiences without unduly constraining the space for improvisation within their games" [46].

While a game plot can be organized with certain temporal and spatial patterns at a high level, it can be shaped at a low level as well. For example, at the high level of a game, the sequence of inevitable events shapes the dramatic arc warranting an overall narrative experience; when these events are bound to specific locations, the spatial structure becomes part of the plot engineering, too. For example, in PaSSAGE, the plot sequencing takes into consideration the character's location in the game space. When the next event is chosen based on the player model, the system manages this selection through triggers. The triggers monitor the game environment and search for the suitable actors within a reasonable distance of the player's current position [45]. At a low level, a plot decision point located between two events can be designed as either a temporal transition or a spatial one. A temporal transition can use one of the four styles discussed in the subsection of Spatial Segmentation whereas a spatial transition can use forking paths, bridges, elevators, and so forth in the game space, just like any transition in the real physical space. In an interactive narrative that is presented in a realistic game world, each event can be bound to specific time and space constraints, instead of appearing in a random fashion. There are two ways to handle these constraints. One way is to build these constraints into the sequencing mechanism (such as in the aforementioned PaSSAGE example) so that the system makes sure of the "eligibility" of the upcoming event. The other way is to design a flexible "transportation" mechanism in the game space so that the player can easily "jump" to the next location following a trigger event (such as in *Fable II*). Most games employ a combination of the two ways.

The design choices for temporal devices and spatial characteristics work together to support, inflect the storytelling style and shape players' narrative experience. The descriptive framework developed earlier in this paper has enabled us to see many techniques and devices within existing narrative designs as well as related gameplay design decisions. To make the connection between analytical finding and narrative design more visible, the following two tables summarize the key concepts we have discussed and their application and function in games. An important note about the tables is that they are not intended to include all concepts we have touched on in this work, let alone all applications in the vast field of digital games.

Tables 1 and 2 provide a high-level overview of the concepts we have explored in this work. We recognize that there are many nonnarrative devices and characteristics that are not included in our discussion. Because the focus of our work is the structure of digital game storytelling, we have limited our discussion to the narrative perspective. Although the use of time as a narrative device is not as rich as in traditional narratives, time is used in multiple ways as a significant and expressive gameplay device. Granting control of time to players has various effects in the gameplay and the game experience. It helps players overcome challenges and creates fun by allowing players to rewind the game (e.g., *Prince of Persia: The Sands of Time, Max Payne*), magnifying the fighting process (e.g., "bullet time"), speeding up the transportation (e.g., "teleporting"), giving hints on puzzles (e.g., orientation cut-scenes for platforming puzzles), and so forth. There is also a time-based device very common in games—the ticking clock, a term proposed for games by Wolf [47]. This device intensifies challenge by setting a time limit for players to finish a task or an action sequence. The tensions that the "ticking clock" creates also shape players' emotional experiences. Similarly, space can be used in many creative ways in gameplay. For instance, space plays a very active role in game puzzles. To conclude, by focusing on the narrative comprehension and experience, our approach generates rich insights for game narrative design.

6. Review through a Case Analysis

In order to fully understand how temporal relations and spatial characteristics act together to structure a game plot and shape narrative experience, it is best to examine a game example in detail and conduct an in-depth analysis. In this section, we use one game level in the historical action adventure game *Assassin's Creed* to illustrate how time and space are structured in game storytelling. We pick an action adventure game for several reasons. Adventure games are famous for their rich stories. Mallon and Webb's empirical study on adventure games shows that a good adventure game demands more of well-designed narrative structure [48]. Adams points out that the designers of adventure games need to "bring not just a story but a world to life—a world in which a story is taking place" [25]; hence the spatial design is crucial to the story. Compared with pure adventure games, action adventures are faster paced and thus players feel more time pressure; therefore, more considerations of temporal design are required as well. We believe that *Assassin's Creed's* open world structure is a good example for the examination of how time and space are designed in games via a variety of devices and techniques.

Since games are essentially complicated systems presenting content hierarchically, both temporal relations and spatial characteristics exist in games at multiple levels. Therefore, we need to decide on the level of granularity for our case analysis. Zagal et al. suggest that a game ontology should start in a "middle-out" fashion because the "most readily observable" categories tend to exist in the middle of the ontology; in this way, both more abstract and more specific concepts can be brought out latter by refined analysis [49]. Similarly, in order for our case analysis to inspire both more abstract and more specific insights, we start out from one specific game level that is easily distinguished and observed by both temporal and spatial standards. According to Zagal et al., a *level* in a game is "a recognizable subspace of the gameworld". Although level can refer to the degree of difficulty as well, "[w]hat helps distinguish a level from other forms of spatial segmentation is the discontinuity in gameplay and in space between one level and another; the more evident the discontinuity, the greater the notion of level" [39]. In our paper, we use this definition for game level. We thus choose the Damascus Poor District in *Assassin's Creed's* Memory Block 2 as an example game level to demonstrate how to look at the time and space in a game narrative. The entire game consists of seven "memory blocks" that can be seen as seven chapters. These blocks are not to be confused with game levels since they are not based on game space. Instead, they are based on temporal sequence, so each memory block can contain events occurring in different spaces. Each block has a set of objectives for players to finish through four types of activities: assassination, scaling viewpoints, investigations and saving citizens. Each activity is enveloped in a "memory strand"; once played, the content of the strand can be viewed in the main menu. In the pause menu, players can check on the game status as well as access the map. Figure 2 shows the in-game map of Damascus Poor District, which is the level of our analysis.

6.1. Temporal Analysis. The story of *Assassin's Creed* overarches the game through the seven memory blocks. On the highest level, the story is presented in a foldback structure,

TABLE 1: Summary of temporal devices discussed that affect narrative and gameplay experience.

Devices for game narrative time	Main forms in games	Function in game narrative	Function in gameplay	Examples cited (selective)
Order flashback	Dialogue, cut-scene, screen caption, text (e.g., diaries, logs)	Provide information; stylistic/genre storytelling	Game mechanic (e.g., Dagger of Time)	*Prince of Persia: Sands of Time*; *Max Payne*
Speed scene	Appeared in the normal state	Create realism	Create realism	*Fable II*; *Animal Crossing*; *Assassin's Creed*
Speed summary ellipsis	Cut-scene, voice-over, screen caption; Direct cut, screen caption	Increase storytelling efficiency	Increase gameplay efficiency	*Fable II*; *Assassin's Creed*; *Max Payne*
Speed stretch	Cut-scene, slow motion	Stylistic/genre storytelling	Game mechanic (e.g., Bullet Time)	*Max Payne*
Speed pause	Orientation cut-scene, pause menu	N/A	Orientation; menu option	*Prince of Persia: Sands of Time*; *Assassin's Creed*
Frequency repetition	Task repetition when died or failed; game replay	Create narrative variation	Ease the challenge; help mastering the skill	*Assassin's Creed*; *Prince of Persia: Sands of Time*
Polychrony	Appeared in all plot structures of games	Create narrative variation; increase interactivity	Create gameplay variation; increase interactivity	*Assassin's Creed*; *Grand Theft Auto III*; *Fable II*, and so forth

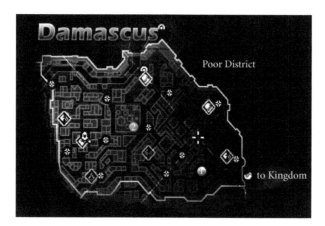

FIGURE 2: Damascus Poor District in *Assassin's Creed* (source: Ubisoft, 2007; image from IGN.com, used with permission).

where the ordering of the main sequence (from memory block 1 to 7) is fixed but the ordering of events within one block is not totally predeterminate. Overall, most parts of the story are presented in the *scene* tempo, which resembles the real-world speed. On the highest level, the repetition is realized through replay. Once a memory block is complete, it becomes replayable; however, one play of a block can be different from another in terms of the selection of activities to do and the ordering of doing them. In the following, we present a temporal analysis of Damascus Poor District in detail; hence, we will discuss the phenomena within the game level. In the Damascus Poor District level, investigation includes three subtypes: pickpocketing, eavesdropping, and interrogation.

6.1.1. Order. Consistent with what we have discussed earlier, flashbacks (retroversion) appear here and there mainly in a typical form of dialogue sequence (cut-scene) but flash-forwards (anticipation) seem to be nonexistent. The most prominent example is the eavesdropping activities. The player character Altair needs to sit on a bench nearby and overhear the conversation between two NPCs in order to get clues about the situation. In one of the eavesdroppings, two assassins are talking about a man named Masun who had let the Templars into the town; he exchanges letters with someone from the fortress and the letters are carried by the basket weaver. This information immediately tells Altair that the letter is important and he needs to find the basket weaver, which will lead to the next pickpocketing activity. The span of flashbacks in this level is typically a few minutes, enough for a brief conversation. Their main function is to provide information and hints for the player.

6.1.2. Speed. In the normal state, the game operates in a *scene* tempo, in which players feel things happen at the same speed as in real world. Of course, if we scrutinize the time used for each action, it tends to be shorter than it would be in a real town the size of Damascus. Hence, our designation as scene tempo is relative, not absolute. Players can use the controller to speed up Altair's walking and running pace, as they would do in the real world. Ellipsis is rarely used in this level. The only ellipsis we observed takes place when the player character finishes a task and naps at the Assassin's Bureau: when he walks out of the room, there is a direct cut to the next scene showing him standing up and looking recharged. This use of ellipsis is mainly for user convenience—assassins do need rest, but the player does not need to wait. The dominant use of scene and minimal use of ellipsis are a result

TABLE 2: Summary of spatial characteristics discussed that affect narrative and gameplay experience.

Characteristics for game narrative space	Function in game narrative	Function in gameplay	Examples cited (selective)
Topographical layout	Affect plot structure	Help create navigational pattern	*Assassin's Creed BioShock*
Topographical spatial opposition	Help group narrative events; Help create conventions (e.g., dangerous space versus safe space) to affect emotional experience	Help shape navigational experience; Help create conventions to affect decision making	*Assassin's Creed; Assassin's Creed II*
Operational character mobility object mobility	Help create the storyworld; Help the plot development; Affect the variability of narrative	Ease or intensify gameplay; affect the variability of gameplay	*Prince of Persia: Sands of Time; Assassin's Creed; Fable II; Heavy Rain*
Operational paths and axes	Help shape/restrain the plot structure	Help create navigational pattern; Affect the degree of repetition of gameplay	*Assassin's Creed; Planescape Torment*
Presentational on-screen space perspective	Stylistic/genre storytelling; Choice of first-person versus third-person help shape emotional experience	Affect the continuity of game space; Affect player control of view; Camera as a guiding device	*God of War; Assassin's Creed; Assassin's Creed II; Prince of Persia: Sands of Time; Max Payne*
Presentational acoustic space	Set the mood, create tension, and enhance the realism.	Provides feedback and hints for players' next moves; Basic game mechanic (e.g., in rhythm games)	*Fable II; Assassin's Creed; Rock Band; Dance Dance Revolution*
Presentational spatial segmentation	Help group narrative events	Set the boundaries of gameplay; help create game levels	*Prince of Persia: Sands of Time; Fable II; Assassin's Creed*
Presentational screen interface	Provide information; stylistic/genre storytelling (e.g., split screen)	Facilitate player control for both gameplay and camera view; provide information and instructions	*Assassin's Creed; Fable II; High Velocity; Heavy Rain*

of the signature fluid design of *Assassin's Creed*. To our knowledge, the other tempi, including summary and stretch, are absent in this level. Pause is not embedded within the storytelling but can be accessed using the player control. Players can pause in order to review the game state and game world or to put the game on standby while they do other things.

6.1.3. Frequency. Iteration is a frequency mode that is not used in this game, consistent with its absence in most games. The story events tend to be presented singularly. However, repetitions—single event being presented multiple times—are not rare in this level. The first type of repetition is typical in games; namely, repetition due to the death of the player character. In *Assassin's Creed*, when the player character dies due to a failed fight, the fight will be replayed so the player can repeat until succeeding. Another form of repetition is related to NPC behaviour in the game. Those NPCs who are bound to a specific location—that is, characters without mobility—tend to repeat what they do and say. Whenever the

player character gets close to a "save citizen" venue, where several guards are troubling a citizen, a soundscape of their conversations will be played. If the player leaves the venue and comes back later, he hears the same conversations. This repetition will only stop after the player character saves the citizen by killing those guards. This second type of repetition reflects poor design for the nonmobile characters. This weakness is shared by many games, decreasing realism and undermining Murray's conception of "immersion" within interactive narrative. In fact, none of the level's use of repetition adds to the quality of the game's storytelling.

6.1.4. Polychrony and Narrative Variation. In the beginning of our temporal analysis, we mentioned that for the same memory block, players can select different tasks and follow different sequences during each replay. In Murray's aesthetic framework, this transformative capacity of the game's design increases a player's sense of agency [33]. Players sense the impact their choices have on the story's variations and the subsequent development of deeper meaning.

FIGURE 3: Damascus operational timeline: four mandatory events with fixed ordering.

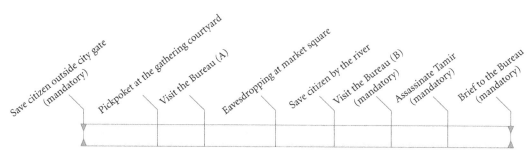

FIGURE 4: Damascus operational timeline: Sequence A.

As a general rule in *Assassin's Creed*, before the player visits a new subspace, that area remains concealed (i.e., black) until the player climbs to the top of a tower and "scans" the area from the vantage point. This scan, or "scaling the viewpoint," is generally the first thing to do in a space. After the scaling, the corresponding area is revealed on the map and the player can then become active in that area. In the Damascus Poor District level, the main objective is to assassinate the black market merchant Tamir. Before entering Damascus, the player character has to save a citizen close to the city gate. After the entrance, another "mandatory" task the player needs to carry out before the assassination is gather information from the leader of Damascus Assassins at the Assassin's Bureau. The player character will then be able to assassinate Tamir after finishing at least two investigation activities (pickpocketing, eavesdropping, or interrogation). After the assassination, he must return to the Bureau for a briefing in order to finish this game level. To summarize, there are only four events sequenced in a fixed order but they are not exactly positioned on the timeline. The inexact positioning is necessary to make room for player freedom. Figure 3 shows the fixed sequence of the Damascus level; other than the first and last events happening at the two ends of the timeline (marked by double triangles in the graph), events in the middle do not own a fixed time point. Figure 4 illustrates the sequence of one possible play. Aside from the beginning and end activities as well as "Assassinate Tamir," the ordering of the activities is determined by the player.

Our analysis reveals that the design of *Assassin's Creed* is very successful in creating variations in the narrative order. By giving the player great control over the ordering and timing of their activities, the interactivity of the game narrative is considerably enhanced. One can easily raise a question here: does the random ordering affect the narrative logic? We went back to the game, performed multiple plays

and concluded that the narrative logic is not influenced by the various sequence orders. Scaling viewpoints only reveals the map whereas saving citizens only enhances the player character's reputation so that the saved citizens will provide help latter. Neither activity entails a plot function that is significant in its own right. There is some low-level narrative logic inherent in the investigation activities. Some of the dialogues deliver useful operational information regarding the assassination, such as the background information on Tamir and the venue where he will appear. But other than the practical implications, the narrative weight is low and no ordering logic is required. We did encounter, in one play (shown as Sequence B in Figure 5), a situation where the logic is affected, but we were pleased to note that the game had intelligently varied the relevant dialogue. Unlike in Sequence A, we did an eavesdropping and the pickpocketing *before* seeing the Bureau leader. In Sequence A (Figure 4), during the first visit, the Bureau leader reveals some information on Tamir and suggests a number of locations in the Souk area where Altiar can begin his investigation; during the second visit, he praises Altair's capability and gives permission (i.e., gives the feather marker) to Altair to assassinate Tamir. In Sequence B, since both investigations have already revealed much information about Tamir, the conversation combines the two dialogues in Sequence A and alters slightly to accommodate what Altair has done in this sequence.

6.2. Spatial Analysis

6.2.1. Topographical View.
Taking the Damascus Poor District as a static space, we see this area as an example of any medieval middle-east city district. In fact, *Assassin's Creed*'s game spaces were modelled after the geography of the actual middle-east cities (around the Holy Land) in 12th century. The architectural design and visual details are based on

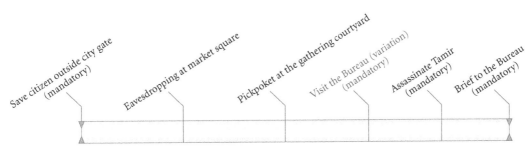

FIGURE 5: Damascus operational timeline: Sequence B.

historical documents and thus look very realistic [50]. The city is guarded with walls and gates. Within the city are the mosques, markets, alleys, and various types of courtyards. Like any populated city, locations are very well connected, which means that more than one path can lead one from one location to another. Thus we can consider the space to be a network layout, with a clear boundary for the district and an evenly distributed density across the area. Figure 6 selectively shows six landmarks that have visually distinct features to make them stand out. Since the real setting of this district is quite dense, we use a limited number of symbolic paths just to show a high-level view of the layout.

As previously mentioned, the game features an architectural style where rooftops of large structures are often connected, and alleys between structures in this poor district tend to be narrow. This two-level vertical structure offers the possibility for the player to take shortcuts by jumping around between roofs, which makes parkour one of the game's most distinct gameplay features. The term parkour is originated from a French physical discipline where participants overcome obstacles and run along a route. The word is used in games nowadays with the general meaning of free running. In general, the security level on the rooftop is low, and the guards on the ground cannot see activities on the rooftop; the rooftop thus facilitates stealth in the gameplay. The two-level vertical design, as well as the network layout, directly influences the space's operational structure by shaping the navigation pattern: the former gives players control of the pacing and the latter creates multiple options for their navigation routes.

6.2.2. Operational View. In the Damascus Poor District, the protagonist needs to complete 2 out of 6 main tasks from Memory Strands 1 to 6. He will then be able to report back to the Bureau (Memory Strand 7) and finally assassinate Tamir (Memory Strand 8), before this level is finished. There are also two types of side tasks in the game operation. One is to scale the viewpoints; the other is to save citizens who are in trouble. Figure 7 illustrates the main tasks based on their locations on the map. These tasks take place in a fixed location, which also implies the immobility of most of the NPCs; that is, characters are bound to one location or to a very limited range. The only exception is the vigilantes, who seem to appear wherever the protagonist is in trouble, providing that he is in good credit (gained by saving citizens).

From the diagram we can see that there is really no axis of centralized actions or happenings. Task locations are evenly scattered around, which means that the player is encouraged to navigate through the entire space.

The immobility of characters and associated actions could potentially make the game dull and lead to poor replayability because after the first time visiting a place, the player will see exactly the same characters and actions during a revisit until the characters are killed or the associated actions are taken, as we have discussed earlier in temporal analysis. However, the large and richly designed space makes up for this weakness in several ways. First, by performing a more-than-required number of tasks, the player can choose to do different things or visit different places for each play. Second, the rich and beautifully rendered environment entices the player to explore and discover new scenery. Third, the network layout provides a number of paths between any two locations, which makes the navigation more interesting and less repetitive.

The provision of a large and well-designed space with full navigational freedom to the player does compensate for the immobility of so many of the characters. However, it also induces another potential problem. With so many options for what to do and where to go, the player can become uncertain about what is the goal for this particular level and what to do next, or how to finish the experience and get out of this town. To make things worse, the game lacks axes in its operational space. The cure for this problem is twofold: one is posting real-time, on-screen instructions and task-indicating marks on the in-game map; the other is creating side tasks that indirectly help unfold the game plot. Scaling viewpoints is such a side task that especially addresses player uncertainty. When the player scales a viewpoint for the first time (by climbing to the top of tower and getting a panoramic bird's eye view), the surrounding area on the in-game city map, originally all dark, will be revealed. This can be related to a game design concept called "fog of war," where the focus area is revealed but other areas on the map are covered; examples can be found in strategy game *Civilization* and role-playing game *World of Warcraft*. When all viewpoints are scaled, the whole Damascus map will be shown clearly on the city map (which can be called up on demand). The viewpoint-scaling endeavour helps players, self-orient by giving a sense of which area has been visited and which has not. With the viewpoints being evenly spread out (see Figure 6), the player

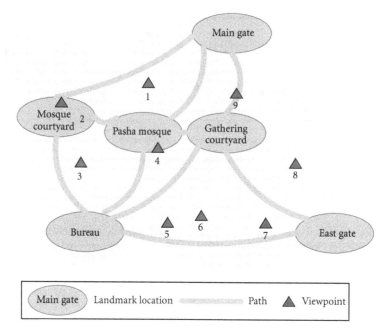

Figure 6: Damascus Poor District: topographical view.

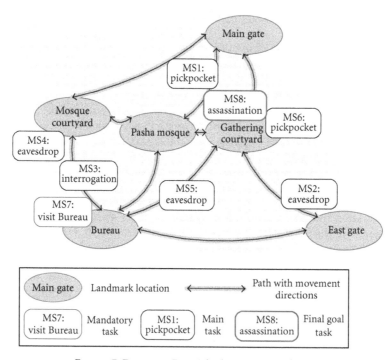

Figure 7: Damascus Poor District: operational view.

is prevented from getting lost in a labyrinth-like space and from neglecting a new area that potentially has a mandatory task to do.

6.2.3. Presentational View. *Assassin's Creed* is very cinematic in its visual style. There is no surprise that we see a lot of cinematic techniques in use here. Having a third-person physical perspective, the player has full control of the camera angles, plus an "eagle vision" that highlights NPCs of

interest. On the other hand, the player assumes a first-person psychological perspective for Altair the Assassin most of the time. The off-screen space and on-screen space together form a 3D story world.

The organization of the game plot is based on locations. Generally speaking, each town is a game level that has its own action style and spatial structure. *Within* Damascus Poor District, however, there is no visible segmentation. The space is continuous, which results in a fluid representation.

The camera follows the protagonist traversing the space and presents the space accordingly. The fluidity is stressed so much that even in some of the cut-scenes (e.g., at the Bureau), the player can keep adjusting his camera view and walking about, while participating in a prescribed conversation. This seamless interaction between the player avatar and NPCs reduces some of the perceived disadvantages of cutscenes (e.g., the player getting bored due to loss of control). This is important—every task scene is interspersed with cutscenes to carry on conversations.

The sound design of *Assassin's Creed* is outstanding. The ambient music creates a mood evocative of the ancient middle-eastern culture. As part of the interactive environment, the soundtrack reacts to what the player does in real time. If the player avatar kills a guard, the NPCs around him will scream and shout out their feelings about him. When the player character is exposed to the city guards, an ambient alert alarm will sound; in the meanwhile, the accompanied background music will change into faster rhythm when the player character is chased by the guards. This dynamic design effectively intensifies the player's narrative, emotional, and gameplay experiences.

The screen layout of this game uses overlays with an alternative interface screen showing the city map (e.g., Figure 2). The play screen presents the game space. Game instructions and hints are overlaid semitransparently on the corners of the screen (Figure 8). At the bottom right corner of the screen lies the mini GPS indicating the direction and distance to the target. In the alternative map screen, players can set a marker on the map interface (Figure 2), which in turn will show up in the GPS on the play screen. *Assassin's Creed*'s interface design creates an interesting, somewhat explicit link between the three levels of the space. It provides players a topographical view in the form of a town map. The map screen has marks for the locations of tasks, providing an overall operational view of the space and hints about appropriate movement and navigation. Not all games have these explicit links between the three views of their narrative space; nevertheless, these links always exist, converging design efforts at all three levels: topographical, operational, and presentational.

6.3. Plot Structure. The interactive narrative structure of *Assassin's Creed* is a typical foldback structure. The plot consists of seven memory blocks. The structure of all the memory blocks is almost identical, except for the first memory block that can be seen as the training block. The sequencing of the seven blocks has no particular temporal design. Within each block, there are two to three assassination missions to complete. These missions are the actual game levels and can also be regarded as plot units. The structure of each mission is again identical. Within a block, players can complete the missions in any order. As we can see, this repetitive structural design and random order of bigger events on the high level does not help build a strong dramatic tension arc—the tension level of each mission or block is equal. However, *within* each mission, although the sequencing mechanism gives players certain freedom, we can see an arc in the general flow of the plot (see Figure 9). The

investigation tasks can be seen as the exposition or setup act where the clues about the assassination target are given or discovered. In the second act, the player character finds the target and kills him, which pushes this unit of plot to the climax. In the third act, the player character makes his escape and the mission is completed.

In *Assassin's Creed*, all missions are bound to a location. Hence, rather than sequencing based on the three-act structure, at a high level the plot is structured based on location. Within a mission, the mandatory investigation tasks are also location-bound. Since the order of investigation tasks is random, the player needs to have a good grasp on the topographical layout of the town in order to engage in efficient play. In this way, the temporal design in effect is woven into the location design and played out in the enactment of plot and gameplay.

7. Conclusion

The study of game time and space has seen many interdisciplinary approaches drawing on a variety of traditions and methodologies. However, there is rarely a systematic discussion of how time and space are structured in game narratives and more specifically, what the key devices and characteristics are involved in the structuring process. We therefore decided to adapt and apply mature frameworks drawn from broader narrative theory in the analysis of story design and experience in games. Through investigations in fields of both narrative analysis and game studies and design, we develop a descriptive framework that organizes important time- and space-related issues into categories and designates characteristics to each category. Our framework for game time consists of the classic narratological categorization of order, speed, frequency, as well as polychrony, a crucial notion originally proposed by Herman addressing fuzzy temporality, which serves as the key to narrative interactivity. Based on these categories, we account temporal devices that support narrative and gameplay. Our framework for game narrative space, inspired mainly by Zoran and Herman's works, consists of three views that show the topographical, operational, and presentational structure of the narrative space in games. Within this framework, we lay out some important characteristics that define the qualities of the space. Through the crosschecking of game examples and a case analysis, our game-specific framework is found to be able to support the understanding of game narrative design.

A survey of the field of game studies encounters several important frameworks that address either time or space in games. Among these frameworks, Nitsche's is one that explicitly adapts narratology in the discussion of the structure of game space in one of the three parts forming his whole book (i.e., structure, presentation, functionality). Nitsche's discussion focuses on the meaning of the story in games and how to understand and adapt the fundamental concepts of story, plot and discourse in the context of game. However, this high-level conceptual discussion leaves the detailed methods for analysis and design of game narrative space largely unaddressed. Moreover, Nitsche's book interconnects the conception of five principle spaces: rule-based space,

FIGURE 8: The play screen and map menu of *Assassin's Creed* (source: Ubisoft, 2007; image from IGN.com, used with permission).

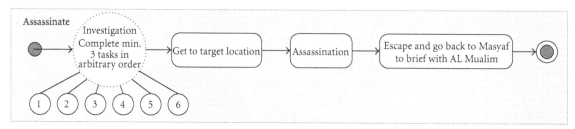

FIGURE 9: A plot unit in *Assassin's Creed*.

mediated space, fictional space, play space, and social space. Although this integrated view on game space is of great value, it is hard to find principles specific to *narrative design*. Jenkin's seminal article on narrative spaces gives us a good starting point to examine the relation between narrative and space, but it contains no specific insights on the structure of time and space. Other frameworks we investigated have even less focus on game storytelling. In Section 2, we introduced several frameworks for game time. These frameworks, built on multiple time schemes or time frames, cover some important concepts of game temporality, though not specifically for narrative comprehension. In addition, in our exploration, we identified the key insight that making narrative interactive lies in the fuzzy temporality that helps create plot variations and thus breaks the linearity of the story. This issue is not addressed in clear terms by any game scholars we have surveyed, although Ryan addresses plot variation in her studies of interactive narrative in terms different from ours [51]. Other frameworks for game space are less comprehensive than Nitsche's and not focused on storytelling, either. For instance, McGregor summarizes six patterns of use of space in games, which is a good descriptive framework to study the relation between space and gameplay [52].

In games, time and space work together to anchor textual, visual, auditory, and other interactive cues in the digital game, from which game players can build their mental story world. Players' narrative experiences are greatly influenced by the ways these cues are embedded in games to form temporal and spatial patterns. Devices and characteristics that facilitate both storytelling and gameplay are especially important in the creation of engaging plot and play. These are the vehicles for conjoining interactive experience and narrative

experience within an integrated dynamic. Treating games as interactive narrative texts, this paper adapts narrative theory in the explication of the structural aspects of time and space in game storytelling. These insights are instantiated within a conceptual framework that incorporates the key factors in the design of game narrative. This framework can be usefully applied in the study of specific games, and can also serve as a basis for critical analysis on a larger scale, providing a methodology for comparing narrative design across different games. As the boundary between digital games and interactive storytelling systems is not clear cut and they share many principles discussed in our work, we believe that our framework can effectively be extended into the domain of interactive storytelling.

References

[1] M. J. P. Wolf, "Narrative in the video game," in *The Medium of the Video Game*, M. J. P. Wolf, Ed., University of Texas Press, Austin, Tex, USA, 2001.

[2] T. Bridgeman, "Time and space," in *The Cambridge Companion to Narrative*, D. Herman, Ed., pp. 52–65, Cambridge University Press, Cambridge, Mass, USA, 2007.

[3] E. Aarseth, "Allegories of space: the question of spatiality in computer games," in *Space Time Play: Computer Games, Architecture and Urbanism: The Next Level*, F. von Borries, S. P. Walz, and M. Böttger, Eds., pp. 44–47, Birkhäuser, Berlin, Germany, 2007.

[4] M. J. P. Wolf, "Space in the video game," in *The Medium of Video Game*, J. P. M. Wolf, Ed., pp. 51–75, University of Texas Press, Austin, Tex, USA, 2001.

[5] D. J. Boron, "A short history of digital gamespace," in *Space Time Play: Computer Games, Architecture and Urbanism: The Next Level*, F. von Borries, S. P. Walz, and M. Böttger, Eds., pp. 26–31, Birkhäuser, Berlin, Germany, 2007.

[6] H. Jenkins, "Game design as narrative architecture," in *First Person: New Media as Story, Performance, and Game*, N. Wardrip-Fruin and P. Harrigan, Eds., pp. 118–130, MIT Press, Cambridge, Mass, USA, 2004.

[7] M. Nitsche, "Mapping time in video games," in *Situated Play, Proceedings of DiGRA 2007 Conference*, pp. 145–151, 2007.

[8] M. LeBlanc, "Tools for creating dramatic game dynamics," in *The Game Design Reader: A Rules of Play Anthology*, K. Salen and E. Zimmerman, Eds., pp. 438–459, MIT Press, Cambridge, Mass, USA, 2006.

[9] D. Arsenault and B. Perron, "In the frame of the magic cycle: the circle(s) of gameplay," in *The Video Game Theory Reader 2*, B. Perron and M. J. P. Wolf, Eds., pp. 109–131, Routledge, New York, NY, USA, 2009.

[10] J. Juul, *Half-Real: Video Games between Real Rules and Fictional Worlds*, MIT Press, Cambridge, Mass, USA, 2005.

[11] J. P. Zagal and M. Mateas, "Temporal frames: a unifying framework for the analysis of game temporality," in *Situated Play, Proceedings of DiGRA 2007 Conference*, pp. 516–522, 2007.

[12] M. Ryan, "Beyond myth and metaphor—the case of narrative in digital media," *Game Studies: The International Journal of Computer Game Research*, vol. 1, no. 1, 2001, http://www.gamestudies.org/0101/ryan/ .

[13] M. M. Bakhtin, "Forms of time and of the chronotope in the novel: notes toward a historical poetics," in *The Dialogic Imagination: Four Essays*, M. M. Bakhtin and M. Holquist, Eds., pp. 84–258, Univeristy of Texas Press, Austin, Tex, USA, 1981.

[14] G. Zoran, "Towards a theory of space in narrative," *Poetics Today*, vol. 5, pp. 309–335, 1984.

[15] D. Herman, *Story Logic: Problems and Possibilities of Narrative*, University of Nebraska Press, Lincoln, Neb, USA, 2002.

[16] M. Nitsche, *Video Game Spaces: Image, Play, and Structure in 3D Game Worlds*, MIT Press, Cambridge, Mass, USA, 2008.

[17] G. Genette, *Narrative Discourse: An Essay in Method*, Cornell University Press, Ithaca, NY, USA, 1980.

[18] M. Eskelinen, "Towards computer game studies," in *First Person: New Media as Story, Performance and Game*, N. Wardrip-Fruin and P. Harrigan, Eds., pp. 36–44, MIT Press, Cambrige, Mass, USA, 2004.

[19] J. Juul, "Introduction to game time," in *First Person: New Media as Story, Performance, and Game*, N. Wardrip-Fruin and P. Harrigan, Eds., pp. 131–142, MIT Press, Cambridge, Mass, USA, 2004.

[20] M. Hitchens, "Time and computer games or "no, that's not what happened," in *Proceedings of the 3rd Australasian Conference on Interactive Entertainment*, pp. 44–51, 2006.

[21] A. Tychsen, M. Hitchens, and A. Drachen, "Game time: modeling and analyzing time in multiplayer and massively multiplayer games," *Games and Culture*, vol. 4, no. 2, pp. 170–201, 2009.

[22] M. Bal, *Narratology: Introduction to the Theory of Narrative*, University of Toronto Press, Toronto, Canada, 3rd edition, 2009.

[23] G. Prince, *Dictionary of Narratology*, University of Nebraska Press, Lincoln, Neb, USA, 2nd edition, 2003.

[24] S. Chatman, *Story and Discourse: Narrative Structure in Fiction and Film*, Cornell University Press, Ithaca, NY, USA, 1978.

[25] E. Adams, *Fundamentals of Game Design*, New Riders, Berkeley, Calif, USA, 2nd edition, 2010.

[26] J. E. Brand, S. Knight, and J. Majewski, "The diverse worlds of computer games: a content analysis of spaces, populations, styles and narratives," in *Proceedings of the Digital Games Research Association Conference (DIGRA '03)*, Utrecht, The Netherlands, November 2003.

[27] L. Soulban and H. Orkin, "Writing for first-person shooters," in *Writing for Video Game Genres: From FPS to RPG*, W. Despain, Ed., pp. 51–68, A K Peters, Wellesley, Mass, USA, 2009.

[28] J. Mechner, "The sands of time: crafting a video game story," in *Second Person: Role-Playing and Story in Games and Playable Media*, P. Harrigan and N. Wardrip-Fruin, Eds., pp. 111–120, MIT Press, Cambridge, Mass, USA, 2007.

[29] H. Kelly, "Animal crossing: a game in time," in *Space Time Play: Computer Games, Architecture and Urbanism: The Next Level*, F. von Borries, S. P. Walz, and M. Böttger, Eds., pp. 180–181, Birkhäuser, Berlin, Germany, 2007.

[30] P. Ruffino, "Max payne: the dream of control over time," in *Space Time Play: Computer Games, Architecture and Urbanism: The Next Level*, F. von Borries, S. P. Walz, and M. Böttger, Eds., pp. 70–71, Birkhäuser, Berlin, Germany, 2007.

[31] M. Kinder, "The subversive potential of the pseudo-iterative," *Film Quarterly*, vol. 43, pp. 2–16, 1989.

[32] N. Montfort, "Ordering events in interactive fiction narratives," in *Proceedings of the AAAI Fall Symposium on Intelligent Narrative Technologies*, pp. 87–94, 2007.

[33] J. H. Murray, *Hamlet on the Holodeck: The Future of Narrative in Cyberspace*, Free Press, New York, NY, USA, 1997.

[34] S. Gaynor, Reorienteering: spatial organization in BioShock, 2009, http://fullbright.blogspot.com/2009/04/reorienteering-spatial-organization-in.html .

[35] L. Manovich, *The Language of New Media*, MIT Press, Cambridge, Mass, USA, 2001.

[36] D. Carr, "Space, navigation and affect," in *Computer Games: Text, Narrative and Play*, D. Carr, D. Buckingham, A. Burn, and G. Schott, Eds., pp. 59–71, Polity Press, Cambridge, UK, 2006.

[37] J. Carlquist, "Playing the story: computer games as a narrative genre," *Human IT*, vol. 6, no. 3, pp. 7–53, 2002.

[38] M. Grimshaw and G. Schott, "Situating gaming as a sonic experience: the acoustic ecology of first-person shooters," in *Situated Play: Proceedings of the Digital Games Research Association Conference*, pp. 474–481, 2007.

[39] J. P. Zagal, C. Fernández-Vara, and M. Mateas, "Rounds, levels, and waves: the early evolution of gameplay segmentation," *Games and Culture*, vol. 3, no. 2, pp. 175–198, 2008.

[40] M. S. Meadows, *Pause & Effect: The Art of Interactive Narrative*, New Riders, Indianapolis, Ind, USA, 2003.

[41] R. Rouse III, *Game Design Theory and Practice*, 2nd edition, 2005.

[42] D. Bordwell, *Poetics of Cinema*, Routledge, New York, NY, USA, 2008.

[43] M. Mateas and A. Stern, "Structuring content in the façade interactive drama architecture," in *Proceedings of the 1st Artificial Intelligence and Interactive Digital Entertainment Conference (AIIDE '05)*, pp. 93–99, June 2005.

[44] L. M. Barros and S. R. Musse, "Towards consistency in interactive storytelling: tension arcs and dead-ends," *Computers in Entertainment*, vol. 6, no. 3, article 43, pp. 1–17, 2008.

[45] D. Thue, V. Bulitko, M. Spetch, and E. Wasylishen, "Interactive storytelling: a player modelling approach," in *Proceedings of the 3rd Artificial Intelligence for Interactive Digital Entertainment Conference (AIIDE '07)*, pp. 43–48, Stanford, Calif, USA, 2007.

[46] H. Jenkins, "Narrative spaces," in *Space Time Play: Computer Games, Architecture and Urbanism: The Next Level*, F. von Borries, S. P. Walz, and M. Böttger, Eds., pp. 56–60, Birkhäuser, Berlin, Germany, 2007.

[47] M. J. P. Wolf, "Time in the video game," in *The Medium of Video Game*, J. P. M. Wolf, Ed., pp. 77–91, University of Texas Press, Austin, Tex, USA, 2001.

[48] B. Mallon and B. Webb, "Stand up and take your place: identifying narrative elements in narrative adventure and role-play games," *Computer in Entertainment*, vol. 3, no. 1, pp. 1–19, 2005.

[49] J. P. Zagal, M. Mateas, C. Fernández-Vara, B. Hochhalter, and N. Lichti, "Towards an ontological language for game analysis," in *Proceedings of the DiGRA Conference: Changing Views—Worlds in Pla (DiGRA '05)*, 2005.

[50] M. Seif El-Nasr, M. Al-Saati, S. Niedenthal, and D. Milam, "Assassin's creed: a multi-cultural read," *Loading*, vol. 2, no. 3, 2008.

[51] M. Ryan, *Avatars of Story*, University of Minnesota Press, Minneapolis, Minn, USA, 2006.

[52] G. L. McGregor, "Situations of play: patterns of spatial use in videogames," in *Situated Play: Proceedings of the Digital Games Research Association Conference*, pp. 537–545, 2007.

Permissions

The contributors of this book come from diverse backgrounds, making this book a truly international effort. This book will bring forth new frontiers with its revolutionizing research information and detailed analysis of the nascent developments around the world.

We would like to thank all the contributing authors for lending their expertise to make the book truly unique. They have played a crucial role in the development of this book. Without their invaluable contributions this book wouldn't have been possible. They have made vital efforts to compile up to date information on the varied aspects of this subject to make this book a valuable addition to the collection of many professionals and students.

This book was conceptualized with the vision of imparting up-to-date information and advanced data in this field. To ensure the same, a matchless editorial board was set up. Every individual on the board went through rigorous rounds of assessment to prove their worth. After which they invested a large part of their time researching and compiling the most relevant data for our readers. Conferences and sessions were held from time to time between the editorial board and the contributing authors to present the data in the most comprehensible form. The editorial team has worked tirelessly to provide valuable and valid information to help people across the globe.

Every chapter published in this book has been scrutinized by our experts. Their significance has been extensively debated. The topics covered herein carry significant findings which will fuel the growth of the discipline. They may even be implemented as practical applications or may be referred to as a beginning point for another development. Chapters in this book were first published by Hindawi Publishing Corporation; hereby published with permission under the Creative Commons Attribution License or equivalent.

The editorial board has been involved in producing this book since its inception. They have spent rigorous hours researching and exploring the diverse topics which have resulted in the successful publishing of this book. They have passed on their knowledge of decades through this book. To expedite this challenging task, the publisher supported the team at every step. A small team of assistant editors was also appointed to further simplify the editing procedure and attain best results for the readers.

Our editorial team has been hand-picked from every corner of the world. Their multi-ethnicity adds dynamic inputs to the discussions which result in innovative outcomes. These outcomes are then further discussed with the researchers and contributors who give their valuable feedback and opinion regarding the same. The feedback is then collaborated with the researches and they are edited in a comprehensive manner to aid the understanding of the subject.

Apart from the editorial board, the designing team has also invested a significant amount of their time in understanding the subject and creating the most relevant covers. They scrutinized every image to scout for the most suitable representation of the subject and create an appropriate cover for the book.

The publishing team has been involved in this book since its early stages. They were actively engaged in every process, be it collecting the data, connecting with the contributors or procuring relevant information. The team has been an ardent support to the editorial, designing and production team. Their endless efforts to recruit the best for this project, has resulted in the accomplishment of this book. They are a veteran in the field of academics and their pool of knowledge is as vast as their experience in printing. Their expertise and guidance has proved useful at every step. Their uncompromising quality standards have made this book an exceptional effort. Their encouragement from time to time has been an inspiration for everyone.

The publisher and the editorial board hope that this book will prove to be a valuable piece of knowledge for researchers, students, practitioners and scholars across the globe.

List of Contributors

Maja Matijasevic and Mirko Suznjevic
Faculty of Electrical Engineering and Computing, University of Zagreb, Unska 3, 10000 Zagreb, Croatia

Jose Saldana, Julián Fernández-Navajas and José Ruiz-Mas
Communication Technologies Group (GTC), Aragon Institute of Engineering Research (I3A), EINA, University of Zaragoza, 50018 Zaragoza Ada Byron Building, Spain

Daniel Schroeder and Howard J. Hamilton
Department of Computer Science, University of Regina, Regina, SK, Canada S4S 0A2

Frutuoso G. M. Silva
University of Beira Interior, Rua Marques de Avila e Bolama, 6201-001 Covilh~a, Portugal
Instituto de Telecomunicacoes (IST), Torre Norte, Piso 10, Avenida Rovisco Pais 1, 1049-001 Lisboa, Portugal

André F. S. Barbosa, Pedro N. M. Pereira and João A. F. F. Dias
University of Beira Interior, Rua Marques de Avila e Bolama, 6201-001 Covilh~a, Portugal

Kazuya Atsuta
Graduate School of Systems and Information Engineering, University of Tsukuba, 1-1-1 Tennodai, Tsukuba, Ibaraki 305-8573, Japan

Masatoshi Hamanaka
Faculty of Engineering, Information and Systems, University of Tsukuba, 1-1-1 Tennodai, Tsukuba, Ibaraki 305-8573, Japan

SeungHee Lee
Faculty of Human Sciences, University of Tsukuba, 1-1-1 Tennodai, Tsukuba, Ibaraki 305-8573, Japan

Peter Vajda, Ivan Ivanov and Touradj Ebrahimi
Multimedia Signal Processing Group (MMSPG), ´Ecole Polytechnique F´ed´erale de Lausanne (EPFL), 1015 Lausanne, Switzerland

Jong-Seok Lee
School of Integrated Technology, Yonsei University, Incheon 406-840, Republic of Korea

Gregg T. Hanold
Oracle National Security Group, Reston, VA 20190, USA

Mikel D. Petty
Center for Modeling, Simulation and Analysis, University of Alabama in Huntsville, Huntsville, AL 35899, USA

David Weibel and Bartholomäus Wissmath
Department of Psychology, University of Bern, Muesmattstrasse 45, 3000 Bern 9, Switzerland

Oriel Bergig, Nate Hagbi, Kirill Pevzner, Nati Levi and Jihad El-Sana
Department of Computer Science, Ben-Gurion University of the Negev, P.O.B 653 Be'er Sheva 84105, Israel

Shoham Blau, Yulia Smelansky and Eyal Soreq
Screen-Based Arts, Bezalel Academy of Arts and Design, Jerusalem 91240, Israel

Kurt Weissgerber, Gary B. Lamont, Brett J. Borghetti and Gilbert L. Peterson
Department of Electrical and Computer Engineering, Graduate School of Engineering and Management, Air Force Institute of Technology, Wright Patterson AFB, Dayton, OH 45433, USA

Nicola Dusi, Maria Federico and Marco Furini
Department of Communication and Economics, University of Modena and Reggio Emilia, Via Allegri 9, 42100 Reggio Emilia, Italy

Alf Inge Wang and Bian Wu
Norwegian University of Science and Technology, Sem Saelandsv. 7–9, 7491 Trondheim, Norway

Li Zhang
School of Computing, Teesside University, Middlesbrough TS1 3BA, UK

John Barnden
School of Computer Science, University of Birmingham, Birmingham B15 2TT, UK

Daniel Örtqvist
Department of Business Administration and Social Sciences (IES), Luleå University of Technology, 971 87 Luleå, Sweden

Mats Liljedahl
Interactive Institute, Sonic Studio, Acusticum 4, 941 28 Piteå, Sweden

Fernando Marson and Soraia Raupp Musse
Graduate Programme in Computer Science, PUCRS, Avenue Ipiranga, 6681, Building 32, Porto Alegre, RS, Brazil

Huaxin Wei, Jim Bizzocchi and Tom Calvert
School of Interactive Arts and Technology, Simon Fraser University, 250-13450 102 Avenue, Surrey, BC, Canada V3T 0A3

Printed in the USA
CPSIA information can be obtained
at www.ICGtesting.com
JSHW051443221024
72173JS00006B/1562